To Chantell

with best

wishes

Ed

Trade Unions Past, Present and Future

Edited by Craig Phelan

Volume 21

PETER LANG

Oxford • Bern • Berlin • Bruxelles • Frankfurt am Main • New York • Wien

Inside the Unions

A Comparative Analysis of Policy-Making
in Australian and British Printing and
Telecommunication Trade Unions

Ed Blissett

PETER LANG

Oxford • Bern • Berlin • Bruxelles • Frankfurt am Main • New York • Wien

Bibliographic information published by Die Deutsche Nationalbibliothek.
Die Deutsche Nationalbibliothek lists this publication in the Deutsche National-
bibliografie; detailed bibliographic data is available on the Internet at
http://dnb.d-nb.de.

A catalogue record for this book is available from the British Library.

Library of Congress Control Number: 2013950950

ISSN 1662-7784
ISBN 978-3-0343-1731-3

© Peter Lang AG, International Academic Publishers, Bern 2014
Hochfeldstrasse 32, CH-3012 Bern, Switzerland
info@peterlang.com, www.peterlang.com, www.peterlang.net

This publication has been peer reviewed.

Printed in Germany

This book is dedicated to my Mum, June Blissett, and my Dad, Ted Blissett. Their unwavering support and encouragement sustained me during the completion of this book. It is also dedicated to my late niece, Ruth, who died in June 2013 aged 18, having endured a lifetime of ill health owing to Behçet's syndrome.

Contents

Acknowledgements

I would like to thank Ed Heery and Bradon Ellem for their advice, encouragement and support in the completion of this book.

I am indebted to all the officers and activists of the British and Australian telecommunication and printing unions, who generously gave up their time to be interviewed. The further help many of these contributors gave, in providing suggestions and contact details of other people to approach for interviews, was also invaluable.

Finally I would like to extend a very special thanks to those participants who, in addition to giving of their time and knowledge, also extended to me hospitality and practical assistance in undertaking my fieldwork. Their help assisted me enormously, but as I promised to protect the identities of all interviewees, I am unfortunately unable to name them here.

Abbreviations

AAOCS	Amalgamated Association of Operative Cotton Spinners
ACAS	Advisory, Conciliation and Arbitration Service
ACIAA	Australian Commercial and Industrial Artists Association
ACOS	Administrative and Clerical Officers Association
ACP	Association of Correctors of the Press
ACTU	Australian Congress of Trade Unions
ADSTE	Association of Drafting Supervisory & Technical Employees
AEA	Actors Equity of Australia
AESA	Amalgamated Engineering and Stores Association
AFMEU	Australian Food Manufacturing and Engineering Union
AJA	Australian Journalists Association
ALHMU	Australian Liquor Hospitality and Miscellaneous Workers Union
ALP	Australian Labor Party
AMEU	Automotive Metals & Engineering Union
AMFSU	Amalgamated Metals Foundry and Shipwrights Union
AMWU	Australian Manufacturing Workers Union
AMWU	Australian Metal Workers Union
APEU	Australian Postal Electricians Union
APTEU	Amalgamated Printing Trades Employee's Union
APTU	Australian Postal and Telecommunications Union
APWU	Australian Postal Workers Union
ASLP	Amalgamated Society of Lithographic Printers and Auxiliaries of Great Britain and Ireland

ATEA	Australian Telecommunication Engineering Association
ATPOA	Australian Telephone and Phonegram Officers Association
ATTCMU	Australian Telegraph, Telephone, Construction and Maintenance Union
AUEW	Amalgamated Union of Engineering Workers
BIFU	Banking Insurance and Finance Union
BL	Broad Left
BWIU	Building Workers Industrial Union
CCPSO	Council of Commonwealth Public Service Organisations
CEPU (P&T)	Communication, Electrical and Plumbing Union, Postal and Telecommunication Section
CEPU (T&S)	Communication, Electrical and Plumbing Union, Telecommunications and Services Section
CEPU	Communications, Electrical and Plumbing Union
CFMEU	Construction, Forestry, Mining and Energy Union
CPGB	Communist Party of Great Britain
CPSA (P&T)	Civil and Public Services Union, Postal and Telecommunications Group
CPSA	Civil and Public Services Union
CSIP	Customer Service Improvement Programme
CWFPU	Confectionery Workers & Food Preservers Union of Australia
CWU	Communication Workers Union
E&SA	Engineering and Stores Association
EETPU	Electrical, Electronic, Telecommunication and Plumbing Union
EOTA	Engineering Officers (Telecommunications) Association
ETU	Electricians Trades Union
FCU	Federated Clerks Union of Australia
FIA	Australian Federated Ironworkers Association

FoC	Father of Chapel
FPA	Federated Photo-Engravers, Photo-Lithographers and Photo-gravure Employees Association of Australia
GMB	GMB Union (formerly General, Municipal and Boilermakers Union)
GPMU	Graphical, Paper and Media Union
GPO	General Post Office
Groupers	Anti Communist Groups
IFOC	Imperial Father of Chapel
ITU	International Typographical Union
LSC	London Society of Compositors
LTS	London Typographical Society
MEAA	Media, Entertainment and Arts Alliance
MEWU	Metals & Engineering Workers' Union
MF	Members First
MoC	Mother of Chapel
MUA	Musicians Union of Australia
NASUWT	National Association Schoolmasters Union Women Teachers
NATSOPA	National Society of Operative Printers and Assistants
NC	National Council
NCU (C)	National Communication Union, Communications Division
NCU (E)	National Communication Union, Engineering Division
NCU	National Communication Union
NEC	National Executive Committee
NGA	National Graphical Association
NGME	National Guild of Motor Engineers
NJC	National Joint Committee of Postal and Telegraph Associations

NSES	National Society of Electrotypers and Stenographers
NSTE	National Society of Telephone Employees
NSW	New South Wales
NSWTA	New South Wales Typographical Association
NTC	National Telephone Company
NUM	National Union of Mineworkers
NUPBPW	National Union of Printing Bookbinding and Paper Workers
NUPT	National Union of Press Telegraphists
NUT	National Union of Teachers
PEPLP	Federated Photo Engravers, Photo-Lithographers and Photogravure Employees, Association of Australia
PIEUA	Printing Industries Employees Union of Australia
PKIU	Printing and Kindred Industries Union
POEU	Post Office Engineering Union
PSU	Public Services Union
PTEU	Plumbing Trade Employees Union
PTTA	Postal Telecommunications Technicians Association
PTTI	Postal, Telegraph & Telephone International
RIRMA	Revisers and Ink Roller Manufacture Auxiliaries branch
SGA	Scottish Graphical Association
SLADE	Society of Lithographic Artists, Designers, Engravers and Process Workers
SOGAT	Society of Graphical and Allied Trades
SPTFC	Sydney Printing Trades Federation Council
STE	Society of Telecom Executives
TA	Telecom Australia
TA	Typographical Association

TGWU	Transport and General Workers Union
The Bloc	The Anti-Communist Bloc
TTEG	Telephone and Telegraph Engineering Guild
TUC	Trades Union Congress
UCW	Union of Communication Workers
UPW	Union of Postal Workers
VBEF	Vehicle Builders Employees Federation of Australia
VPOU	Victorian Print Operatives Union
VPTGWU	Victorian Printing Trades and Graphical Workers Union

CHAPTER I

Introduction

The questions that form the core of this book started to take shape in the late 1980s. At that time I was working for the Banking, Insurance and Finance Union (BIFU) as a National Official, having recently left the University of Warwick, where I had been a Research Associate in the Industrial Relations Research Unit (IRRU). During my time at Warwick, I had become increasingly interested in what factors shaped union policies and in those theories which sought to explain union behaviour. This interest heightened during my time at BIFU, where I participated in national policy-making and observed the influences on those of us who were making policy choices. The decisions that we made were often markedly different to those taken in similar circumstances by the other unions that I had been active within, the GMB and the TGWU. Significantly the reality of policy formation, in all three unions, did not seem to be explained by any of the analytical frameworks that had been put forward by scholars to explain union policy-making. It was this disparity between the theory and the reality of policy-making that prompted the following questions, which were eventually to form the basis of this book: how, and why, do unions adopt specific policies? What factors explain the different behaviour of similar unions, when faced with comparable policy choices?

My interest and practical knowledge of trade union policy-making originated whilst I was a lay union activist. I joined the Transport and General Workers Union (TGWU) on my first day at work and by the age of 19 had become a shop steward and branch secretary. My TGWU activism involved me in policy-making at the Regional and Trade Group level, as well as at Biennial Congresses. I also accepted an invitation to join the TGWU Broad Left faction, in which I became active. Thanks to the help of TGWU officers I gained a place at Newcastle Polytechnic, where

I started studying industrial relations, a subject I then pursued further by undertaking an MA in Industrial Relations at the University of Warwick.

During my time as a student I was struck by the disparity between the various explanatory frameworks of union policy-making, set out by various scholars and my experience in the TGWU. This sense that there was a gap between union policy-making theories and reality did not disappear when I became more familiar with the various analytical frameworks. However I was aware that I had had little practical involvement in national decision making, and no experience of policy formation from the perspective of a full time official. These gaps in my knowledge clearly handicapped any serious attempt to critique any of these analytical frameworks, particularly 'rank and filism', which stressed the moderating role of full time officials (Webbs, 1897, 1920; Michels, 1915; Zeitlin, 1983; Cliff, 1970; Offe et al, 1985; Callincos, 1982).

Working at IRRU involved me in research which, whilst not directly focused on union policy-making, provided further insights into union decision making at the national and local level (Blissett, 1989). This understanding increased my misgivings over whether any of the various, policy-making theories accurately explained union behaviour. These doubts deepened further during my five years as a National Officer at BIFU. My work involved me in national policy-making bodies, including the National Executive Committee (NEC), and in undertaking national negotiations with a selection of finance employers. Whilst working at BIFU I became an active member of the GMB Union (thanks to the operation of a post-entry closed shop) and became Branch Secretary of the 900 strong Westminster Trade Union and Political Staffs branch. My GMB activism also involved serving on the London Regional Council and attending GMB Annual Congress.

This additional direct experience of policy-making at a national, regional and local level, in two trade unions, reinforced my conviction that there were serious flaws in all the major theories of union policy-making. Specifically my experience contradicted the contention of classical theorists (Webbs, 1897, 1920; Michels, 1915) that union policy-making was shaped by an oligarchy of senior officers, whose undertaking of their role resulted in them becoming more conservative than their members. Neither did my experience fully support the assertion of 'institutional contextualist' authors (Bain, 1970, Clegg, 1976) that a union's policies and structures were largely shaped by employer and State policies. Whilst it was undoubtedly true that the institutional and political environment impacted on all the unions' policies, they also made a series of policy selections, which, I believed, profoundly affected their performance.

Similarly the relationship between full-time officers and activists did not conform to the portrayal drawn by rank and filist authors (Callincos, 1982; Cliff, 1970; Beacham, 1970; Offe et al, 1985). My experience, across all three unions, was that officers did not, as rank and filist scholars suggest, act constantly as a brake on membership militancy. Instead, in some cases the exact opposite was the case, with officials frustrated at members' reluctance to support their calls for a more combative industrial approach. The argument put forward by political factionalist authors (Edelstein and Warner, 1975; Davis, 1987; Frenkel and Coolican, 1984; Dickenson, 1982) that it was the operation of factional groups which ensured that members had a 'democratic' choice between candidates with different policy agendas, also failed to adequately describe the reality of unions, such as BIFU and the GMB. Here, powerful and complex informal internal groups certainly operated and greatly influenced policy-making, but their cohesion was based on geographical, occupational or personal loyalty, rather than ideology.

I was aware that a number of scholars had similarly critiqued the theories of policy-making outlined above and made alternative suggestions. Undy et al's (1981) proposal that union policy-making was shaped by both 'internal and external change factors' which included the institutional context the union operated within and the operation of internal factional groups, certainly resonated with my experience. However, their work did not seem to identify which factors played a dominant role in influencing policy, nor did they recognise the influence of informal factors in policy-making such as personal loyalties friendships and enmities, which so strongly shaped BIFU, GMB and TGWU policy. Heery and Kelly's work (Heery and Kelly, 1988; Kelly, 1988, 1990; Heery, 1990; Fosh and Heery, 1990) which suggested that unions enjoy the ability to take 'strategic choices' at the local as well as national level and that those decisions are affected by ideology, gender and generation, resonated with my experiences in all three unions. However even this analysis did not fully encompass the various *micro-political* forces that I had observed strongly influencing union policy direction, in all three unions.

This gap that I perceived in the literature motivated me to produce a research proposal, the aim of which would be to discover empirical answers to the question: How, and why, do unions adopt specific policies? What factors explain the different behaviour of similar unions, when faced with comparable policy choices? I also wished to test my hypothesis that union policy-making was significantly affected by micro-political factors, such as personal friendships, loyalties and enmities. Having decided upon this area of study I then attempted to define the scope of the investigation and refine the research questions.

In the first instance, the decision was taken to locate and evaluate industrial or occupational unions which organised similar groups of workers in a specific industry, thereby allowing a comparison of policy-making in an alike industrial and institutional environment. The intention was to examine four unions, two of whom would operate discretely in one industry or profession and a further two who organised solely in another profession or industry. This would allow for a cross comparison of unions who operated in different sectors, as well as those who organised in the same industry. As Chapter 2 explains, finding unions which discretely organised similar groups of workers in two separate industries or professions, within Britain, proved to be highly problematic. This eventually led to the adoption of a comparative approach, and the choice of unions who organised in the British and Australian telecommunications and printing industries. The reasons behind the selection of these two countries and the telecommunication and printing industries unions are also outlined in the methodology.

At this initial stage, it was important to decide which areas of union policy-making was to be the focus of the study. A decision was taken to concentrate on three key areas of strategic significance; recruitment, amalgamations and union efforts to influence the labour process, which were all important to the direction and performance of any union and, in my experience, were often the subject of intense debate. Having defined these three policy areas and taken the decision to focus on the Australian and

British telecommunication and printing unions, a framework needed to be devised that would guide the analysis and allow the central questions to be addressed. To this end, a series of informal subsidiary questions were developed and then applied, to all three policy areas, in each of the featured unions.

The first of these questions was: Who makes policy? This is a query which has generated considerable debate in the literature, with various authors positing, that different groups within a union control policy-making. The classical theorists (Webbs, 1897, 1920; Michels, 1915) assert that an oligarchy of senior officers dominate decision making, whilst rank and filist's (Callincos, 1982; Cliff, 1970; Offe 1985; Fairbrother, 1990; Fairbrother and Yates, 2003) hold that policy-making authority has to be constantly wrested by lay activists from officers. Other scholars alternatively argue that policy-making is the product of a more complex and interdependent relationship between different groups operating at diverse levels of a union's structure (Edwards, 1983; Kelly, 1988; Fosh and Heery, 1990; Kelly and Heery, 1989). One of the objectives of the research was to ascertain who the key decision makers were, in all of the different unions, and to determine what factors allowed them to wield policy authority. If this question could be successfully answered, it would constitute an important contribution to this debate.

Linked to the above investigation was another question: How is policy formed? Behind this question lay the desire to explore the different strength of various formal decision making bodies within a union's structure, and the influence on policy-making of informal, often less visible groups, such as political, occupational and geographical factions. The question also allowed for an exploration of how the dynamics of the relationship, between full-time officers and lay representatives, affected policy formation in all the unions. This subject is also a source of considerable contention in the literature and the intention was that the evidence gathered would allow this book to make an informed comment on the nature of policy formation.

Developing this line of inquiry further was the subject of the next question: How is policy implemented? This question sought to focus on the responses of different strata of union representatives to policy decisions, and whether these various groups can alter, subvert or even simply ignore the national policies of their union. What factors determine whether groups in a union have this ability to adjust or ignore policy was also examined. The ability of employers and the State to respond, often negatively, to union policy, and the impact that these reactions have on policy implementation was also considered.

The next two subsidiary questions were closely linked and related to the factors that shape union policy makers decisions. The first was: What are the internal influences on policy makers? Specifically, this question sought to investigate the level of influence craft and occupational loyalty, democratic structures and political factions play in shaping policy makers views. This question also allowed for an enquiry into how micro-political factors such as personal respect, friendships and enmities affected policy-making in all the unions surveyed.

How decision makers' views were shaped was also the subject of the next, related question: What are the external influences on policy makers? Discovering to what extent legislation, technological change, Government policies, employer actions and industrial relations structures affected union policy makers, was the aim of this question. Whilst it was acknowledged that there can be myriad external forces which influence individual union's policy choices, it was these wider contextual external forces that were the focus of this element of the research.

The final, subsidiary question was: How successful were the policies the unions adopted? In seeking answers to this question, the various policies the unions selected were evaluated, and judgements were then reached as to whether the policies adopted were the most effective available, given the circumstances the union faced. A comparison of the relative success of the different unions' policy responses, when they were faced with corresponding institutional or political challenges, was also undertaken.

Once the central and subsidiary research questions were put together in a formal proposal, I was successful in an application for a three year Commonwealth Scholarship to undertake a PhD at the University of New South Wales. The field research was completed by 1996, the final year of my scholarship. Unfortunately I then fell seriously ill and by the time I had made a full recovery in 1997, my funding had ceased. It was imperative that I secured paid employment and I was successful in an application to become a GMB Organising Officer. Over the next twelve years I held a number of full-time officer positions in the GMB including Regional Organiser, Senior Organiser, National Secretary and London Regional Secretary. All of these roles involved me in policy-making at the workplace, branch, regional and national level, with my period as London Regional Secretary seeing me serve on the Regional Committee and the national Central Executive Council. During my time working for the union it was impracticable to complete my research and it was only when I was made redundant in 2009, that I was able to contemplate finishing the PhD that I had started fifteen years earlier.

Having applied successfully to restart my PhD at Cardiff University the decision was taken to update the fieldwork in both countries, but to still maintain a strong focus on policy-making during the period from 1980 to 1996. These were the years which were the primary focus of the original empirical research. This choice allowed for a full use of the interviews, observations and data that had been gathered in the mid-1990s, whilst it also provided the benefits of retrospection in assessing the policy choices the respective unions had made, in what had proved to be a tumultuous period in all of their histories. It is this research which provides the empirical substance of this book.

The book is comprised of thirteen chapters. Following this introduction (Chapter 1), there is a description of methodology (Chapter 2) which describes why the British and Australian printing and telecommunication unions were selected as the comparators and the reasons for the adoption of an interview rich, qualitative, approach to the field research. The following chapter, Union policy-making – theoretical perspectives (Chapter 3), consists of a broad evaluation of the literature that surrounds union policy-making, plus an appraisal of the work that considers union recruitment, amalgamations and efforts to influence the labour process. In the next four chapters (chapters 4–7) the historical evolution of policy-making, and those factors which influenced decision makers in the respective Australian and British telecommunication and printing industries unions, are analysed. Each chapter charts the organisational, occupational and ideological development of the unions, which shaped their internal structures and informed their policy approaches. These four chapters also explore the external and internal influences which helped to shape the specific policy positions towards recruitment, amalgamation and the labour process, which the unions had adopted by the start of the 1980s.

The main body of the empirical research is then set out in the next four chapters (Chapters 8–11). These chapters encompass a detailed examination of the recruitment, amalgamation and labour process policies adopted by the Australian and British printing and telecommunication unions. Each one of the chapters incorporates a detailed analysis of the factors that shape policy makers decisions; these include internal influences such as occupational, craft, ideological and micro political loyalties as well as external institutional, political and technological pressures. Comparisons are also made of the policies adopted by the various unions in each of the three areas. A summary and findings chapter (Chapter 12) follows which précises the findings of the book and juxtaposes the empirical data gathered, against the theories of union policy-making set out in Chapter 3. The final chapter of this book (Chapter 13) is the conclusion. It seeks to draw together the key findings of this book, whilst also reflecting on what the implications of the results of the research are for the wider union movement and the debate over union policy-making.

CHAPTER 2

Methodology

Introduction

This chapter explains why a qualitative, interview rich, methodology was adopted, in order to answer the two central research questions: How, and why, do unions adopt specific policies? What factors explain the different behaviour of similar unions, when faced with comparable policy choices in three specific areas; recruitment, amalgamations and influencing the labour process?

Initially the chapter will concentrate on why a comparative approach was adopted in order to try and answer these questions. As part of this section, an explanation will be provided as to why Britain and Australia were selected as the comparator countries. The reasons for the choice of the respective nations' printing and telecommunication unions will also be addressed.

The strengths and weaknesses of the adopted methodology, in testing the research hypothesis that informal micro-political influences inside trade unions – such as personal friendships, enmities and loyalties – affect union policy-making to a greater extent than is acknowledged in union policy-making literature, are also considered.

Finally the various problems and limitations with the adopted methodology are highlighted, as are the reasons why other methodological approaches were not deployed.

The reasons for the adoption of comparative research

In the early 1990s, when the book was at its gestation phase, the aim was to focus solely on British trade unions. The original intention was to undertake a detailed examination of a small number of unions, who faced similar industrial and technical challenges, organised like memberships and possessed closely comparable internal structures. Finding unions with these industrial, organisational and structural similarities would, it was hoped, eliminate variance in union policy and behaviour, which were simply the results of vastly different institutional contexts. I also anticipated that the knowledge and contacts, I had gained over 20 years as a lay activist and full-time officer, would assist me in securing the cooperation of the relevant unions.

Preliminary research quickly identified the difficulty in locating unions who not only possessed similar internal structures, but who had also confronted parallel industrial challenges, whilst organising directly comparable memberships. A number of British unions which appeared initially to be good comparators, such as the NUT and the NASUWT, displayed on closer examination many significant structural and contextual differences, which made meaningful comparisons problematic.

This difficulty in locating suitable domestic comparator unions, led to consideration being given to the possibility of comparing unions who organised alike workers, in different countries. The hope being that close comparators could be found which would provide better data for addressing the research questions. In exploring the possibility of an international comparison at least two countries were sought, that had related institutional structures and possessed unions which had similar memberships, alike internal structures and who faced comparable industrial challenges. In seeking comparator countries, there was a strong wish to retain Britain as one of the comparators, so as to utilise the knowledge and contacts I had within the British union movement. A careful trawl of possible comparator nations resulted in the decision that a valid comparison of Australian and British unions was possible. This was owing to their extensive economic, political and institutional similarities, whilst they also possessed trade unions that had similar organisational and policy-making structures.

The reason for these similarities, as subsequent chapters chart, rested largely upon the legacy of Britain's colonisation of Australia in the eighteenth century. The subsequent period of imperial rule resulted in the creation of political, social and legal structures, which closely resembled those of Britain. Equally as importantly, the British (and Irish) migrants who populated the Australian colonies, either formed branches of British unions, or created unions which were structurally and organisationally similar to their British unions. For a number of Australian unions this commonality of structure and organisation did not alter with independence, federation or the evolution of the arbitral system. Crucially, at the start of the fieldwork in 1994 there were still unions in Australia who organised identical groups of members, in a nearly identical organisational fashion, as their British counterparts. These structural similarities encompassed both nations possessing just one major national union confederation: the British Trade Union Congress (TUC) and the Australian Confederation of Trade Unions (ACTU), whilst many unions were also affiliated to their respective Labour/Labor Parties.

The similarities in the evolution of the Australian and British economies during the latter part of the twentieth century also provided the basis for comparison of union responses to similar industrial and technical challenges. Both nations had suffered declines in their manufacturing sectors, from the early 1970s onwards, owing to the growth of global competition. The resultant attempts by Australian and British employers to introduce new technology provided a significant challenge to the unions' influence, over the labour process in heavily unionised sectors of the economy. The widespread replacement of full-time manufacturing jobs, with part-time and temporary employment in the service sector, occurred in both economies, creating similar recruitment challenges for the unions.

Politically, the two union movements have also faced comparable challenges in the last three decades. In Britain (1979–1997) and then Australia (1996–2007) conservative political parties gained and retained power for four terms of office, during which time they introduced a host of legislative constraints on union ability to operate closed shops and to take industrial action. In addition, the Liberal/Country National Party Government was able to effectively dismantle large tranches of the federal arbitral model of industrial relations. This left Australia by 2007, with a system of industrial relations that closely resembled the British model, as fashioned by the Thatcher Conservative Government.

This convergence in the two nations' national industrial relations systems was mirrored in the economic and social spheres, with the Liberal/ Country National Federal Government's enthusiastic adoption of the British Conservative Government's (1979–1997) polices of wholesale economic deregulation and privatisation. It should, though, be acknowledged that elements of these deregulatory economic policies had, controversially, first been introduced by the ALP Federal Government (1983–1994).

By the mid-1990s the increasing convergence of institutional factors in Britain and Australia created the circumstances in which the industrial, political and membership challenges faced by the two trade union movements were increasingly similar. The requirement now was to discover if a small number of unions could be located, in both countries, which faced parallel industrial and technical challenges, organised alike memberships and possessed closely comparable internal structures. At this stage, in order to try and achieve a balance between being able to conduct the requisite depth of study and securing an analytically robust set of comparative data, the decision was taken to try to find comparator unions in two industries in both countries.

Selecting the comparator unions

The need to locate unions which faced similar challenges to their influence over the labour process ruled out a substantial number of potential comparators. In industries such as mining or forestry, the differences in industrial methods, ownership and scale, to say nothing of internal structures ruled out such a comparison. Major structural differences in the public sectors of both nations also made cross-national evaluations problematic. The nature of the constitution, which gave the Australian States authority over public services, was then reflected in the public service unions' structures. Many

Australian public services unions only organised in a specific State, or were highly autonomous branches of a loosely federated national union. This was dissimilar to Britain where public service workers were organised by national unions.

An examination of both countries did though result in the locating of two industries, printing and telecommunications, where the unions faced similar challenges to their influence over the labour process, thanks to corresponding technological, political and economic developments. The unions also displayed closely comparable membership makeups and related corresponding internal structures. This was the case at the start of the empirical research, in 1994, when all of the industries were organised, principally, by a single industrial union. In Australia these unions were the Printing and Kindred Industries Union (PKIU) and the Communication Workers Union (CWU), whilst in Britain it was the Graphical Paper and Media Union (GPMU) and the National Communications Union (NCU).

During the course of the fieldwork, amalgamations took place which saw these industrial unions become part of larger general or multi-industrial unions. However the structural similarities and parallel membership coverage of the two printing and the two telecommunications unions, at the start of the research, was pronounced. The structural and organisational similarities between the PKIU and GPMU could be traced back to the nineteenth century, when British emigrants to Australia formed identical printing craft unions. The strength of this model of print unionism was considerable, and its structures remained firmly in place up until the 2000s. These similarities involved the unions having financially and constitutionally strong branches and chapels, who enjoyed considerable policy-making autonomy. There were also parallel rivalries between the various craft and non-craft unions, which resulted in comparable demarcation disputes and strained inter-union relationships. The industrial and technological challenges that the respective print unions had faced, were also comparable, whilst the successful adoption and implementation of the pre-entry closed shop had secured impressive levels of control over the labour process and high membership density. In the 1980s both nations' print unions faced significant employer and State opposition to these long-standing organisational and industrial methods. The analysis of the Australian and British unions' policy responses to these challenges forms an important component of this book.

In the telecommunications industry, the Australian CWU and the British NCU also displayed similarities in their internal structures and membership coverage. Unlike the print unions this resemblance was not the result of the conscious creation by British emigrants of identical unions. Instead, the British and Australian telecommunications unions developed along comparable lines thanks in large part to the operational similarities found in the two countries' General Post Offices. This likeness extended into the introduction of similar occupational divisions and grading structures, which, when added to similar collective bargaining structures resulted in unions being formed along comparable occupational lines.

Uniting these occupationally differentiated unions proved to be problematic in both nations, with demarcation rivalries adversely affecting inter-union relationships. The similarities between both nations' telecommunication unions also extended into their branch structures, where a large proportion of collective bargaining and membership representation, was undertaken by local branch officers, without national union assistance. This level of branch autonomy resulted in all the national unions struggling to exert policy control over the branches, which had a history of taking unilateral action. There were also strong political factions operating within both countries' telecommunications unions, and they played a very significant role in shaping union policy.

The nature of the two nations' telecommunications industries had also been similar since the early twentieth century, when telegraph and telephony services were nationalised. The State remained the monopoly provider of telecommunication services in Britain until the 1980s and in Australia until the 1990s, when deregulation introduced competition and the privatisation of the respective national carriers. Following the introduction of deregulation both national carriers experienced loss of market share which, when combined with rapid technological advances, greatly reduced the labour force. The subsequent privatisation of BT and Telstra resulted, by 2008, in BT shedding over 90,000 jobs, whilst Telstra had cut its workforce by over 30,000. How the Australian and British unions responded to these seismic shifts in their industrial, political and technological environments, is addressed in this book.

Selecting the most effective methodology

Selecting a methodology, that would most effectively provide answers to the research questions, was an important consideration. Adopting a predominantly quantitative methodology was considered and then rejected at an early stage. There were two keys reasons for this decision. Firstly, the inquisitorial nature of the research questions and hypothesis did not lend themselves to a quantitative research approach, as various research methods authors have stated (Bryman, 2004; Bryman and Bell, 2007; Silverman, 2000). Secondly I knew, from practical experience, that many unions regularly distorted their published membership and recruitment figures, whilst union officers and activists were also extremely wary of responding openly to any form of survey, where they did not know and trust those undertaking the research. At first hand I had seen unions deliberately manipulating their participation in such quantitative research by regularly distorting membership and recruitment figures and giving less than truthful responses to questionnaires. In some instances this was for good industrial reasons, relating to recognition agreements and the retaining of bargaining rights. In others the reasons were political, with union leaderships wishing to either exaggerate their membership in order to retain status and delegates to labour movement bodies, or to understate their membership, so that they reduced their affiliation fees to the same organisations. There were also instances where very strong recruitment figures would be under-declared in order to build up a pool of recruits, which could be drawn upon, when recruitment slowed. In order to overcome these barriers and to successfully undertake the exploratory nature of the research a predominantly quantitative methodology was rejected.

After rejecting the quantitative approach, a qualitative methodology, which relied heavily upon secondary sources, specifically official journals, minutes and union histories, was also considered. There were a number of benefits to such an approach (see Bryman and Bell, 2007) as the vast majority of the relevant unions kept – thanks to their craft and occupational traditions – meticulous minutes of all their meetings, from their

National Executive Committee down to the smallest Chapel meeting. Many of these minutes, and other documents such as journals, were held at either the unions' offices or in British and Australian academic institutions. Gaining access to these materials, preliminary enquires confirmed, would be relatively straightforward and the resources available would cover a long historical time-frame, which would allow for the study of the development of union policy over an extended period. This, as Chapter 1 identified, would be beneficial, as it would allow for the analysis of how policy was formulated and then modified, with the opportunity to focus on what factors altered the policy direction of a union.

However, there were a number of serious difficulties with the adoption of such a methodological approach. In all the unions I had worked for, or been active within, union documents either deliberately excluded, or sanitised, all records of policy debates and the alternative policy options that were discussed. This was even the case in those meetings where a 'verbatim' minute was taken of the meeting. Here the editing process, which was meant to simply correct 'typographical errors' became an exercise in expurgation. The union verbatim records therefore became a mechanism for the recording of policy decisions, with only limited mention of any debates and no detailing of arguments over alternative policy options, which were considered and rejected. As research methods authors note (Silverman, 2000; Bryman, 2004) this form of distortion, is a potential difficulty faced by scholars, when they rely simply on the official published records of any organisation. Whilst these official union documents still provided a useful source of information, they were not a source that could be relied upon to answer many of the detailed questions over policy choice that this book posed.

There were a number of reasons why unions produced these less than candid official records. Primarily they feared being portrayed as disunited, which they believed would weaken their negotiating position with employers and undermine the faith their members had in the organisation. To this end any reporting of internal disagreements was suppressed. This wish was particularly powerfully expressed during industrial negotiations or disputes, when the desire to appear unified led to official records being heavily censored. Preliminary discussions with the officers of the British printing and telecommunication unions, suggested that their unions had also acted in a very similar fashion. There were also, often justified, concerns that a predominantly hostile media would distort any debates over policy, by portraying them as evidence of internal divisions. This depiction could, some senior officers' feared, then translate into members losing confidence in their union's prosecution of a dispute.

Another reason that unions were reticent about openly discussing the true nature of their policy process was apprehension over the reaction of 'ordinary' members if the role and nature of, often strong, political factions was highlighted. Many officers, including paradoxically many who were faction members, were keen to stifle mention of internal political factions, and their links to radical political parties. Their fear was that the members would react negatively if they believed their union's policies were being influenced by members of radical political parties. For this reason, the role of various parties – in particular Communist and Trotskyist parties – inside BL groups was not highlighted in factional literature. As for official union literature there was seldom, if ever, any mention of factions or their activities. This was the case even in unions where no candidate had been elected to serve on the NEC, or in a senior full-time officer position, without factional support.

All of these concerns over the possible adverse consequences of candidly documenting the internal workings of their union led to official union materials being a less than wholly reliable source of information about union policy-making. To rely on them could potentially lead to serious misapprehensions about the reality of policy formulation, in particular the forces which shape its creation and amendment. These are issues which a number of scholars of archival sourcing (Bryman, 2004; Silverman, 2000) have also noted.

Aside from official internal union publications the other major secondary source of information are official union histories. These books were clearly a rich source of data, as they related the sweep of a union's historical development, whilst also focusing on major industrial conflicts and significant policy decisions. Many of the print and telecommunication union histories were written by noted scholars (Hagan, 1966; Gennard, 1990; Gennard and Bain, 1995; Bealey, 1976). However, personal experience had shown that when union leaders commissioned official histories they were keen for themselves and their union to be portrayed in a positive light. This led to considerable restrictions being placed on the freedom of authors to write candidly about internal conflicts within the union, or to criticise the policy choices of the current union leadership, who had commissioned the work (see Callow's, 2012, history of the GMB). This desire to ensure that their official histories were not overtly critical also saw leaders demand editorial control over the final draft.

Preliminary interviews with officers of the printing and telecommunication unions, confirmed that all their official union histories were subject to this type of restriction. Having read the relevant unions histories (Howe and Child, 1952; Bundock, 1959; Fitzgerald, 1967; Hagan, 1966; Gennard, 1990; Gennard and Bain, 1995; Gennard and Hayward, 2008; Waters, 1978; Bealey, 1976) and then commenced interviews with officers and lay activists, it quickly became clear that all the authors had written versions of events, which often expunged or sanitised major internal arguments, factional conflicts and bitter personal rivalries. They also tended to write very favourably about the current leadership of the relevant union. The collective result was that these accounts were partial, and in some cases thoroughly bowdlerised, versions of history. As one senior British printing union officer observed when commenting on his own union's official history:

> We weren't going to pay for the truth of our internal backstabbing and infighting to be published.

All of these doubts over the reliability of union histories, alongside the problems with the accuracy of union records and journals, led to the conclusion that adopting a methodology which rested extensively on these secondary sources would be unwise. This is not to say that these sources should be ignored, as official histories, journals and minutes are invaluable sources of information on the official viewpoint of the union's leadership over a whole host of issues. Where though these sources need to be treated with great circumspection is in their portrayal of contentious policy issues, inter union disputes, or the success of industrial policies, such as recruitment campaigns and official strikes. Over such subjects the subjectivity of union publications and histories means that it would be prudent to use a multiplicity of primary, as well as secondary sources, in order to try and establish a more authentic depiction of the policy formulation and modification process. Once this has been achieved, then the danger of building an analysis of policy-making, based upon unreliable data, is greatly lessened.

Aside from union commissioned or produced publications, there are a number of different books and articles that cover not only the broader subject matter of print and telecommunication union policy-making, but also specific events in the unions history (Melvern, 1986; Littleton, 1992; Richardson, 2003; Gennard, 1988; Bain, 1998; Dickenson, 1984; Parker, 2009), or of particular groups of workers (Cockburn, 1984, 1991; Darlington, 1994). All of these authors' works are addressed in greater detail in Chapter 3. What is significant is the way in which authors who gathered primary data from interviews, were able to reveal more about national union policy-making, than scholars who relied more heavily on secondary sources. Equally as significantly authors such as Bain (1998), freed of the editorial constraints of co-authoring SOGAT's official union history, was more forthright in documenting the internal discord over policy direction, which afflicted the print unions during the News International dispute. The problems with the reliability of secondary data meant that it was essential to adopt a methodology which would ensure access to considerable quantities of primary information, in order for the research questions to be addressed.

The selected methodology

For all the reasons outlined above it was a relatively straightforward decision to adopt a methodological approach which relied heavily on the collection of primary data directly from participants in union policy-making. However, realising a methodology which successfully provided reliable data, for comparison and analysis was a considerable challenge. For reasons that have been documented, union officers are often reticent about providing accurate information and offering candid comment, over contentious policy issues. It was therefore necessary to identify a methodology that would give lay activists and officers sufficient confidence, in order that they participated and contributed candidly.

In contemplating how best to gather the views of officers and activists the use of questionnaires, face-to-face interviews, telephone interviews and observation were all considered. The sensitive nature of the research questions, which sought to delve into influences on an individual's policy choices and the role of factional allegiances, led to the more impersonal questionnaire and telephone interviews methods being rejected, a decision which is in line with the recommendations of many qualitative research methods scholars (see Silverman, 2000). This decision was also strongly informed by my experience as a full-time officer. I knew that academic questionnaires were often not answered by officials (unless a senior officer was conspicuously supporting their completion), and that they were treated with suspicion by those who felt obliged to undertake them. The chances therefore of eliciting frank contributions from a lay or full-time officer, whom you may never have met, over internal policy issues and factional struggles, would be next to nil. Similarly, attempting to build up a sufficient rapport with an interviewee you did not know, over the telephone, so that that they would speak openly about such issues, would be extremely difficult.

The wariness of union officers and activists towards external researchers also made observation a difficult method to initially employ successfully. Union officers and activists, I knew from experience, would often be extremely suspicious of being observed and may well behave in a different manner than they would normally, if an observer was present. However I did not rule out observation as a research method, if and when a high level of trust had been established with the relevant participants, which would ensure they behaved naturally when being observed. Such levels of confidence were eventually established amongst many participants and observations of numerous meetings did take place, which are detailed later in this chapter.

The total, or partial, rejection of these various methods of data collection left face-to-face interviews, as the chief means of gathering primary evidence. Whilst this process involved the consumption of considerably more time and resources than the other methods, it was this approach, as a number of research methods scholars concur, that was most likely to provide accurate information in these types of circumstances (see Silverman, 1984, 2000; Bryman, 2004; Bryman and Ball, 2007). In order to ensure that the interviews were as effective as possible in eliciting the candid views and opinions of interviewees, a semi-structured format was adopted. This technique was embraced so as to allow as much latitude as possible, in the interview, for the exploration of the interviewee's opinions, whilst still retaining a structure which would provide readily comparable information from each interview (see Silverman, 1984, 2000; Bryman, 2004; Bryman and Ball, 2007).

The requirement to place interviewees at their ease also informed the manner in which the interviews were documented. Drawing upon personal experience, and conversations with former union colleagues, I was aware that union officials (including myself) became less open if they were being tape-recorded during interviews. This was the case even if the interviewer was an academic as opposed to a journalist. The reason was the fear that any unguarded comment could, potentially, be disseminated to a third party or used against them internally. The nature of the subjects that would be raised in the interviews meant that such reserve would be damaging to the quality of the information gathered. Therefore the inconvenience of not having an audio record was preferable to having an interviewee made more reticent, by the presence of a tape recorder. The lack of audio recordings meant that short hand notes were made of interviews, although there were a large number of occasions when the nature of the discussion warranted the cessation of note taking altogether. In these circumstances, summaries of what had been said were recorded immediately after the interview concluded. This was also the method used to record conversations with officers and activists when discussions took place at informal social events, or union meetings.

Having decided upon a methodology which would provide good quality information, it was imperative that the British and Australian printing and telecommunication unions, agreed to allow their officers to participate. Without such an agreement it was unlikely that full-time officers of the union would participate in the study, whilst the ability to access internal documents would be severely restricted. Gaining this agreement of all the nominated unions was by no means assured. The nature of the proposed research and the reluctance of unions to disclose their internal affairs, made the process problematic. Other authors (Watson, 1988; Kelly and Heery, 1994; Heery, 2004, 2006) who had conducted attitudinal research amongst full-time officers had previously been denied access by certain unions. Whilst the relatively large sample size of their studies meant that these rejections did not undermine the validity of their work, this would not be the case with this research. Its methodology depended on a small number of unions granting full co-operation; if one union was not to do so the whole comparative framework would be badly damaged. The need therefore to secure the co-operation of each union was critical.

In order to achieve this agreement, informal contacts were initially made with colleagues and friends inside the relevant British unions, to ensure that when the formal written request for access was made, there would be individuals who could vouch for me and the legitimacy of the research. The importance of this approach was later confirmed by a senior officer of one union, who stated that if other officers had not vouched for me, then the General Secretary would have refused to allow any of his officers to participate in the study.

Even after securing the assistance of the selected unions, I was made aware that there was still concern, inside some unions, over exactly how sensitive information on policy-making, would be gathered, stored and used. These concerns manifested themselves in the reluctance of some officers, of one union, to commit to being interviewed. As it was so important to the validity of the fieldwork that a broad spectrum of officials and activists, from the different strands of industrial, occupational, geographical and political groups participated, steps were immediately taken to overcome these potential contributors concerns. All prospective interviewees were reassured that all records of their comments would be kept completely confidential, that all published documents would protect their anononimity, and that there would be no audio recordings made of the interviews.

More importantly, I benefitted from the assistance of friends inside this union who reassured their concerned colleagues that I was not engaged in a project hostile to them, or their union.

Thankfully these assurances and the intervention of their colleagues worked with the overwhelming majority of potential contributors. Understandably some interviewees were not minded to give up their free time, or to travel to be interviewed. The decision to give an assurance that I would travel to any part of Britain or Australia, at a time and date of the interviewees choosing, to conduct the interview, helped secure the contribution of a number of reluctant contributors. It also resulted in a number of memorable and lengthy trips across Australia, including a 400 mile drive into the bush to meet a retired officer at his country NSW smallholding. A trip, which thanks to the kindness of the relevant union's, State Organiser, I undertook with him in a union vehicle suitably equipped for the task. Other interviewees understandably agreed only to meet whilst at work, which in the case of one newspaper Father of Chapel (FoC) involved conducting the interview, whilst the presses were running, at two o'clock in the morning.

Having secured the assistance of the vast majority of interviewees there was only a tiny minority of officers and activists left who had declined to be interviewed. This small group did though contain two very senior officers of one union, whose non-participation would leave a gap in the empirical evidence, which in a study which relied so heavily on primary research, would be damaging to the validity of the findings. Great efforts were therefore made to persuade these officials to change their mind. Informal direct contact was engineered at social functions, in order to try and persuade the prospective interviewees, face-to-face, to participate. Further phone calls and letters were also sent, which sought to deal with any concerns that these officers may have had about the project. Most importantly (as it later transpired), friends of those refusing to contribute intervened and were able to persuade their senior colleagues to participate. By the end of this process of reassurance and persuasion all of those officers and activists who were approached agreed to be interviewed. The only exceptions being those retired officers and lay officials who sadly either died, or became so seriously ill, that they could not participate in an interview.

At the conclusion of the fieldwork over 220 officers and activists, from the two nation's telecommunication and printing unions, had been interviewed.[1] A number of participants, who were central to their union's policy-making, were interviewed more than once with 46 contributors being interviewed twice, whilst a further group of 27 participants were interviewed three times or more. In addition to these interviewees a small number of British and Australian telecommunication and printing industry managers also contributed to the study.

These interviews were though only part of the process of gaining information about the views of policy makers and the influences upon their decision making. The relatively loose structure of the interviews and the unusual experience of being interviewed by an officer of another union generated a number of questions from the interviewees, which allowed the interview to become more discursive. This trend I welcomed as it provided the platform for a more relaxed environment in which it was possible to undertake an exploration of contributors' views and the factors that influenced their decision making choices.

During and after the interviews a sizeable number of participants wished to hear more, either about the recruitment and organisational policies of the unions I had represented, or the industrial developments that were occurring in the industries I had organised, or studied. This led to a series of invitations not only to have further discussions but also to speak to their colleagues at a variety of different forums. These included branch, sectional and Federal/National meetings, Federal and National Delegate conferences, officer and shop steward training seminars and a joint management and union training weekend.

All of these invitations I was delighted to accept, as they allowed me to reciprocate the assistance I was receiving, whilst also gaining excellent access to policy makers and union decision making forums.[2] Having spoken

---

1   An anonymised list of all participants is provided in Appendix 1.
2   It should though be acknowledged that I made a number of speeches to unions who were not the subject of the study, in a fraternal effort to assist in their efforts to recruit members and build their industrial strength.

at a number of these union meetings and conferences it was noticeable that interviewees became more relaxed in my presence. This, gratifyingly, occurred in all the unions, and made securing multiple interviews with key policy makers more straightforward. It was also noticeable that interviewees who had heard me speak were subsequently more prepared to discuss the nuances of policy-making and the factional, occupational and personal influences that had shaped their policy choices. This greater level of confidence that senior officers and lay members felt in me, manifested itself in other ways. I was allowed to observe significant policy-making meetings including three unions Federal/National Executive's committees. This level of access was highly unusual, with senior officers from two of the unions informing me that, as far as they could recall, I was the first person from outside the union to observe the whole of a National/Federal Executive meeting.

As the study progressed, central figures in union factions also decided to speak more openly about their factional organisation and to allow me access to factional meetings. Pleasingly, given my factional background, the unions Right, as well as Left, factions felt sufficiently confident in my discretion to discuss their factional activities and the influence they wielded over policy. To my surprise, in two of the unions, both the Right and Left factions allowed me to attend their pre-meetings, held before National/ Federal Executives, and openly discussed their plans for electorally defeating the opposing faction. This provided me with a fascinating and privileged insight into the operation of these factions, and their influence on policy formulation.

In establishing this remarkable level of access I was assisted not only by my union background and contacts, but also by the longitudinal nature of the field work. Undertaking detailed research initially over three years and then subsequently over fifteen years, allowed lay and full-time officers to get to know me well, not only via interviews, but also at union social events and in unplanned conversations that took place, when I was in their offices attending meetings or conducting further research. Whilst I ensured that all participants were aware that I was undertaking research and that their views may be used, albeit in an anonymised form, the informal nature of the contact in a relaxed social setting assisted in putting contributors at ease and led to an enormous amount of extremely useful information being provided. The benefits associated with conducting qualitative fieldwork over a substantial period of time, and the advantages of having 'insider' status are also acknowledged by a number of research methods authors (Silverman, 1984, 2000; Bryman, 2004).

Another advantage of the research being spread over many years was the ability it provided for participants to test whether I would respect confidentiality. By the second and third interviews, with key policy makers, they were aware that I had not shared the contents of their initial contribution with any third party, be they inside or outside their union. This realisation was invaluable, as the participants were, in their latter interviews reassured that they could speak candidly to me, with no possibility of their views being disseminated. This confidence led to second and subsequent interviews being more open, which allowed me to probe more deeply into the micro-political influences and those factors which influenced their policy choices. Once again the importance of acting in this type of ethical fashion is prominent in the works of many research methods scholars (Bryman, 2004; Bryman and Ball, 2007; Silverman, 1984, 2000).

The success or failure of the adopted methodology largely rested upon whether high levels of confidence and trust could be engendered amongst the participants. Without certainty that their opinions would be treated with complete discretion, the likelihood was that little of value would be elicited from the interviews. The ability to politely deflect the often skilful probing of union leaders into what individuals from opposing groups had told me, alongside the recording of interviews and information in a hard to decipherer personalised shorthand,[3] all contributed to securing the candid views of participants, which were often at odds with their public pronouncements. This success allowed for access and insight into areas of union behaviour that had previously been hidden from outside observers.

---

3   This method was adopted so that if the notes of interviews fell, temporarily or permanently, into third parties hands, they could not be deciphered easily.

Problems and limitations with the selected methodology

Adopting a methodology, which relied so heavily on the collection of primary data, had disadvantages, as well as benefits. Whilst there were good reasons, detailed earlier in this chapter, not to rely significantly on secondary union sources, the resultant reliance on information gathered from interviews and first hand observations presented difficulties in relation to testing the validity of the information provided. The nature of the policy questions meant that it was necessary to try and elicit candid statements from contributors about the reasons why they had taken specific decisions, and what those forces were which influenced their policy choices.

Judging whether an interviewee is telling the truth about their actions is difficult; whilst deciding if they are being candid over the reasons for their behaviour and what factors influenced their action, is extremely problematic. Whilst it is possible to substantiate the validity of an interviewees' recall of their actions, by asking others present for their recollections; it is not possible to validate an individual's account of their own motivations, or the factors that influenced their decisions. Whilst therefore all steps were taken to ensure that interviewees were confident that their views would only ever be reported in an anonymous form and their confidences would never be breached, there can be no guarantee that individual participants did not ascribe motivations to themselves, or influences upon them, that were in reality false. However the large sample size and the consistency of views that were provided, does suggest that this inherent problem with this type of research, was largely negated.

Another drawback to depending so heavily upon interviews, as Bryman (2004) and Silverman (2000) note is the natural distortion that occurs when contributors attempt to recall the actions that were taken decades previously. This was a particular problem as the research necessitated reviewing the manner in which changing institutional environments and alterations to a union's internal micro politics, had affected policy decisions, which necessitated participants recalling events and decisions made many years earlier. The fragility of the health and memory of participants also meant that there was only a very small band of interviewees who could recall the policy debates from before the early 1960s, which led to the focus of the research gravitating towards events that occurred in the two decades preceding the start of the research in 1994.

Although considerable amounts of time and effort were devoted to finding comparable countries that possessed unions who had similar internal structures, organised corresponding memberships and had confronted parallel industrial challenges, the reality is that no union faces identical policy challenges nor is indistinguishable from another in their membership and structure. Whilst the two countries printing and telecommunication unions had faced very similar industrial challenges there were noteworthy differences in the size and geographical concentration of both industries. The Australian printing and telecommunication sectors employed fewer workers than in Britain (although as a proportion of the population the employment ratios were similar) and concentrations of employment were more geographically dispersed in Australia, reflecting the size of the country and its State based, federated, history.

Institutional differences between the two countries also caused difficulty in comparing the Australian and British unions accurately. The Australian arbitral system created a wholly different, legislative structure for wage fixation, union recognition and dispute resolution. Although from the 1980s onwards, when the ALP Federal Government initially introduced Enterprise Bargaining, Australia started to move away from the arbitral model towards a de-regulated system, the historic influence of the arbitration system was still strong, up until 1997. The direct legislative intervention by the ALP Federal Government to create larger industrial unions in the late 1980s and early 1990s, by threatening to de-register small federal unions, is another example of divergences in State policy, which affected the political and institutional framework in which the unions operated.

These variations in the comparator unions and in the institutional and political context in which they operated, limit the ability of the research to accurately compare and contrast the response of a union to a specific industrial or political challenge. These difficulties when coupled to the problems of judging the accuracy and clarity of memory, and the levels of honesty being displayed by interviewees, placed limits on the capacity of this form of qualitative research to provide totally reliable evidence (see also Bryman, 2004; Bryman and Ball, 2007; Silverman, 2000).

Conclusion

In this chapter the reasons why a qualitative, comparative, methodology was adopted, have been outlined. As this chapter has conceded, it was impossible to identify unions, which were identical and confronted matching industrial challenges. However it has been demonstrated that it was possible to identify unions in Australia and Britain, who possessed similar histories, parallel organisational coverage, comparable structures and who had confronted similar industrial challenges in comparable institutional environments. The subsequent securing of access to the key policy makers in the identified comparator unions then ensured that the interview dependent methodology could be effectively implemented.

In the subsequent empirical chapters (Chapters 4–11) the findings of the empirical research, which encompassed in excess of 290 interviews undertaken over 16 years, are set out. These research findings are then juxtaposed, in the summary and findings chapter (Chapter 12), against the theories of union policy-making which are set out in Chapter 3. It is in this chapter and the conclusion (Chapter 13) that answers to the research questions and an assessment of the hypothesis, based on analysis of the empirical evidence, are also provided.

Union Policy-Making: Theoretical Perspectives

Introduction

This chapter outlines and reviews the main bodies of literature which frame the two central questions posed by this book: How, and why, do unions' adopt specific policies? What factors explain the different behaviour of similar unions, when faced with comparable policy choices in three specific areas; recruitment, amalgamations and influencing the labour process? The chapter is comprised of four sections. The first considers general theories of union policy-making, the second work on the labour process, the third literature appertaining to amalgamations, and the fourth literature relating to recruitment. The value of these different perspectives, in explaining what was revealed by the research, is then commented upon in the empirical chapters.

In the first section the 'classic' texts of the Webbs, Michels and Turner, concerning union policy-making, democracy and control of the decision making process are considered (Webbs, 1920; Michels, 1913; Turner, 1962). This is then followed by a consideration of rank-and-filist writers who argue that full time officials act as conservative force in policy formulation (Cliff, 1970; Offe et al, 1985; Callincos, 1982; Fairbrother, 2000; Bramble, 2008). Those scholars who assert that democratic control over policy-making can only exist if there is factional competition for policy authority, are then examined (Lipset, 1956; Edelstein and Warner, 1979). The first section also considers the later literature on the role played by political factions in determining union policy-making in Australian and British unions (Dickenson, 1982; Frenkel and Coolican, 1984; McIllroy et al, 1999, 2007; Daniels and McIllroy, 2009).

The work of authors who declare that union policy is largely determined by institutional and contextual forces is the focus of the next part of the chapter (Bain, 1970; Clegg, 1976). Included here are the arguments of scholars who state that a greater diversity and individualism in society has significantly altered the context in which unions operate, forcing them to develop new policies to accommodate a changing workforce (Hyman, 1999; Dickens, 1998; Colling and Dickens, 2001). The case of authors who favour an institutional explanation of union behaviour, but place a stronger emphasis on the effect of the State, are also considered (Howell, 2005). Finally in this section, the work of writers who have developed the concept of unions being able to exert, 'strategic choice', in their policy-making are examined. This assessment will also examine the various typologies of strategic choice, which have emerged (Boxall and Haynes, 1997; Kelly, 1998; Heery and Kelly, 1994; Kelly and Heery, 1994; Heery, 2000, 2003, 2006).

In the second section authors who have focused on how unions have been able to control the labour process are examined. The central emphasis here is on the institutions of the closed shop, work demarcations and the different interpretations of these phenomena that have been developed by researchers (Dunn and Gennard, 1984). The section concludes with a discussion of work that has sought to explain the diminution of union influence over the labour process in more recent years.

The chapter's third section examines the literature concerning union amalgamation. It considers the work of scholars who propose that there is a close relationship between the capitalist economic cycle and merger 'waves' (Waddington, 1988, 1995; Waddington et al, 2005). It also examines the argument that the roles of union leaderships and legislative change have had a major impact on amalgamation activity (Undy, 1996, 2008). The discrete Australian work considering the impact on union amalgamations of federal legislation and Federal Government policy is also reviewed (Davis, 1999; Griffin, 2002; Griffin and Scarcebrook, 1989; Dabscheck, 1989).

In the final section, the literature on union recruitment and organising is reviewed. This will encompass work on the successful organising strategies of the unions in the 1960s and 1970s, and the subsequent literature on union recruitment strategies designed to reverse membership losses, in the period since the early 1980s (Terry, 2000; Willman, 2001; Heery, 2001; Heery et al, 2000a, 2000b, 2003a, 2003b; Gall, 2004; Frenge and Kelly, 2004; Cooper, 2003).

Section 1: Theoretical explanations of union policy-making

The 'classical' theorists

Attempts to theorise union policy-making, reach back over a century. In their study of British trade unionism, the Webbs (1897), suggested that as unions grew, the policy influence of full-time officers expanded, because members lacked the experience, skill and knowledge, to run their own affairs. These officials would they believed become 'marked off by capacity, training and duties from the bulk of the rank and file' (Webbs, 1897: 16). This phenomenon, they asserted, would lead to a decrease in militancy and the adoption of more moderate industrial policies as full-time officers became detached and more conservative in their views. As they observed:

> We see sturdy leaders of many trade union battles gradually and insensibly accepting the capitalist axiom that wages must necessarily fluctuate according to capitalist profits (Webbs, 1897: 338–9).

To counteract this acceptance by union officers of capitalist values the Webbs believed that union policy-making structures needed to resemble that adopted by the Amalgamated Association of Operative Cotton Spinners (AAOCS). Its structure comprised a lay central executive that was responsible for policy-making, and to which all local branches, and officers, were subordinate. Without such a structure, the Webbs believed that policy-making would always gravitate into the hands of the officials, who they felt were effectively irremovable from office, even if they faced regular elections. So convinced were they of this theory that they asserted that annual votes for union officials 'invariably resulted in a permanence of tenure exceeding that of the English civil servant' (Webbs, 1897: 16).

A contemporary of the Webbs, the German sociologist Robert Michels, drew upon their work in his book *Political Parties* (1915). Here Michels outlined his 'iron law of oligarchy', that he claimed was applicable to political parties and trade unions. The core of his argument was that governance by the people (or union members) was impractical, and that all those parties who sought to govern on their behalf, would quickly become large and bureaucratic, with a small elite dominating decision making. The leadership of these parties was further distanced from the membership and the electorate by what Michels termed 'intellectual factors', which made educated leaders indispensable to the governed masses. This dependency, Michels believed, resulted in gratitude towards, and even veneration of, those holding leadership positions. Furthermore, those in the elite, enjoyed their comfortable well-paid jobs, and developed a 'greed for power' (Michels, 1915: 205).

In common with the Webbs, Michels also stated that once established in office, union leaders would become conservative, taking on board the values of the ruling elite, against the interests of the working class. He wrote that union leaders, 'although they belong to the class of the ruled; come to form part of the ruling oligarchy' (Michels, 1915: 284). To ensure their continuation in power leaders would seek to put down any membership radicalism, as it may threaten their control of the union. If however the ruling elite should be deposed, Michels believed that those that follow them into power will quickly undergo a transformation which 'renders the revolutionaries of today into the reactionaries of tomorrow' (Michels, 1915: 187).

Aspects of Michels' theory have been accepted and developed by writers from a wide spectrum of ideological positions, ranging from pluralists through to Trotskyists. One of the most prominent of the pluralist authors who adopted Michels' theory was Seymour Lipset. His research into the American International Typographical Union (ITU) in the early 1950s discovered that the ITU enjoyed a system of democratic internal government in which two clearly defined political factional groups contested elections for union positions. Lipset, having satisfied himself that a democratic structure existed inside the ITU, did not draw the conclusion that Michels' iron law of oligarchy was incorrect. Instead he asserted that:

> This study has not disproved Michels' theory; rather in a sense it has given additional empirical support to his analysis of the connection between oligarchy as a political form and the overwhelming power held by the incumbent officers...where an effective and organised opposition does exist, it does so only because the incumbent administration does not hold a monopoly over the resources of politics (Lipset et al, 1956: 413).

In seeking to explain why the ITU was the exception to Michels 'iron law of oligarchy', Lipset went to great lengths to set out the specific circumstances necessary before democratic control was possible, within a union. These criteria included the union having to operate a decentralised structure; the work that the unions' membership undertook being of both a high status and a homogeneous nature; and the membership exhibiting a high level of interest in their union's affairs. These were only three, of a list of the twenty two specific conditions, which needed to exist if the 'iron law of oligarchy' was not to apply (Lipset et al, 1956: 414–17). Without the existence of all these factors, Lipset asserted that, 'the real and often permanent power rests with the men who hold with the highest positions' (Lipset et al, 1956: 4–5).

The conclusions of Lipset, Michels and the Webbs about the nature of union policy-making were remarkably similar. Intriguingly in the case of the Webbs (1920) and Lipset et al (1956) they undertook empirical research, whose results contradicted their own theories, yet still they continued to assert that the democratic structures they uncovered were atypical.

Subsequent to Lipset et al's work on the ITU, Turner (1962) undertook a wider empirical study of British cotton workers' unions. Arising from this work he outlined a theory which developed the Webbs' (1920) and Lipset et al (1956) arguments. He asserted that not just unions with specific characteristics, but all craft unions, were intrinsically democratic in their policy-making structures. Turner's (1962) hypothesis proceeded to divide trade unions into two broad groups, which he christened 'open' and 'closed'. The 'open' union category comprised all general and industrial unions. These unions, he asserted, did not have the ability to control the labour supply and therefore depended upon mass recruitment of workers, in order to attain high membership density levels and wield collective bargaining strength. 'Closed' unions encompassed all the craft unions, and unlike 'open' unions, they could exert control over the labour supply and the labour process.

These differing typologies led, Turner asserted, to different patterns of policy-making structures, and varying levels of lay membership participation. 'Open' unions would be centralised, with a high degree of officer control, owing to low levels of membership activity. This pattern of union policy-making, Turner colourfully entitled, 'popular bossdom'. Conversely, 'closed' unions, would display high levels of membership participation within democratic structures (Turner, 1962). His theory therefore still accepted that, in non-craft unions, policy-making was dominated by an oligarchy of full-time officers.

By the early 1970s there were a considerable number of scholars, from both the radical and pluralist traditions, questioning the validity of what Hyman christened the 'industrial relations orthodoxy' (Hyman, 1971: 21). Marxist and Pluralist scholars, most notably Clegg (1970), were dismissive of the 'iron law of oligarchy' being applied to trade unions:

> ...to assert that power in most British unions is highly centralised in the hands of an oligarchy of leaders, or even of a single autocrat...is so wide of the mark, so inconsistent with the facts of trade union life, as to be laughable (Clegg, 1970: 92).

In substantiating this assertion, Clegg outlines the many limitations on trade union leaders exercising of power. He points to various restraints on union leaders' policy authority, which included: the operation of political factions; the autonomy of different levels of union government; and the industrial power of shop stewards and shop-floor organisations.

Clegg's criticism of 'industrial relations orthodoxy' was further substantiated by detailed empirical studies by Lane and Roberts (1971) of Pilkingtons Glass; Beynon (1973; 1984) of Ford and Batstone et al (1977, 1978) of Massey Ferguson, which highlighted the growing policy-making strength of shop stewards and workplace union organisations. Other authors, such as Brown (1981), England (1981), and Batstone (1988), also charted the trend during the 1960s and 1970s towards a greater devolution of union policy-making power. In many cases this shift was then incorporated into the rulebooks of the unions (Terry, 1995: 204).

A large scale study of trade unions, by Undy et al, led these authors to also cast doubt on the veracity of Turners 'open' and 'closed' union hypothesis. They wrote:

> We would argue that our study demonstrates that these classifications are of doubtful utility, and are subject to more and more exceptions, in the contemporary situation (Undy et al, 1981: 348).

Specifically Undy et al (1981) contended that Britain's then largest, general union, the TGWU, was becoming increasingly decentralised, whilst the craft based AUEW was increasingly, 'dependent on an unofficial party system that has no place in Turners morphology' (Undy et al, 1981: 342). Having deployed considerable empirical evidence to counter the assertions of the 'classical theorists', scholars from both Pluralist and Marxist traditions, put forward a variety of alternative hypothesis to explain union behaviour.

Rank and filism

By the mid 1970s a growing number of Marxist authors had rejected the Webbs' (1920) and Michels' (1913) key assertions that only a small coterie of full time officers dominate policy-making. Whilst other radical scholars also questioned the assertion that Marxist candidates, once they are elected as officers, would automatically become more conservative.

Hyman (1971), Hinton (1973) and Holton (1976) all contended that union policy-making was not simply controlled by full-time officers but was instead the result of a struggle for policy control between union officers and an increasingly powerful shop steward movement. This analysis drew heavily upon empirical evidence of the growing strength of the shop stewards movement, detailed by authors undertaking studies of workplace unionism (Lane and Roberts, 1971; Beynon, 1973, 1984; Batstone et al, 1977, 1978). Authors who adopted this rank and filist view of union policy-making, assert that gaining effective control of union policy-making is dependent on the successful mobilisation of shop stewards and members in order to challenge 'unrepresentative union officialdom' (Fairbrother, 2000). This belief in the need for a 'challenge from below' is part of the wider view of policy-making that perceives there to be a dichotomy in the roles of full-time officers and lay activists (Fairbrother, 2000).

The growth of rank and filism was linked, according to Zeitlin (1983, 1989) to the upsurge in lay member militancy, which saw the movement of policy control away from full-time officers to lay members. Rank and Filist authors stressed that such a change was necessary for any given union to become more radical (Callincos, 1982; 1983; Cliff, 1970; Offe et al, 1985; Bramble, 1995). As Bramble stated:

> Similar pressures operate on left wing and right wing officials, with the result that changes to the political complexion of leadership personnel, usually do not herald the advent of fundamentally different relations with members and employers (Bramble, 1995: 420).

This simple, dichotomous, view of the role of full-time officers and shop stewards has been criticised, not least by Hyman himself, in his later work. In 1979 he wrote that there was a growing 'bureaucratisation of the rank and file', which meant that, 'the simple dichotomous conception of power misrepresents the problem and thus ultimately confuses strategy' (Hyman, 1979: 157). By 1984 his position had evolved further. He asserted that the idea of full-time officers being a separate and distinct bureaucracy is 'virtually empty of theoretical content' (Hyman, 1984: 181).

Other authors have produced powerful critiques of the view that there is a clear dichotomy in the interests of full-time officers and shop stewards, which leads inexorably to a struggle for control of union policy-making (Edwards, 1983; Kelly, 1988; Heery and Fosh, 1990; Kelly and Heery, 1994). The work of Kelly and Heery (Kelly and Heery, 1989, 1994; Heery and Kelly, 1994; Kelly, 1998; Heery, 2006) powerfully marshals evidence which indicates that the political ideology of full-time officers is important in informing their dealings with employers, stewards and members. It also plays a major role, these authors assert, in determining an officer's desire to empower and strengthen shop steward structures. Kelly and Heery (1994) and Heery (2003) also produce empirical evidence which demonstrates that far from seeking oligarchical control of policy-making, or acting as an inherently conservatising force, officers often aim to shift decision making authority to shop stewards. As they state, over 90% of officials from all the unions they surveyed agreed that, 'wherever possible work place representatives should handle their own collective bargaining' (Kelly and Heery, 1994: 113).

This desire is motivated not only by an officer's ideology, but also because of plain practicality. As authors note (Heery and Kelly, 1990; Callus et al, 1991), relatively small cadres of full-time officers often cover thousands of workplaces, which enjoy various levels of decentralised bargaining. In order to operate effectively they physically require shop stewards to control and implement their own workplace bargaining policies. Callus et al (1991) stated that far from struggling for policy authority, the relations between delegates (shop stewards) and officers was founded on mutual interdependence, which fostered co-operation. These findings, based on solid empirical evidence, are a powerful and persuasive critique of the rank and filist argument.

Political factions

Since the publication of Lipset et al's (1956) work, which highlighted the operation of political factions in the American ITU, there have been a number of other studies, which have focused on the operation and significance of political factional groups and their impact upon union internal democratic processes. Edelstein and Warner (1975) undertook a study of union democracy inside fifty-one American, and thirty-one British trade unions. Their work concluded that a number were, what they termed, 'democratic' unions. By this they meant that there were clearly defined opposing factional groups in place, contesting elections for lay and full-time officer positions. Disappointingly, if perhaps unsurprisingly given the number of unions studied, Edelstein and Warner (1975) do not expand on why some unions are more 'democratic' than others. Whilst their work is therefore useful in documenting the existence of factional groups, it does not assist in explaining their policy-making influence or why factions are strong in some unions, but not in others.

The Australian authors Dickenson (1982) and Davis (1986) also studied the operation of differing 'democratic structures' in various Australian unions. Davis' study led him to unequivocally state 'democracy rather than oligarchy governed these unions' (Davis, 1986: 196). His work though, primarily focused on the levels of membership and activist participation in the unions he examined. The influence of political factions on policy-making, and the internal dynamics of those factions, was not tackled in any detail. The examination by Dickenson (1982) of the Australian Federated Ironworkers Association (FIA) and the Administrative and Clerical Officers Association (ACOS), concluded that both these unions had effective internal democratic process and functioning, opposing, political groups. Yet Dickenson, in a similar fashion to Edelstein and Warner (1975) and Davis (1986), was highly circumspect about why these unions enjoyed such structures and what influence they had on policy-making.

In Britain, Martin (1969) also examined the internal democracy of the union movement and noted the existence of political factions. He argued that within British unions there was an analogy with eighteenth century British democracy, in that there was a dominant governing party opposed by a smaller solely oppositional, non-governing party. The form of factional politics that Martin (1969) portrays, differs from that which Lipset et al (1956) depicts, in that the factional groups are loose and transient, united only by their opposition to the polices of the leadership.

Work by England (1981) on the TGWU Broad Left, in part contradicts the findings of Martin. England's research uncovered a coherent factional group which has a clear ideological and industrial agenda and a strategy for mobilising members in order to attain election success. As a former, long term, active participant in the TGWU BL, my experience confirms the accuracy of England's observations. Where England's (1981) work is less illuminating is in measuring the level of influence that the BL had, as an organisation, on the policy choices of its full-time officer and activist members.

Undy et al's (1981) large scale study of what the authors described as 'change' in the union movement, placed emphasis on the role of political factions, in engendering alterations to the policy direction of various unions. The authors argued that the role of factions was one of a series of 'internal and external change factors' that predicated policy change. Their definition of external factors included; technological change, Government policy, the actions of other unions, economic circumstances, and the role of employers' organisations. Internal factors were described by the authors as concerning the:

> attitudes and polices of particular union groups, and those that concern the influence of particular decision making structures – most notably the provisions of the union's rule-book (Undy et al, 1981: 324).

Whilst the empirical research undertaken by Undy et al (1981) undoubtedly provides a rich source of data, the theoretical side of their work has been criticised (Kelly and Heery, 1994). Kelly and Heery point out that their work provides little theoretical help for those attempting to analyse the specific factors that cause an alteration in union policy. Their compelling argument being, that simply describing a variety of agents of change, does not give a clear picture as to why the individual union decides upon a specific policy option (Kelly and Heery, 1994).

Other authors (Frenkel and Coolican, 1984; McIllroy et al, 1999, 2007; Daniels and McIllroy, 2009) have highlighted not only the role of trade union factions in union policy-making, but also the part played by various political parties in the operation of those factions. Frenkel and Coolican (1984) in their study of Australia's Amalgamated Metals Foundry and Shipwrights Union (AMFSU) and the Building Workers Industrial Union (BWIU) suggested that the dominant political party ideology of a ruling union faction was the most pertinent factor in informing the union's decision making. They put forward the theory that unions could be categorised into either 'Radical' or 'Labourist' camps. 'Radical' unions would, they held, display higher levels of industrial militancy than Labourist unions, who attempt to work in a co-operative fashion with employers (Frenkel and Coolican, 1984: 332–3). Frenkel and Coolican's (1984) work has been critiqued by Gardner (1989) who points out that similar industrial policies were pursued by Right and Left wing unions in Australia. She suggests, that a simple reliance on political factional control to indicate policy direction is simplistic and inadequate (Gardner, 1989: 63).

McIllroy et al (2007) more explicitly address the role of specific political cal parties, most notably the Communist Party of Great Britain (CPGB) and various British Trotskyist parties, in helping to create union Broad Left factions. They also consider their on-going influence in the functioning of these factions. McIllroy's latter work with Daniels (Daniels and McIllroy, 2009) charts the splits in the Broad Lefts in a number of unions and the role played by various parties of the Left in these factional schisms. McIllroy et al (2007), and Daniels and McIllroy (2009) also differ from Frenkel and Coolican (1984), in that they do not assume that the simple attainment by a Left faction of majority control of a National Executive and senior full-time officer posts, will automatically translate into greater industrial militancy. They carefully chart the manner in which control by Left factions of NECs and the election of Left faction backed General Secretaries (in particular in Unite and PCS) has not led to those unions tackling what they describe as the 'economic and industrial neo-liberal agenda' (Daniels and McIllroy, 2009: 157). Whilst the authors acknowledge this phenomenon is partly to do with an adverse economic and industrial climate, along with the difficulty in ensuring membership support for more militant policies, they doubt the 'nerve, will and tactical acumen of left-wing leaders in combat with neo-liberalism' (Daniels and McIllroy, 2009: 157).

The work of Daniels and McIllroy (2009) and McIllroy et al (2007) whilst displaying a thorough knowledge of the political composition and success of different unions' political factions, does not address other potential internal influences on policy makers, whatever political factional grouping they belong too. Whilst the effect on union policy of external economic and industrial factors is acknowledged, the influence on union policy-making of other factors such as craft, occupational and geographical loyalties, or micro-political influences such as personal friendships and rivalries, is largely ignored. This is perhaps unsurprising as full-time and lay union officials are often less than candid with external researchers about the influence upon their policy decisions of such factors. It is one the aims of this book to address this issue both empirically and theoretically.

Institutional contextualism

A number of pluralist authors (Flanders, 1965; Bain, 1970; Clegg, 1976; Boraston et al, 1975), having robustly rejected the theory of oligarchical control of unions, also refuted the rank and filist explanation of union behaviour. They asserted instead that union policy was largely shaped by formal bargaining structures and the policies of employers and the Government.

Flanders (1965) in explaining what he termed the 'challenge from below', which involved a struggle for policy-making authority between workplace shop stewards and full-time officers, asserted that this phenomena had occurred because private sector employers had switched to local plant, as opposed to national, bargaining. Bain's (1970) work placed even greater emphasis on the role of employers in shaping union policy-making. He stressed the dependence of unions on the acquiescence of employers in providing opportunities for them to represent and recruit members. Clegg (1976) underlines the manner in which collective bargaining structures affect the manner in which unions conduct their internal affairs and are a primary element in shaping internal governance structures, such as the creation of trade/occupational groups or sections.

This argument that 'institutional' external influences are the dominant elements in union policy-making was developed by Dickens and Colling (Dickens, 1998; Colling and Dickens, 2001) in relation to equal opportunities. These authors also agreed with Hyman (1999: 99) when he declared that there was a crisis in the model of trade unionism which had been developed in the twentieth century. Hyman (1999) describes this mode of trade unionism as being based on 'mechanical solidarity' of male manual workers working in areas of mass production. Economic and societal change he asserts had led to a fracturing of class and union solidarity, with workers taking a more individualistic view. This requires unions to engage in policy reform which creates what he describes as a wider 'organic solidarity' in order to respond to the very different institutional and societal environment. This organic solidarity would encompass the growing variety of diverse individual interests such as race, ethnicity, gender and sexuality. The latter points are developed by Dickens and Colling (Dickens, 1998, 2000; Colling and Dickens, 2001) who stress the need for unions to alter their bargaining priorities and systems of internal governance to display a greater institutional focus on the importance of equality issues, which often reflects legislative change.

These broad societal and institutional contextual frameworks tend, as Kelly and Heery (1994) state, to view unions as being swept along on the tide of employer and State policies, without the ability to effectively shape their own destiny. Boxall and Haynes (1997) and Heery (2005, 2006), writing from different ideological standpoints, both suggested that scholars who favour institutional determinism of union policy-making, fail to acknowledge sufficiently the role of unions' governmental and managerial processes, in shaping their policy direction (Heery, 2005: 103).

State contextualism

There are authors, who have adopted an institutional perspective towards union policy-making, who have focused particularly on the influence of political factors. Howell (2005) for instance states that there has been a tendency by scholars to overestimate the autonomous strength of British trade unionism, whilst they have underestimated the power of the State to mould union policy (Howell, 2005).

In defending his assertion Howell (2005) argues that there have been three distinct systems of industrial relations in Britain during the twentieth century, which largely shaped union behaviour. These three systems he contends have all been created by the British State in order to deal with distinct crises in the economy. The first occurred in the early part of the twentieth century, when the Government instituted industry level collective bargaining, as a mechanism for limiting both industrial conflict and market competition. The second developed in the early post-war decades when there was a necessity to regenerate and reorganise capital, in order to improve productivity. In this instance the state, Howell contends, permitted the decentralisation of bargaining, which allowed the locus to shift to the company level, whilst the scope of collective bargaining coverage broadened to include a wider range of work issues. Finally, in the 1980s, the state responded to a climate of heightened international competition and a shrinking manufacturing base by placing greater emphasis on 'flexibility in all its myriad forms and on increasingly individualised relationship between employers and employees' (Howell, 2005: 191). This, third system of industrial relations, which Howell dubbed 'hyperflexibility', was characterised by the dismantling of the political and economic institutions that co-ordinated industrial relations and imposed collective regulations.

In all three systems Howell asserts that the State's role a legislator, employer, and as a role model for the private sector, had a determining influence on the conduct of employers and unions in Britain (Howell, 2005: 192–3). Howell's (2005) claim that the State can play a critical role in shaping the British industrial relations framework and thereby effectively control the parameters within which unions are able to operate, is shared by a number of other authors. Wedderburn (1986), Ewing (2006) and Lewis (1986) all chart the manner in which not only the strength of British unions, but also their ability to self-govern and to make policy decisions were severely constrained by the legislation of the 1979–1997 Conservative Governments. These authors though do not subscribe to Howell's (2005) broader State contextualist historical theory; instead they focus on the detrimental impact of Government legislation on union ability to act independently and effectively, whilst acknowledging, unlike Howell (2005), the successful repulsion of similar Conservative legislative efforts in the early 1970s (Wedderburn, 1986; Ewing, 2006; Lewis, 1986).

Strategic choice

The determinist and universalist manner in which academics, who subscribe to an institutionalist or state contextualist view, write of union behaviour has been the subject of numerous critiques (Gallie, 1978; Streeck, 1992; Child, 1997; Hyman, 1997; Kelly, 1998; Boxall and Hayes, 1997; Heery and Kelly, 1994; Heery, 2000, 2003). All of these writers, from a variety of different ideological standpoints, assert that trade union decision making is not simply determined by the industrial, societal or political environment. Instead they contend that unions make a series of 'strategic choices' about the manner in which they represent their members' interests. These choices are made, because individual union members hold a multiplicity of different interests, many of which may be contradictory, and from which a union must select. At the same time a union must also decide upon policy priorities. Hyman expresses this succinctly:

> The articulation of a coherent employee voice requires the filtering and prioritizing of multiple, fragmentary and often contradictory grievances. (Hyman, 1997: 310)

Other scholars ascribing to this view of 'strategic choice' by unions, further emphasise that in sorting interests and deciding on priorities, union policies will be 'influenced by the preferences and values of activists and those in in formal representational roles' (Heery, 2003: 291).

Authors in this tradition (Kelly, 1998; Heery and Kelly, 1994; Kelly and Heery, 1994; Heery, 2000, 2003, 2006) have developed the concept of strategic choice by suggesting that union activists and officers play a crucial role in 'interest formation' amongst members. Their hypothesis involves union activists instigating 'social identification', which consists of lay and full-time officers suggesting to members that they have common, as opposed to individual, interests. These collective interests are typically in opposition to those of their employers. Union philosophy, as well as individual officer ideology, also plays an important role in this process of 'shaping' union members interests, and their subsequent readiness to take industrial action.

Other scholars who favour the 'strategic choice' model have focused more on the ability of unions, specifically union leaders, to make decisions on how they represent their members interests. This branch of strategic choice theory emphasises the ability of decision makers to take proactive decisions in the face of industrial challenges, which determine the success or failure of the union's response. In this analysis great emphasis is placed on the internal, national decision making process, which results in a union making a series of strategic choices (Boxall and Hayes, 1997; Boxall, 2008; Child, 1997). This approach differs substantially from the 'strategic choice' model adopted by Heery and Kelly (Heery and Kelly, 1988; Kelly and Heery, 1994; Heery, 2003, 2006) which stresses the ability of unions to decide between policy options at the workplace, as well at the national level. Their work also emphasises the effect on policy, of the beliefs, values and ideology of key lay and full-time officers.

Kelly (1988), along with other authors (Darlington, 1994, 2001; McIllroy and Campbell, 1999; McIllroy, 2007; Daniels and McIllroy, 2009), advances this argument further by declaring that ideology is a key source of variation in the policy choices of union officers and activists. He and others stress the role played by Left factional activists in creating collective organisation, building campaigns over specific industrial issues, where they carefully 'frame' their arguments to promote greater industrial militancy. These views are not held by other strategic choice scholars such as Boxall and Haynes (1997) who state that the key policy decisions of any union occur only at the national level, and that whilst unions can make a series of policy choices, in a Neo-liberal environment 'partnership unionism' is the only logical, viable, long term strategy (Boxall and Haynes, 1997: 587).

As is illustrated above there are a variety of different strands to the 'strategic choice' theory. However all scholars who adhere to this position agree that a union has the scope to select between different policy options, and that this selection can manifestly affect their success.

The strategic choice model has been the subject of critiques by various authors, including, unsurprisingly, those holding an economic or societal contextual viewpoint. Critics stress that union ability to make strategic choices is constrained by the political, economic and social environment in which they are operating. As scholars from, for example, the feminist perspective stress, unions cannot strategically choose to ignore the growing issues surrounding gender and the changing role of women in the labour market and society. This would be the case even if they wished so to do (Wajcman, 2000; Cockburn, 1993; Coglan and Ledwith, 1996).

In assessing the merits of the strategic choice model it is striking that, unlike the institutional and political contextualist theories, this hypothesis provides an explanation as to why unions who operate in the same industries, and organise similar groups of members have historically seen such variations in their recruitment, organising and negotiatory policies and performance. The strategic choice hypothesis, as expressed by Kelly and Heery (Kelly, 1998; Heery and Kelly, 1994; Heery, 2000, 2003), also provides reasons why a union may make dissimilar policy choices at different local levels of its organisation. These policy variations which Heery (2003) ascribed to influences such as 'gender, generation and ideology' (Heery, 2003: 294) are less easily explained by State and institutional theorists, who adopt a more determinist perspective on union policy-making.

In the empirical chapters, the different policy-making theories outlined above, will be juxtaposed against the reality of policy-making in British and Australian telecommunication and printing unions. This exercise will allow a judgement to be made as to which provides the most accurate analysis of policy-making.

Section 2: Labour process, amalgamations and recruitment

The labour process

The literature focusing upon trade union efforts to exercise influence over the labour process is large and diverse. In part this is owing to the nature of the theoretical discussion over the definition of the term 'labour process'. In this section there is not the scope for a review of the literature debating what activities should, or should not be, covered by the term labour process. Instead for the purposes of this chapter a broad definition of the term is used, based on Braverman's (1974) definition and the subsequent work of Burawoy (1979). This encompasses the control of the recruitment and regulation of labour, the operation of the production process (including the introduction of new technology), and the ability of employers to deskill and fragment their employees work. Using this definition, the literature relating to union efforts to control the labour process will be considered.

A considerable proportion of the labour process literature has focused on union efforts to modify employers' control of the production process and the hiring of employees. Specifically, the role of the pre-entry, and post-entry, closed shops has received considerable attention. The literature encompasses contrasting opinions on the effect the closed shops has had upon union ability to recruit members, regulate the production process and influence the selection of new employees (McCarthy, 1964; Dunn and Gennard, 1983, 1984; Stevens et al, 1989; Zappala, 1991; Hart, 1979; Gennard et al, 1979; Gennard and Bain, 1995; Gennard, 1990; Cockburn, 1983).

A number of authors (McCarthy, 1964; Dunn and Gennard, 1983, 1984; Gennard et al, 1979; Gennard, 1990; Gennard and Bain, 1995) are clear that the development of the closed shop, in all its forms, represents a conscious strategic choice by unions, with the aim of increasing their membership and strengthening their influence over the labour process. They conclude that compulsory unionism was highly successful in delivering these policy objectives and that the pre-entry closed shop was also effective in overcoming resistance to union organisation by hostile employers.

Other writers (Weeks, 1990; Hart, 1979) take issue with this view and instead adopt a more institutionally contextual approach. They suggest that the growth in closed shops reflected a desire by employers in the 1960s and 1970s to embrace the idea, in order to avoid multi-unionism, and to allow unions officials (be they lay or full-time) to reach potentially unpopular collective agreements, which were necessary to guarantee the long term future of a company, plant or operation. Hart (1979) specifically argues that the closed shop was adopted by a significant number of employers for these reasons.

The research of Dunn and Gennard (1984) which challenged the assertion that numerous employers welcomed compulsory unionism is comprehensive and persuasive. Their argument is further strengthened by subsequent developments, which saw British employers making full use of the provisions of employment legislation to rid themselves of compulsory unionism and to weaken the influence of unions over the production process (Gennard, 1990).

Other scholars, who accept that the application of the closed shop was an active policy choice by unions, do not concur that such a policy was in the long term interests of the wider labour movement. Cockburn (1983, 1991) is particularly critical of the exclusionary aspects of the pre-entry closed shop, which effectively debarred any non-indentured trade unionists, particularly women, from the opportunity to undertake printing craft work. This policy, Cockburn (1983) holds, led to division and disunity between groups of workers which served the print unions and their members ill, when they faced seismic technological change in the 1980s. This argument is vehemently rejected by authors, such as Gennard, who point to the unique strength the pre-entry closed shop granted to employees (Gennard, 1990).

The inability to sustain all forms of the closed shop,[1] in the face of hostile Government legislation, was an experience shared alike by Australian and British unions. Whilst legislative attacks on compulsory unionism occurred at different times in the two countries – the 1980s in Britain, the late 1990s and early 2000s in Australia – there is broad agreement, that the ability of unions to affect the labour process was seriously weakened (Batstone, 1988; Daniel and Milward, 1983, 1984; Zappala, 1991; Dunn and Gennard, 1984; Gennard and Bain, 1995; Gennard, 1990; Cockburn, 1983).

Authors addressing this subject, from the various viewpoints outlined in the first section of this chapter, have offered a variety of different explanations for the decline in union influence over the labour process. Those from a political contextual outlook such as Howell (2005) attribute the decline principally to a political shift, which saw the election of a Conservative Government, committed to unitarist industrial relations policies. Other scholars stress the shift in societal values away from collectivism, so powerfully embodied in the very notion of the closed shop, to a more individualistic society (Hyman, 1999). Whilst those who favour an economic and institutionalist explanation focus on the move in developed industrial economies from a Fordist to a post–Fordist, industrial model. This they argue necessitates the adoption of a 'partnership' approach by unions, if they wish to regain influence over the labour process (Bacon and Storey, 1993; Osterman, 1996).

Those writers who assert that the British economy is shifting towards a neo-Fordist model disagree with the post-Fordist thesis. They highlight the manner in which the union movement is losing control over the labour process owing to increasing fragmentation of the labour process, which has

---

1   Including union preference clauses that had previously been present in Australian State and Federal 'awards'.

resulted in growing numbers of low paid workers, on temporary contracts (Beynon, 1997; Crouch, 1999; Heery and Salmon, 2000). Rank-and-filist authors, whilst accepting there has been a decline in union influence over the labour process, highlight the role of union leaderships in not supporting members involved in major industrial conflicts (Bramble, 2008; Darlington, 1994). Other scholars (Kelly, 1990, 1998; Waddington and Whitston, 1997) attribute the loss of union influence over the labour process to a wider counter-mobilisation policy by the Conservative Government and employers. This policy incorporated economic measures which resulted in a recession and mass unemployment, which when allied to a legislative assault on union ability to take industrial action, led to a, 'vicious cycle of union ineffectiveness, worker fatalism and decline' (Kelly, 1998).

In Australia during the 1980s and early 1990s authors from a variety of ideological viewpoints noted a less dramatic, yet clearly discernible, weakening of union ability to affect the labour process. This was the case even though the Australian unions faced a less overtly hostile political environment (Bamber et al, 1997; Hearn and Costa, 1997; Davis, 1999; Kelly, 1993; Dabscheck, 1995; Ford and Plowman, 1989). A rapid acceleration in this decline followed the election of a Liberal/Country National Coalition, Federal Government in 1996. Their commitment to economic and industrial policies, which closely resembled those of the 1979–1997 British Conservative Government, precipitated a dramatic collapse in union membership and influence over the labour process. This, according to many writers, was linked to the protections afforded to the union movement, by the arbitral system, being stripped away (Cooper and Ellem, 2009; Bramble, 2008).

Amalgamations

Undy, writing in the mid 1990s, notes that in relation to union amalgamations, 'detailed studies of this important aspect of trade-union behaviour have been rather limited' (Undy, 1996: 125). Since he made this observation, the amount of literature devoted to analysing union amalgamation policy in Britain has, in comparison to other policy areas, remained sparse. Undy

(1996, 2008) and Waddington (Waddington, 1988, 1995; Waddington et al, 2005) have been the main contributors to the debate over amalgamation strategies in Britain and the effect mergers have had on union behaviour. There have though also been examinations of specific mergers (Terry, 1996) and accounts in union histories of amalgamations (Gennard and Bain, 1995; Gennard, 1990). In Australia there has been a greater academic interest in amalgamations (Hearn and Costa, 1997; Davis, 1999; Kelly, 1993; Griffin, 2002; Dabscheck, 1995) owing in large part to the ACTU and the Australian ALP Federal Government's (1981–1996) determination to press for the creation of large industrial unions, as part of their industrial relations modernisation programme.

As with the more general debate over union policy-making, there are disagreements between scholars over the causes and consequences of various types of amalgamations. Waddington's work (Waddington, 1988, 1995; Waddington et al, 2005) examines the patterns of British union mergers and consists of a deductive research method that focuses on aggregated data. He proposes that since the start of the twentieth century that there have been two periods of merger waves; 1918–1924 and 1966–1987. These 'waves' Waddington concluded are linked to periods in the economic cycle when the economy moved from the upswing to the downswing. This movement in the economy adversely affected many unions bargaining and membership strength and provided the critical economic, political and unionisation factors which creates 'the urge to merge' (Waddington, 1995: 44–70). Waddington (Waddington, 1988, 1995; Waddington et al, 2005) also asserted that specific internal factors, whilst less important than the external economic context, also contributed to the merger waves. He went on to state that, 'trade unionists merge their organisations to strengthen their bargaining positions' (Waddington, 1995: 68)

Undy (1996; 2008) and other authors, such as Chaison (1996), agree with Waddington that a rise in merger activity was caused by a combination of external and internal factors. They also believe that primarily external economic factors, which adversely affect a union's financial, membership and bargaining strength, are the key motives for amalgamations, and that the majority of merger activity has been overtly defensive.

Where Undy (1996, 2008) is critical of Waddington is over his assertion that there was an amalgamation wave from 1966 to 1987. He argues (Undy, 2008) that a phenomenon that has stretched from 1966 to 1987 cannot be described as a wave. Undy (1996) instead describes it as a 'merger movement'. Furthermore Undy also takes Waddington to task for failing to devote sufficient attention to legislative changes in the 1960s[2] which removed the necessity of the acquiring union having to ballot their membership over an amalgamation with a smaller union, and allowed any minor union to transfer their membership, if they attained a simple majority in favour of a merger (Undy, 1996: 130). The increase in the number of transfer of engagements, which followed the legislative changes, supports Undy's thesis. From 1974 to 2004 over 90% of all British union mergers consisted of transfer of engagements, with the vast majority involving transfers into one of Britain's five largest unions. In conjunction with the easing of the legislative constraints Undy also asserts that the leaders of Britain's largest unions adopted a more pro-active approach to persuading smaller unions to amalgamate (Undy, 2008). These policies, Undy claims, all assisted in the increase in merger activity (Undy, 2008: 58–109).

Chaison (1996) adopts a similar emphasis on the importance of an adverse external economic environment. He, like Undy (2008), believes that greater merger activity, in Britain since the 1960s, owes much to changes to the legal frame-work and the more positive attitude of senior officers of larger unions (Chaison, 1996). Chaison (1996) also discusses union merger policy in Australia, which as he and others note, had been different to Britain, owing to the involvement of the Federal Government and the ACTU since the late 1980s (Griffin, 2002; Kelly, D, 1993; Davis, 1999; Dabscheck, 1995). This intervention consisted of political, industrial and legislative pressure being placed upon all unions, by the ACTU and the ALP Federal Government to form large industrial unions.

---

2   The Trade Union (Amalgamations, etc.) Act, 1964, relaxed the restrictive conditions for union transfers of engagements imposed by The Societies (Miscellaneous Provisions) Act, 1940.

Prior to this period, as Griffin notes (2002: 7), merger activity in Australia had been relatively restrained, with 94 mergers occurring in the period 1905–1986. The majority of these mergers had involved unions who has organised occupations or trades which had become obsolete, owing to technological advances. By 1996 a dramatic alteration in amalgamation activity had occurred. The total number of Australian unions fell from 316 to 132 thanks in large part to 172 mergers being concluded during this decade (Australian Bureau of Statistics, 1996).[3] If, using Waddington's analogy, Britain had experienced amalgamation waves, then Australia in the period from 1986 to 1996, had experienced a merger tsunami. This high rate of merger activity rapidly dissipated after 1996, with only two further federally registered unions merging in the period up to 2002 (Griffin, 2002).

The reason for this remarkable upsurge in amalgamations can be traced to the policy decisions of the ACTU leadership and ALP Federal Government. They believed that reversing declining union membership, and the successful implementation of their joint Prices and Incomes Accords, required the formation of large industrial unions. Crucially, as scholars from different ideological viewpoints agreed, there was by the late 1980s a consensus amongst the majority of ACTU affiliates, that such an aggressive amalgamation policy should be urgently pursued. At its 1989 Congress, the ACTU affiliates adopted a policy which called on all small and medium sized unions to merge (Davis, 1990, 1999; Griffin, 1994, 2002; Dabscheck, 1989).

The pressure on all unions to conform to this ACTU policy was then considerably increased by the passing of the *Industrial Relations Act 1988* (Griffin, 2002; Davis, 1999; Bramble, 2008). This legislation gave powers to the Australian Industrial Relations Commission (AIRC) to review the registration[4] of trade unions with less than a specified number of members. In 1990, after extensive ACTU lobbying, the initial Federal Government

---

3 The Australian Bureau of Statistics stopped collecting data on Trade Unions after 1996.

4 A union's de-registration would effectively mean that they were unable to use the Federal arbitration system. Their membership coverage protection and use of the Federal industrial awards system would also, effectively, be removed.

decision that all unions with 1,000 members or less would be subject to AIRC review, was extended to 10,000 members. As Australian writers from a wide range of ideological viewpoints agree, it was this legislation, which applied to 232 unions in 1992, that provoked the massive increase in amalgamations (Davis, 1990, 1992, 1999; Griffin, 1994, 2002; Griffin and Scaresbrook, 1989; Dabscheck, 1989; Kuhn, 1993; Tomkins, 1999).

Recruitment

Over the last three decades the British literature concerning union recruitment policies has been closely interwoven with that which has examined the decline in union membership (Waddington and Fairbrother, 1990; Hyman, 1989; Edwards, 1986, 1994; Terry et al, 2000; Daniels and McIlroy, 2009; McIlroy, 1988). Many authors have sought to diagnose and prescribe how the union movement may revitalise itself, via new recruitment methods, following the legislative demise of compulsory unionism and the decline in membership numbers Heery et al, 2000a, 2003a; Heery, 2005; Heery and Alder, 2004; Heery and Simms, 2008; Cooper, 2003; Gall, 2003; Milkman, 2000; Kelly and Badigannavar, 2004). Prior to the 1980s, scholars had written of the effectiveness of the closed shop in efficiently recruiting millions of members (Dunn and Gennard, 1984; Bain, 1970; Roberts, 1962; Clegg, 1976). Bain (1970) specifically focused upon the manner in which the trade union movement used compulsory unionism to successfully recruit members in growing, white-collar, areas of employment. In particular he notes the manner in which trade unions in the late 1960s were able to persuade amenable employers, who already implemented post entry closed shops for their manual employees, to extend these provisions to their white collar workers (Bain, 1970: 186). Other authors, from Australia and Britain, who adopted a similar institutional contextual analysis (Flanders, 1965; Clegg, 1976; Bain, 1983; Lansbury and Spillane, 1983; Howell, 2005), agree that whilst the success of unions in recruiting could vary, the primary determinants of growth was the political, economic and institutional environment in which a union was operating.

Another group of scholars, predominantly from the rank and filist tradition, argue that the upsurge of shop steward movements, in both countries during the 1970s, led to greater lay member activism which facilitated higher levels of direct recruitment and a growth in the application of the closed shop (Lane and Roberts, 1971; Beynon, 1973; 1984; Fairbrother, 1990, 1996, 2000; Cohen, 2006; Darlington, 1994).

After the decline in union membership, which occurred in Britain during the 1980s and 1990s, the focus of the British recruitment literature moved to address possible approaches to achieve union revitalisation. Heery (2003) groups these works into three categories, which he describes as evolution, renewal and agency (Heery, 2003: 297).

The evolutionary theory is, Heery (2003) points out, advocated by many of those authors who also propound a wider institutional contextualist explanation of union policy-making (Bacon and Storey, 1993; Osterman, 1999; Poole, 1997; Thomas and Wallis, 1998; Bassett, 1986; Bassett and Cave, 1993). These writers propose that in order to recruit more successfully, unions need to adjust their policies to ensure that they remain relevant and attractive to potential members. In order to do so these authors assert that unions need to engage in partnership agreements with employers. Here the union agrees to resolve disputes without recourse to industrial action, in return for recognition and unhindered recruitment access to employees (Ackers and Payne, 1998; Basset, 1986; Bassett and Cave, 1993; Bacon and Storey, 1993; Osterman, 1999).

As well as seeking these partnership arrangements authors such as Bassett (1986) urge unions to provide individual services, such as discounted insurance, consumer goods and legal advice to persuade non-members to join. As Heery et al (2000a) state this form of organising has a long history in unions organising professionals, managers and freelancers. Unions such as the Union of Shop, Distributive and Allied Workers (USDAW) have adopted this partnership thesis wholeheartedly and have reported strong membership growth. Other unions though who have espoused this approach have been far less successful; Community for example has experienced a dramatic membership decline. (Certification Officer reports 2012). Whilst some unions who entered into such partnership agreements, have experienced widespread dissent from members that have led to attempts to renegotiate the arrangements (unpublished GMB London Regional Council minutes, March and October 2006 and 2007).

Other writers, who espouse a political contextualist explanation of union policy-making (Howell, 1999, 2005; Brown et al, 1997), question whether union recruitment initiatives can have a positive impact. They outline the manner in which a hostile political and economic landscape leads inexorably to union decline and makes any recruitment strategies liable to failure (Howell, 1999: 68; Brown et al, 1997). There are also other scholars, who favour a strongly institutionally contextualist explanation of union policy-making, who see such recruitment initiatives as 'defensive', in that they help, but only marginally, to protect the integrity of the union movement, until the economic and political climate improves (Chaison, 1996: 110).

Renewal theorists, Heery (2003) asserts, can be broken down into two broad groups. Rank and filist authors favour a revivalist policy that is based on what Fairbrother describes as 'membership participation' as opposed to the 'principle of leadership predominance' (Fairbrother, 1990). This analysis articulates the need for union members and their stewards to regain control of recruitment policy, and drive an agenda which challenges not only employers but also ineffectual and consensual union leaderships (Fairbrother, 1996, 2000; Fairbrother and Stewart, 2003). This view has a strong antecedence and can be found in the work of other rank and filist theorists from the 1970s onwards (Hinton, 1973; Holton, 1976; Callincos, 1982, 1983; Freeman, 1985; Cliff, 1970; Beacham, 1970; Offe et al, 1985; Bramble, 1993). Central to this form of renewal theory is the necessity for members and their stewards to 'build the challenge from below' (Fairbrother, 2000) with stewards not only recruiting but also engendering militancy which makes unions attractive and relevant to employees in the workplace.

Other authors, who also hold the view that unions can substantially affect their membership levels, through their recruitment strategies, have provided critiques of this rank and filist renewal argument (Heery, 1998; McIllroy, 1995; Terry, 2000). They assert that effective union recruitment campaigns, in the starkly altered industrial landscape of the post 1970s, require the co-ordination of organising campaigns by union leaderships. This is in order to ensure that resources are effectively concentrated on

specific recruitment targets rather than simply on servicing large groups
of members in already well organised workplaces (Terry, 2000; Willman,
2001; Heery, 1998).

Those scholars who support a renewal analysis, but do not subscribe
to the rank and filist view, do not put forward a single homogenous theory.
Heery (2003) has attempted to characterise a number of the distinctions
that appear in these versions of union renewal theory. In 'managerial
renewal' unions are urged to arbitrate between the wide variety of valid,
yet narrow, competing workplace, occupational and sectional interests,
in order to form a 'general' interest. Supporters of this thesis argue that
the union movement must ensure that resources are devoted to organising potential members, and not solely dedicated to servicing the current
membership, if unions are to regenerate themselves (Terry, 2000; Willman,
2001; Heery, 1998, 2001; Heery and Kelly, 1990; Cooper, 2005; Costa
and Hearn, 1997). Willman (2001) in particular advocates a central role
for union officials in this process. He states that full-time officers bring a
union-wide perspective and are therefore more likely to withstand sectional
membership interests which wish for resources to be devoted to servicing
rather than recruiting non-members.

The manner in which this 'managerial' organising is undertaken can
take different forms. Heery et al (2003a) describes unions adopting a
'bottom up' approach in which they use an adversarial organising strategy, to attempt to identify and exploit workplace grievances over issues
such as discipline, pay, managerial style and health and safety (Heery et
al, 2000b; Waddington and Whitson, 1997). In this model the onus is on
recruiting members without employer assistance and relying on gaining
above 50% of a bargaining group to secure recognition, via the provisions of
the 1999 Employment Relations Act. Another approach alluded to earlier,
involves unions seeking to organise a company, by offering a cooperative,
'partnership' approach. In appealing to employers in this fashion, unions
seek to secure agreements which allow unfettered recruitment access to
employees. USDAW's agreement with Tesco is a classic example of this
approach (Heery et al, 2003a; Waddington and Whitson, 1997).

Other authors who support the view that unions need to adopt renewal
strategies advocate a new 'organic solidarity' (Hyman, 1999) in which

unions appeal to the diverse ethnic, gender, sexuality, disability and social interests of potential members. In campaigning for the rights and interests of these groups in the workplace and in society, it is argued that unions can strengthen their membership appeal outside of the male, white, able-bodied, heterosexual norm (Dickens, 2000; Colling and Dickens, 2001; Heery, 1998; Murray, 1994).

There are other scholars, according to Heery (2003) who adopt an 'agency theory' approach to union revitalisation. They believe that union renewal rests upon unions having the ability to take a series of meaning-ful 'strategic choices' between various alternative strategies. These choices determine the manner in which a union selects policies and can determine their success or failure in recruiting members. Part of this thesis involves the 'action determinism' of the actors involved, particularly full time officers (Child, 1997). 'Action determinism' in this context refers to the manner in which an actor's choices are 'selected according to in-built preference and information processing systems' (Whittington quoted in Child, 1997: 49). Various empirical studies of union officers' behaviour have supported these assertions (Heery and Kelly, 1988; Healy and Kirton, 1999; Colgan and Ledwith, 1996). The gender, age cohort and educational qualifications were all factors which were found to colour officials' actions. The research by Heery and Kelly (1988) in particular indicated that younger and better educated officers responded differently to their older and predominantly less formally educated counterparts, when faced with a variety of policy choices (Heery and Kelly, 1988; Heery, 2006).

According to a number of scholars (Kelly, 1998; Kelly and Heery, 1994; McIllroy and Campbell, 1999; Daniels and McIllroy, 2009) the most important of the above determinants was the ideological views of a union official or activist. These they assert shape the manner in which the officer approaches recruiting and organising. Kelly particularly focuses on the manner in which officers and activists, from a radical ideological viewpoint, 'frame' policy questions, and then act, so as to develop a collective definition of members' and workers' interests, which sits within the construct of the wider class struggle (Kelly, 1998). This in turn affects the manner in which officers and stewards seek to recruit and organise around specific issues which they 'cast' in such a way, so as to build a wider union organisation, that seeks not only prosecute narrow workplace issues, but also to affect wider societal change (Kelly, 1998; McIlroy and Campbell, 1999, England, 1981; Daniels and McIlroy, 2009). These authors also focus on the role of political factions, specifically the Broad Left, in motivating their members to not only recruit and organise non-members, but also to campaign inside the union for the adoption of specific strategies, including recruitment policies (McIlroy, 1988; England, 1981; Daniels and McIlroy, 2009).

In all of the agency theory literature, as Heery et al (2003a) note, it is believed to be critically important that unions operate internal democratic structures that allow for the renewal and replacement of their leaderships. Heery's hypothesis being, that if unions are to 'strategically innovate' they must have the ability to, 'renew their leaderships with those of a different gender, generation and ideology' (Heery, 2003: 297). Where such structures are not present, or are, for a variety of reasons, not implemented,[5] then, the agency thesis predicts, such revitalisation is thwarted (Heery et al, 2003a).

Pressed to their extremes, there are contradictions in the various prescriptions for union revitalisation. The idea that unions are able to make strategic choices which determine their levels of growth and the belief that membership levels are determined by the nature of the political environment, the economic cycle, or technical innovation, are inherently contradictory. Similarly the belief that the role an individual holds, governs the approach they take to recruitment, is inconsistent with the view that it is the beliefs, values and motivations of an organisation, which determines an officer or activist's approach.

---

5   See for example Britain's third largest union the GMB, where the General Secretary was elected unopposed in 2006 and 2010 and the union's lay President has not faced a contested election since the 1990s.

Conclusion

This chapter has laid out many of the different theoretical explanations that have been put forward to explain union behaviour. It has also outlined the arguments that have been presented concerning the labour process, recruitment and amalgamations policies of unions. In the following empirical chapters these different, and in many instances contradictory hypotheses will be juxtaposed against the evidence gathered on policy formulation in the Australian and British printing and telecommunication trade unions. In doing so, the value of these different perspectives in helping to address the central research questions, will also be assessed.

CHAPTER 4

The British Printing Unions: Pre-1980

Introduction

In this and the subsequent three chapters, the historical structures and political processes of the British and Australian telecommunication and printing unions are outlined. How these frameworks helped to shape contemporary policies, and the attitudes of policy makers, is a major feature of all four chapters. More specifically the respective unions' development of labour process, recruitment and amalgamations policies is analysed, and the manner in which these strategies shaped contemporary decision making is considered.

This chapter focuses on Britain's printing unions and the manner in which the printing craft and non-craft unions historically developed in markedly different fashions. Initially the chapter details the evolvement of the craft and non-craft unions' structures and political process, before turning to the development of the unions' recruitment, amalgamation and labour process policies. In doing so it highlights how, firstly the craft, and subsequently the non-craft unions, came to rely heavily on the efficient operation of the pre-entry closed shop, in order to deliver high membership density and significant levels of influence over the labour process. How the various print unions' historical approaches to policy-making, in all three featured areas, shaped contemporary decision makers attitudes and affected the print unions policies is also investigated.

Structures and political processes: the craft printing unions

The knowledge and respect that all the interviewees from the British printing craft unions displayed towards their respective union's history and structures, was striking. This was not the norm amongst participants from non-printing unions and it reflected, as a number of craft union interviewees stated, the manner in which they had been taught their trade unionism, along with their craft skills, by their FoC.

The FoC's combination of the union's representative's role along with a training and supervisory function, went far beyond the role played by shop stewards in other industries. Performing these tasks granted the FoC's, as interviewees stated, an enormously powerful position in the working lives of apprentices, and it was a system that lasted well into the latter half of the twentieth century. As a senior officer recalled:

> On my first day at work, in 1980, I was met by the FoC. He told me that I'd be joining the union and that he would be teaching me my trade. No one else, including management, was to tell me what to do. If they did, I was to tell him, and he'd sort the buggers out.

In addition to their training and supervising of apprentices the FoC's also decided how the chapel's work would be allocated amongst members and were responsible for members timekeeping and their standards of performance. This granted the FoC's a remarkably powerful role in the lives of all chapel members. As a retired machine minder observed:

> The most important man at work was the FoC. He decided what you did, when you did it and whether you got overtime. There was little contact with management – they mainly dealt with the FoC.

This powerful role in the workplace for the craft union chapels and their FoC's had its origins in the role played in the industry by the printing craft guilds. These guilds were local associations of craftsmen who were formed to administer and protect the practice of the various printing trades. Their history stretched back to the seventeenth century (see Moxon, 1683 in

Cockburn, 1984) and as demand for printed matter grew in the eighteenth and nineteenth century, the guilds, started to metamorphose into craft associations. All of these various craft associations retained their trade autonomy and organised alongside each other in what became the newspaper and general printing industry (Howe and Child, 1952; Bundock, 1959; Gennard, 1990; Cockburn, 1984).

The craft associations jealously guarded many of powers they inherited from the guilds. This allowed them to regulate apprentice entry to the trade, to supervise the training of apprentices, whilst also deciding upon the provision of labour to individual employers. This high level of control by the craft associations over the supply, training, allocation and management of labour granted the printing craft associations the ability to operate what became known as pre-entry closed shops, and to exert a profound influence over the labour process (Turner, 1962; Clegg, 1976; Howe and Child, 1952; Bundock, 1959; Gennard, 1990; Gennard and Bain, 1995; Cockburn, 1984).

The success of this model of union organisation, in providing regular employment and good wages for their members, led to a considerable demand for apprentice entry to the various printing trades. Union control over apprentice entry numbers, meant that it was often the chapels who decided who would gain entry to a trade. As Cockburn (1984) notes, and interviewees agreed, such was the demand for apprenticeships that craftsmen would often be willing to pay sizeable sums of money to secure their son's entry to their trade. As one former NGA Officer recalled becoming a printing craft apprentice was viewed as "a bloody good number".

Interviewees also recalled how they were made aware, from their first day at work, how lucky they were to be a printing trade apprentice and that they, like all other members, had to abide by the democratic decisions of the union and the chapel. If they failed to do so, or their work was in anyway shoddy, then they would be disciplined, not by the employer, but by the chapel committee. Punishments for either union or work related offences ranged from fines, through to the most drastic sanction of all; the withdrawal of the union card. This punishment was, owing to the operation of the pre-entry closed shop, effectively a dismissal from not only the job, but also the trade.

Attendance at chapel and in many instances branch meetings was compulsory, with non-attendance attracting a fine. Yet the importance of their union to the lives of members was such, that as one former NGA officer commented:

> All the members would have gone to the chapel even if it had been voluntary. The chapel controlled our working lives, so we all wanted to have a say in the decisions.

This type of comment was made by many printing craft union participants, when they reflected on the role the chapel and the union had played in their formative years. The strength of the chapel influence, and that of the FoC's, on all the print unions policy makers conception of the nature of the trade unionism was clearly profound, and, as they stated themselves, it strongly coloured their values and attitudes.

The craft unions' development from numerous, small, locally based associations also resulted in considerable financial and industrial policy autonomy being granted to the chapels and branches. These structures reflected the fact that the constituent regional unions, when they had amalgamated, had insisted on retaining their local autonomy. The chapels, and in some areas the branches, therefore remained at the centre of the union's relationship with members and employers. When eventually the unions which represented the different printing crafts started to amalgamate with one another, they all insisted on their chapel and trade structures being protected in the amalgamation agreements.

One of the results of this pattern of internal development was the ability of chapels and branches to negotiate without recourse to the national union. Such chapel autonomy was particularly pronounced, by the early part of the twentieth century, in the burgeoning newspapers and magazine sector. Here the chapels would negotiate agreements on staffing, pay and conditions, which were often superior to national or regional agreements. Some of these agreements were the cause of internal union conflict, particularly when they enshrined the chapel's ability to exclude members, who were not from their branch, from working in a specific shop. As a former NGA machine manager recalled:

> There was a lot of ill feeling in the union towards newspaper chapels who started running themselves as unions within a union. It built up a lot of resentment and disunity.

These high levels of local autonomy were jealously defended by the strongest newspaper chapels and branches, who charged their delegates to national policy forums with protecting their autonomy. Failure to do so as one former official of the NGA wryly observed: "would have seen the delegate having the briefest of tenures".

As interviewees stated, in the period from 1945 to 1980, when many of the contemporary policy makers entered the industry as craft apprentices, they and their colleagues enjoyed comparatively high wages and good conditions, owing to the strength of the chapel and branch structures. The success of this model of trade unionism generated an almost doctrinaire belief in the defence and perpetuation of chapel and branch autonomy, which, as a number of interviewees candidly conceded, made altering their strategies to cope with a transformed institutional and industrial environment, post 1980, extremely problematic.

Structures and political processes: the non-craft printing unions

The printing unions who organised the non-apprenticed workers did not, initially, have craft union organising methods open to them. Their strategy was to recruit sufficient membership numbers in order to generate collective industrial strength, which could then be deployed to improve their members' terms and conditions. The subscriptions they charged were, in comparison to the craft unions, low, and there was no provision of sick and unemployment benefits. However, by the early part of the twentieth century, in those areas of the printing industry where the non-craft unions' members were in close contact with the craft unions, their organisational structures and industrial strategies started to change to resemble the craft unions (Bundock, 1959; Gennard and Bain, 1995).

Unions such as National Society of Operative Printers and Assistants (NATSOPA), which organised predominantly in newspaper and general print shops, adopted policies to regulate the labour supply, that were very similar to the craft unions. They succeeded in implementing these policies mainly thanks to many of their members being highly skilled, although they were not classified as craft workers. NATSOPA also adopted similar policy-making structures to the craft unions, with a large degree of policy authority residing in the hands of the chapels.

The industrial and organisational model adopted by NATSOPA was not the only structure operated by the non-craft unions. The National Union of Printing Bookbinding and Paper Workers (NUPBPW), whose membership was predominantly located outside of the newspaper industry, did not adopt so completely the craft unions industrial methods, nor did they have the same level of strong chapel organisation. Instead the NUPBPW devolved considerable policy authority to their branches, with the Branch Secretary, as opposed to the FoC, enjoying considerable influence over day-to-day policy-making. The autonomy of the NUPBPW branches is captured by a NUPBPW Branch Secretary recalling his period in office from the mid 1950s:

> In 35 years I only ever asked for help of a National Officer on three occasions. We dealt with all the negotiations with employers and ran the call office[1] ourselves. Yes, three times in over thirty years, and on each occasion they were no bloody use whatsoever.

Encapsulated in this quotation is the manner in which the development of the NUPBPW structure, although different to that of the craft unions and NATSOPA, also created a local tier of the organisation with considerable policy autonomy, self-reliance, and a similar belief in their own industrial abilities.

---

[1]   The call office was a facility run by the branch to place members into vacant posts. Employers would contact the call office with details of vacancies, and the call office would send applicants to fill the posts. Call offices (which had alternative names in different printing unions) were operated by all the printing craft unions.

The two largest non-craft print unions post the Second World War, NATSOPA and the NUPBPW, continued to develop these subtly different structures, in a burgeoning number of workplaces, thanks to their growing industrial strength which forced more employers to accept the pre-entry closed shops. By this time the NUPBPW as well as NATSOPA were using the craft union organisational model, which relied on the pre-entry closed shop, but they retained a branch, rather than a chapel, based structure. These structural differences developed further as the large NUPBPW branches started to employ full-time staff and officers, whilst NATSOPA retained a FoC led chapel structure.

These differences over structures and the locus of local policy authority were never fully resolved, even after the unions amalgamated, to form SOGAT. As many interviewees observed, disagreements over what representational structure SOGAT should adopt, contributed significantly to the split which saw NATSOPA secede from SOGAT in 1972. It was also, as contributors from both sides confirmed, a major reason for the deep fissure that existed within the SOGAT NEC, between the former NATSOPA London delegates and ex-NUPBPW provincial NEC members. This was to be a division that was to seriously handicap SOGAT's efforts to defend its influence over the labour process in the 1980s, and to successfully prosecute the News International dispute.

The labour process: The craft printing unions

The development of the printing craft unions from the guilds entailed an adoption not only of their local structures and processes but also the manner in which they sought to control various elements of the labour process. The key to these efforts was the control of the labour supply, a power the guilds had enjoyed and the craft unions fought jealously to guard. This regulation of the supply of labour provided the basis for the craft union chapels and branches to negotiate relatively high wage levels for their members, in a rapidly expanding and increasingly profitable industry (Gennard, 1990; Cockburn, 1984). The high wage levels in turn permitted the associations to charge high membership fees, from which they were able to provided unemployment and sickness benefits, thereby ensuring members were not forced, owing to financial hardship, to seek work without the agreement of the union.

As the industry grew in the nineteenth century and transportation improved, the local chapel based associations had increasing problems with controlling the supply of labour. They largely solved this difficulty by reaching a series of agreements between themselves to ensure that their members did not all seek work in a particular area. Instead they agreed on a 'tramping system' in which unemployed members would be paid an allowance, by their union, in order to follow a specific route in their efforts to seek work. These arrangements allowed the regionally based unions to retain control of the labour supply in their area. The need to cooperate in order to keep this level of regulation also encouraged a number of the craft unions to enter into amalgamations, so that they had direct control of a wider geographical area and a larger pool of craftsmen (Gennard, 1990; Cockburn, 1984).

Once these larger craft unions were in existence they sought to tackle those employers who had sought to address skilled labour shortages by hiring more apprentices than the union had agreed. The unions' tactical response was to pay unemployed members not to take work in these shops, and to ensure that members working for other employers, refused to handle any product that was destined for, or emanated from, the 'blacked' shops. Those craftsmen who defied the union and took up employment in the 'blacked' shops faced expulsion, which resulted in them being unable to work in companies that recognised the union. These forms of secondary industrial action and internal discipline proved to be highly effective not only in restricting the labour supply, but also in increasing union strength in the workplace, where the chapels were able to greatly influence the regulation of labour and the production process.

Secondary industrial action also proved to be efficient in resolving pay and recognition disputes, which led to the craft unions to use this mode of action regularly up to the mid-1980s. It was only the combination of legislation (which prohibited secondary action in 1982) and the fines, injunctions and sequestration that the NGA suffered in the Messenger Newspapers dispute, which led to this form of official secondary action being abandoned.

The ability of the printing craft unions to so powerfully influence the labour process also relied on their ability to exclude other employees from undertaking their members work. To this end, the craft unions fiercely defended demarcation lines and jealously guarded the concept that only apprenticed workers could undertake any task they judged to be craft work. This policy led to an insistence that all members rigorously policed demarcation lines. As a NGA officer recalled:

> When I started as an apprentice Compositor the FoC made it explicitly clear that Natty men[2] must never be allowed to get near to the stone. If we ever saw them doing so we were to fetch the FoC, or a Chapel committee member, straight away.

Other officers and activists also described regular stoppages, called by the FoC, whilst similar demarcation disputes with the non-craft unions and their members were resolved. Whilst this protection of their trade bred a strong spirit of camaraderie amongst the craft union members, it also led to comparable, deep levels of resentment from non-craft union workers. The methods developed by the printing craft unions, from their guild origins, to influence the labour process were highly successful in achieving tight control over the labour supply and an enviable level of impact on all aspects of the labour process. However their methods for achieving this control rested on exclusivity and employers requiring the craft skills their members possessed. When technology started to undermine this demand for the various trades the craft unions controlled, they sought to retain employment for their members by attaining 'ownership' of the process that had replaced their trade. This policy often bought them into conflict with other unions, particularly those who organised the non-craft employees, who worked in corresponding areas. These disputes added to the antipathy that existed over craft demarcation lines, and militated further against any cross union unity in disputes with employers. As this book documents in

2   NATSOPA members.

Chapter 8, this was to prove to be a considerable handicap in the 1980s
and 1990s, when employers sought to use new technology to undermine
print union influence over the labour process.

The labour process: The non-craft printing unions

The non-craft printing unions, adopted not only structures and policy-
making processes that were similar to the craft unions but also organisational methods designed to influence the labour process. Both the largest
non-craft unions, NATSOPA and, later in their history, the NUPBPW
exploited the fact that employers could not simply replace many of their
more highly skilled members with untrained workers to secure not only
improvements to pay and conditions but also a growing number of pre-entry
closed shops. The non-craft unions efforts to increase their influence over
the labour supply and other aspects of the labour process, was also aided by
the craft unions absolute refusal to countenance their members undertaking non-craft work. As interviewees recall this meant that during non-craft
union strikes, even if the craft unions members continued to work, their
action was highly effective (see Bundock, 1959; Gennard and Bain, 1995).

The major non-craft unions also deployed their increasing influence
over the labour process in places where they were well organised, to spread
their organisation and the application of the pre-entry closed shop to businesses who supplied, or received goods from, companies where they were
strongly organised. In order to achieve this wider organisational coverage
the non-craft unions' branches and chapels once again adopted similar
tactics to the craft unions, by using secondary industrial action. This policy
helped to extend the non-craft pre-entry closed shops, into a wider range
of employers as well as into white collar and ancillary areas of the industry.
These tactics proved to be increasingly successful in the 1960s and 1970s,
as the non-craft unions secured more pre-entry closed shops and greater
influence over the labour process, in many previously unorganised sectors
of the industry.

However, in a number of these ancillary and white collar areas the non-craft unions had difficulty in building strong local organisations at either the chapel or branch level. This often meant that the application of the closed shop was not closely policed, and this left SOGAT's organisation very vulnerable, when they attempted to rebuff attacks by employers on their influence over the labour process in the 1980s.

Recruitment: The craft printing unions

The recruitment policies of the printing craft unions have, as this chapter has already demonstrated, historically been connected to their efforts to control the labour process. As far back as the Guilds the craft unions succeeded in achieving tight regulation of the labour supply, through the application of what was in effect a precursor to the pre-entry closed shop (Gennard, 1990; Cockburn, 1984). By successfully controlling the training and supply of skilled labour, through the sophisticated application and policing of the pre-entry closed shop, the printing craft unions did not have to engage in active recruitment up until 1980. Instead apprentices had to join the union if they wished to gain entry to the trade, and they had to remain in the union if they wished to work in the trade (Gennard, 1990; Cockburn, 1984). The strength of this organisational model rested therefore on the ability of the unions to ensure that employers abided by, and meticulously implemented, the pre-entry closed shop.

For over a hundred years this single, highly effective, organising strategy remained in place and delivered very high levels of membership density in small as well as large workplaces (Dunn and Gennard, 1984; Gennard, 1990). Even when individual craft skills became obsolete, the craft unions used their industrial strength to gain control of the operation of any new machinery or processes that replaced that which they controlled, thereby allowing the organising model to continue undisturbed. It was not until the 1980s, that this method of recruitment was seriously contested by employers and the State. Up until that time although there were a number of isolated challenges by companies to the application of the pre-entry closed shop, the vast bulk of employers, sometimes reluctantly, accepted this form of compulsory unionism.

The reliance of the printing craft unions on the pre-entry closed shop also meant that they had no experience or expertise within their activist and officer corps in direct recruitment. As Chapter 8 charts, this put the NGA at a considerable disadvantage, as they attempted to adapt to the rapid and dramatic industrial, technological and legislative alterations which occurred in the industry in the 1980s. These were changes which also effectively undermined the NGA's ability to use compulsory unionism in their efforts to organise a growing pool of non-apprenticed, white collar, printing workers.

Recruitment: The non-craft printing unions

Unlike the printing craft unions, a number of the non-craft unions had historically had to adopt a variety of different approaches in order to recruit members. However during the latter half of the twentieth century many of the non-craft unions were able to impose on employers, the pre-entry closed shop. This policy was highly successful in boosting membership density in already organised areas and in recruiting large numbers of members in areas of the printing industry where previously there had been little or no union organisation. The increased prevalence of the closed shop also led, as a number of older SOGAT lay and full time officers stated, to a declining use of the recruitment and organisational skills that they possessed. As one SOGAT branch officer recalled:

> When I started as a FoC we didn't have a closed shop. I remember that we pressed for one and we got it in the late '60's. Looking back, I believe that we lost as much as we gained, with important recruiting skills being lost, which we could have done with when the Tories made the closed shop illegal.

Other interviewees endorsed this view, whilst many added that in some areas covered by closed shops the union's organisation was poor or even non-existent. As a retired officer observed:

> We embraced the pre-entry closed shop and it delivered us tens of thousands of members. However in many areas we had no activists to police it and some members were even allowed by employers to stop paying their subs. Look, lots of employers only ever introduced it so they could trade with organised shops. When the closed shop was removed, what was left of our membership often simply collapsed.

The failure to build strong workplace organisations across all areas in which the closed shop operated, was dissimilar to the experience of the craft unions, where the central role played by the chapel and the FoC in union structure and the local labour process, guaranteed high levels of activism. This was not the case in many of the non-craft areas and when the closed shop was removed membership fell away rapidly, particularly in the ancillary and distribution areas of the industry. In attempting to address this decline SOGAT, like the NGA, no longer had officers and activists who possessed the recruitment skills needed to persuade members to join, who were not compelled to do so.

Amalgamations: The craft printing unions

The nature of the printing craft unions had, since they metamorphosed out of the guilds, predisposed them against amalgamations. The original regional craft union desire was to rigorously control the supply of skilled labour, by limiting membership of the union through the local control of apprentice entry to the trade. This organisational method was at odds with any notion of building a wider national craft federation, let alone an industrial union. As has been documented earlier, improved transportation and the resultant increase in the mobility of labour, forced the craft unions firstly to co-operate and then, in a number of instances, to amalgamate, in order to retain their prized control of the labour supply.

However, this process of amalgamation was neither straightforward nor swift. As late as 1964, the British compositors were still organised into three separate unions, the Scottish Graphical Association (SGA), who organised Scottish compositors, the Typographical Association (TA) which represented all English and Welsh compositors working outside of Greater London, and the London Typographical Society (LTS) who covered compositors who were apprenticed and worked within a 15-mile radius of Charing Cross. These divisions, as Cockburn (1983) states, had lasted for decades owing to LTS and their predecessors' absolute refusal to allow any compositor, who had not been apprenticed within a 15-mile radius of Charing Cross, to work in Greater London. This policy assisted the LTS in preserving a substantial pay differential between their members and the TA (Cockburn, 1983: 73). The LTS behaviour led the TA to reply in kind, and they barred LTS members from working outside of the Greater London area. Unsurprisingly these policies engendered considerable antipathy between the two unions' officers, activists and memberships, which remained even after the two unions finally merged.

The motivation for the amalgamation between the LTS and the TA was linked to changes in printing machine technology which allowed employers to relocate out of London, to larger, cheaper, industrial premises where they could employ the lower paid TA members. Employers were also then able to use the improving road network to freight their goods onwards to customers, rather than having to rely on the rail network. These changes precipitated a fall in LTS membership which resulted in the union having to seek a merger for the type of economic and membership reasons that many scholars of union amalgamation put forward as precursors for amalgamation (Undy et al, 1996; Undy, 2008; Waddington, 1995).

The industrial and institutional reasons behind the TA and the LTS merger, to create the NGA in 1964, also drove other, often unwilling, craft unions to amalgamate. By the late 1960s a number of significant amalgamations had taken place. The Association of Correctors of the Press (ACP) put aside their historical antipathy towards the LTS and joined the NGA. The National Union of Press Telegraphists (NUPT) amalgamated with the NGA in 1967 followed by the National Society of Electrotypers and Stenographers (NSES) and the Amalgamated Society of Lithographic

Printers and Auxiliaries of Great Britain and Ireland (ASLP), in 1969. This left, by 1970, only two major craft unions, the Society of Lithographic Artists, Designers, Engravers and Process Workers (SLADE) and the SGA (Scottish Graphical Association) outside of the NGA.

Efforts to bring SLADE and the SGA into the NGA proved to be problematic. SLADE, whose membership base was in Lithoset printing, refused to merge at this time and only finally agreed to amalgamate with the NGA over a decade later in 1982. The reason for SLADE's refusal to merge centred on a series of bitter demarcation disputes with the NGA, in a number of different employers. The SGA's antipathy towards the NGA was also caused, in part, by a geographical demarcation dispute, surrounding the NGA's and previously the TA's, attempts to organise Scottish compositors. Interviewees also highlighted the fact that there was deep seated mutual antipathy between the two unions' General Secretaries, which played a very significant part in ensuring the tentative amalgamation talks were unsuccessful. This evidence supports the belief that micro-political factors, in this instance a personal enmity, profoundly affects union policy.

The mergers that took place between the printing craft unions, in the period up until 1980 were all characterised by a number of common features. Each amalgamation was entered into by at least one union that was suffering significant membership decline and a contraction in industrial and financial strength, reasons which scholars of union amalgamations (Waddington, 1988, 1995; Waddington et al, 2005; Undy et al, 1996; Undy, 2008) cite as the most common cause of mergers. These membership losses were all directly linked to changes in technology and resultant diminutions in employment levels in the various trades the craft unions organised. Unlike a number of amalgamations involving the British telecommunications unions (which are covered in later chapters), none of the printing craft union mergers reflected any ideological desire to form an industrial union. Instead, the mergers were pragmatic attempts to ensure that the merging union could maintain its ability to provide benefits to its members, whilst continuing to function coherently in those workplaces where it retained chapel agreements. To this end the smaller unions who were amalgamating with the NGA all strove to retain as much sectional and chapel autonomy as possible (Gennard, 1990; Cockburn, 1984).

This desire to retain sectional and chapel independence led to a number of the merger agreements protecting sectional independence. In the case of the original TA merger with the LTS, the agreement enshrined the two merging unions' separate rulebooks in the NGA's constitution. Owing to this arrangement the LTS continued to function autonomously as the NGA London Region, whilst the TA's former constitution covered NGA members in the rest of England and Wales. The rulebook also guaranteed the NGA London Region the ability to pursue different industrial and political polices, if they so wished. This was a freedom which they were to exercise on numerous occasions. As one NGA officer recalled:

> In reality there was never a merger in anything but name. The London Region was never willing to accept the authority of the national union.

This divide did not disappear quickly after the merger. Thirty years later some of the officers and members of the London Region made it clear in their interviews that their allegiance was to their Region not the national NGA.

Similar arrangements were also put into place for other amalgamating unions, which meant that officers and activists continued to have a strong loyalty to, and an electoral dependence on, the trades, geographical areas and chapels from which they had emanated. These loyalties outweighed, any factional or ideological or even wider union loyalties. The structure of the NGA that was created by these amalgamation agreements also guaranteed a high degree of policy autonomy for sections and chapels and ensured that chapel and trade interests remained highly influential in determining national decision makers' policy choices.

Amalgamations: The non-craft printing unions

After the Second World War the non-craft print unions, started to effectively divide themselves into two separate groups. The first of these groupings consisted of unions who practised 'quasi-craft unionism', which entailed the adoption of internal structures and industrial tactics, which mirrored those of the craft unions. NATSOPA was the largest of these unions and they organised workers who although not apprenticed craft workers possessed skills which allowed them to operate in a very similar manner to the craft unions. They sought to amalgamate with other comparable non-craft print unions which had developed similar structural and industrial models. The second grouping included unions who organised members, who did not have the levels of skill that allowed them to adopt craft union methods, or who represented workers across a whole industry, such as ink and paper production. The organisational tactics they adopted can be loosely defined as 'industrial unionism' with a structural emphasis on organising workers into multi-employer branches rather than workplace chapels.

Amalgamations between these two groups of unions were uncommon up until the 1960s, with mergers taking place between unions who were in one or other of the two groupings (Gennard and Bain, 1995). This process led to the formation by 1960 of two large non-craft printing unions; NATSOPA, who were a 'quasi-craft' union, and the NUPBPW, which, although it organised members with quasi-craft skills, operated more like an industrial union. By the 1960s NATSOPA and the NUPBPW members were, owing to technological advancements, increasingly coming into conflict with each other and the craft unions, over demarcation issues.

Both unions agreed motions at their Conferences, which stated that it would be logical to merge, in order to ensure that they were better placed to resist the craft union policies of 'following the work' into what they both viewed as non-craft areas. Bringing the two unions together however, proved to be profoundly difficult. During the lengthy negotiations there were fundamental disagreements over the merged union's structure, with particular conflict over whether local policy authority should lie with the branches or the chapels. Finally in 1966 a merger was agreed. The new union's structure resembled in many ways that of the NGA, in that it was intrinsically federalist. SOGAT as the new union was to be named embodied two separate divisions; Division A contained the NUPBPW membership, whilst Division 1 encompassed NATSOPA's members. Both divisions had their own discrete NEC's (who would retain policy-making authority), their own rule books, and separate General Secretary's (Bain and Gennard, 1995)

The two unions also agreed in the amalgamation agreement to enter into post-merger discussions to agree on a unified rule book, a single NEC, and to stage elections for a single General Secretary, all by the end of 1969. Whilst these discussions were taking place the highly federated, division based, union structure, saw the adoption by the divisions of contradictory industrial and political policies, which as former NATSOPA and NUPBPW officers recalled, created tensions and confusion amongst SOGAT members. Resolving all these outstanding issues by the end of 1969, proved to be impossible, owing in significant part, interviewees confided, to a strong personal animosity between the General Secretaries. After a series of acrimonious meetings and a fractious SOGAT Conference in 1968, the union far from coming together as agreed, started to split asunder.

The official reasons for the split, which followed in 1972, revolved around the refusal by the Division 1 Executive (formerly NATSOPA) to accept the passing of greater policy authority into the hands of a united SOGAT NEC and to consent to a unified rule book, which granted branches and their officers a more prominent role than chapels (Gennard and Bain, 1995). Interviewees however stated that the personal antipathy that existed between the General Secretary of NATSOPA, Dick Brigenshaw, and senior officers of the NUPBPW, was the primary reason why NATSOPA seceded, a view which Gennard and Bain (1995) endorse. This is further powerful empirical evidence of the important role that micro-political factors play in amalgamation policies.

The secession of NATSOPA did not alter SOGAT's belief that accelerating technological developments in the pre-press and press areas would inevitably lead to a plethora of demarcation and coverage disputes, between all craft and non-craft unions. In order to address this problem SOGAT's national leadership suggested that the best way to resolve these problems was through creation of one industrial printing union. Significantly SOGAT approached the NGA to take part in these print unions' merger talks, even though at that time, relations between the two unions were very poor, owing to industrial disagreements and the NGA's decision to resign from the TUC in 1972. They had taken this decision, prior to their probable expulsion, following their choice to register as a trade union under the provisions of the Industrial Relations Act (1971). Whilst SOGAT, SLADE and the other print unions had followed TUC guidance and deregistered, the NGA's membership had rejected their National Council recommendation to deregister and stay in the TUC (Gennard, 1990: 294). As NGA activists and officers of the time conceded this reflected the outlook of many NGA chapels, which were reluctant to put at risk their sizeable chapel funds by allowing the national union to deregister. The NGA chapels and branches also reacted negatively, to suggestions from the NGA's senior national officers that they should even consider attending amalgamation talks with SOGAT and the other printing unions.

The merger talks however went ahead, although NATSOPA, as well as the NGA, had refused to attend. Whilst agreement on a merger could not be reached between all the unions, the SGA and SOGAT, after lengthy negotiations agreed on amalgamation terms. This was to be the first merger involving two major craft and non-craft unions, and its success was largely attributed to the profound coverage disagreements, and personal animosity, that existed between officers and activists of the SGA and the NGA. The SGA's decision to amalgamate with SOGAT also owed much, as interviewees and Gennard and Bain (1995) agree, to the considerable autonomy that was offered to the Scottish union. The generous amalgamation package that SOGAT proposed to the SGA, substantiates Undy's (1996, 2008) assertions that the efforts of larger unions to persuade smaller unions to amalgamate, played a more significant part in explaining patterns of amalgamations than is acknowledged by authors who stress the economic and industrial motivations for union mergers (see Waddington, 1988, 1995; Waddington et al, 2005).

The merger of the SGA into SOGAT was followed shortly thereafter by NATSOPA approaching SOGAT to suggest they entered into discussions about re-amalgamating. This volte face by NATSOPA's leadership was, former officers confirmed, linked not only to increasing membership losses, but also to the retirement of senior officials who had been at the centre of the acrimonious split from SOGAT. These discussions, as Chapter 8 charts, took many years but were eventually to lead to NATSOPA merging again with SOGAT in 1982; the same year that SLADE finally merged with the NGA.

The different industrial, structural and organisational natures of the printing unions had historically militated against the creation of such an industrial union. So too had the industrial success of the craft and 'quasi-craft' organisational model, which was exclusionary rather than inclusionary in its nature. The success of this model in delivering high membership density also weighed against mergers. These factors, when combined with a lack of powerful Left factions (who in other British unions were campaigning for the creation of larger general or industrial unions), meant that amalgamations had only been entered into when technological and institutional changes started to undermine union organisational and industrial strength.

Conclusion

The historical success of the printing unions in establishing a model of trade unionism which delivered considerable influence over the labour process and guaranteed very high membership density, through the operation of the pre-entry closed shops, has been shown to have had a profound effect on contemporary printing union policy makers. The influential function of the respective unions' chapels and FoC's in 'educating' apprentices and in workplace supervision, ensured that the union had a prominent and respected place in all of its members' lives. The strength of this role bred an allegiance, amongst contemporary craft union policy makers, to their union's very specific mode of unionism, which stressed the centrality of the chapel, the branch and their trade.

So strong was the success of this style of craft unionism, in the first eighty years of the twentieth century, that it led to many non-craft unions adopting 'quasi-craft' organising and industrial methods. Whilst this resulted in large scale membership increases, considerable local policy-making autonomy and significant industrial success, it also led to non-craft unions' becoming as dependent as the craft unions, upon the effective application of the pre-entry closed shop.

Chapter 8 will examine the consequences for the print unions of their strong dependence upon these homogenous organisational and industrial polices, when they were forced to respond in the 1980s to what Kelly (1996) identified as a powerful 'counter-offensive' launched by employers and the State.

CHAPTER 5

The Australian Printing Unions: Pre-1980

Introduction

In this chapter, the manner in which the contemporary structures and industrial polices of the Australian print unions have been influenced by the historical development of their organisation and political processes will be addressed. Specifically the development of the Australian printing unions' labour process, recruitment and amalgamations policies will be charted and the effect of these historical strategies on modern policy in the three areas will be analysed. What affect the unions' structures and political process had upon contemporary policy makers' values and views will also be considered.

The reasons why the Australian unions polices either varied from, or were similar to, those of the British print unions, will be investigated, as will internal variations across the States and Territories of Australia. These latter differences are particularly important as they affected the creation of the national unions and their subsequent policies.

Unlike Britain, in the majority of Australian States, the craft and non-craft printing unions merged relatively early in their history. For this reason this chapter, unlike its predecessor, is not divided into separate craft and non-craft sub-sections. Instead the structures and political process of all the Australian printing unions are considered, followed by a charting of the development of the unions policies in the three selected areas.

Structures and political processes

In common with their British counterparts many Australian print union officers from craft backgrounds had a strong pride in, and knowledge of, their unions' history. Many related with considerable approval how in the early nineteenth century, groups of skilled British immigrant printing workers, set up unions in Eastern Australia's embryonic printing industry. These were, as many interviewees correctly stated, some of earliest unions to be formed in Australia. This knowledge had been passed down to them by their FoC's, who, as in Britain, had taught their apprentices union history, as well as their trades.

The early Australian unions closely resembled the British printing craft unions, which was unsurprising given that their founders had all originally been union members in Britain (Hagan, 1966). As in Britain during that period, the Australian craft unions were small; organising workers from a specific trade in a particular town. By 1858 there were over a dozen towns, in Victoria alone, with their own separate compositors' unions (Hagan, 1966: 23–4). This level of localism, as in Britain, made the unions' viability susceptible to downturns in the local economy and influxes of skilled labour from other areas. In order to address this problem the small, town based unions started to amalgamate, in order to create organisations which had wider geographical coverage.

Amalgamating in this manner and retaining the traditional British print union craft structures was called into question in the 1890s by the leaders of many of Australia's print unions, as deep economic depression caused a huge loss of membership. As Hagan notes (1966: 138) the Australian printing unions lost over two thirds of their membership in this decade along with a number of industrial disputes, called to protect wages and compulsory unionism (Hagan, 1966: 109–10). The print unions' struggles were a small part of the wider labour movement's efforts to actively resist redundancies and wage cuts. This resistance most famously encompassed the Maritime Union strike of 1890 and the Shearers' Union strikes of 1891 and 1894. These unsuccessful disputes saw the State making a series of hostile interventions, including the use of the military force to breach picket lines.

Importantly for the print unions these industrial defeats led to a policy split which was to affect their industrial unity until the 1990s. Across most of the then Australian colonies the printing craft unions had, independently, concluded that they needed to organise all grades of print workers in order to retain viability and influence over the labour process. This argument was rejected in Victoria, where the unions remained organised along tightly demarcated craft and non-craft lines, and in Hagan's words, decided to 'lie low and hope for the return of better days' (Hagan, 1966: 135). This divergence in attitude went further with the majority of the printing unions supporting the creation of Labour[1] Parties and the introduction of compulsory arbitration, which the Victorians opposed (Hagan, 1966; Fitzgerald, 1967).

This sharp division in policy responses by similar unions to comparable institutional pressures is at odds with the type of homogeneous response that institutionalist authors (Bain, 1970; Clegg, 1976) suggest would occur when alike unions are faced with corresponding external factors. The considerable variation in policies does though support the views of scholars who assert that unions make rational strategic choices between different policy options, decisions which are often dictated by the views and ideology of the policy makers (Kelly, 1998; Boxall and Hayes, 1997; Heery and Kelly, 1994; Heery, 2000, 2003).

The divergence in the structures of the Australian printing unions grew wider as unions outside of Victoria sought to form federations, which brought together both craft and non-craft workers. Whilst these efforts to bring all the different printing unions in each State together proved to be problematic, what did occur in all States, bar NSW and Victoria, was the formation by the 1930s of one union, the Printing Industries Employees Union of Australia (PIEUA), which represented both craft and non-craft printing workers. In NSW after a series of amalgamations and splits, the picture was more complicated with Amalgamated Printing Trades Employee's Union (APTEU) organising the bulk of craft and non-craft workers whilst the Printing Industries Employees Union of Australia (PIEUA) represented compositors. Victoria in contrast retained the craft and non-craft union divisions, which like Britain, were only finally being bridged after 1980.

---

1 The Australian Labour Party changed its name to the Australian Labor Party in 1912.

The consequences for the structures and political processes of the Australian printing unions of the widespread, but not universal, adoption of industrial print unionism were intriguing. Older interviewees, from all the States bar Victoria and NSW, recall how the structures of the PIEUA resembled those of their State craft union predecessors, with a strong emphasis being placed on chapel autonomy. The unions had though to put in place structures and processes to deal with demarcation clashes that occurred between craft and non-craft chapels. The structures they used to resolve these problems were State branch committees, whose role it was to arbitrate between the different parties. However as a former PIEUA officer admitted:

> It was always the comps that dominated the branch. They turned up in big numbers, were better educated, had louder voices, and voted as a block. This meant that nine times out of ten – they got their own way.

This compositor domination was repeated in elections to all tiers of the PIEUA structure with full-time officer and lay activists positions at the State and national level being dominated by Compositors. The scale of this control is reflected in the fact that up until its merger in 1966, every PIEUA Federal and State Secretary had been a compositor, whilst over 85% of the union's full-time officials were also from the composing trade.

The filling of chapel and branch activist and officer policy-making posts by craftsmen, was replicated in the NSW's APTEU, which did not organise Compositors. Here the various policy makers emanated instead from the various craft chapels that organised skilled press shop workers. When APTEU interviewees, from both craft and non-craft backgrounds, were asked to explain this disparity they pointed to the eloquence and organisation of the craft workers. Given this control of both 'industrial' unions by craft activists and officers it is perhaps unsurprising that their industrial focus tended to be on the craft, rather than the non-craft, areas. Even after the merger to form a single industrial printing union the PKIU in 1966 (which is described later in this chapter), the dominant focus continued to be on craft worker issues.

As in Britain, outside of newspapers and the general print, the non-craft areas, whilst organised thanks to the pre-entry closed shop, also tended to have lower levels of union activism. This was particularly the case in the less skilled distribution and ancillary areas, where the Australian unions, similarly to SOGAT, achieved membership coverage, but lacked a strong activist base. There were exceptions to this rule, with non-craft members in paper mills and the large cardboard packaging plants, forming sophisticated workplace structures. Yet these union chapels tended to function as almost 'semi-detached' entities within the union, intrinsically different in their organisational and representational structures, and participating less than the craft chapels in the operation of the State branches.

The manner in which the Australian industrial print union structures and political processes resembled those of their craft predecessors is a testament to the organisational strength of the printing craft trade unionists. This dominance allowed the craft officers and activists to make a series of policy choices which prioritised their issues at the expense of those of non-craft members. These findings once again support the assertion that unions have the ability to make a series of strategic choices which can profoundly affect the policy direction they follow (Hyman, 1997; Kelly and Heery, 1989, 1994; Heery and Kelly, 1994; Kelly, 1998; Heery, 2006). Whilst this structural and industrial model, which depended so heavily on the closed shop, delivered impressive organisational and labour process outcomes, it also made the PKIU organisationally vulnerable to the economic and technological transformation which affected the sector in the late 1970s, which made their powerful craft areas industrially obsolete.

The labour process

At their outset the Australian print unions' adopted policies to influence the labour process which were identical to those of British printing craft unions. This pattern of behaviour did not radically alter until the 1970s, with the Australian unions adopting very similar policies to their British counterparts. The similarity was most pronounced in the policies the Australian unions used to control the labour supply. Like the British craft unions, they followed the policies of the printing guilds and rigorously applied the pre-entry closed shop and ensured through primary and secondary industrial action that they controlled the number of apprentices entering the various trades.

Building on the strength that this tight control of the labour supply granted, the Australian unions' chapels, in common with their British counterparts, also trained apprentices and effectively managed the day-to day activities of their members. As the Australian unions became more industrial in nature, they expanded their coverage in the non-craft areas by using secondary industrial action to 'persuade' recalcitrant companies, who supplied goods or received products from union organised shops, that they should recognise the union and the pre-entry closed shop. As in Britain this process led to the unions operating sophisticated employment systems which placed members into jobs, that the employers had informed the union were vacant. This was done via the branch call (employment) offices, whose officers decided who would be sent to the employer, as the solitary applicant, to fill the vacant post. Only members who were not in financial arrears could use the call office facilities and the print unions would frequently use secondary industrial action against any employer who either rejected the union candidate, or hired workers not sent by the branch (Hagan, 1966).

The similarity with British print union policies also permeated other aspects of the labour process, with the chapels running their affairs in a comparable fashion, even though in the majority of States there was only one industrial printing union. As a PKIU official who arrived in Western Australia in the early 1960s recalled:

> When I got a start I was worried about not understanding how the demarcs operated in a union that represented all the print workers on the paper. So it made me laugh when on my first day the FoC said to me – remember, only the Comps are allowed near the stone. It was amazing, I was half the world away, but I could have been back in the NGA chapel where I served my apprenticeship.

As has been discussed earlier in this chapter, part of the reason for these similar patterns of behaviour relates to the Australian unions retaining their demarcated chapels, whilst their branch and national structures were dominated by craft activists and officers.

By the early 1970s the ability of the PKIU and the Victorian unions to use these methods to wield a high level of influence over the labour process started to come under a concerted challenge, as employers sought to introduce new pre-press technology. The Australian printing industry was not as large, or as concentrated, as Britain's, and the demand for newspapers was falling. The geographically vast, federated nature of Australia meant that there had never been a centre of newspaper and general print similar to that found in London. Instead Australia had a series of regional newspaper and general print centres, based in the State capital cities, which were both experiencing contraction as State television and radio expanded. The dispersed nature of the industry meant that the unions found it exceptionally difficult to generate the level of cross title solidarity and industrial influence, which the British unions wielded in Fleet Street. Even where a company, such as Rupert Murdoch's News Limited, owned a string of newspapers in different States, there was not a parallel PKIU structure, which could collectively respond if the employer introduced new working practices on one title.

In 1976 these problems became acute when John Fairfax Newspapers Ltd, introduced computers which allowed direct text inputting by Journalists, at its biggest selling newspaper the *Sydney Morning Herald* (Cryle, 2006: 3). There had been no consultation with the PKIU over the introduction of a process which effectively removed the role of the compositor and other pre-press employees. Unsurprisingly this action sparked strike action involving all 1400 PKIU Fairfax production members. The strike, which lasted two months, was marked by a number of clashes with the police as pickets attempted to stop journalists from entering the plant. Crucially, for future relations between the Australian Journalist Association (AJA) and the PKIU in NSW, the AJA refused to instruct its members not to cross the PKIU picket line, which incensed the print workers and caused a rift which, as Chapter 9 charts, had not healed by the 1990s.

After 60 days of strike action, and the intervention of various prominent NSW Labor Council figures, the PKIU NSW branch and the Fairfax
chapels, were finally persuaded to call off their strike, and allow the NSW
Industrial Court to make a determination on the dispute. Justice Cahill,
the presiding Judge, took until August 1977, to reach his decision, and
in the interim Fairfax was forced to revise and moderate their proposals.
However, when the judgement was finally handed down, it proved to be
disastrous for the union. Justice Cahill made it clear that he was seeking
to deal with 'matters of general principle' in the newspaper and printing
industry rather than just settling 'specific grievances' raised by the PKIU
(Cahill; 1977: 8). He ruled that the AJA members should be responsible
for direct text entry and all the subsequent editing and composition of the
newspaper, whilst members of the Federated Clerks Union of Australia
(FCU) should directly input classified advertisements, received over the
telephone (Cahill; 1977: 15).

This decision was to damage the PKIU's strength in the pre-press areas,
across Australia, as the Federal Industrial Relations Commission and the
other State Industrial Relations Commissions and Courts, indicated that
they would follow Justice Cahill reasoning if they were called upon to make
judgements in similar cases. In the wake of the judgement no other State
branch or large newspaper chapel chose to test the resolve of the employers or the Commissions by taking strike action over the introduction of
the new pre-press technology. Instead as a number of officers and activists
recalled, often unhappily, the PKIU proceeded to deal with the introduction of new technology in all areas of the industry, not just the pre-press
rooms, in a highly pragmatic fashion. News Ltd for instance managed to
avoid industrial disputes in all their Australian newspapers, as they reached
agreements with the PKIU which saw very large numbers of employees
accept voluntary redundancies, with only a small minority of time served
workers retrained for other work (Cryle, 2006: 6).

The straightforward causal link that has been made by authors such
as Cryle (2006) between the judgement and the PKIU subsequent policy
is though questionable. Interviewees point to other reasons aside from the
judgement, for the lack of resistance to job losses in the pre-press areas. As
a former senior PKIU officer commented:

> A lot of the skilled blokes were only a few years off retirement and they were offered
> a bloody great pay-out. Asking them to take action to defend their jobs was a total
> non-starter. That horse just wouldn't run; they wanted the money.

Many officers expressed their frustration at this willingness of their members to accept the redundancy packages, believing that with greater membership resistance more members could have been retrained and redeployed. The difficulty the print unions experienced in getting members to take action is at odds with the view of rank and filist authors such as Bramble (1993, 2008) who state that it was full-time officers' lack of willingness to call for industrial action that discouraged greater membership militancy.

The ability and willingness of the major newspaper employers, Fairfax and News Limited to offer generous redundancy packages, led to a rapid, unchallenged, decline in the employment of printing craft workers. Alongside this numerical decline came a diminished influence over the labour process, as technology reduced the level of physical skill needed to produce the finished product. This trend accelerated further during the late 1970s as magazine production and large parts of the general print sector started to relocate their operations to Asia. This was partly due to the easing of Australian tariff barriers which had previously restricted imports from Australia's neighbours. Once again there was a lack of strong industrial resistance, owing in these instances to the weak industrial position that the PKIU and its members suddenly found themselves. This was pithily summed up by a former NSW PKIU officer:

> We had a meeting with one employer to try and keep the printing of his magazines
> in Sydney. He told us he could produce twice the run, in Asia, with a third less
> labour, for half the cost, including transportation. He then said: You mongrels can
> go on strike 'till kingdom come; it'll make no difference – we're going, end of story.

Following the 1976 *Sydney Morning Herald* dispute, the findings of this book clearly show that a series of strategic choices were taken, often at the local chapel level, which resulted in the PKIU adopting a highly pragmatic approach to the introduction of new technology and a resultant diminution in their influence over the labour process. This strategy allowed the new equipment and working practices to be introduced in return for

generous severance packages and a continued role for the union in representing the workers that remained. In part these decisions were coloured
by environmental and political factors as the institutional contextualist
authors suggest (Flanders, 1965; Bain, 1970; Clegg, 1976; Boraston et al,
1975; Howell, 2006), but they were also shaped by members choosing to
accept redundancy packages, rather than engage in what they viewed as
unwinnable fights. The evidence of these types of local strategic choices
supports the assertions of authors such as Kelly and Heery (Kelly and
Heery, 1989, 1994; Heery and Kelly, 1994; Kelly, 1998; Heery, 2006) that
unions make critical labour process policy choices at the workplace as well
as the national level.

Recruitment

In the period prior to 1980 all the Australian printing craft and non-craft
unions successfully sought to introduce and implement the wide spread
use of the pre-entry closed shops as their primary recruitment tool. As in
Britain, this had not been the original recruitment method adopted by
the non-craft unions, but they had rapidly adopted similar organisational
methods to the craft unions. This trend accelerated more quickly than in
Britain, owing to many of the non-craft unions amalgamating with the
Australian craft unions, in the first half of the twentieth century. The craft
chapels' industrial strength was then harnessed, to ensure pre-entry closed
shops were agreed in non-craft areas.

   Unlike the British unions the Australians were also able to use the
Federal and State arbitral system to 'rope in' a company, to the appropri-
ate printing award. This action, if approved by the relevant Commission,
granted the company's employees the minimum terms and conditions,
provided by the relevant award. The ability of the Australian printing
unions to use these methods of organising allowed them to significantly
increase their membership numbers and industrial coverage. However as

with the British non-craft unions, this model of organising whilst boosting membership numbers was less successful in developing activists who could build a local organisation. Many PKIU officers reflected that they should have done more to build a robust activist base in the 1960s and 1970s when they had the opportunity. As one officer reflected:

> If we are honest, we dropped the bundle. We could have organised thousands of members in the industry, and built a much stronger organisation. A lot of officers got shitty about going into these shops, because they were small with few members or potential members. Instead they wanted to visit the big shops where there were a lot more votes. In the end we ended up taking the easy road and never used the strength we then had to build up our structures and expand even further into the growing sectors of the industry. This proved to be a major blue, which then bit us in the arse.

These problems, with establishing powerful workplace organisations, outside of areas where the PKIU had large numbers and industrial strength, did indeed prove to be a weakness in the 1980s and 1990s, when technological change saw an expansion in the number of employers, who operated small jobbing, instant print or graphic design shops. Even without the type of legislative restrictions that the British print unions were to face in the 1980s, the Australian unions found it impossible to use the pre-entry closed shop in areas of the industry where from the 1980s onwards industrial and technological changes meant that employers could not be substantially affected by secondary action, and non-union employees could be hired. These changes, plus the PKIU's lack of officers with physical organising skills, were to prove to be a considerable barrier to effective recruitment in the period post 1980.

Amalgamations

As has been detailed earlier in this chapter, the Australian printing unions entered into amalgamations across the craft/non-craft union divide over seventy years before their British counterparts. These amalgamations followed part of wider strategic decisions by the print unions in all of Australia's States, bar Victoria, to respond to highly adverse industrial and economic conditions in the 1890s, by seeking wider labour movement co-operation to generate political solutions to the devastating industrial and membership problems they faced. In contrast the Victorian's chose to remain in separate craft and non-craft organisations up until the latter part of the twentieth century (Hagan, 1966). As Hagan noted (1966) the decision of the Victorian printing craft unions not to engage in amalgamations with non-craft unions was in keeping with those taken by British printing craft unions. This attitude reflected the strong tradition, which both Hagan (1966) and Gennard (1990) note, of craft exclusivity and independence, which saw the craft unions only ever merging with other printing craft unions.

Moving away from this tradition proved to be difficult, for the craft unions in the rest of Australia. In the largest printing centre, NSW, all the major craft unions took the decision to enter into Sydney Printing Trades Federation Council (SPTFC) in the early 1900s. However a demarcation dispute between the different craft union chapels at a Sydney general printer, Simmons Limited, led to acrimonious meeting, after which the NSW Typographical Association left the organisation. Crucially the other craft unions did not follow suit, but instead decided to stay in the Federation and to turn it into a State-wide general printing union. This they succeeded in doing in 1921, when they formed the Amalgamated Printing Trades Employees' Union (APTEU).

The reason, according to Hagan (1966), for this decision was the Federation leaders' anger and personal animosity towards the NSWTA senior officers, who they felt, had behaved arrogantly over the Simmons issue. In response they now wished to isolate and eventually destroy the NSWTA. The decision surprised the NSWTA who responded by forming a new national printing union the Printing Industries Employees Union of Australia (PIEUA) with a stated remit of bringing together, not just all the Compositor unions, but every printing union in Australia. These decisions give credence not only to Undy's (Undy et al, 1996; Undy, 2008) argument that unions can enter into mergers for political as well as economic reasons, but also the powerful role that micro-political factors can play in amalgamation policy choices. The two unions also now engaged in a competition for merger partners, which led to the APTEU merging with a number of printing unions in NSW and the PIEUA establishing itself as an industrial union in all the States, bar Victoria and NSW, where it only organised Compositors.

As has been noted earlier in this chapter, both the PIEUA and the APTEU were organised along similar, craft union structural lines, with retention of a devolved organisation that granted considerable autonomy to the chapels. However, even though by 1940 both unions' Conferences had asserted that it was anomalous to have two industrial printing unions in Australia, securing an amalgamation proved to be elusive. A number of older interviewees, reflecting on the reasons why bringing the two unions together proved to be so difficult, focused on the animosity, which existed between the senior officers of the two unions. The nature of this rivalry was such that even in Hagan's (1966) official history, the hostile personal relationship between the two, long serving Federal Secretaries, was cited as the reason why all merger negotiations failed up until 1966. Indeed the relationship was so bad in 1945, that the PIEUA supported its Federal Secretary, E.C Magrath, in a successful High Court defamation action against Tom Bell, the APTEU Federal Secretary. The cause of this action was a series of letters from Bell to Magrath, described by Hagan (1966: 297) as, 'sometimes abusive and occasionally even obscene'.

The strong personal animosity between the two leaders is further evidence of the importance of micro-political factors in shaping union policy direction. It also led to an exacerbation by the leadership of the industrial and political differences that had existed between the unions for decades. As another elderly, former senior APTEU Officer, recalled:

> Look, the Comps were small minded and conservative. Most of the bastards didn't have a political bone in their body. The APTEU was different. We were skilled men, but we weren't snobs like the Comps. Tom Bell always believed we should be 'militant craftsmen', yes 'militant craftsmen', not a bunch of no good bastards who'd rather run a mile than have a blue.

The political divide the retired officer referred to also encompassed the APTEU activists and officers being more engaged in labour movement politics than PIEUA officials, or indeed those from the British print unions.

Yet the impression that the political and industrial divide between the unions was so great that it could not have been bridged was dismissed not only by Hagan (1966), but also by interviewees who pointed to the manner in which the PIEUA was able to operate in other States. As an elderly PKIU officer reflected:

> Look the reason it took so long to merge was Magrath and Bell. They couldn't stand to be in the room with each other, let alone negotiate a merger. It wasn't to do simply with politics or trade unionism – they simply didn't like each other. All the other reasons put forward are garbage. The real barrier to a merger was at the top, not amongst the chapels or the members – that was just a smokescreen.

This argument is given credence by the overwhelming majorities that both unions returned in favour of a merger, when negotiations finally produced an amalgamation deal in 1966. Importantly negotiations that led to the amalgamation terms being drawn up had only been started after both Bell and Magrath had retired.

After the formation of the PKIU in 1966, the only other sizeable printing unions left in Australia were located in Victoria. The Victorian Printing Trades and Graphical Workers Union (VPTGWU) had for many years had discordant relations, at both the chapel and State level, with the PIEUA and, subsequently, the PKIU. The VPTGWU refused all offers to merge with the PKIU in the period up until 1980, by which time they themselves had merged with other small Victorian printing unions, becoming the Victorian Print Operatives Union (VPOU). Yet even after these mergers, the decline in the employment levels in the sector detailed earlier in the chapter meant that the VPOU had become a very small organisation indeed. Not amalgamating with the PKIU was, even VPOU officers agreed, industrially illogical by the end of the 1970s. However the level of animosity was such that the VPOU refused all the PKIU overtures.[2] As a former VPOU officer explained:

---

2   The VPOU finally merged with the PKIU in 1992, the events leading up to which are covered in Chapter 9.

> We didn't want a bar of the PKIU. The Comps had treated us like mongrels for years. You've got to understand our dislike of the Comps ran very deep.

This ill feeling, and parallel desire for independence, was shared by another predominantly Victorian union, the Federated Photo Engravers Photo-Lithographers and Photogravure Employees Association of Australia (PEPLP). Even in the face of rapidly tumbling membership and the eradication of the trades their members practised, PEPLP refused to merge with the PKIU in the period up to 1980.[3]

Yet when questioned more closely as to why they had refused to merge for so long when their membership base was so weak, it became clear from contributors that other factors aside from demarcation and membership coverage disputes were more important. As a number of senior officers of the VPOU admitted, the primary reason for not merging by the late 1970s was micro-political, in that they did not wish to become part of a Victorian PKIU branch whose internal, highly personal, infighting (which is reviewed in detail in Chapter 9) had made it operationally dysfunctional. Here once again, in relation to the amalgamation policies of the Australian printing unions, the role of micro-political factors in deciding policy direction is shown to be profound, whilst also being partly concealed from the public and the members' gaze.

Conclusion

By 1980, the Australian printing unions had already suffered considerable industrial setbacks in their efforts to control the introduction of new technology and protect their influence over the labour process. The PKIU's defeat at the *Sydney Morning Herald* in 1975, led them to accept

---

3   The PEPLP amalgamated with the PKIU in 1986, an event which is also covered in Chapter 9.

the introduction of new technology and changes to the labour process across the industry, far earlier than in Britain. In return, unlike in Britain, employers continued to accept the PKIU's supervisory, negotiatory and labour supply roles, but only in those, ever shrinking, areas of the industry where the union was strongly organised. As a consequence, by 1980, the PKIU was still heavily dependent on traditional recruitment and organising methods, even though the number of employees covered by these agreements was rapidly contracting. The combination of all of these factors was to pose enormous challenges, in all three policy areas, for the union in the post 1980 period.

This chapter's examination of the Australian printing unions' pre 1980 policies has shown that the unions responded to very similar institutional, political and technological challenges in a variety of different ways. This diversity of response corroborates the theory put forward by strategic choice authors (Heery and Kelly, 1994; Kelly and Heery, 1994; Heery, 2000, 2003, 2006; Kelly, 1998) that similar unions, when faced with alike industrial or political challenges, can engage in a series of strategic choices, which result in a range of different policies being pursued. The evidence has also shown that these strategic choices, whilst clearly in part shaped by institutional and ideological factors, were also very significantly fashioned by micro-political factors, particularly personal animosities.

In Chapter 9, the manner in which the PKIU dealt with major challenges in all three key policy areas, in the post-1980 period, will be analysed. In doing so the chapter will seek to discover those factors which helped shape the policy responses of the PKIU's policy makers.

CHAPTER 6

The British Telecommunication Unions: Pre-1980

Introduction

At the beginning of the 1980s British Telecom was the publically owned, monopoly supplier, of Britain's telecommunication services. The telecommunication unions who organised its staff had operated solely within the public sector for over seventy years, following the Government's nationalisation of all telecommunication services. This chapter charts the development of the structures and political processes of the telecommunication unions and considers how they were affected by organising only workers who worked for one specific public sector organisation. The focus then shifts onto how the labour process, recruitment and amalgamation policies of these unions evolved. How these policies, structures and political processes helped to shape the attitudes and beliefs of contemporary policy makers, and the strategies they adopted, is then analysed. Finally the manner in which British telecommunication union polices either varied from, or was similar to, those of the British and Australian printing unions, will be examined.

Structures and political processes

The British telecommunications unions, unlike the print unions, did not have hundreds of years of guild organisational history, to provide a blueprint for their contemporary structures and political processes. Instead the telecommunication unions grew out of small linesmen's associations, who organised within regional telegraph companies in the early decades of the nineteenth century. These associations were not particularly large or effective, and it was only after 1870 when the British Government nationalised the telegraphy service, owing to its inefficiency, that the industry grew rapidly. This presented the unions with the opportunity to make greater, nationwide, organisational progress (Bealey, 1976: 22). These prospects were improved even further when the Government acted in 1880 to ensure that the calls made on the newly invented telephone were legally classified as telegrams. At the same time they also placed legal restrictions on who could operate telephone services and took direct control of all telephone trunk lines.

These decisions played a significant role in creating an institutional environment in which the telecommunication unions were able to build a national membership base and stabilise their organisational structure. However, initially the Government actively discouraged trade unionism, with activists in the 1890s and early 1900s, being victimised and dismissed for undertaking union activities (Bealey, 1976: 34). Even in the face of this hostility the unions grew, as Government investment in the industry resulted in an expansion in employment numbers, and more workers sought a vehicle to improve their relatively poor wages and conditions.

Shortly after nationalisation the various regional unions met, not to try and merge their organisations but instead to agree a common submission to a Royal Commission, which was considering the role of the General Post Office (GPO). As Bealey (1976) notes, the meeting did not concentrate on pay or recognition, but instead focused on how to convince the Royal Commission to recommend that the regional unions were treated by the GPO as 'associations of professional engineers'. This aspiration for greater status was to be a goal that dominated the approach of the telecommunication unions up until the 1970s. As older interviewees recalled this desire was very important to the national leadership and much of the membership of the union, as they perceived the acceptance of their status as skilled craftsmen as being critical in determining how they were treated by management. To this end from the time of nationalisation the leaderships of the regional unions were very keen not only to press forward their status claims but also to be seen as organisations that sought to act in a professional conciliatory manner, over questions of pay and conditions (Bealey, 1976).

To this end, the unions did not seek to use industrial action as a tool to gain recognition and to stop victimisation. Instead they jointly undertook a co-ordinated political campaign from the early 1890s onwards, in which they supported parliamentary candidates, who pledged to support their quest for recognition. In return, these candidates received financial and practical assistance from the unions. In 1902 many of the regional telegraphy unions amalgamated to form the Engineering and Stores Association (E&SA) and the new union gambled that their recognition goals could be achieved by political, as opposed to industrial, means. Their success in gaining recognition in 1906 entrenched the belief that this lobbying and negotiatory approach, as opposed to industrial action, was the most effective way to achieve their industrial goals.

The British telecommunication unions' determination to find solutions to industrial issues by changing the institutional and political environment in which they operated was strikingly similar to the Australian printing unions approach during the same period. Their effectiveness challenges the assertions of authors such as Howell (2005), who fail to acknowledge the considerable historic ability of unions to shape the political and institutional environment in which they operate.

At the same time the E&SA were achieving recognition in the GPO through lobbying and negotiation, there was a parallel effort to gain recognition amongst private sector telephone service employers. The largest of these was the National Telephone Company (NTC), who by 1902 employed some 10,000 workers. Partly in response to the political campaigns of the unions, the Government declared in 1902, that they would bring all telephone services under the auspices of the GPO by 1911. As a result the telephone companies refused to improve pay and conditions for their staff, which prompted NTC employees sought to seek to join the Electrical Trades Union (ETU). The ETU rejected their advances, stating that NTC telephone engineers were, 'only skilled labourers not craftsmen' (Bealey, 1976: 60). This rejection infuriated the NTC engineers and was, as interviewees confirmed, to have long term adverse consequences for relations between the ETU and the POEU.

Having been rejected by the ETU, the NTC employees formed their own union, the National Society of Telephone Employees (NSTE) in 1905. The NSTE, whilst wishing for their skilled craft status to be recognised, differed from E&SA in their willingness to take industrial action. As 1911 approached, the NSTE, through a mixture of negotiation and industrial action, succeeded in persuading the Government that they should transfer all the telephone company staff into the employment of the GPO when they took control of all telephone services. This victory created a position, inside the GPO, where telecommunications engineers were represented by two unions. Discussions between the unions over a merger (which are analysed later in this chapter) proved to be problematic, and it was only when the Government refused to continue to recognise both unions in 1915 that a merger finally occurred. This amalgamation created the Amalgamated Engineering and Stores Association (AESA), which changed its name to the Post Office Engineering Union (POEU) in 1919.

The two merging unions had a number of structural, industrial and policy differences that they sought to resolve after amalgamation. Initially there was a major disagreement over affiliation to the Labour Party, with the NSTE, unlike the E&SA, being an affiliate (Bealey, 1976). The POEU, after much debate, finally decided to affiliate to the Labour Party. However there was a significant minority of former E&SA officers and activists who opposed the affiliation, because they feared it would adversely affect relations with Conservative or Liberal Governments. This disagreement rumbled on until 1927 when the union was forced (along with all other Civil Service unions) by the Trades Dispute and Trade Union Act to disaffiliate from the Labour Party. Even when they were able to re-affiliate in 1946, the POEU did not do so. Instead they stayed outside the Party until 1966, when the Labour Government persuaded them to re-affiliate by giving a commitment to expand employment in telecommunications and, critically, granted the union a National Executive Committee seat.

Upon amalgamation the two unions' structures were dissimilar, with the E&SA's organisation being more devolved, which reflected their antecedence as a series of regional occupational associations. The NSTE on the other hand was more centralised, with a stronger national structure and less autonomous branches. The structure they agreed for the POEU sought to marry these two models together, by retaining the occupational branch structure whilst putting into place a large, lay member, National Executive Committee (Bealey, 1976). The role of the lay activists who filled these posts was to change profoundly after the adoption by the GPO of the Civil Service Whitley system of collective bargaining. (The Whitley system is described in detail later in this chapter.) These alterations followed meetings between the POEU and GPO management at which the employer accepted the union's argument that if the national Whitley Council's and Committees system was to work, then the POEU's delegates needed to meet and decide upon their policy positions prior to meetings. This logic was also applied to the various local Whitley committees, resulting in POEU gaining full time release for the members of the POEU National Executive Committee (NEC), who sat on the national Whitley bodies, and the branch secretaries, who sat on the local Whitley councils.

The arrangement was to have a profound effect on the union's structures. The full time release of NEC members, from their GPO duties, meant that they were based full time in London, so that they could attend the various national Whitley meetings. When they were not at these meetings the NEC attended the POEU's London head office, where they were able to intervene in the union's day-to-day policy decisions, to a far greater extent than the Australian or British print unions' national governing bodies. Senior POEU full-time officers and NEC members agreed that this led to a position in which the NEC took upon itself negotiating and internal management roles, which would have been played by national full-time officers in many other unions.

The release of the branch secretaries from their GPO roles also allowed the branches to undertake all the representational and negotiatory roles that were fulfilled in many industrial, occupational and general unions by regional full-time officers. As many contributors observed, this meant that the POEU did not create a regional structure with offices and full time officers, but instead relied on branches to perform this role. This combination of functions ensured that the branches and their officers assumed a very important local negotiatory and representational role in the structures of the union.

Whilst these adaptations to the POEU's structures seem to adhere to institutional and state contextualist authors (Bain, 1970; Clegg, 1976; Howell, 2006) assertions that as 'secondary institutions' union structures will alter to mirror those of the employer and the State, it is important to note that the POEU itself actively sought these alterations to their political and institutional environment. This ability to alter their environment is a feature of union activity that institutional and political contextualist scholars often overlook.

Following the POEU's success in securing recognition, extensive facility time and the introduction of the Whitley Council system, the union's leadership, as older interviewees and Bealey (1976) observed, became committed to influencing their employer through 'reasoned debate' (Bealey, 1976: 41). This conviction, as contributors agreed, suffused the national union's policy outlook up until the mid-1960s, during which time there was not one national industrial dispute. The conciliatory approach also resulted in the POEU's structures and internal political process being designed to enhance this outlook.

Perhaps the most striking illustration of this policy was the union's unusual method of appointing, rather than electing, their General Secretary. As one elderly former NEC member recalled, the union's NEC were determined to be regarded as "statesmanlike professionals" by the GPO, which led them to decide to advertise the post of POEU General Secretary only in *The Times* newspaper. The result was that the NEC proceeded to appoint four General Secretaries, who led the union from the 1920s to the 1970s, who had never worked in the industry, but did have degrees (unrelated in every case to either telecommunications or industrial relations) from Oxford or Cambridge University. It was not to be until the 1970s that the union finally appointed a General Secretary, Bryan Stanley, who had worked as a telephone engineer. The reason for the policy was explained by a former POEU NEC member:

> We wanted a GS who was well educated and could hold his own in meetings, and was at ease in social gatherings with managers and Government Ministers.

This consensual, status conscious, approach to trade unionism was not universally popular with the whole of the POEU membership. As Bealey (1976) and older interviewees concurred, it contributed to a series of conflicts with branches and occupational groups that led to breakaways which beset the POEU from the 1920s until the 1950s, which are analysed later in this chapter. The success that those candidates who supported this 'moderate' approach enjoyed in POEU elections prior to the 1940s was based upon informal, micro-political contacts rather than the operation of a formal faction. Senior lay and full-time officers sought to encourage likeminded individuals to stand for office and then campaigned for their election (Bealey, 1976).

In the aftermath of the Second World War there was a significant adverse reaction to the NEC's continued consensual, restrained approach, to bargaining with the GPO. The Communist Party of Great Britain (CPGB) played a significant role in marshalling activists and members who opposed the approach of the POEU leadership. They successfully ran candidates for branch officer positions in many of the large city branches and then, in 1947, they won as many seats as the 'moderate' group, in the NEC elections. The election, which then took place at Annual Conference, came as a tremendous shock to the union's leadership, who only retained control of the NEC thanks to the casting vote of the President (Bealey, 1976).

Their response was to form a formal factional group, the Anti-Communist Bloc, which soon became universally known as 'The Bloc'. The Bloc ran a successful anti-communist campaign at the 1948 NEC election, which saw them increase their majority. They then immediately made major alterations to the NEC's constitution, expanding the number of seats from 16 to 23 and introducing regional and sectoral electoral divisions. Following these changes The Bloc started to operate as a highly secretive and effective factional group, who successfully retained control of the NEC and of all senior officer positions, until the 1980s. The Bloc's success in controlling the union owed much to what one prominent member described as 'ideological flexibility'. He went on to explain:

> We tried to ensure that we had candidates from all the different occupational and geographical groups. If we spotted a capable activist, who wasn't a Commie, or a

fellow traveller, we would invite them to a Bloc meeting. Our aim was to ensure that we pursued sensible industrial policies and kept the Commies out.

The Bloc leadership also used its control of the NEC and full time officer positions to dispense patronage to supporters. Delegation places to the TUC, Labour Party or even a fraternal visit overseas were all in the gift of The Bloc controlled NEC. As one former NEC member commented, "If you wanted to get on in the union, you joined The Bloc".

An important feature of The Bloc's operation was its secrecy. You could not join the organisation, or attend its meetings, without an invitation. Whilst positions on Annual Conference motions were taken by a meeting of members before the start of annual conference, the day to day affairs of The Bloc were dealt with by a group referred to as the 'inner wheel'. The inner wheel consisted of selected representatives from different parts of the country, who decided the policy line that The Bloc would pursue at the NEC and in its negotiations with management. As one former NEC member observed, "In reality the inner wheel ran the union."

The establishment of a powerful national ideological faction, whose members controlled all tiers of a union's policy-making for an extended period, was a phenomenon that distinguished the POEU from either country's printing unions. The more centralised nature of bargaining and the union's internal structures assisted The Bloc in gaining and retaining a strong hold over policy-making up until the 1980s. The nature of the POEU's structures and policy-making processes also meant that when the Broad Left (BL) factional group started to make industrial and electoral progress, from the late 1960s onwards, it was able to relatively rapidly secure effective control of significant parts of the union's internal and industrial policy-making bodies. The functioning of these factional groups was a feature of the POEU political processes, which played an important part in shaping the union's policy direction, as a number of authors (McIlroy, 1988; Undy et al, 1981; Parker, 2009) have previously asserted. However as this and later chapters will illustrate, there were a series of other, often micro-political, influences on the POEU's policy direction, which these authors tend to overlook.

The labour process

The nationalisation of the telegraphy and the telephone services in the early part of the twentieth century meant that the unions only dealt with a single, publicly owned, monopoly provider of telecommunications services. This allowed the POEU to focus on establishing influence over the labour process in just one employer, which they achieved, without ever attaining the control the print unions enjoyed over labour supply. The basis for their influence over the labour process came from the operation of post-entry rather than pre-entry closed shops, the building of a vibrant lay officer structure, and the ability of their members to take effective industrial action.

The ability of the unions to influence the labour process, post nationalisation, was aided by the GPO's decision to operate a Whitleyist model of industrial relations. This system involved high levels of lay union officer activity, which was facilitated by the employer who accepted that the unions were a key participant in the administration and management of industrial relations. The remit of the Whitley Councils, which remained in place to the 1960s, included wages and conditions, promotions, disciplinary procedures and work practices. Such was the volume of work that such a comprehensive structure generated, that the National Whitley Council was empowered to appoint divisional, occupational and local committees to deal with issues that occurred at those levels. All the Whitley Councils and Committees consisted of representatives from management and the union. This multi-layered, hierarchical, consultation and negotiatory framework created a stable and highly bureaucratic system in which the unions played a central part.

The Whitley system was greatly valued by The Bloc as it granted the union an effective collective bargaining mechanism, influence over many aspects of the labour process, and a system for resolving disputes, without having to engage in industrial action. Many interviewees recalled that by the 1960s, this adherence to the Whitley system was being called into question, by both management and POEU BL branch activists. The BL branch activists explicitly rejected the consensual approach that the system depended upon and wished to see it replaced with straight forward, adversarial, collective bargaining.

It was though to be the Government's decision in 1969, to break the GPO up into Postal and Telecommunication divisions, which was to herald the end of the Whitley system. The management of the new Telecommunications division replaced the Whitley system with a novel arrangement which involved the negotiation of overarching national collective agreements. These agreements were designed to allow flexibility in their implementation, so as to grant regional and occupational managers greater scope for realising divisional managerial priorities. This change in the negotiating structure also granted POEU branch officers an important new role in negotiating the local implementation of national agreements.

The branch officers who undertook this new role were increasingly young, politically radical, and industrially militant. They had joined the GPO in the 1960s, as telecommunications employment expanded rapidly, and many of them wanted to replace the consensual industrial policies of The Bloc with a more dynamic and confrontational approach. As interviewees recalled, they pressed at branch meetings for the adoption of more militant local industrial strategies and they successfully stood for office at branch elections. Once elected, interviewers from both factions agreed, these branch officers were often able to secure advantageous local agreements. The reason for this success, and a notable increase in influence over all aspects of the labour process, was directly related to the union's growing industrial strength. Domestic and business customers were by the end of the 1960s increasingly demanding a more sophisticated and comprehensive telephone service. The new exchange and distribution technology, which was installed to meet this demand was unreliable and required considerable maintenance to function efficiently. The fragility of the new systems presented the POEU with the scope to take highly effective, short term, industrial action, which many branches embraced with alacrity.

Buoyed by their growing local influence over the labour process, many branch delegates pressed the POEU national leadership to be more industrially militant. This demand crystallised into a call for the POEU to campaign for a thirty-five hour working week. The national leadership of the union refused to do so, and it was industrial action at the branch level, co-ordinated by local activists which secured a reduction in the working week from forty to thirty seven and a half hours. Equally as important, according to interviewees, it also established the extremely popular 'nine day fortnight' working roster. The campaign proved too many branch activists just what could be achieved by taking industrial action. As many contributors also recalled it acted as a catalyst for activists, who opposed The Bloc's moderate industrial approach, to come together to discuss how the POEU national leadership could be removed. This meeting agreed that a Broad Left (BL) political faction should be created, whose aim it would be to wrest control of the national POEU from The Bloc in order that more radical industrial policies would be implemented.

Chapter 10 will evaluate how the internal factional power struggle that followed, affected the policy responses of the union to the substantial changes to the labour process that occurred in the 1980s, following deregulation, privatisation and profound technological change.

Recruitment

Prior to the nationalisation of the telecommunications industry in 1911 the telecommunications unions, unlike the print unions, had to recruit employees at their workplace. As a method of recruitment this was difficult and time consuming, as many potential members spent their days walking across the countryside, tracking and repairing line faults (Bealey, 1976: 37). These difficulties were further compounded by the fact that many union activists who voluntarily undertook recruitment work also suffered from employer victimisation.

After the POEU were successful in their campaign to secure recognition and stop victimisation of their activists, they also sought a post-entry closed shop in the GPO. The arguments they deployed are illustrative of the generally conciliatory approach the union adopted towards management.

They asserted that it would be beneficial for the GPO to agree to a POEU closed shop, as it would negate the possibility of aggressive, and potentially disruptive, inter union competition for members (Bealey, 1976). These arguments, as Dunn and Gennard (1983) note, were used successfully by many unions in the public and private sector to persuade employers to enter into compulsory union agreements, but did not directly secure the POEU a post-entry closed shop. As Bealey (1976) and older interviewees observed, the GPO were able to resist the call for a closed shop for many years, owing to the reluctance of the POEU to use any form of industrial action to pursue their claim. This is dissimilar to the British and Australian non-craft printing unions, who readily deployed secondary industrial action to secure pre-entry closed shops (Gennard et al, 1979; Dunn and Gennard, 1983; Gennard, 1990; Zappala, 1991).

Apart from an aversion to industrial conflict there were a number of other reasons why the POEU did not zealously pursue a formal closed shop agreement. The GPO's formal recognition of the POEU and the subsequent implementation of the Whitley system in the 1920s increased the union's industrial influence and assisted greatly in recruiting members. The subsequent agreement by the GPO that POEU delegates to the various Whitley Councils and Committees would be granted extensive time-off, in order to engage fully in the Whitley system, created a sizeable pool of lay activists who were able to use their facility time to recruit members. Whereas previously the POEU and its predecessors had to either deploy full-time officers to recruit members, or rely on activists operating in their own time, they now had a significant number of lay officers who could undertake union work, including recruitment, in company time. All of these concessions, plus the GPO's administration of check-off assisted the union's recruitment efforts. This was further aided, following the Second World War, by what interviewees stated was the expectation of local managers, that all new starters, in POEU organised areas, would join the union. It is then unsurprising that when the post-entry closed shop was finally granted by the GPO, the positive effect upon the POEU's high membership density levels was insignificant.

The refusal by successive Governments to agree to a formal post-entry closed shop casts further doubt on Hart's (1979) theory that employers, including the State, actively sought to introduce closed shops, for their own industrial benefit. It does however add weight to the argument that unions had to actively pursue the case for the closed shop in the face of employer resistance, even in workplaces with high union density (Gennard et al, 1979; Dunn and Gennard, 1984).

By the end of the 1970s the POEU, having achieved a post-entry closed shop across BT, also possessed a sophisticated and comprehensive lay representational structure. This granted the POEU and its successor, the NCU, greater membership organisation resilience than that enjoyed by the British non-craft printing unions when the closed shop was proscribed in the 1980s by the Conservative Government. However, similarly to the print unions, the POEU's officers and members' lack of physical recruitment experience, owing to the application of an informal post-entry closed shop since the 1940s, did lead to difficulties for the union in recruiting in the deregulated telecommunications industry of the 1980s. As one Branch Secretary very candidly observed:

> I had spent twenty years as a branch officer in the 1960s and 1970s, and I never had to recruit anyone. I didn't think we should refuse to recruit Mercury members. No, my problem was I had no experience of how to go about it.

As with the printing unions the recruitment benefits they enjoyed from having established compulsory unionism, were ironically to prove to be a handicap when the unions sought to organise sectors where workers had no need, or pre-disposition, to join a union. How the POEU and subsequently the NCU sought to deal with the profound organisational difficulties that they encountered in a privatised and deregulated industry, post 1980, will be examined in Chapter 10.

Amalgamation

The regional telegraphy unions, who eventually combined to form the POEU, were initially anxious to remain independent. It was only, as Bealey (1976) notes, when they realised the impracticality of remaining as separate

regional unions, after the Government nationalised the whole telegra-
phy service, that they finally, 'reluctantly agreed' to form a national union
(Bealey, 1976: 36). After nationalisation the primary objective of all the
GPO unions was securing collective recognition from the Government.
The unions formed a National Joint Committee of Postal and Telegraph
Associations (NJC) to achieve this objective. As Bealey (1976) states the
unions' success in gaining recognition was widely attributed to the manner
in they had worked cooperatively together (Bealey, 1976: 39). The achievement led the postal unions to suggest that all the GPO unions merge.
However the E&SA were uncomfortable with this proposed amalgamation, as they viewed themselves as skilled engineers, and they did not wish
to be in the same union as 'unskilled postmen' (Bealey, 1976: 57). They also
harboured fears that the larger postal unions would dominate any merged
union to the disadvantage of their members.

These concerns and prejudices contributed significantly not only to
the E&SA rejection of a merger but also the POEU's subsequent rejection of all amalgamation suggestions by the postal workers unions up until
1980. Following the decision to remain separate from the postal unions
the two main telecommunication unions the E&SA and the NSTE had
difficulty in agreeing a merger. It was only after the intervention of the
Postmaster General, who made it clear in 1915 that the Government was no
longer prepared to recognise both unions, that the unions finally merged
(Bealey, 1976).

This wary attitude towards mergers was to characterise POEU policy
over the next sixty years. As one former NEC member recalled, the principle
reason for this policy was the preoccupation with ensuring there was no
"dilution of our occupational craft status". However the POEU did spend a
considerable amount of time and energy negotiating and concluding merger
agreements, not with other trade unions, but instead with organisations
which had seceded from the union. That the POEU devoted significant
resources to persuading various break-away groups to re-join, owes much
to the success of the seceding organisations in recruiting POEU members.

The reasons the POEU was beset by so much secessionism relates,
older interviewees and Bealey (1976) agree, to a complex combination of
structural, political and micro-political issues. The POEU's historically

centralised policy-making and negotiating structures, were perceived by a number of regional and occupational groups, as granting them insufficient influence over specific local or trade related issues. In particular these groups felt aggrieved that the union's NEC, which was elected by the whole of Annual Conference, failed to address their sectional or regional issues. This was because, they believed, it concentrated on its largest component membership group, the telephone engineers (Bealey, 1976). Additionally within the telephone engineering section there were frequently occupational tensions, with groups of internal engineers believing they had greater skills, which were not recognised by the POEU or the GPO. Internally this conflict also manifested itself in internal engineers wishing to be in separate branches to external engineers, construction labourers and storeskeepers (Bealey, 1976).

These conflicts led to a series of secessions from the POEU, the first of which involved Birmingham internal engineers leaving the union, after the NEC refused to put forward a separate wage claim on their behalf. Their organisation, the Telephone and Telegraph Engineering Guild (TTEG), made no secret of its dislike of being in the same union as 'unskilled' workers. Their journal stated: 'the greatest mistake that the old Linesman Associations ever made was to admit construction hands and storesmen' (Bealey, 1976: 37). The TTEG remained separate from the POEU for over a decade, only finally agreeing to return in 1931. The long term effect of these types of internal dispute is clearly illustrated by the case of the TTEG. As late as 1996, more than a decade after nearly all internal and external geographical engineering branches had merged, the Birmingham internal and external branches remained determinedly separate. As interviewees candidly admitted, the relationship between the branches, was poor and had been strained for as long as any member could remember. In this instance the ability of internal conflicts to have a long term influence on contemporary policy behaviour, are clearly evident.

By the end of the 1940s there were a number of other secessions from the POEU, one of the largest of which was in 1945, when the Branch Secretary of the London Central Branch, Fred Smith, resigned and set up the Engineering Offices (Telecommunications) Association (EOTA). He did so after his branch committee invited a CPGB area organiser to address a branch meeting, without his consent. His subsequent demands for an inquiry into CPGB infiltration of the branch were rejected by the POEU leadership. Smith then resigned and formed the EOTA (Bealey, 1976, 1977). The EOTA like the TTEG stressed the need for higher pay for internal engineers, and a change in their job title from 'Skilled Workman' to 'Engineering Officer'. The new association recruited heavily within London, claiming 6,700 members by 1950. However, like the TTEG, the EOTA's claims for recognition were rejected by the GPO and they finally re-joined the POEU in 1954.

Apart from demonstrating, once again, the craft tensions that existed inside the POEU, the EOTA secession also illustrates the influence micro-political factors have in shaping policy. The Bloc controlled NEC's refusal to grant Smith an inquiry into CPGB infiltration is at first sight very surprising. When questioned as to why they refused, two interviewees with intimate knowledge of The Bloc's decision were clear that it was due to the London Bloc's delegates dislike of Smith. It is this type of intra-factional, personal conflict, which tends to be overlooked in the work of authors (McIllroy et al, 2007; Daniels and McIllroy, 2009) who have analysed the influence of factions within unions.

Sectional grievances which led to POEU activists forming secessionist organisations were not restricted to groups of internal engineers. Various other minority national occupational groups were also sufficiently exasperated by their lack of representation in POEU's internal and negotiatory representational structures that they seceded from the union. The largest of these was the National Guild of Motor Engineers (NGME), who separated from the POEU in 1949 and recruited over 30% of the GPO's Motor Mechanic workforce, within eighteen months. This secession, so soon after the creation of the EOTA, led the POEU NEC to make considerable concessions. They granted occupational groups, such as the Motor Mechanics, greater autonomy and guaranteed different geographical areas and occupations NEC seats. These concessions, plus the GPO once again refusing recognition, led the NGME to return to the POEU.

There was a discernible pattern as to why groups seceded from the POEU and then merged back into the union. In each case, the secessionist organisation was made up of a homogenous occupational group who, at either a national or local branch level, harboured a grievance against the POEU national leadership over the way they were being represented. Having broken away, the secessionist organisation often recruited strongly, but was denied full recognition by the GPO, at which point they then negotiated re-entry. In every case, as Bealey (1976) notes and interviewees confirm, the POEU were eventually prepared to negotiate re-amalgamation terms with the secessionist organisations because of those organisations success in removing a significant body of members from the union.

Eventually and somewhat reluctantly, as POEU officers of the time recollect, The Bloc controlled NEC decided in 1954, that they must grant greater autonomy to occupational groups in order to prevent further secessionism. This decision led to various occupational groups having their own guaranteed seats on the NEC, whilst being granted greater policy-making autonomy. It also heralded the protection of occupational branches, a policy which was still in operation in the 1980s. Combined together these policy alterations were successful in stopping further, large scale, membership secessions.

The desire of the POEU's dominant faction to retain its integrity as the trade union for telecommunications engineers powerfully informed its amalgamation policies up until the 1980s. Whilst overtures from the postal workers unions were rebuffed, the POEU were prepared to negotiate with, and then readmit, secessionist groups. By 1980 this wish to be solely a telecommunications engineering union was starting to wane. The increasingly powerful BL faction was pressing for the union to move away from its craft traditions and shift towards a more inclusive industrial unionism. The success of the BL in achieving this goal, and the consequences for the POEU, is appraised in Chapter 10.

Conclusion

The POEU's desire to be regarded as a 'professional engineering union', representing skilled craftsmen, dominated its policy-making in the period up until 1980. The POEU's fixation with status during this time can, in part, be explained by the institutional framework in which the union operated.

The GPO, as the sole employer of Britain's telecommunications workers, ran a complex, profoundly hierarchical, grading system that recognised status and seniority more than skill or performance. It also operated a Whitleyist system of industrial relations which partially incorporated the union into management's policy-making structures. Such an explanation would accord with the argument of authors (Bain, 1970; Clegg, 1976) who propose that union policies are profoundly shaped by their institutional environment. Yet this explanation fails to acknowledge the success of the telecommunication unions in altering their political and institutional environment at the beginning of the twentieth century, when they adopted a series of policies which helped to persuade the Government to fully nationalise the telecommunications industry and grant the unions recognition. This ability to take strategic decisions which fundamentally alter the environment that a union operates within is in line with the argument of authors (Kelly, 1998; Heery and Kelly, 1994; Heery, 2000, 2003) who assert that the strategic choices a union makes can help to determine their future.

The manner in which POEU policy was also shaped by the influence of The Bloc faction also substantiates the argument of those authors who assert that the influence of factional groups and the ideological perspectives of decision makers are important in determining the policy direction of a union (Heery, 2003; Kelly, 1988; Darlington, 1994, 2001; McIllroy and Campbell, 1999; McIllroy, 2007; Daniels and McIllroy, 2009). This chapter has also produced empirical evidence which substantiates the hypothesis that micro-political factors play a critical role in determining the POEU's policies in all three areas. In Chapter 10, the labour process, recruitment and amalgamation policies the POEU adopted, in response to the Government's deregulation and privatisation of the telecommunications industry, are considered. How these policies were affected by the rise in industrial and electoral strength of the BL faction will also be evaluated.

CHAPTER 7

The Australian Telecommunication Unions: Pre-1980

Introduction

This chapter focuses upon the policy-making of the Australian telecommunications unions' from their formation up until 1980. Initially it outlines the evolution of their structures and internal political processes. It then concentrates on the unions' approaches to influencing the labour process, recruitment and amalgamation.

In performing this task the chapter considers the influence on the unions of operating within an industry, which had been controlled by the Federal Government since nationalisation in 1905. How the industrial, economic, political and demographic variances between the Australian States affected the unions' policies, will be explored. The reasons for any similarities and differences in the policies of the Australian and British telecommunications unions will also be addressed. Woven throughout the chapter, there is an examination of the reasons for the acute historical antipathy that existed between Australia's two major telecommunication unions, and an assessment of how this antagonism affected policy formulation.

Structures and political processes

The Australian telecommunication unions, unlike their printing counterparts, were not formed by British trade unionists who had emigrated specifically to work in the industry. Instead the Australian telegraphy industry trained its own employees, many of whom were first or second generation British migrants. The structural and organisational similarities between the British and Australian telecommunication unions are not therefore explained by a common lineage. However, as Turner (1983: 31) notes, it would have been surprising if British migrants had not drawn upon the trade union structures they were familiar with, when they formed their own organisations. Crucially the telecommunications unions in both countries also evolved to deal with similar managerial structures, which themselves reflected the decision of Governments to nationalise the industry in the early years of the twentieth century.

Prior to nationalisation, the majority of manual telegraphy workers were employed as linesmen, by small, regionally based companies. They worked, as in Britain, in small disparate groups who covered vast amounts of territory in constructing the network and repairing line faults. The unions that the workers formed were occupationally organised, with a base in a specific town. Many of these small unions merged to form State wide unions after the various Colonial Governments took direct control of their telegraphy networks. When in 1901 the Colonies formed the Commonwealth of Australia they granted the Federal Government; 'full control of postal, telegraphic, telephonic and other like services' (1901 Australian Constitution).

The nationalising of telecommunications led a number of the State based organisations to consider forming a national union. This stimulus was increased considerably when in 1911 the Federal Labor Government announced it would grant federally registered, public sector trade unions, full recognition. Such recognition granted unions' full use of the Commonwealth Arbitration Court, which had the power to hand down legally binding decisions on wages and conditions: a right that was denied by most State governments.

The outcome of the amalgamation negotiations was the creation of not one, but two, national telecommunication unions, representing different occupational groups. These two unions were the Australian Postal Electricians Union (APEU), and the Australian Telegraph, Telephone Construction and Maintenance Union (ATTCMU). The APEU represented employees who, in Britain, would have been described as internal engineering grades, whilst the ATTCMU organised Telegraph and Telephone Lines-workers, the British 'external' engineering grades. The division between the unions deepened in 1919, when the APEU refused to merge with the ATTCMU and six other postal unions. This decision marked the start of an uneasy eighty year relationship between the two unions, which was distinguished by regular periods of hostility and conflict.

These amalgamation decisions were to have a profound and lasting effect on the structures and policies of Australia's two largest telecommunication unions. Unlike in Britain, where the POEU fought to counteract secessionist demands, in Australia these divisions were reinforced by discrete occupational trade unionism. An APTU officer recalls his early childhood in a small town in New South Wales in the late 1920s:

> My dad was a linesman and he told me there had always been trouble with the Techs'. They really pissed our blokes off. One example was that the tech's union put up a sign in the local exchange, reminding linesmen to wipe their boots before they walked in. All bloody hell broke loose. There was even talk of a stop work meeting, before management finally took the sign down.

Here, as in other recollections of activists and officers from both unions, a deep seated, visceral, occupational enmity was evident.

These divisions were exacerbated by the topography and demography of Australia. The concentration of Australia's population in the State capitals, particularly Melbourne and Sydney, led to the majority of exchange work and therefore the membership of the APEU being focused in a few large urban conurbations. The APWU's membership in contrast was more dispersed, owing to their role in maintaining the geographically vast Australian telecommunications infrastructure. This divergence in location often led the unions into conflict over the Federal Government's investment priorities. The APWU pressed hard for investment in rural areas, whilst the ATEA sought greater expenditure on the urban exchanges. These conflicts further aggravated the two unions' occupational rivalry.

The internal structures of the unions, also partly contributed to their historically poor relationship. The APEU and the APWU both had a single branch for each State. Owing to the concentration of employment in Sydney and Melbourne, this meant that both unions possessed NSW and

Victorian branches which were twice the size of the next largest branch. These branches, thanks to the agreements that were reached to form the national unions, enjoyed considerable policy autonomy. This, in turn meant that a disagreement between the respective NSW or Victorian branches was often difficult for the national unions to resolve, owing to the autonomy and the considerable national policy influence of these branches. The APWU's constitution, which guaranteed substantial industrial autonomy to the telecommunications division, also meant that disputes with other unions remained the provenance of the division.

With both telecommunication unions historically organising exclusively within the same single employer, there were, as many interviewees agreed, often great difficulties in resolving inter union disputes. As a former federal ATEA officer recalled:

> Everyone, at whatever level of our two unions always had a dog in the fight. Unlike other unions, where many senior branch and federal officers could take a more detached view of a dispute, in our unions, everyone had a stake in every dispute.

Conciliatory interventions in local disputes, by either the branch or federal leaderships of either union, were therefore problematic. A number of interviewees also highlighted the fact that difficulties between the unions were heightened because both unions' constitutions insisted that all their officials faced regular elections. They stated that it was 'electorally dangerous' for any officer to adopt a conciliatory approach towards the other union, because of the level of membership animosity. These comments were born out by the fieldwork and reflect a reality that is in sharp contrast to the rank and filist theory of Bramble (2008) who suggests that members are constantly being restrained by a 'conservative bureaucratic leadership from acting in a spirit of solidarity and militancy' (Bramble, 2008: 23).

The conflict between the two unions was at its worst in NSW and Victoria. Many reasons were put forward for this, but two factors were most commonly cited. The first was the larger numbers of employees in the two States generated more occasions on which conflicts over demarcation issues could occur. The second was the remarkably high level of factional activity in the NSW and Victorian branches of both unions.

Turning initially to demarcation disputes, owing to greater volumes of telecommunications traffic in NSW and Victoria the employer tended to launch any new telephone technology in the larger Melbourne and Sydney exchanges. The introduction of new technology would often produce coverage disputes, as the unions disagreed over whose members should install and maintain the new equipment. This was unlike in the more sparsely populated States where there were often tacit agreements between the unions and their members, that demarcation lines could on occasion be overlooked, in order that vital telephone services could be maintained in very isolated rural areas.

As for the role of political factions in the NSW and Victorian branches this went back to the early 1920s (Waters, 1976). From that decade onwards branch elections were fierce contests between various Left and Right factions. The intensity of these clashes can be gauged by the fact that even the APWU's heavily expurgated official history states that NSW branch election campaigning 'went too far' in the 1920s and 1930s (Waters, 1976: 45). Recollections of retired officers of the telecommunication section of the APWU, supply a less euphemistic description.

> It was pure bloody murder in the branch in the thirties. There was some very ordinary behaviour with blokes being regularly bashed. I can tell you had to be pretty bloody tough if you were going to stand for branch office.

Aside from the violence, the NSW and Victorian branch elections of both unions were marked by the distribution, by all factions, of luridly scurrilous, anonymous leaflets. These were colloquially known as 'shit-sheets'; a title which accurately captures their contents. In addition to these practices, the Industrial Relations Commission upheld various charges of ballot rigging in a number of APWU elections, whilst unproven allegations of election misconduct were commonplace. There was also evidence of the involvement of the criminal underworld in a number of the APWU's NSW branch elections (Whitton, 1987). This extreme level of factional conflict inside the NSW and Victorian branches was not replicated, over a sustained period, in any of the other unions studied. Why the factional battles in the unions Victorian and NSW branch were so ferocious is a topic over which nearly all interviewees held a variety of strong opinions.

A number of contributors argued that the Federal Government's control of the industry resulted in the unions having close links with the ALP, which led to the unions' involvement in the Party's own factional conflicts. Other participants focused on the extremely close personal relationships between the ALP leadership and APWU officials, which they alleged resulted in the ALP assisting the APWU factional leaders in 'placing' supporters in postal and telecommunications jobs, so that they could influence the predominantly immigrant workforce to support the relevant APWU and ALP faction. As an elderly APWU former official recalled:

> There were large numbers of migrants working as posties and linies in NSW. Many could be intimidated into voting for particular candidates, or into handing over their [ballot] papers. Vote gathering was common. The organisers of these operations had been placed into jobs so that they could gather votes.

The multi-ethnic makeup of the APWU, which allegedly encouraged this behaviour, was certainly unlike that of the predominantly Anglo-Saxon ATEA, the POEU or either nation's printing unions.

Racial and cultural diversity was also cited in explanations of the bitter internal divisions that occurred between the Right factions in NSW and Victoria during the 1940s and 1950s. The argument being that members who migrated to Australia from Southern Europe and Ireland in the 1940s were likely to support the Catholic Church sponsored 'Anti-Communist Groups'[1] (known colloquially as 'Groupers') in their efforts to take control of the NSW and Victorian branches. Significantly for this book's hypothesis, retired APWU officers recalled how the non-Grouper, Right factional leaders drew on personal support and friendships with key delegates (who many contributors stated were fellow Masons) in order to secure enough votes to defeat the Groupers challenge in NSW (Waters, 1976).

These accounts of why the NSW and Victorian branches were so affected by factional politics were not universally accepted. Officers from

---

1   The 'anti communist groups' which operated inside the Australian labour movement were emanations of the Roman Catholic church supported National Civic Council which sought to 'counter' the influence of the Communist Party of Australia (CPA) in Australian Society in the 1940s and 1950s.

the former ATEA point out that their NSW and Victorian branches did not organise large numbers of recent migrants, nor did they enjoy a particularly close relationship with the ALP, yet they still had high levels of factional activity. Their explanation focuses instead on the factional divisions between the Groupers and 'Masonic' Right factions within the two States wider labour movement, and the regular interference in ATEA affairs by the APWU. Officials of the APWU similarly complained of 'meddling' by the ATEA in their business. Such regular factional involvement in another union's affairs, whilst found on occasions in the British print unions, was not a regular occurrence in any of the other unions studied. Its presence, which was deeply resented by officers and activists of both unions, undoubtedly added to the vituperative relationship that developed between the unions NSW and Victorian leaderships.

Factional interference in another union's affairs is not a subject which has been widely charted by those who have written about factional activities (Daniels and McIllroy, 2009; Undy et al, 1981; Dickenson, 1982; Davies, 1987). This may be because scholars have had difficulty in identifying such covert behaviour, but the lack of coverage does not diminish the poisoning of relationships that such action caused.

The ability of charismatic senior branch officers, who had a strong antipathy for officers of the other union, to powerfully influence branch policy was also cited as a reason for the dysfunctional relationship that existed between the NSW and Victorian branches. The empirical evidence supports these observations, as it became clear that long serving senior officers, who had led their factions into power, largely through the strength of their own personality, organising skills and micro-political astuteness, nearly all harboured a deep personal antipathy for senior officers of the other union's State branch.

Whichever of the various explanations outlined above best explains the acrimonious relationship between the respective unions' NSW and Victorian branches, the effect their disputes had on each of the union's political processes was undoubtedly profound. How these formal and informal structures, political processes and inter-union relationships influenced the telecommunication unions' recruitment, amalgamation and labour process policies, will now be considered.

The labour process

As with the British POEU, the earliest records of the Australian telecom-munication unions illustrate their belief that they would be better able to influence the labour process, and improve wages and conditions in the public, rather than the private sector (Waters, 1976). However the move-ment of all telecommunication employees into the public sector did not immediately assist the unions in their efforts to exert more influence over the labour process. The Colonial GPO's, who were predominantly con-trolled by Conservative parties, were disinclined to recognise and negotiate with the telecommunication unions. Neither did the transfer of telecom-munications into the Federal Government's hands immediately resolve the unions' problem of marginalisation. It was not until they were granted collective recognition and the ability to use the federal arbitration system by the Federal Government that their ability to influence the labour pro-cess increased.

Following recognition, the two main unions sought to improve not only members' terms and conditions but also their occupational status. This desire for increased status, which they shared with the POEU, often brought the two unions into conflict. The Postal Telecommunications Technicians Association (PTTA), as the APEU had been renamed, had the objective of achieving a separate grade for telephone technicians and prohibiting all other employees from working in technical areas (PTTA Journals May 1946–June 1955). At the same time the APWU wished for their skilled members to be placed onto the same grade as the postal electri-cians and for demarcation lines to be removed. When in 1944 the Federal Government agreed to change the mechanics job title to technicians the PTTA's leadership were delighted, whilst the APWU's were incensed (Waters, 1976). However the Government refused the PTTA's long stand-ing claim that all technical telecommunication work should be undertaken by their members. This demand was to remain PTTA and then ATEA policy until the 1990s.

The contrast between the two Australian unions' policies and that of the POEU is striking. Throughout its history the POEU sought to balance the demands for demarcation protection of different internal occupational groups. By contrast, in Australia, pursuing occupationally divisive policies were priorities for both major unions, leading to a focus on job demarcation, union coverage and grading issues. In NSW and Victoria, these problems were particularly acute. As one interviewee described it "a vicious circle" of demarcation disputes, coverage arguments and political interference in each other's affairs resulted in the unions refusing to negotiate jointly with the employer. As union and management contributors candidly agreed, these divisions were made worse by management policies. From the early part of the twentieth century the technicians and linesmen groups were placed in different divisions and were managed separately, with local managers frequently concluding discrete agreements over working patterns, staffing levels and rosters. These arrangements could cause resentment as both organisations believed that the other was being treated more favourably. The result was regular rounds of 'leapfrog' bargaining at the local and divisional level. As a long serving manager reflected:

> In retrospect we mismanaged the Linies and the Techs. They should have been treated as one entity, on a State by State basis. We also should have been stronger and insisted on one set of negotiations. Instead when either of the unions spat the dummy, we gave in and negotiated separate deals.

Union contributors noted that it was management who initially divided the occupations, so that they could 'divide and rule'.

The divisions that existed between the two unions did not totally preclude them from negotiating jointly with the employer at the national level. This they did through the auspices of the Council of Commonwealth Public Service Organisations (CCPSO). The CCPSO was made up of the various recognised telecommunication unions and associations along with PMG management and it operated in a similar fashion to Whitley Councils. The CCPSO's structure though, unlike the British Whitley Councils, encompassed binding arbitration, an attribute which was supported by the leaderships of both unions. Until the early 1970s, this machinery resolved all the national pay negotiations, without the unions taking official national industrial action. It was not until 1974 that the first official national strike was called by the telecommunications section of the APWU.

As many interviewees observed, one of reasons for industrial peace was the national unions' leaderships' wish to use political lobbying and the arbitral system, rather than industrial action to enhance terms and conditions and boost employment numbers. The APWU, in particular, campaigned not only to influence the ALP but also the Country Party (which was part of the Liberal/Country Coalition which held federal office from 1949–1972) to provide telephone services to the remotest areas of Australia at heavily subsidised rates. They also placed pressure on all political parties to locate telephone equipment manufacturing in Australian country towns. These campaigns were so successful that the PMG department became the largest employer in many parts of rural Australia in the 1950s and 1960s. Such was the success of the APWU's jobs campaign that the ATEA expressed concern that the Federal Government were diverting too many resources into the 'bush', at the expense of upgrading the network in the major Australian cities. In addition both unions combined to call for the protection of 'untimed' local calls.[2] The success of these campaigns helped to grow telephone usage to a point where, by the 1970s, Australians were one of the largest users of telephony services, per person, in the world (Katz, 1997). This growth helped offset reductions in labour caused by the introduction of new technology.

Technological and organisational change did however usher in a period of alterations to the labour process during the late 1960s, which sparked industrial conflict, particularly within the two largest States. The changes followed the building and operation of larger mail and telephone exchanges. The first to be built was in Redfern, Sydney, and it housed over 500 PTTA members. Prior to Redfern's construction, the bulk of telecommunication work in Australia had been undertaken by small groups of technicians and

2   Local 'landline' telephone calls in Australia have always have been charged at a flat rate, whatever their time duration. Local, in this context, can cover many hundreds of miles.

linesmen working out of a series of small telephone exchanges. However in Redfern there were large numbers of staff working in what one former ATEA officer described as a "factory like environment, in which managers were breathing down the necks of members everyday". Industrial relations at Redfern quickly deteriorated, with the catalyst, ironically, being a strike by local APWU postal members. The PTTA Federal Executive and the NSW Branch leadership both directed its membership to cross APWU picket lines, much to the annoyance of the local PTTA members. After a heated debate with full-time officers, the PTTA sub-branch agreed to work, but the resentment that ensued from members towards the employer and the union was considerable. As a lay activist of the time, who went on to be a PTTA/ATEA official, recalls:

> Our blokes were no great mates with the linies and the posties. However asking us to scab was a mongrel act. We never forgave the Feds or the Branch for threatening to disown us if we didn't cross the picket line.

Another ATEA officer, who was a technician at the time recollected:

> After that dispute our members had had enough. If a manager so much as looked at them, they were ready to have a blue. Over the next three years there were walk-outs over shift patterns, demarcation lines and manning levels. At the end of '68 the managers claimed that the tech's had taken 29 separate pieces of unofficial strike action.

In Melbourne a similar large telephone exchange was opened and there was also an upsurge in the levels of local industrial action.

The parallel between these events and those taking place in the POEU are striking. Both groups of interviewees recollect similar upsurges in political awareness and militancy during the late 1960s, as growing numbers of young members, who entered the industry during a period of rapid network expansion, rejected the arbitral approach to bargaining and dispute resolution. Interviewees recall that this growing level of membership belligerence, particularly in the Redfern exchange, was viewed with horror by Right dominated PTTA Federal Executive and the NSW State Executive. The federal leadership of the union acted to control what they viewed, as 'industrial anarchy' at the Redfern exchange (Waters, 1976). They launched an enquiry and attempted to instruct the New South Wales branch to close down the Redfern sub-branch. The NSW branch, although hostile to the activities of members at Redfern viewed this directive as an attack on their industrial policy-making autonomy, and refused to close the sub-branch down. This sparked a power struggle on the Federal Executive, which was eventually won by NSW after the Victorian branch instructed their delegates, who had originally backed the federal leadership to reverse their position and support NSW.

This decision heralded a sea change in the industrial and political direction of the union. Soon afterwards a group of younger, more politically and industrially militant officers won the Victorian branch elections, whilst in NSW many of the activists from the Redfern exchange won officer positions. This change in the leadership of the union's two dominant branches led to a more combative industrial strategy in NSW and Victoria. This yielded positive results with significant pay increases, longer holidays, shorter working weeks and higher rates of penalty premiums (overtime rates), all being secured. Guarantees of no reductions to staffing levels, when new technology was introduced, were also obtained in many areas.

The primary reason for this success was the susceptibility of the telephone network to disruption. Strikes of even a short duration by key workers could lead to major failures in the service. As a former telephone technician of the time, and now a senior state officer commented:

> We could pull a few dozen techs out, in the main Sydney or Melbourne exchanges, and within a few hours there'd be total bloody chaos.

Federally, support for the more militant approach of the NSW and Victorian branches grew after a controversial national agreement was reached in 1970. The deal was entered into by the Federal Secretary, Ken Turbet, without the agreement of the branches or the membership. Part of the agreement saw the job classification of technicians being changed to that of telecommunication tradesmen. Turbet's decision, which he had been given leave to unilaterally sign by the Federal Executive, proved to be highly controversial. As a senior ATEA officer recalled:

> Look the title technician was incredibly important to us. That's what we were – technicians. It wasn't just a job title, it was part of us. I tell you Turbet must have been as mad as cut snake to sign, and the Executive just as crazy to let him.

Incensed by the grade title change ATEA members took strike action, without Federal leadership support, and succeeded in getting the technician grade reinstated and a new assistant technician grade created. The NSW and Victorian branches, in response to Turbet's actions, also attained changes to the union's constitution at Federal Conference, which prohibited the Federal Secretary from acting in this manner again and granted the state branches and sub-branches even greater industrial autonomy.

The APWU NSW and Victorian branch leaders also came under membership pressure during this period to adopt industrial tactics similar to the ATEA's. As a result there was an increase in militancy which saw the two unions considerably strengthen their levels of influence over the labour process. These gains not only heralded improvements in members' terms and conditions, they also allowed the unions to resist employer efforts to undermine demarcation lines. If anything, during the 1970s the political and industrial changes in the ATEA Victorian and NSW branches led to sharper demarcation divisions, owing to the further deterioration in political and personal relationships between the branch leaderships. It was not though until the 1980s, as Chapter 11 documents, that the employer felt sufficiently confident to start to mount a serious challenge to the unions' influence over the labour process.

Recruitment

In common with their British counter-parts and the non-craft print unions of both countries, the Australian telecommunications unions initially recruited members in the face of employer and State hostility. That they were able to gain what was often a precarious membership foothold was testament to the endeavour and commitment of activists, often in the face of disciplinary sanctions (Waters, 1976). It was only when the unions achieved recognition that membership numbers increased significantly. By the late 1920s the two unions sought to build on this growing membership strength by seeking compulsory unionism from the Federal Government. As in Britain, this was resisted by the ALP, as well as by Coalition Governments. However management did tacitly conceded the closed shop in many areas, in order, as one former APWU officer recalled, "to keep the peace with the unions". Interviewees stated that these informal agreements were strongly policed by both unions and management (Martin, 1975: 51), a claim which is substantiated by the unions reporting membership density levels of over 95% by the late 1950s (PTTA annual reports 1956–1960).

The achievement of such high density levels in their coverage areas allowed the two unions to concentrate on those developing parts of the industry where they did not have established coverage. Neither union was clearly victorious in this struggle although the importance they both placed on being able to lay claim to operating and maintaining the new satellite and microwave technology can be gauged by the fact that both unions changed their names.[3] Aside from these efforts to gain membership in new areas of the industry, the unions continued to successfully use 'informal' compulsory unionism in order to recruit members up until 1980. In line with all the other unions featured, officers and activists of the telecommunication unions agreed that whilst this recruitment method was highly effective, it failed to provide them with the skills they needed to recruit workers in the deregulated industry of the 1990s.

3   In 1974 the APWU changed its name to the Australian Postal and Telecommunications Union (APTU), prompting the PTTA to change its name to the Australian Telecommunications Employees Association (ATEA) owing to fears it could be viewed by the Federal Industrial Relations Commission, as simply a craft union.

Amalgamations

Before 1980, the Australian telecommunications unions engaged in one significant period of merger activity, which lasted from the late 1880s to the early 1920s. During this time various small, regionally based, occupational telecommunication unions firstly came together to form State unions and then, after nationalisation, these unions amalgamated again to form national unions. That this process did not result in the creation of one federal union for all manual telecommunication workers, but instead created two such unions was to have a profound effect on policy, as this chapter has already shown.

Prior to the formation of the two federal unions the negotiations to form State based unions had been complex. The various small occupational unions were anxious not to lose their identity whilst acknowledging the need to become part of a State-wide organisation, which could deal with the Colonial Government. Importantly it was at this stage that the developing division between electrical engineers and linesmen started to become formalised in State wide union structures. Unlike the Australian printing unions there were no instances of the small telecommunication unions amalgamating across occupational lines to form State wide industrial unions. The reason for the rejection of such an amalgamation policy was, as interviewees and Waters (1976) noted, linked to the antipathy that had developed between lines workers and electrical engineers, following the occupational separation that had been originally installed by management. Elderly former officers of the APTU, interviewed in 1994, offered an insight into why there was a refusal to contemplate such mergers:

> When I started work in the late 1920s, it was soon clear that the Techs saw themselves as a cut above everyone else and were treated better by the bosses than us Linies.

On the technicians side the powerful desire to be viewed as a group of skilled engineers was evident in the recollections of a former lay officer:

A lot of us were unhappy with being known as a Postal Electricians union. We weren't two bob electricians, we were highly skilled technicians. If we had merged with the Linies, our demands for our skills to be recognised would have been side-lined.

It was these types of sentiments, and the managerial separation of the trades, which contributed to their being no mergers between the various State-based, Postal Electricians unions and the Linesmen's unions. Instead State wide occupational unions were created, who then came together to form national occupational unions, after the industry was nationalised.

In 1919, the NSW Linesmen union branch put forward a radical proposal that these divisions should be bridged and a union formed for all manual workers who were employed by the Federal Post Office (Waters, 1978: 12). After a series of what were described, as 'difficult' internal debates the postal unions agreed to amalgamate but the APEU rejected the offer (Waters, 1978: 12). Having suffered considerable internal opprobrium for suggesting an amalgamation with the APEU, the NSW branch was deeply frustrated at the APEU's attitude. According to a number of older interviewees, such was the branch leadership's exasperation that they resolved to ensure that the APEU were never again approached over an amalgamation. The amalgamation discussions between the linesworkers and the postal unions though were successful, with the APWU being formed in 1924. The nature, as well as the outcome, of these amalgamation negotiations saw an entrenching of the strong occupational and personal divisions, which were to last until 1980.

These findings cast further doubt on Waddington's (1995) assertion that 'unionists merge their organisations to strengthen their bargaining positions' (Waddington, 1995: 68). As interviewees from both unions admitted, the creation of a single union for Australian telecommunication workers would have granted greater industrial strength than that enjoyed by two separate unions. The reasons why such a merger did not take place until the 1990s are, as this chapter has shown, linked to a series of complex industrial, political, personal and structural factors. The evidence supports Undy's (2008) observation, that the success of amalgamation negotiations is dependent on a wide variety of internal and external influences, not just industrial logic.

Conclusion

Throughout this chapter the influence on the labour process, recruitment and amalgamation policies of the Australian telecommunications unions of the decision to remain independent unions has been shown to be profound. Many of the external institutional factors that the Australian unions historically confronted were very similar to those faced by the POEU. Yet the policies they adopted, particularly in terms of the labour process, were significantly different. One of the primary reasons for this variation, the empirical evidence indicates, was the decision of the two Australian unions to utilise, rather than address, the occupational and craft prejudices which were so powerfully exhibited by the workforce. This was in contrast to the British POEU, which as the sole industrial union for manual telecommunication workers sought to dissipate (not always successfully) similar occupational divisions.

The different choices of the Australian unions, in all three policy areas, reflect the ability of unions to make a series of strategic choices. These findings support the assertions of scholars who argue that such choices are important in determining a union's future, and are influenced by the policy makers' beliefs, values and ideology (Kelly, 1998; Heery and Kelly, 1994; Kelly and Heery, 1994; Heery, 2000, 2003, 2006). The empirical evidence also suggests that the 'beliefs, values and ideology' of policy makers' were themselves shaped by a rich and complex combination of influences. These included the nature of union internal structures, the strength of political factions, and the effect of numerous micro-political factors, particularly personal loyalties and enmities.

CHAPTER 8

The British Printing Unions: 1980–1996

Introduction

In this and the following three chapters, the main body of empirical evidence gathered for this book is outlined and analysed. All the chapters cover the period from 1980–1996 and consider the labour process, recruitment and amalgamation policies of the Australian and British printing and telecommunications unions. The manner in which these policies developed is outlined, whilst an analysis is undertaken of the reasons why specific policy choices were implemented. Comparisons are also drawn between the responses of the unions to similar institutional challenges in all three key policy areas. The reasons for similarities and variations in policy approaches are evaluated.

This chapter specifically charts the labour process, recruitment and amalgamation policies of the British print unions from 1980–1996. The period was arguably the most tumultuous in the print unions' history, during which their powerful influence over the labour process and their ability to enforce compulsory trade unionism was contested by employers and the State. This challenge was epitomised in two of the most significant industrial disputes of the late twentieth century; the Messenger Group Newspapers strike and the News International dispute. The policy choices that affected the prosecution of these disputes, and the effect the outcome the disputes had on the subsequent policies of the print unions, are major themes of this chapter.

Interwoven throughout the chapter there is an examination of why the strained and fractious relationship, between SOGAT and the NGA, improved in the early 1980s before deteriorating markedly from 1984 onwards. The manner, in which this corrosive relationship affected both unions' policies, is also considered.

The labour process

As the NGA and SOGAT entered 1980, they were faced with a formidable array of industrial and political challenges to their strong influence over the labour process. During the previous ten years technological advances had granted employers the ability to produce their products without utilising many of the craft skills that the printing unions' members possessed. At the same time the election of the Conservative Party, in May 1979, heralded the return of a Government who were explicitly committed to curbing the ability of trade unions to influence the labour process and to enforce compulsory unionism (Conservative Party Manifesto, 1979: 2–3).

This section focuses on the policies that the printing unions adopted in order to try and retain their influence over the labour process in the face of a rapidly altering industrial and political environment. In doing so those reasons that lay behind specific policy choices will be examined, with particular emphasis being placed on exploring the influences that shaped policy makers' decisions.

Reflecting in 1997 on the industrial strength of the NGA at the start of the 1980s a former national lay activist observed:

> We were a powerful, well organised union. We didn't fear any employer, nor the new Tory Government.

These sentiments were not mindlessly hubristic. Both the NGA and SOGAT had previously been successful in defending their considerable influence over the labour process, in the face of employer and State efforts to weaken their control in the 1970s (Gennard, 1990; Gennard and Bain, 1995). However by 1980, as former senior union officers of both unions recalled, the immense threat that new technology posed to both unions influence over the labour process was understood clearly by their respective General Secretaries. The NGA's General Secretary, Joe Wade, was so exercised by the dangers of direct inputting that he floated the radical proposal that the print unions should review how they operated their craft demarcation lines. Wade became convinced of the need for such an alteration, after the Newspaper Society[1] approved a policy, codenamed 'Project Breakthrough', which sought to introduce single key-stroking by journalists in all provincial newspapers by 1984. Wade's proposal, entitled 'The Way Forward', suggested that the NGA, SOGAT and the NUJ should collectively organise a series of joint closed shops, in which members of all the unions would be able to directly input data (Gennard, 1990: 161–2.)

The policy sought to set aside the craft and occupational demarcation lines upon which the NGA's control of the labour process had largely been built. After what participants described as a heated debate, he got this proposal through the National Council. This was a feat, many contributors suggested, which reflected more on his personal standing amongst National Councillors, rather than their belief in the policy. These observations add weight to the evidence that micro-political factors, such as personal respect, can affect a union's policy direction.

The National Council's willingness to adopt 'The Way Forward' was not though the precursor to the plan being accepted and implemented across the union. The national newspaper composing chapels were enraged by the policy and made it clear that they would never implement it. Instead, they stated, they would continue to defend their right to input all copy. The NGA national leadership viewed this position as totally unrealistic, reflecting the national newspaper pre-press chapels' failure to acknowledge technological realities. As a former NGA National Officer observed:

> Some of our national newspaper chapels thought they were invincible. The truth was that direct inputting was the death knell for the compositors, and we all knew it. The problem was the IFoC's and FoC's stuck their heads in the sand and refused to deal with reality.

On the other side of the argument the leaders of the powerful and fiercely independent national newspaper chapels put forward a contrary view. A former Fleet Street FoC recalled:

---

1   The Newspaper Society was the employers' association which represented hundreds of regional newspaper publishers.

> What 'The Way Forward' was really saying was that we should simply give up everything we had won. As far as we were concerned they could bugger off. We had just won our dispute at *The Times* over single keystroking[2] and even if we had wanted to adopt this policy, our members would never have worn it.

The refusal by the national newspaper chapels to enact the type of compromises agreed in 'The Way Forward', was often cited by contributors as the primary reason why the NGA was unable to reach negotiated agreements with newspaper employers over the introduction of 'single keystroking' in the early 1980s. This is another clear example of how union policy can often be shaped, as Kelly and Heery suggest (Heery and Kelly, 1988; Kelly and Heery, 1994; Heery, 2003, 2006), by the decisions of local workplace activists, as well as national union policy makers.

Whilst the NGA was struggling to internally implement 'The Way Forward', the policy was effectively made unworkable by SOGAT's rejection of the document. Joe Wade had been hopeful that his opposite number, Bill Keys, could deliver his NEC's support for the policy, owing to Keys sharing the view that the print unions needed to be adaptable in order to mitigate the effects of new technology on union influence over the labour process (Gennard, 1990; Gennard and Bain, 1994). However, the SOGAT NEC rejected the NGA's proposal, for reasons that a former NEC member recalled:

> Many Exec members felt that the NGA simply wanted to move into our areas, because technology was making them redundant. They had always jealously guarded their control over the composing room, which we were not allowed to even enter. Now they wanted to come into our areas. As far as many newspaper delegates were concerned, they could just piss off.

Although SOGAT rejected 'The Way Forward', Wade was correct in his assumption that Bill Keys favoured a more flexible approach to defending the unions influence over the labour process. In an effort to address

---

2   In 1978/79 there was a twelve month strike at Times Newspapers Limited which was, in part, called over the employers wish to allow their journalists to directly enter copy, known as 'single keystroking'.

these issues Keys put forward a policy document entitled, 'Programme for Action'. This proposed that members in the national newspapers worked more flexibly, in return for job security agreements. Keys' proposal was accepted by the NEC in the face of fierce opposition from the national newspaper delegates. However, as with the NGA, the powerful national newspaper branches and chapels made it clear that they would not implement the policy.

The problems that both unions faced in imposing policy decisions on their national newspaper chapels were reflected upon by a former senior NGA official:

> Throughout our history our power came from the strength of the chapels. By the early 1980s this had also become a handicap. The union couldn't implement national policy if the powerful national newspaper chapels refused to co-operate. To be honest it became almost anarchical.

Similar views were expressed by other senior officers of both unions, who also reflected on the unfeasibility of imposing sanctions on the national newspaper branches and chapels, at this time, when they refused to follow national policy. In part this reflected constitutional protections provided by the rulebook, but chiefly it revealed the reality of devolved policy authority in both unions, where attempting to force the industrially, electorally and financially powerful national newspaper chapels and branches to undertake an industrial policy with which they vehemently disagreed, was unachievable. There was also, as interviewees conceded, a great reluctance on the part of senior lay National Executives/National Council members, to agree any curbs on the autonomy of the chapels and branches, which they represented.

At the same time as these internal debates over how to protect their influence over the labour process were unfolding, there had been a significant alteration in how the unions sought to prosecute industrial disputes. The NGA, following a rare industrial defeat at T. Bailey Forman in 1973 (where members had worked during an official dispute), had adopted new picketing tactics. Historically the NGA had not organised mass pickets during strikes, owing to their members' strict observance of all official disputes. However in 1975 the NGA adopted a new approach which it first deployed at the regional newspaper printer, Sharman's of Peterborough. The new strategy, which drew heavily on the tactics deployed by the NUM in their 1974 national strike, saw the deployment of mass 'flying' pickets. This approach proved to be highly successful at Sharman's, where some members had continued working during an official strike, with the site being shut and the dispute being successfully resolved. This achievement ensured that the NGA now adopted more widely a robust picketing approach, which was seen by many interviewees as part of a wider shift in the industrial policy direction of the union. As one officer recalled:

> By the early 1980s we had adopted a more combative industrial approach, in which we were prepared to use more robust industrial tactics.

This alteration in policy was linked by a number of interviewees and Dickinson (1984), to a generational change that was taking place inside the leadership of the NGA. Younger lay and full-time officers were being elected who, in printing craft unionism terms, were more industrially militant. Chief amongst this 'new' generation of NGA officials was Tony Dubbins, the then Assistant General Secretary, who was in the vanguard of this new approach, and who had persuaded the National Council, against the advice of the General Secretary, to endorse and pay for a mass 'flying picket' at Sharman's (Dickinson, 1984: 37; Gennard, 1990: 472–3). This change in the NGA's policy, which drew inspiration from the National Union Of Mineworkers (NUM) picketing tactics, supports Heery's (2003) theory that unions can achieve alterations in policy direction when they operate internal democratic processes which allows for the 'renewal and replacement of their leaderships with those of a different gender, generation and ideology' (Heery, 2003: 297).

Significantly, this 'generational shift' was also taking place in the leadership of SOGAT where a number of senior officers, including Bill Keys, were approaching retirement. Importantly for relations with the NGA, these changes did not result in the election of officers who espoused a more radical industrial approach. Instead they heralded the replacement of senior officers from the London newspaper branches, with officials who emanated from the industrially more moderate provincial branches (Bain, 1998; Gennard and Bain, 1995; Dean, 2007). The most important of these elections was that of SOGAT's first female General Secretary, Brenda Dean, who came from a provincial branch, and who was elected when Bill Keys retired in 1985.

Prior to these changes taking place the relationship between the two unions had improved significantly. This was partly owing to Bill Keys and Joe Wade sharing similar views on the need to be pragmatic in dealing with the introduction of new technology, but it also reflected the two unions' belief that the TUC must be proactive in defying the legal constrictions placed upon secondary action and the closed shop by the Conservative Government's 1980 and 1982 Employment Acts. This unity was on public display at the Special TUC Conference held in April 1982 where the print unions moved and seconded a motion opposing the Employment Acts, whilst calling for TUC financial and practical support to unions who refused to obey the legislation (Dickinson, 1984; Gennard, 1990; Gennard and Bain, 1995).

By 1983 the two General Secretaries fears that their respective unions' ability to defend their influence over the labour process was about to be severely tested, proved correct. Contrary though to the scenario that they had both independently painted to their national governing bodies, the challenge to their influence over the labour process did not initially occur at a major national or provincial newspaper, but instead at a small, North Western, free newspaper publisher: Messenger Group Newspapers.

The Messenger Newspaper Group dispute

Speaking in 1996 a senior NGA lay activist recalled the start of the Messenger Newspaper Group strike:

> Looking back at it, we slept-walked into the Messenger dispute, we should never have involved ourselves in the way we did over a dispute that was so small and insignificant.

Significantly though, even with the benefit of hindsight, this did not represent the majority of NGA activists and officers' views. Interviewees overwhelmingly expressed a very different opinion, which are succinctly encapsulated by a former senior NGA officer:

> Look we had no choice. Shah[3] was basically saying to us I'll produce my papers with non-union labour. The consequences if we had simply let that happen across the whole printing industry would have been devastating. We'd have been derecognised left, right and centre. So yes, even with all that happened, we were right to stand up to Shah.

These conflicting views reflect the diversity of opinions that were expressed prior to and during the strike, by different NGA policy makers who shaped the union's prosecution of what became a major dispute. Unlike the subsequent News International strike, which involved from its outset thousands of print workers, the Messenger strike initially involved just a handful of NGA members. They were employed at a Fineward Typesetting, a small company in Stockport, which was part of the Messenger Newspaper Group.

The origins of the dispute can be traced back to 1982, when Fineward Typesetting refused to offer its workers, at its new premises in Bury, the same terms and conditions as employees received in Stockport. The company at that stage operated a NGA pre-entry closed shop and had previously accepted that they would extend this agreement to cover the new Bury office (Dickenson, 1984: 64; Gennard, 1990: 486). Negotiations between the NGA and Messenger Newspaper Group were complicated, as they involved three NGA branches,[4] who all had discrete responsibility for Messenger's three separate sites. All three branches conducted totally separate negotiations with no co-ordination between the branches, or with the NGA's Regional or National Officers. There was also considerable tension between the branches, which importantly revolved around

---

3   Selim 'Eddie' Shah was the owner of the Messenger Newspaper Group, of which Fineward Typesetting was part. The Messenger Newspaper Group published free newspapers across the North West of England.
4   The West Pennine branch covered Bury, whilst the Manchester branch had responsibility for the Warrington printing plant; and the Stockport branch represented the Messenger Group workers employed in the town.

poor personal relationships between the respective branch officers. As one branch activist recalled:

> There was no love lost between Owen[5] and the officers at Stockport. I'm sure that's why he went and negotiated rates for Bury without even speaking to the Stockport branch.

The rates agreed for the Bury site were £40 per week less than those paid at Stockport. Unsurprisingly, the Stockport branch were incensed at this undercutting of their members wages; however in an action that displayed the union's highly devolved policy-making structure they called on the West Pennine branch committee, not the national union, to reverse this decision. The West Pennine branch did overturn the agreement, which according to Shah (in evidence he gave to a Court hearing on 10 July 1984) made him determined to make Messenger Newspaper Group a non-union company (Dickenson, 1984: 73).

Unsurprisingly, given Shah's intentions, all the negotiations failed to make progress, and in the autumn of 1982 the Stockport and West Pennine branches decided to take the unusual step of seeking assistance from their National Officer. The onus for such a request rested upon the NGA branches and chapels, unlike in the POEU where negotiations that involved more than one branch would automatically involve the intervention of national officials. Following the intervention of the National Officer, John Ibbotson, the negotiations seemed to have reached an agreement in early September 1982. However these hopes were dashed when the Fineward Stockport chapel reported that they had discovered that the copy being sent to them was being produced by non-union staff working in Bury. Shortly thereafter it also became clear that the company was also printing newspapers, using non-union labour, at the new Warrington plant.

Although angry at being actively deceived, the NGA did not immediately take industrial action. As a then NGA branch officer stated:

---

5   Owen Coop was then the NGA West Pennine branch, Branch Secretary.

> We went to extraordinary lengths to avoid a strike. We gave Shah every opportunity to reach a sensible settlement, and the lads at Fineward kept working, even though they were accepting copy in breach of Rule 43.[6]

Part of the reason for this reticence was reflected upon by a former NGA national officer:

> We realised that Shah was attempting to organise a non-union operation and that any action by the lads at Fineward's would have little effect. This meant we'd have to call on other members to 'black' Messenger Newspaper Group as a whole. In light of the Tory Employment Acts we knew there'd be legal consequences and we were keen to see if we could negotiate a deal.

Owing to this apprehension amongst the union's national leadership the NGA General Secretary, Joe Wade asked the Assistant General Secretary, Tony Dubbins, to personally lead negotiations with Messenger Group. Following these talks, and in direct contravention of the union's own rules, the National Council agreed to Shah's proposal that the NGA visit Bury and Warrington and attempt to recruit the non-union workforce. As a National Officer observed:

> Some National Councillors thought that attending these meetings was not only in contravention of our rules but also a sign of weakness. However the role of Tony Dubbins was very important. He was the heir apparent to Joe and he had a lot of influence over the National Council. I know he hoped to find a solution so that we didn't have a dispute with a company where we were so weak. Like a number of us he was worried we were being suckered into a dispute where we had little to win and lots to lose.

This quotation reflects the views of a number of other officers and lay activists who recalled how, in a fast changing legislative environment, Tony Dubbins, predominantly for micro-political reasons, was looked to for a solution. This was partly owing to the success of the tactics he had previously put forward in the Sharman's dispute. As interviewees also recall the

6   The NGA's rule 43 stipulated that all copy handled by NGA members must emanate from a unionised workplace and must be transferred onto a, approved, unionised workplace.

trust the NC displayed in Dubbins proposals did not relate to his position as Assistant General Secretary; instead it reflected their personal faith in him and his negotiating ability.

This evidence illustrates how suggestions by some strategic choice authors (Boxall and Hayes, 1997; Child, 1997; Willman, 2001) that senior officers can simply shape union policy by using the powers that are granted by their office is overly simplistic. Instead in the diffused, democratic, structure of a union such as the NGA, where significant policy-making authority is devolved to lay members, it is imperative for a senior officer to be able to generate lay activist support, in order that the strategies they propose are adopted and implemented. To be able to generate such support, in the NGA, which had weak political factions, interviewees confirmed that NGA officials relied on micro-political factors, such as respect, friendships and craft loyalty.

The meetings arranged in the autumn of 1982 with the non-union Messenger staff proved to be unsuccessful. This was perhaps unsurprising given that staff later confirmed that they were asked to give assurances at their interviews that they were prepared to cross picket lines work and work during an industrial dispute (Dickenson, 1984: 82). By November 1982 further protracted negotiations, led again by Tony Dubbins, had made no tangible progress. Inside the NGA tensions over how to respond to the use of non-union labour increased as negotiations failed to reach a resolution. The Fineward NGA Chapel were now dissatisfied that they were still handling non-union copy and that no effective action was being taken by the national union. They pressed in meetings with officers to go on strike and for the union to institute the blacking of all Messenger products. However there was great unease amongst senior officers and the National Council over their weak industrial position at Fineward, which they feared would lead to all their members being dismissed if they took action. As a former senior NGA officer stated:

> We were effectively trying to square the circle. We knew we were in a very weak industrial position, yet we also knew we had a small group of loyal NGA members at Fineward, who were well pissed off that they were being told by the national office to work normally.

The negotiations continued for months but in June 1983 the NGA's protracted efforts to negotiate a solution finally ended. As another former NGA national official recollects:

> In the end it was Shah who bought the situation to a head, when he advertised the Fineward lads' jobs. Effectively he left us with no choice: we had to take the bastard on.

The NGA national leadership, now totally exasperated by Shah's behaviour, wrote to the company with an ultimatum; either reach an agreement by the 22 June 1983, or the NGA would declare an official dispute with the Messenger Newspaper Group. The 22 June came and went with no agreement and on 4 July 1983 the NGA called an official strike of the Fineward members.

At the outset of the dispute the union did not immediately seek to deploy the tactics they had used successfully in the Sharman dispute. Instead only the Fineward members picketed their Stockport workplace and there was only very limited secondary action. The reasons for their reticence related to the desire of the union's leadership to balance exerting pressure on Shah, with trying to protect the NGA from legal action. The decision to proceed in this fashion was not universally welcomed. Members of the Fineward Chapel, days before the dispute, made it clear that they no longer wished to go on strike. As an officer who met the Chapel members in early July 1983 recalled:

> The lads told us that the strike was being called too late. The horse had bolted and any action would now have no chance of being effective.

Inside the National Council there was also fierce debate over how to proceed. Some delegates were of the opinion that the dispute was a grave tactical error. As one former National Council delegate recalled:

> At the meeting I made it clear I thought it was madness to embark on a dispute where the company had been producing papers with non-members for months. Look, let's just get this straight, there are times when you have to walk away from situations – simply because you cannot win – and this was one of them.

Other officials were critical for wholly different reasons, as a former National Councillor recollected:

> We made a terrible error in not acting decisively, much earlier. We should have called a strike and mass secondary action, as soon as we knew he was producing papers with nons.

The variety of different policy options that were discussed prior to the start of the Messenger strike provides convincing evidence of the way in which the NGA were making strategic choices between clear policy options, in a manner that Kelly and Heery describe (Kelly, 1998; Heery and Kelly, 1994; Kelly and Heery, 1994; Heery, 2000, 2003, 2006). Importantly for this book's hypothesis, those policy choices have also been shown to be profoundly influenced by micro-political factors, in particular the respect and confidence that many senior lay and full-time officials placed in the opinions of Tony Dubbins.

During the first weeks of the strike the NGA continued with its cautious approach, picketing only the Stockport site as opposed to the non-union, Warrington and Bury workplaces. This was coupled to secondary action being taken against Messenger Newspaper Group's suppliers and investors. The NGA had calculated that these companies were unlikely to launch legal action against the union, owing to their heavy dependence on NGA organised labour. The companies included Reed International, the then owners of Mirror Newspapers, who following disruption of the *Daily Mirror's* production in both Manchester and London, announced that they were selling their Messenger Newspaper Group investments. Shah immediately responded by issuing proceedings against the NGA claiming that the union was in contravention of the 1980 Employment Act, in that it had induced Reed International to repudiate a contract with the Messenger Newspaper Group. The company was successful in their action, with the Court awarding damages against the NGA of £13,000. This came, as a former NGA officer admitted, as an unpleasant surprise to the NGA leadership, who had believed that any legal cases relating to their secondary industrial action would have had to be instigated by the company directly affected. The action was to be the first of many which were successfully brought by Shah against the union.

Alongside their campaign to bring commercial pressure to bear on Messenger, the NGA also sought assistance from the other union recognised by the company, the NUJ. Although the NUJ's National Executive was sympathetic and sanctioned secondary action, at the local level, the NUJ Messenger chapel was split over taking action. At a NUJ Messenger chapel meeting a small majority of journalists did vote in favour of taking secondary action. However after the declaration of the result half the NUJ's members left the union and continued to work normally, thus ensuring that the various Messenger Newspaper Group titles continued to be produced.

The splintering of the NUJ Chapel, plus the company's successful legal action were major blows to the NGA's strategy to win the dispute, without having to resort to significant levels of secondary action or mass picketing. Inside the union there was growing unrest over the prosecution of the dispute. As many lay and full-time officers recalled, they were aware that other printing employers, who were hostile to the levels of influence the NGA wielded in their workplaces, were taking a keen interest in how the dispute was unfolding. As an NGA National Officer of the time recalled:

> A few weeks into the dispute, there was a lot of publicity surrounding the court case and we were hearing back from the Branch Secs and FoC's that employers were starting to get more leery on the back of what was happing at Messenger. They made it clear we now needed to win this dispute and they were asking me: How the hell is a tin pot clown like Shah being allowed to print his papers, whilst our boys are on strike?

By October 1983 criticism was also increasing from the six Fineward members themselves who were frustrated that there was only a picket at Stockport, whilst the paper was being produced at Bury and Warrington. These criticisms had particular resonance inside the union as they were expressed by members who had loyally answered the call to take strike action and had then remained on the picket line for over three months. National Officials, who were close to Dubbins at the time, recalled that he was by now well aware that the policy of limited secondary action was failing to win the dispute and that he had concluded that it was now necessary to escalate the action, if the Union wanted to win the strike and defend its wider ability to influence the labour process (See Dickenson, 1984; Gennard, 1990).

In order to test the levels of support for possible escalation of the action an open meeting was called of all printing unions members at the New Century Hall, Manchester on 27 October 1983. This meeting was to have a profound effect on the NGA's conduct of the Messenger dispute. The meeting, to the surprise of some local branch officers, was attended by over 600 print workers. Many of those attending were highly critical of the NGA's failure to organise a mass picket at all Messenger Group premises and to institute large scale secondary industrial action. This condemnation of the union's tactics was led by the Liverpool NGA Branch Secretary, Ray Williams, who demanded that mass pickets should be deployed in the same manner as at Sharman's. His proposal was overwhelmingly endorsed by the meeting (Dickinson, 1984: 91). Interviewees recalled that whilst Dubbins and Ibbotson were angered by Williams' castigation of their tactics, they were also privately pleased with the meeting's support of mass picketing, which a number of local branch officers had insisted their members would not endorse.

The General Secretary and the National Council, having heard of the support from activists and members for a change of policy, endorsed the adoption of mass picketing. This led to the NGA's North West Region writing to all their chapels and branches asking for members to picket the Stockport Messenger Newspaper Group office. This written request was quite clearly in direct breach of the prohibitions placed on secondary picketing by the 1982 Employment Act, and led to the Messenger Newspaper Group successfully seeking an injunction to stop the secondary picketing. The issuing of the letter was seen by some (Dickinson, 1984) to reflect the union's reversion to its Conference policy of ignoring the legal limitations placed upon both secondary action and secondary picketing by the Conservative Government. According though to former senior officers, the letter was not an act of pre-meditated defiance, but was instead an error by a long serving Regional Officer, who was not cognisant with how his letter contravened the 1982 Employment Act. That subsequently the NGA decided only to issue requests for members to take part in 'demonstrations of support', gives credence to these statements.

The aggressive use of legal action by the Messenger Group left the NGA, as officers recalled, with a key strategic choice: either retreat and abide by the injunction, or escalate the action. As a National Councillor recalled at that time there was a significant majority in support of taking further action:

> By early November '83 we knew it was shit or bust. Shah's position was crystal clear; he wasn't interested in a settlement, and the Courts and the Government supported him. We all now realised that this dispute had taken on national significance. Other employers, who had no love for us, were lining up to act like Shah – if he could defeat us.

At the NGA's Biennial Delegates Meeting held in early November, Joe Wade reflected this view when he spoke of the need for the union to act nationally in order to win a dispute that was critical to its future (Dickenson, 1984; Gennard, 1990). There was overwhelming support for his speech, with many delegates expressing surprise that the union had not been able to stop Shah's efforts to produce newspapers with non-union labour. These were sentiments that reflected the expectation of activists that their union's historic control over entry to the industry and considerable influence over the labour process, should allow them to deal robustly and effectively with employers who sought to derecognise the NGA.

In response to the views being expressed at the Biennial Delegates Meeting the NGA announced that the Bury and Warrington, non-union, sites were now to be picketed. Early in the evening of 9 November the NGA was successful in deceiving both the employer and the police into thinking that the mass picket would be at Bury, whilst they secretly moved their secondary pickets to the production plant in Warrington. Having secured this tactical advantage the NGA's lack of experience of mass picketing proved to be a considerable handicap. Union officers who were in charge of the picketing were unclear as to what to do next having arrived at the plant, where they found very few security guards and Police officers. As a former NGA officer recalls:

> The problem was no one really knew what to do next. Our officers and activists had next to no experience of picketing. You know yourself how difficult it is to organise and control mass picketing; particularly when the pickets are wound up with little or nothing to do. I believe our lack of experience led to what happened that night, which of course turned out to be a gift for Shah and the Tories.

The events referred to involved groups of pickets kicking and hammering on the outside of the building using any implement they could find to hit its corrugated metal external shell. According to those present, a regular beat developed, that mimicked the 'banging out' rhythm that print workers used when an apprentice had served his time. As Dickenson notes (1984: 95) even at a time of violent anger the pickets strong craft traditions still permeated their behaviour. No one inside the Warrington plant was injured during this noisy demonstration, and production of the Messenger newspapers was not affected. However the events of 9 November 1983 catapulted the dispute into the full glare of the national media with almost universally hostile coverage. Eddie Shah was extensively reported likening the pickets to "Nazis", whilst editorials in the national newspapers described the pickets as "vicious mindless thugs" (Dickenson, 1984: 96–7).

After they met the next day, the NGA leadership publicly expressed satisfaction at the scale of picketing and that the distribution of the Messenger titles had been delayed by eight hours, privately though they were deeply concerned. A then NGA officer reflected:

> Joe was worried that the picketing was completely out of control. He took a lot of persuading not to abandon it then and there. It was only Tony's intervention, where he stressed that there had been very few officers present that led to a compromise, in which we assigned every national officer to the dispute and all the North West branches were asked to help in stewarding. We also sent up a van, floodlights and a generator and basically did everything we could to coordinate and control the picketing.

These adjustments in policy illustrate not only the manner in which the NGA were constantly making a series of strategic choices throughout the dispute in a manner that Kelly and Heery suggest (Kelly, 1998; Heery and Kelly, 1994; Heery, 2000, 2003), but also the importance to the conduct of the strike of micro-political relationships, in this instance between Wade and Dubbins.

Having been convinced of the need to continue with mass picketing, Wade sanctioned the preparation of an even larger picket of the Warrington plant. As preparations were put in place, Messenger Group's lawyers returned to the Manchester High Court, where on the 17 November

1983 Mr Justice Eastham found the NGA to be in contempt of court and ordered it to obey the previous injunctions, and to desist from secondary picketing and the 'blacking' of Messenger copy. He also fined the union £50,000 plus costs and warned the NGA that if they failed to obey the Court Order then they could face sequestration of their assets.

Former NGA National Officers and NC members admitted in their interviews that they were all shaken by the size of the fine and the threat of sequestration. At a series of informal and formal meetings there was a debate, amongst the senior officers, over how to continue their prosecution of the dispute. As interviewees stated the strike had by this time altered from being a regional newspaper dispute into a challenge to the ability of the union to influence the labour process across the whole industry. Abiding by the Court Order was discussed but was swiftly dismissed, even though the union were clear that the consequences could be the sequestration of all their assets. The reason, as interviewees recalled, was the strong belief that to withdraw from the dispute would have given the 'green light' to employers who the NGA leadership knew were contemplating adopting a similar strategy to Shah's. It was therefore decided that all options designed to win the dispute must be considered. These included a one day national strike of all NGA members, a two day stoppage of all the national newspapers, or a further escalation of the mass picketing.

There was then a considerable debate at both the National Council and prior to the meeting informally amongst senior lay and full-time officials over what strategy should be adopted. Those favouring a national strike believed that it was would generate tremendous pressure on Shah from other employers, whilst also demonstrating to the industry the strength of the Union. Other senior officers disagreed, preferring instead to seek secondary action by the national newspaper chapels, which had the ability to create extensive disruption without the risk of a significant minority of members refusing to answer the strike call. That these two strategic choices could be seriously contemplated is a reflection of considerable internal cohesion and industrial strength of the NGA at this time. Interviewees recalled that after considerable deliberation, Joe Wade's unease over the idea of a national stoppage led to agreement that a national strike would only be called as a last resort. Instead it was decided that the secondary picketing would be increased and, if sequestrated, the NGA would call on their national newspaper chapels to undertake secondary strike action.

Furthermore the NGA national leadership also decided to press the TUC for assurances that it would honour the 1982 Special Conference policy and financially support the NGA, if they were sequestrated. The evidence that, once again, complex strategic policy choices were being made by the union is overwhelming. The results of the NGA leadership's deliberations also throws into doubt those State and institutional contextualist authors (Howell, 2005; Bain, 1970) who place such emphasis on union policy being shaped by legislation and the policies of the Government and employers.

By the middle of November 1983 the NGA's continuing efforts to stage a mass picket as well as increase secondary action were being met with an increasingly belligerent police response. Urged on by statements from the Home Secretary the police were now regularly man-handling pickets, as newspapers were transported out of the printing plant. As injuries to pickets mounted the NGA altered its policy, abandoning the use of physical weight of numbers to block the entrance to the plant, which they had used successfully at Sharman's. Instead pickets were now instructed to sit down in the road. This alteration did not lead to any of the anticipated moderation in the Police's response. As one former NGA officer observed wryly; "the Coppers then simply kicked seven bells out of us whilst we sat on the ground".

The NGA's difficulties continued to mount, as all efforts to negotiate a settlement at ACAS failed, whilst the TUC General Council refused, at their meeting on the 23 November to give financial assistance to the NGA, owing to their fears that they would be party to the Court's injunctions. The NGA were though bolstered by an offer from the TGWU to pay the NGA's total wage bill and provide premises for the union's officers and staff, if the NGA had their funds sequestrated. On 25 November the NGA went back to the High Court where their solicitors were predicting they would receive a further heavy fine and possibly be sequestrated. The pressure at this point on the senior officials of the NGA was intense. As a former senior officer stated:

> You know yourself what it's like when employers successfully take out injunctions against you. The lawyers tell you that if you don't do as the Court says then they'll issue more injunctions and possibly sequestrate your union's assets. It feels like the weight of the world is on your shoulders. We knew that it was possible that if we did the right thing by our Messenger members that the union itself could fold; with hundreds of years of history and the livelihoods of all the officers and staff, possibly disappearing overnight. The stress was almost unbearable.

Even under this stress the NGA's leadership remained steadfastly committed to their policy of refusing to abide by the Court's injunctions and to call for secondary strike action in the national newspapers, if they were to be sequestrated. To this end Wade and Dubbins met the Fleet Street chapels, who agreed to set aside their still simmering discontent over 'The Way Forward' and support the strike call. As one FoC present commented:

> Whatever our differences with head office, we realised we had to act to defend the existence of the NGA. That's why we agreed to a 48 hours stoppage, if we were sequestrated.

This comment reflects not only the reasons why the Fleet Street FoC's supported secondary action, but also their substantial industrial strength and policy-making autonomy. As all interviewees concede if the IFoC's and FoC's had failed to support the call for action, the two day strike would not have been feasible, even if the General Secretary himself had called upon the members to take action. Here, once again, the diffusion and complexity of the NGA's policy-making was revealed, with different layers of the union's structure having to agree, if a policy is to be implemented. This pattern of behaviour is at odds with the suggestion of authors such as Boxall and Haynes (1997) who assert that key policy decisions in unions are taken at the national level.

During this phase of the dispute, SOGAT started to play an increasingly important role, predominantly through Bill Keys. It was Keys who, contributors recall, persuaded the SOGAT NEC to offer financial assistance to the NGA, and who intervened on their behalf at the TUC General Council. Significantly he also worked with the ACAS conciliators and Tony Dubbins to try and find a formula to resolve the dispute. These efforts reflected the importance Keys placed upon the outcome of the dispute which as one contributor remarked he viewed as "crucial to the future of print unionism not just the NGA".

On 25 November 1983, the Manchester High Court imposed a further fine of £100,000 and decided to sequestrate the whole of the union's assets for failing to respect previous Court Orders. The NGA appealed instantaneously and were granted a temporary stay until that night, when the Master of the Rolls Sir John Donaldson upheld the High Court's sequestration order, but limited the sequestered amount to £175,000 of the NGA's assets. The Fleet Street chapels, as agreed, immediately commenced a 48 hour strike, which halted all national newspaper production. The national newspaper proprietors met and announced that they would be dismissing all the NGA members who were taking strike action and that they would be launching individual proceedings against the NGA for the maximum permissible damages of £250,000. These writs were duly served on 26 November and the NGA faced a liability of over £3,000,000.

Whilst the consequences were potentially grave for the finances of the union, the action did create pressure on Eddie Shah. A number of the national newspaper proprietors who were investors in, or suppliers to, the Messenger Newspaper Group, informed Shah that they wanted to see a resolution to the dispute. Indeed Robert Maxwell claimed he offered to buy the Messenger Group in order to resolve the dispute. Negotiations were arranged by ACAS for Sunday 27 November, which Tony Dubbins, for the first time, agreed to attend alone, whilst Shah consented to attend with only his solicitor accompanying him. At the meeting, according to Dubbins, an agreement was reached which included the introduction of a post entry closed shop and the reinstatement of the 6 strikers, whom Shah had dismissed. Shah's solicitor, Dubbins stated, was charged with setting out the agreement in writing, so that all parties could sign the document the next day (Dickenson, 1984). However when the document arrived on the Monday it had been fundamentally altered, with the company now refusing to reinstate the 6 dismissed strikers. Whilst Dickenson (1984) and Gennard (1990) both accept this version of events, it is deeply puzzling that a verbal agreement reached at a meeting held under auspices of ACAS was not, as is the norm, immediately typed up by the ACAS officer and signed by the parties involved. Whatever the facts of the matter, interviewees agreed that the failure of Messenger Group to abide by the 'agreement' created intense anger inside the NGA, which led them to escalate the picketing at Warrington, even though their previous efforts had not stopped the paper's distribution and had led to many injuries along with the fines and sequestration.

In retrospect many NGA officers and activists openly questioned this decision as did Gennard (1984: 11) in his overwhelmingly supportive account of the dispute. Asked to reflect on the NGA tactics immediately post the 27 November 1983 many senior officials and activists had remarkably similar views. These are encapsulated in one officer's recollections:

> Tony definitely believed he had a negotiated a resolution that Sunday and he told not just Joe, but also Bill Keys. When on the Monday Shah welshed on the deal Tony was absolutely raging. There we were with our funds seized by the bloody Courts and this arsehole Shah was pissing us about. We wanted to hit back hard at him. Hence plans were made to organise a truly huge mass picket.

The role played in this policy choice by anger and frustration was a common theme in contributors' memories of the time. It was an emotion that was unsurprising, given that the historically powerful NGA were unused to being treated with such contempt by any employer. The annoyance the NGA felt was, some contributors believed, heightened by the fact that Tony Dubbins had informed Bill Keys that an 'agreement' had been reached on the Sunday evening. That Keys was one of the first people Dubbins called is significant; it reflects the strong relationship that had developed between Dubbins, Wade and Keys during the dispute. As a senior SOGAT officer of the time observed:

> There was great respect from the NGA leadership for Bill's efforts throughout the Warrington dispute, which grew further when he convinced the NEC to support the NGA when they were sequestrated.

The strong personal rapport between the print unions' leaders had seen a marked improvement in relations between their unions, which, was not to continue after Bill Keys was replaced by Brenda Dean. Here again the effect on inter union relations of micro-political as well as ideological and industrial factors is evident.

On the night of 29 November the NGA, in a remarkable logistical effort, succeeded in transporting 4,000 members to the Warrington picket line. Given the location of the plant, the sub-zero temperatures and the short notice, this was a tremendous feat for a union of only 120,000 members. The pickets were met by 2,000 Cheshire Police, whose Chief Constable had received an open letter from the then Home Secretary, Leon Brittan, making it clear that under no circumstances should pickets be allowed to stop the Messenger newspapers being published and distributed. The Police engaged in a series of baton charges at picket lines, which resulted in hundreds of people being injured, whilst dozens of pickets were also arrested. This tactic, which as Geary (1985) notes had been developed by British colonial police forces in Northern Ireland and Hong Kong to deal with 'serious violent disorder', was now being deployed in Britain to deal with industrial disputes.

On the morning of the 30 November the NGA senior national officers, who had been in meetings at the TUC the night before, were horrified at the scale of injuries sustained by their members and activists. They were now acutely aware of the lengths the Police, strongly encouraged by the Conservative Government, would go to support the Messenger Newspaper Group. An NGA officer close to Wade and Dubbins recalls that the decision to abandon mass picketing was taken that morning:

> Both Joe and Tony realised that they couldn't ask our members to undertake a mass picket of Warrington again after so many of them had taken such a terrible kicking. They realised they had to try and find another way to win the dispute.

The NGA leadership now entered into a further intense round of formal and informal meetings over how best to conduct the dispute, whilst protecting the overall viability of the union and its continuing ability to retain influence over the labour process in the rest of the industry. The need to do so was made even more pressing when on 9 December, at another High Court hearing, the NGA were fined a further £525,000, for their continued secondary action.

The following day, when the NGA NC met, they were faced with what one interviewee described as, "a number of very grave problems". All efforts to deploy selective secondary action had so far failed to force Messenger Newspaper Group to settle the dispute, but had seen the NGA incur huge fines. Mass picketing had failed to stop the Messenger newspapers production and distribution, but had resulted in a large number of pickets being injured or arrested. Financially the NGA's decision to disregard Court Orders and to refuse to co-operate with the sequestrators had resulted in the union's financial viability being at risk.

In seeking to address these difficulties, a number of different policy alternatives were put forward. A number of NGA London Region delegates proposed that the union should withdraw from the dispute, place the six members in new jobs, and purge their contempt of court, thereby saving the NGA from financial ruin. Another suggestion, put forward by members of the small NGA BL, involved the call for a national strike of all members. Both of these propositions were opposed by the union's senior officers, who were unconvinced that a national strike would force Messenger Newspaper Group, with its non-union workforce, to reach an agreement. They were however acutely aware that simply abandoning the strike could have disastrous internal consequences, because so many activists wanted to see the dispute escalated, not cancelled. There were also concerns amongst the senior officials that conceding defeat would encourage employers to attack the closed shop and the NGA's ability to influence the labour process across all sectors of the industry.

The solution Joe Wade and other senior officers proposed was intriguing. They stated that the NGA should call on the TUC to implement its 1982 Special Conference policies in full, thereby giving substantial financial support to the union. Without such support, and with the continued sequestration of the union, the senior officers stated they believed the dispute could not be won and would have to be abandoned. A lengthy, and what many contributors described as an angry debate ensued, which lasted nearly eight hours. Finally a new policy position was agreed by the NC. The union would call a national one day strike of all NGA members on 14 December 1983, but only if the TUC indicated that they were prepared to issue a statement of support for the union's position.

On the 12th December the TUC Employment, Policy and Organisation Committee (EPOC) met and a motion offering the support the NGA sought was passed. However later that evening TUC General Secretary, Len Murray, made a statement that TUC policy was not dictated by its EPOC and that the TUC would not be issuing any statement of support for the NGA, unless the General Council instructed him to do so. The NGA NC met on 13 December and postponed the national strike set for the 14 until the outcome of TUC General Council, which met later that day. At a well-attended TUC General Council, a lengthy and often bitter debate took place which resulted in the TUC refusing to issue a statement of support. On 15 December the NGA NC reconvened and agreed unanimously not to proceed with the national strike. They also resolved to continue the strike but not to take any further illegal industrial action. In reality, as interviewees conceded, this marked the end of all serious efforts to win the dispute. At a further meeting on 18 January 1984, the NC having received reports that negotiations with Messenger Newspaper Group had failed to make progress agreed, with the Fineward chapel's support, to purge their contempt of court so that the NGA could come out of sequestration.

The manner in which the NGA NC adopted a policy which, de facto, moved responsibility for the prosecution of the dispute into the hands of the TUC is significant. In recollecting the reasons behind this change in policy direction, there was a split between those NC members and officers who stated that the policy simply reflected the reality that the dispute could not continue without active TUC support, and those who believed that seeking an endorsement for unlawful secondary action from the TUC was a manoeuvre by senior officers to extricate themselves from the dispute by proxy.

Those who put forward the latter view focus on the fact that a TUC statement of support was of little practical significance. As one former NGA National Officer commented:

> The request for a TUC statement of support was a smokescreen. We all knew that the Right wing unions wouldn't lift a finger to help us. But their predictable decision not to even issue a pathetic statement of support allowed Tony and Joe to convince some weak NC members that they had sufficient reason to abandon the strike. It

was a convenient way out, and allowed a lot of the NC who had been under intense pressure from their chapels and branches to support a national strike, to get off the hook when they supported abandoning the strike.

This interpretation is flatly denied by many former senior officials of the NGA, who remain adamant they could not continue without TUC support. Yet others, who supported the decision not to proceed without the TUC statement, did give substance to the allegation, whilst defending the decision. As one former officer observed:

> Yes we did know that the General Council were unlikely to back us, but by December 10th we needed to find a way to persuade the majority of the NC that the truth was we couldn't continue with the dispute, because it threatened to destroy the union. By insisting on TUC support for a national strike it allowed delegates to report back that they had supported a national strike, without placing the Union in jeopardy, which would have happened if it had gone ahead and we had been fined. It also helped to avoid massive recriminations when we had to bring the dispute to a conclusion without a settlement.

If this was indeed the true purpose of the policy decision of 10 December 1983, it was broadly successful. In the main, as Dickinson (1984: 188–96) notes and interviewees confirmed, NGA activists and members blamed the TUC, not their leadership, for what was a major industrial defeat.

The rich and often complex nature of policy formation with various groups and individuals needing to be able to justify their actions to their constituents, whilst following a subtly different course to that which they have been mandated, are ably demonstrated by the NGA's NC policy debate and decision of 10 December 1983. Nearly thirty years on after the NC debate, the policy choice is still shrouded in ambiguity and acrimony. As many interviewees who were involved candidly admitted, the reason for continued controversy rests on their desire not to be portrayed as having acted disingenuously, in order to engineer an end to an unsuccessful dispute.

The labour process: after the Messenger dispute

Following the conclusion of the Messenger Newspaper Group strike there was what one interviewee described as "noticeable alteration in attitude rather than formal policy" within the NGA. The changes, as other contributors agreed, manifested themselves in a more cautious approach to the use of 'blacking', a distancing of the official union from unofficial action and a reluctance to deploy mass pickets. These were not official policy changes, but they were alterations in behaviour which all NGA interviewees noted. There was also what a number of interviewees characterised as 'a draining of confidence' amongst officials and activists in the traditional industrial methods the NGA had deployed to defend its remarkable level of control over the labour process. As one senior lay activist from the regional newspapers commented:

> Post Warrington there was a definite shift in the balance of power at the workplace. The employers were cockier and we were, in truth, less certain of our ability to effectively defend ourselves.

These changes also affected SOGAT, whose leadership was increasingly aware of what one former officer described as "increasingly bullish employers' attitudes". These findings support Kelly's (1998) assertion that in the 1980s there was an employer and State counter-offensive against powerful trade unions.

It was in this rapidly changing industrial environment that both unions found themselves electing new General Secretaries. The NGA membership, following the retirement of Joe Wade in 1984, elected Tony Dubbins who, as many contributors stated, had been viewed the heir apparent since the mid-1970s. Importantly Dubbins had managed to keep his reputation intact after the loss of the Messenger dispute. Dubbins took up office in 1984, which was the same year that SOGAT's Bill Keys announced he would be retiring.

Following Keys' early retirement announcement, a campaign was launched by a number of senior North Western branch secretaries to get the union's President, Brenda Dean, nominated for the post of General Secretary. This was a bold tactical move, as SOGAT had an overwhelmingly male membership and there was a widely held belief, as all interviewees confirmed, that they would not elect a female General Secretary. In addition Dean, unlike all previous NATSOPA and SOGAT General Secretaries, did not emanate from one of the London production branches, instead she had worked as a secretary in a Lancashire printing company, before working her way up to become the Manchester Branch Secretary and National President. Her remarkable rise, as contributors acknowledged, owed much to her considerable skills as an organiser and administrator, which were complemented by her poise and ability as a public speaker. Under her leadership, the Manchester branch had grown to become the largest branch outside of London.

Aside from the obvious gender, industrial and geographical differences, Dean's attitudes and negotiating style were also very different from that practised by the powerful Fleet Street chapels and the large London branches. As Chapter 3 described, their traditions were closely aligned to that of the printing craft unions, which often involved a robust negotiating style and the use of industrial action in order to gain, and retain, control over the labour supply and the labour process. Dean, who in her role as Manchester Branch Secretary negotiated directly with the national newspaper employers, adopted a less aggressive and more conciliatory attitude than the SOGAT Fleet Street chapels FoC's and London branch secretaries. As a SOGAT branch secretary of the time recollects:

> There was a culture clash between Brenda and the Fleet Street FoC's. Brenda would research and prepare her case prior to entering negotiations and once there she would reason and cajole management into accepting the union's position. On the other hand the Fleet Street Chapels simply told the management what they wanted and that if they didn't get it, then their paper wouldn't be coming out. It really pissed them and the NGA off, if Brenda was able to negotiate the better deal.

Dean's active support for Keys' 'Programme for Action' policy, along with her public backing of the London Women's branch in an internal demarcation dispute with SOGAT's largest branch, London Central branch (LCB), at Format International in the late 1970s, only added to the antipathy between her and London branches. This antipathy convinced many commentators, as Gennard and Bain note (1995), that Dean could not be successful in the General Secretary election. Interviewees agreed that her victory came as a surprise to many and owed much to her extremely well run campaign and Dean's considerable personal charm. The large number of candidates (twelve in total), the lack of coherent national political factions, plus the decline in membership strength of the previously dominant London branches, also contributed to Dean's victory.

Upon taking up office Dubbins and Dean were faced with fresh challenges to their unions' influence over the labour process, in both national and regional newspapers. These confrontations often involved employers seeking to introduce direct text inputting and new production machinery, the deployment of which they sought to link to new collective agreements involving only one union. This led to a series of disputes between SOGAT and the NGA over who should retain coverage, less than a year after the two unions' leaders had worked so closely during the Messenger Newspaper dispute. The relationship between the two unions swiftly became highly acrimonious, with Tony Dubbins launching a public attack on SOGAT in the NGA's journal (July, 1985) following SOGAT members crossing NGA picket lines during strikes at the Wolverhampton Express and Star and the Kent Messenger. Dubbins wrote, 'I have never seen, from a TUC affiliated union, such acts of treachery and opportunist behaviour' (July, 1985: 4). Such public accusations were rare, even in the printing unions' often troubled history, and the SOGAT leadership were so incensed that they went to the considerable cost of publishing a special edition of their journal in order to publicly refute the charges made against them and to counter that the NGA were attempting to undermine their News International machine minders' recognition agreement (July 1985: 2).

Asked why relations between the unions had worsened so rapidly and dramatically participants from both unions, focused principally on the dysfunctional personal relationship that existed between Tony Dubbins and Brenda Dean, rather than political or industrial differences between the unions. As a former NGA officer related:

They were very different people, with different views and attitudes. Whereas Joe and
Bill were similar people who were both from the print and would be able to sort out
their differences, Tony and Brenda were very different. He was from the print and
he understood his members and was happy in their company. Brenda was different,
she was very charming and pleasant, and came across really well in the media, but
she never seemed comfortable with the type of trade unionism that Tony believed
in. That I think always placed a distance between them; a distance that never existed
between Joe and Bill.

These reflections, and those of other NGA officials, often stressed Dean's
failure to have worked 'in the print'. A number of SOGAT supporters of
Dean believe that these views illustrate an inherent insularity and sexism
amongst NGA officers and activists, a view that Cockburn (1983, 1991)
endorses. As one SOGAT activist commented:

Look the NGA wasn't known as No Girls Allowed for nothing. I was never a fan of
Brenda's politics or her industrial policies, but if anyone ever tells you that she wasn't
the victim of male chauvinism, they're either daft or lying.

Whatever the reasons for their strained relationship, the antipathy that
existed between Dean and Dubbins meant that when inter-union disputes
occurred, there was not the same ability that Keys and Wade had had to
informally resolve such conflicts. This is another example of micro-political factors having a powerful effect on inter-union relations and policy
direction.

By the latter half of 1985 a series of major industrial problems were
besetting both unions in national as well as regional newspapers. Robert
Maxwell's Mirror Group Newspapers (MGN) was seeking to move the
publication of his newspapers out of London, and to re-negotiate working
practices and staffing levels. Following a brief period of industrial action,
when employees stopped work to attend chapel meetings on 21 August
1985, Maxwell dismissed all 4,500 NGA and SOGAT members. This
type of behaviour was not unusual for Maxwell, who by the mid 1980s
was, according to a NGA National Officer, "volatile, contradictory, and
totally unstable". The MGN membership was only reinstated on the 12th
September, when an agreement was finally reached over the relocation of
The Sporting Life. In the same period there was unofficial industrial action

at the *Financial Times* over staffing levels and the NGA's bête noir, Eddie Shah, concluded a single union deal with the EETPU for their members to print his new national daily paper *Today*. It was during this period of considerable industrial strife and inter-union conflict that rumours started to circulate that News International was preparing to produce all of its papers at its new Wapping site, whilst planning to replace the whole of its current production workforce.

The News International Dispute

The rumours as to the plans News International had for the Wapping site came from inside the plant itself. Importantly it was chapel officers from the AUEW and the SOGAT Revisers and Ink Roller Manufacture Auxiliaries (RIRMA) branch, who knew workers fitting out the plant, who first leaked the information about the company's plans to produce all their titles at Wapping without their current workforce. Although the RIRMA branch were sufficiently concerned that they organised an open meeting in June 1985, which all the News International chapels and the London branches were invited too, not one FoC attended from the other News International chapels. As interviewees admit, the reasons why they failed to attend arc shrouded in controversy. Many interviewees point out that the Fleet Street chapels and branches operated a highly hierarchical system, which led the production and composition chapel FoC's to doubt information provided by maintenance chapel activists. As a former News International FoC explained:

> The assistants were at the bottom of the food chain. As far as the production and pre-press chapels were concerned no bloody tool carrier could tell them anything about printing newspapers.

Other contributors, while acknowledging that craft prejudices were a factor, also point out that fallacious rumours were common in Fleet Street and that News International were constantly reassuring the FoCs that their members would be going to Wapping if they negotiated staffing reductions. As one News International FoC recalled:

> If truth be told we didn't want to believe that the paper could be produced without our members. So we believed Murdoch's managers when they assured us that after any move to Wapping we'd still be printing his titles. It was, I admit, a terrible bloody error.

These negotiations had been on-going throughout the latter part of 1984 and had resulted in January 1985 in the *News of the World* Machine Chapel reaching an agreement with the company over machine room staffing levels when the transfer to Wapping took place (Gennard and Bain; 1995: 604).

The information obtained by the RIRMA branch had however created greater concern amongst SOGAT and NGA senior national officers. Brenda Dean and Bill Miles, the SOGAT National Officer for the national newspapers, were sufficiently concerned to arrange to meet Tony Cappi the RIRMA chapel officer who had obtained the information. As a result Dean held a meeting with *The Sun* and the *News of the World* IFoC's and FoC's which resulted in an urgent meeting being arranged with the NGA and News International. At the meeting News International gave further categorical assurances that all the activity at Wapping was owing to the company preparing to launch *The Post*, and that the transfer of location discussions would be completed in the next couple of months. The unions were also told that Rupert Murdoch would meet with them at the end of September 1985. In addition to this meeting there were also discussions with the EETPU (Electrical, Electronics and Plumbing Trade Union) who explicitly stated that their members working at Wapping were only installing and testing equipment. Although still concerned, both national leaderships, the branches and the chapels, all agreed to continue to negotiate with News International.

In early September, the assurances the unions had been given were thrown into question when a copy of *The Sun* newspaper, which had been produced at Wapping, was smuggled out of the plant and given to the unions. According to senior officers of both unions there was a strong assumption that the physical production of a newspaper was proof that the EETPU members in Wapping were running, not simply installing the presses. There was also a strong belief, contributors stated, that this would result in unofficial strike action by the chapels at News International.

Such action as Bain (1998: 103) and Richardson (2002: 91) point out would have had a devastating effect on Rupert Murdoch's plans to relocate News international to Wapping, as he was not then ready to produce newspapers at the new plant. Shawcross goes further, asserting that Murdoch was so financially exposed in the USA at the time that he could not have financially withstood the loss of revenue caused by a strike on *The Sun* and *The News of the World*, which were Murdoch's "cash cows" (Shawcross, 1992: 334–7). These assertions are all substantiated by then then editor of the *Sunday Times*, Andrew Neill (1997: 154). Interviewees agree that the decision not to take action in early September played a decisive role in the print unions' eventual industrial defeat at News International, a view which is endorsed by a number of other authors (Gennard, 1988; 1990; Gennard and Bain, 1995; Bain, 1998; Melvern, 1986; Littleton, 1992; Richardson, 2003). As a former SOGAT officer stated:

> That was it. That was our great chance. If we had gone then we could have won. He was not ready to produce his papers without us, and we now know how financially stretched he was. I'm certain he'd have cut his losses and our people would have been in Wapping.

The reasons why the News International chapels decided not to take industrial action in early September 1985 were complex and subject to host of different interpretations, which themselves reflect the diverse and multifaceted forces that played a part in shaping major policy decisions. In recalling these events all contributors accepted that on Friday 6 September 1985 the IFoC's and the FoC's of *The Sun* LCB Chapel met with the branch committee and decided not to call for unofficial action before the meeting with Murdoch later in the month. The London Machine Branch (LMB) committee also met with their News International FoC's and they resolved to recommend an immediate 24 hour strike, to a meeting of all their News International membership. At that meeting the LMB News International members voted 520 to 306 not to take industrial action. The respective NGA chapels, in the wake of this meeting, also chose not to take action, citing the resolutions of the larger SOGAT chapels as the primary reason for their decisions.

It is the reasons behind these crucial policy choices which are highly contentious. The LMB and LCB officers are adamant that the General Secretary's decision to make it known that she wanted no unofficial action before they met Murdoch affected the outcome of the respective meetings. Those close to Dean have a different version of events; they state that whilst she made no call for unofficial strike action, she did not intervene to try and stop the chapels from taking unofficial action, which, knowing them well, she had expected. Former senior national officers of the NGA are also clear that they expected their *Sun* and *News of the World* chapels to take unofficial industrial action.

Pressed over why London branch NEC members should have portrayed Dean as being hostile to unofficial action, the SOGAT senior officers stated it was either a deliberate misrepresentation or a misunderstanding of the public position that both unions had to take in order to avoid legal action. These assertions are denied by those close to the NEC members involved, who are adamant that the official and unofficial line emanating from SOGAT and the NGA's headquarters was that action should not be taken until after the Murdoch meeting. A number of former SOGAT and NGA national officers, support this view, stating that whilst the two General Secretaries expected unofficial strikes in early September they were against such action. As one former SOGAT officer recalled:

> At the time we were in a major conflict with Maxwell. Brenda loathed Maxwell and wanted Murdoch to print more copies of *The Sun*, to replace *The Mirror* where our people were locked out. She certainly wasn't keen on having a dispute with Murdoch as she thought this would be a case of fighting on too many fronts at once.

Whilst Dean (2008) agrees that she had a deep personal loathing for Maxwell and preferred to deal with Murdoch (which is another example of the influence of micro-political factors on union policy makers) she and other interviewees dispute that the leadership of the two unions opposed instantaneous action by the News International chapels.

Whatever the truth of the role played by Brenda Dean, it is undeniable that in many previous instances the Fleet Street chapels had often taken action without the support of the national union. Whether therefore any alleged intervention by either General Secretary could have had a significant effect on the decision of the Fleet Street chapel activists and members is questionable. These doubts are given further credence by the views of members and FoC's who were present at the various meetings. As a News International SOGAT FoC stated:

> I spoke and voted in favour of taking action. But before and after the meeting a lot of blokes were saying; why are we always taking action? We had supported Warrington and the Miners and some lads were pissed off at how they had lost money supporting disputes which had been lost. You could see some of them didn't want another fight. The position of national office was not relevant at all.

A former senior Fleet Street personnel manager reflected on the mood in the chapels at this time:

> A lot of the chapels put an enormous amount of time and resources into supporting the Miners strike. When the NUM lost their strike, it was a big body blow to their morale and self-confidence.

Having decided not to act in early September 1985 the unions met Murdoch at the end of the month, where he stated that he wished 'in a spirit of unity' to reach an agreement with the print unions by Christmas over *The London Post* and the move of *The Sun* and the *News of the World* to Wapping (Bain, 1998: 80). However following the meeting his management team proceeded to present a list of demands (which was dubbed by the chapels, 'The serfs' charter'), which included: no negotiations with chapels or branches, no closed shops, no industrial action, total flexibility, legally binding collective agreements and the right of management to decide staffing levels, work methods, and whether new technology was to be introduced (Littleton, 1992: 68–9). In other words total managerial control of all aspects of the labour process.

All the print unions, including the EETPU, initially rejected the proposals, whilst stating they were willing to negotiate on greater flexibility and avoiding disruption. At a meeting with the company on 10 December, the EETPU broke ranks and said it was prepared to accept News International's demands. Complaints were made by the NGA and

SOGAT to the TUC over the EETPU's behaviour, which were initially upheld before being overturned at a subsequent TUC General Council. The NGA and SOGAT also sought assurances from News International about job security for its members on its established titles, whilst presenting the annual wage claim for 1986. News International rejected the claim and stated it would no longer negotiate with SOGAT, the NGA, or the AUEW and on 6 January 1986 the company served a six month notice of termination of all its collective agreements.

Now clear that the company were planning to derecognise them, SOGAT and the NGA chose to remain within the legislation and instituted a strike ballot of their News International members. SOGAT members voted 3,534 – 52 in favour of strike action, whilst the NGA's membership voted by 843 – 117 votes to go on strike. The unions continued to try and negotiate an agreement for the transfer of work to Wapping and on the 23 January 1986 they met Murdoch himself again. He refused to move on any of his labour process and bargaining demands, and offered to keep only a few hundred jobs for current printing staff in the company's production sites outside of Wapping. He also made it clear there would be at least 4,000 redundancies.

At this stage there was unanimity between the affected chapels, branches and the national union leaderships that official strikes now had to be declared. Whilst there was still simmering disagreement over who was responsible for the unions finding themselves in this position, these conflicts were less pronounced whilst the different tiers of the two unions remained united over how to conduct the dispute.

On 24 January 1986 SOGAT's NEC issued notice of an official strike, as did the NGA and the AUEW. The company responded on 25 January by dismissing all of the strikers. In doing so the company was acting upon legal advice that, thanks to the 1982 Employment Act, they could avoid paying the striking workers redundancy compensation if they dismissed *all* those taking part in strike action. The two major print unions, from the start of the dispute, realised that in order to change Murdoch's decision to dismiss their membership and hire an alternative workforce they had to disrupt News International's ability to publish and distribute their titles. Equally as important, the unions' national officers, owing to the size and strategic importance of the dispute, took direct responsibility for negotiations, somewhat to the annoyance of the relevant chapels and branches. It quickly became evident that the company had switched to using TNT, an Australian distribution company to move all of their papers by road, not rail, to the wholesalers' distribution depots, rendering any support from the rail unions ineffective.

In order to counteract this distribution ploy SOGAT and the NGA initially adopted two specific tactics, which were endorsed by the relevant chapels and branches as well as the national union executives. The first comprised a twenty-four hour picket of the Wapping site, which the chapels organised and was well attended by the dismissed members. The aim of the picket was to stop or delay TNT vehicles from exiting the plant. Unlike at Messenger Group, the unions realised that if their picket lines could seriously delay the distribution of News International titles, the time sensitive nature of the daily newspaper market meant that they could totally derail the company's distribution operation. The second part of the strategy involved SOGAT seeking to persuade its members in the newspaper wholesalers to refuse to handle News International titles.

On paper this second element of the unions plan seemed powerful, as SOGAT possessed post entry closed shops in all three of the largest wholesalers; John Menzies, W.H. Smith and Surridge Dawson. In some areas such as London, Glasgow and Liverpool the action was immediately effective, but in many other areas the SOGAT closed shop had in reality ceased to function, with large numbers of part-time, low paid, workers not in the union and weak workplace organisation (Richardson, 2003: 10). This organisational frailty had been highlighted by the National Officer, Bill Miles, at the 1983 BDC, yet the problem had not been remedied by 1986. Alongside this organisational difficulty it also became clear to senior SOGAT officers that there was a major difficulty in persuading provincial wholesale activists and members to take secondary action. As a former SOGAT branch secretary for a small provincial branch recollects:

> The London branches weren't well liked and many of our members viewed Fleet Street members as arrogant and over paid. Their earnings in comparison to our members were colossal, and this caused a lot of resentment. Add to this that our members could get sacked for refusing to handle Murdoch's papers and you can see the problems we faced.

Another NEC member whose branch did support the secondary action gave a subtly different explanation:

> Look a lot of the senior provincial branch secretaries weren't fans of the Fleet Street FoCs and they certainly weren't busting a gut to make sure secondary action was taken at the wholesalers.

These micro-political animosities were confirmed by other contributors and figure large in Dean's (2008) own account of the dispute. Here the difficulties caused by the personal antagonism that existed between the London branch officers and a number of the provincial branch secretaries figure very prominently. Allied to these micro-political problems were the sectional rivalries that survived between former officers and activists of NATSOPA and SOGAT, many of whom still harboured resentments over the manner in which NATSOPA had seceded from the SOGAT in 1972. Whichever of these factors was the primary motivation for the half-hearted response of many provincial branches, their lack of action proved to be a considerable handicap in the dispute.

To add to SOGAT's and the NGA's problems in stopping the distribution of News International titles, the unions were unsuccessful in the High Court in defending their secondary action. Injunctions were issued against SOGAT for instructing members not to handle News International papers, whilst both unions were prohibited from attempting to stop TNT from distributing News International papers. The Post Office was also successful in gaining an injunction against the UCW for directing their members not to deliver *Sun* bingo cards. Finally the NGA's instruction to members not to print News International supplements was deemed unlawful, which after a very close workplace ballot resulted in NGA members resuming the printing of the supplements.

Although the unions were suffering a series of legal reverses, the first part of their strategy, to stage a mass picket of the Wapping plant, was having a considerable effect. TNT lorries were badly delayed in leaving the plant which meant that papers arrived at the wholesalers too late to be delivered onto newsagents. News International revenue was badly affected and in January 1986 a deeply concerned Rupert Murdoch spoke to the

Home Secretary and the Prime Minister, and gained assurances that in future the Police would do all in their power to ensure that Newspapers got out of Wapping on time (Neill, 1997; Shawcross, 1992). In the following weeks the Metropolitan Police went to extraordinary lengths to ensure TNT vehicles exited the plant promptly. Roads around the plant were regularly sealed off, local residents were not allowed to leave or enter their homes at certain times, and TNT lorries were allowed to flout traffic laws on a regular and systematic basis. Whenever there were large demonstrations organised by the unions outside the plant, hundreds and on occasion thousands, of Metropolitan Police would be deployed in full riot gear and there were numerous incidents of police, sometimes on horseback, baton charging picket lines and causing serious injuries.

Inside the two print unions there was intense debate as to how to best respond to legal action and the Police violence. The two unions picketing policy, unlike in the Messenger dispute, resided predominantly in the hands of the News International chapels and branches. They drew up the picketing rosters, paid strike pay and organised rallies and demonstrations. Even in the face of increasingly violent police tactics, the News International chapels were adamant in discussions with national officers that the mass picket should remain in place, owing to the disruption it was causing to the newspapers distribution. This was a policy that was largely supported at this stage by the two national unions. The SOGAT NEC and the NGA's NC response to the High Court's injunctions was also similar; they both refused to withdraw their explicit instructions to their members not to handle News International titles. These decisions were in line with the two unions' conference policies, and were viewed by a large majority of policy makers, as critical to the successful prosecution of the dispute. As a consequence of their refusal to call off secondary action SOGAT were again taken to the High Court, where on 10 February 1986 they were found to be in contempt of court, resulting in a £25,000 fine and the sequestration of all their assets. The High Court further ruled that the union could only come out of sequestration if it purged its contempt of court.

It was at this stage that Brenda Dean took the decision that, unlike the NGA or NUM during their periods of sequestration, SOGAT would fully co-operate with the sequestrators. This decision incensed many SOGAT officers and activists, particularly those from News International. As a then London branch secretary reflected:

> Why the hell would you want to help the Sequestrators? What we should have done is moved money onto sympathetic third parties or converted it into cash. We knew when we refused to stop taking secondary action that we would face sequestration. Yet we did nothing to salt money away. I thought at the time, that Dean's behaviour was very fishy, now I'm sure she was up to no good.

Another SOGAT officer who was hostile to Brenda Dean was blunt:

> Brenda never wanted to be in contempt of court. I'm sure she thought if we allowed the sequestrators to stop the union functioning effectively, then the provincial branches would support her in purging our contempt.

This conspiratorial view of Dean's actions is dismissed by her supporters who point to the manner in which she skilfully articulated the sacked members' case at meetings and via the media. The reason, they state, that Dean in conjunction with other senior SOGAT officers agreed to co-operate was in order to appear as a reasonable law abiding trade union, which had been placed in contempt of court by unjust laws (see also Dean, 2007).

The fissures, which as Chapter 4 documented, had always been present between different elements within SOGAT, now started to widen dramatically. The issues the various parties disagreed over were wider than just the prosecution of the News International dispute. They also now encompassed how the union should be attempting to defend its influence over the labour process in the industry as a whole. Broadly the union split into two camps with the London branches and a small BL group on one side and the General Secretary and the full-time branch secretaries from many of the large provincial branches on the other.

The London branches and the BL's supporters pressed for an escalation of the secondary action in the News International dispute, including a stoppage on all the national newspapers and if necessary a national strike of all SOGAT members. There was also a smaller element from the London branches, who wished to take direct physical action against News

International's production premises.[7] More broadly this group also argued that it was imperative that SOGAT prepared itself to take industrial action in order to defend its members against the growing trend of employers who were unilaterally introducing new technology and weakening the union's influence over the labour process. Taking the opposite view, the General Secretary and her supporters favoured staying, wherever possible, within the law and in protecting the ability of the union to function for all its members, many of whom were not involved in the dispute. To this end they were particularly concerned that the sequestrators were not able to seize the considerable funds of the SOGAT branches. Across the industry those supporting the General Secretary also wished to engage with employers in order to try and negotiate the introduction of new technology, which they viewed as inevitable.

The debates over the prosecution of the News International dispute, and the disagreements over how the union nationally should counter employers' attempts to undermine SOGAT's influence over the labour process, whilst unilaterally introducing new technology, are further examples of unions making strategic choices. These choices were made at the local as well as the national level in a manner that Kelly and Heery contended would be the case (Heery and Kelly, 1988; Kelly and Heery, 1994; Heery, 2003, 2006). The influence of occupational, geographical and micro-political factors in shaping these policy decisions was also apparent.

Added to the mounting internal policy disagreements within SOGAT, there were also growing policy differences with the NGA. Inside the NGA there was apprehension that the union, having been fined £25,000 by the courts for taking secondary action, was in a position where SOGAT's policy decisions could leave the NGA exposed. A former senior officer of the NGA explained their position:

---

7   These plans revolved around a physical attack on the Wapping printing plant. Interviews and further research suggest these were serious plans, involving third parties, who had the knowhow and equipment necessary to cause serious damage to the News International plants.

> Remember this was primarily a SOGAT dispute. They had over 4,000 members involved whilst we had only 900. There was no way that we were going to escalate our secondary action and get ourselves sequestrated, only to find that Dean had done a secret deal with Murdoch.

These doubts about the commitment of the SOGAT leadership to the dispute were repeated by a number of former NGA lay and full-time officers and reflected a fundamental lack of trust between the unions' leaders. Unsurprisingly many former SOGAT officers have a different explanation for the NGA's approach to the dispute. One ex-SOGAT officer's comment encapsulates their views:

> The NGA remained behind the scenes throughout the dispute. They knew that Brenda was a far better spokesperson than Dubbins. She came across well on the TV, where she did a tremendous job putting the sacked workers' case. The truth is the NGA were keen not to get sequestrated in the way they did at Warrington. So it suited them for SOGAT to take all the hard decisions in the dispute, and then claim that as a minority union they could not go 'out on a limb'. That way they didn't cop the flak we did from their chapels.

These quotes illustrate the distrust that existed between SOGAT and the NGA, which, interviewees from both sides agree, was greatly exacerbated by the dysfunctional relationship that existed between Dean and Dubbins. Contributors agreed that the distrust they had for one another proved to be a handicap in negotiations and in the efforts being made by SOGAT officers to try and get the News International chapels and branches to work with their own General Secretary. As a former SOGAT National Officer commented:

> Unlike at Warrington, where Bill busted his balls to help the NGA, at Wapping I always had the feeling that behind the scenes Tony was making trouble for us.

By March 1986 the internal policy divisions inside SOGAT had worsened. Sequestration had meant that all the national union accounts were frozen, officers' cars were impounded and crucially the High Court had further ruled that the sequestration extended to chapel and branch funds. These actions made the core activities of the union, in particular full-time and lay officers conducting negotiations and representing members at disciplinary and grievance hearings, extremely problematic. SOGAT's decision to co-operate fully with the sequestrators also meant there was no illicit cash held by the union, or its supporters, to pay for its core operations. These effects of the sequestration led the NEC to call a meeting of all branch secretaries on 14 April 1986 to discuss how to respond. There was, participants' recall, an impassioned debate, with many of the branch secretaries from the provinces calling for the 'contempt of court' to be purged so that the union could regain the use of their assets and function normally. On the other hand the London branch secretaries accused those seeking to purge the union's contempt of court of betraying the members in dispute.

The majority of the branch secretaries supported Dean's position, which was that the union should await the outcome of their legal challenge to the sequestration of SOGAT branches funds. At the subsequent NEC on the 21 April there was a further delay in deciding whether to purge the union's contempt of court. Interviewees, from both sides, agree that although the majority of the NEC was now in favour of purging the contempt of court, but that they held off for tactical reasons, related to the mass rally and picket due at Wapping on 3 May. This was also the date the News International members, who had marched all the way from Kinning Park in Scotland, were due to arrive at Wapping. The rally was attended by over 12,000 people and was met by what one interviewee described as a "frightening degree of force" by the Police. Over 250 demonstrators were injured when mounted Police staged a series of charges into the picket line.

On 6 May 1986 the branch secretaries and subsequently the NEC both met again. The Court of Appeal had by this time ruled that some 80 SOGAT branches funds were separate from the assets of the national union and were therefore released from sequestration, but that the other branches funds would remain sequestrated. At their meeting the branch secretaries and then the NEC (by 22 votes to 11) agreed to purge their contempt of court. The majority opinion, supported by senior officers, was that the 'blacking' was not working outside of London and it was nonsensical for the union to be sequestrated over a policy that was ineffective. Unsurprisingly the London delegates were incensed, with one describing the decision as "a total betrayal". Two days later Dean withdrew the instruction to members not to handle News International papers and purged SOGAT's contempt of court, thereby gaining release of the union's funds.

The abandonment of the secondary action caused the London District Committee of SOGAT which was comprised of the London branches, to register their "disgust and abhorrence" at the actions of the NEC and the General Secretary. They also called upon Dean to explain the NEC's decision at a meeting of News International members on 19 May 1986. By this stage the relationship between the London branches and the General Secretary had deteriorated to such an extent that they both believed that the other's actions were stopping any chance of resolving the dispute. Those close to Dean, thought that a number of the London activists were totally unrealistic in their expectations of how the dispute could be resolved, and were also actively seeking to remove the General Secretary from office. As one former SOGAT officer stated:

> Some of the London branches were intent on using the strike for their own ends. They were wreckers, who did not have the interests of the sacked members at heart, but were simply trying to remove Brenda from office.

On the other side FoCs and activists from the London branches described how they felt the national union had let them down. Their often bitter views are encapsulated in the words of one former News International FoC:

> We felt utterly betrayed. We'd been on the cobbles for over 4 months and now our own union was kicking us in the teeth. Dean and the NEC had never escalated the action, by calling out the other papers or for a general print strike. We'd always stood by other strikers and now, when the chips were down, Dean kicked us in the teeth.

The visceral and highly personal nature of SOGAT's internal conflict was to be heightened by what transpired at the meeting of News International members on 19 May 1986. Prior to the meeting senior officers advised Brenda Dean that owing to the anger of the News International members, it would be unwise for her to attend the meeting. Dean, however, was adamant that as the union's senior officer she would attend to put the NEC's view. The meeting proved to be stormy; jeers and catcalls punctuated Dean's speech, and the questioning was extremely hostile and peppered with personal criticisms. One SOGAT London official who was present commented:

> The only thing that I was thankful for was that there was no violence. Apart from that the meeting was totally bloody awful.

At the end of the meeting a resolution was overwhelmingly carried, calling for the escalation of the dispute and condemning the NEC. During the meeting many of the FoCs had accused the NEC and the General Secretary of undermining the strike, and seeking to destroy the role of chapels in the union, by their centralising of the negotiations with News International.

Following the meeting the division between the two groups became greater still. Those who supported the General Secretary believed that it was unlikely that Murdoch would ever reinstate the sacked workers and that the union should now negotiate an acceptable compensatory settlement. As they stated in their interviews, this would have allowed SOGAT to focus on dealing with other employers who were attacking the union's closed shops and making huge numbers of redundancies, as they unilaterally introduced new technology and outsourced production and distribution roles.

It was these concerns that led Dean, according to her supporters, to engage in secret direct talks with Murdoch and other News International directors, without the knowledge of either the FoCs or the NGA. As a former senior SOGAT officer admitted:

> We deliberately held negotiations with News International without the FoCs or the NGA. If we had tried to do so with some of them, it would have been a complete waste of time.

When they got to hear of the meetings the reaction of the London branches was, unsurprisingly, very angry, with further accusations of treachery and a undermining of the union's constitutional structure. The belief that SOGAT's leadership no longer wished to pursue the dispute was also shared by senior figures in the NGA, as a former national officer recalls:

> By the end of May 1986 a lot of our people got the distinct feeling that she was distancing herself from the strike and was seeking a deal without our input.

Further talks between both print unions and Rupert Murdoch took place at the end of May. At the meeting Murdoch, who was suffering from significant falls in circulation and revenues made an offer which encompassed; redundancy pay, the lifting of the bar on strikers working at Wapping, a review in a year's time of union recognition, and the 'gift' of the Grays Inn Road premises and printing plant. He also offered to lift all legal action, but insisted on a response from the unions within one week.

The NGA considered and then recommended their members reject the offer, with the affected members voting via a workplace ballot conducted by the branches. SOGAT acted quite differently. The NEC decided to dispense with a workplace ballot and instead issued a postal ballot directly to the members involved. Enclosed with the ballot paper was a five page letter from the General Secretary which, without specifically recommending acceptance, encouraged members to vote yes to the offer. Reflecting upon this decision a number of senior officers candidly admitted that the postal ballot was undertaken in order to bypass the influence of the FoC's.

This decision further exacerbated the deep divisions between SOGAT's national leadership and the London branches, not now just over the conduct of the News International strike but also the way in which policy-making was being centralised. The view of the London branches was that the NEC conduct of the News International ballot was contrary to the union's rules. Interviewees from the London branches also recalled that they felt that the NEC and the General Secretary were now seeking to remove policy-making authority from the chapels and branches. So exercised were they that the London Machine Branch sought a High Court injunction to stop the postal ballot. The application failed on what the Court described as 'the balance of convenience' for the union.

The ballot itself resulted in SOGAT members rejecting the offer by 2081 votes to 1415. The NGA membership, at their workplace ballot also voted, by 648 to 165, to reject the offer. As the dispute continued into the latter half of 1986 various alternative strategies were put forward. One of the most remarkable was proposed by a group of senior NGA lay officers who developed a sophisticated plan to enter and occupy the News International Kinning Park site. The arrangements were all in place when, by a narrow majority, the NGA NC rejected the plan, on the grounds that it was too dangerous to those members involved. Significantly in this joint union dispute, the NGA never consulted or involved SOGAT at any stage in the planning of this action, an act which reflected the distrust that existed between the unions.

Soon after the rejection of Murdoch's offer SOGAT's Biennial Conference met in June 1986. Prior to its opening efforts were made to avoid public confrontation over the conduct of the dispute. This proved to be a very difficult set of internal negotiations and in her opening address Dean decided to openly attack what she called 'wreckers' in SOGAT. Many interviewees' stated that her speech was well received by a substantial majority of delegates, which assisted senior NEC members in brokering an agreement with the London branches. This agreement entailed the NEC agreeing to assist in increasing the number of pickets at Wapping and giving an undertaking that any negotiated resolution to the dispute would involve jobs and recognition for the sacked workers. In return the London branches agreed to support the NEC's express position that the union would do everything possible to avoid sequestration. The deal resulted in a relatively peaceful conference with the only major argument occurring over the LMB branch's motion calling for the resumption of blacking of News International titles, which was opposed by the NEC, and then overwhelmingly defeated.

Immediately after the SOGAT BDC there was the increase in picketing at News International. The company took further legal action which resulted in limitations being placed upon picketing and demonstrations at both News International and TNT sites. At this time Neill (1997: 187) states that News International directors still believed they could lose the dispute, leading Murdoch to make what he described as 'his best and last offer. This was a similar to the previous offer, but it did contain the acceptance that SOGAT and the NGA could represent members individually within Wapping. The offer was again rejected by the members of all three unions; with SOGAT members voting 2372 – 960 against the offer, a sizeable increase in the No vote compared to the previous ballot.

After seven months in dispute, and with no sign of a settlement being negotiated that would be acceptable to the members concerned, SOGAT faced mounting financial problems. Although efforts had been made to gain financial support from British and overseas trade unions, the union and its London branches and chapels were incurring huge costs in running the dispute, which when allied to rapidly reducing income levels, led to a financial crisis. Inside the NGA the financial position was slightly better, owing to the smaller number of members involved in the dispute and the larger financial income that the union generated from its relatively high subscription charges. However the financial costs incurred during the Messenger strike, when added to the expenditure on the News International dispute and falling membership income, also meant that the NGA were starting to experience financial difficulties.

As all efforts to negotiate a settlement failed, SOGAT's monetary problems grew worse. Those branches with large numbers of members in dispute were, by the autumn of 1986, in acute financial difficulties as they continued to support their dismissed members. The LCB had spent £500,000 on the dispute, whilst the RIRMA branch had paid out over £750,000, and SOGAT nationally had spent in excess of £3 million. The branches and national union were rapidly approaching a position in which they could not assist the members in dispute. In order to address this crisis, the NEC proposed a temporary six month membership levy of 58 pence per week. The increase was put to the members, and although the union's Journal campaigned for acceptance, it was rejected by 51,187 votes to 44,265. In the recollections of many officers and NEC members, including those from London, this was the point when they knew that it would not be feasible to continue with the dispute. As a former senior SOGAT officer recalled:

> When that vote came in I knew the game was up. It's not like we'd asked for the world – no sympathy strikes, no blacking; all we asked for, was 50p a week for 6 months – and the members said no. Much as I wanted it to be different, I knew that was it.

Shortly after the ballot result was declared, News International sought to exploit SOGAT's weak financial position (Neill, 1996) by issuing writs for contempt of court against the print unions, in relation to their continuing organisation of mass pickets. Dean and other senior officers were advised by their solicitors that the action may well succeed, and the General Secretary called an emergency NEC on 5 February 1987. At the meeting she strongly advised the NEC that to continue with the dispute would result in sequestration, which would be in contravention of BDC policy. Her recommendation therefore was that the NEC should terminate the strike, without a ballot of the members involved. Contact had been made with News International, who stated that they would implement their previous offer and withdraw legal action, if they received a letter from SOGAT terminating the industrial action and all boycotts, within 24 hours. The NEC then voted 23–9 to end the News International dispute. Recalling the vote a SOGAT NEC member stated:

> The vast majority of us felt we had simply no choice. The union could simply not survive another bout of sequestration. If we did not end the strike, then we'd go bust. In those circumstances I felt we had no other option but to end the strike; but I felt physically sick that we ended it without the News International members getting to vote.

The next day, the NGA NC met and agreed, by 27 votes to 5, that they should not carry on the News International dispute alone, and that they would therefore also call off their official action.

These were momentous decisions, not simply because they ended one of the major industrial conflicts of the late twentieth century, but because they did so without the agreement of the members involved. For two unions whose industrial strength had been built on the strength and policy-making autonomy of their chapels and branches, this was a remarkable turn of events. Unsurprisingly the decisions were greeted with incredulity and outrage amongst the News International membership. More than a decade later a former London SOGAT FoC commented:

> For me, it was one of the worst days of my life. I had always been totally loyal to the union. I gave everything in that strike; I lost my house, as well as my job, in trying to defend basic trade union principles. Then my own union betrayed me by ending the strike without a ballot. I literally could not believe it. It was like a waking nightmare.

Views similar to these were expressed by other News International FoC's and members. The anger many felt led to a number of members continuing to picket Wapping unofficially, until they finally withdrew after the London District Council met in February 1987 and passed a motion praising the strikers for their determination and loyalty, but also advising them to apply for their compensation packages.

As sources from within News International admitted (Neill, 1997; Shawcross, 1992), a dispute which had so nearly been won by the unions, finally ended in failure. This defeat, the evidence gathered has shown, was caused in large part by organisational failures, occupational fissures and micro-political divisions. These differences, which beset relations between the unions and within SOGAT, prevented the dispute from being pursued in a unified and disciplined fashion and contributed enormously to the unions defeat.

The labour process: – after the News International dispute

The NGA NC suffered considerable criticism from its News International chapels after they abandoned the industrial action. However, as interviewees from the chapels confirm, the majority of NGA members accepted the argument put to them by National Councillors and senior officers that they could not win the dispute on their own. Therefore the locus of criticism was directed at the SOGAT national leadership, thereby allowing the NGA to exit the News International dispute, as they had the Messenger strike, defeated yet still relatively united. This unity though did not allow the union to stave off a wave of attacks in the national and provincial newspapers, where a large number of companies insisted on direct inputting by journalists, resulting in huge reductions in staffing levels and major changes to the labour process. In other instances, particularly in the newspaper industry, other publishers followed News International's example and moved to new premises, where they introduced new technology and derecognised the NGA altogether.

The position within SOGAT, post the News International dispute, was even worse. Not only was the union in severe financial difficulties, it was also severely weakened industrially, with arguably its most powerful branches and chapels no longer able to defend their influence over the labour process. Worse still, SOGAT's organisation in many employers, which had depended upon the strength of its newspaper production chapels to impose closed shops on various distribution and ancillary companies, was now disappearing. This resulted in the loss of thousands of members. In addition to this toxic industrial and organisational cocktail the union was also suffering, by the end of the dispute, from large festering internal wounds.

Those chapel and branch activists, who represented News International members, were excoriating about the national leadership, openly stating that the General Secretary had colluded with the News International management to end the dispute.[8] They also claimed that if some provincial branches, which had not supported the blacking of the News International titles, had done so, then the dispute could have been successfully resolved in its opening few months. This is an assertion that has subsequently been supported by Richardson (2003: 91–3) in his analysis of the role of provincial braches in the dispute.

Countering these accusations, supporters of the General Secretary, along with Dean herself (2007), point out that if the News International chapels had not ignored warnings about Murdoch's plans for the Wapping site they may well have been able to secure jobs at the new site. They also assert that by the end of the dispute, the London branches were simply looking for scapegoats, whilst refusing to accept that they had lost the dispute (Dean, 2007).

In the years that followed the ending of the dispute SOGAT's internal fissures, and their fractious relationship with the NGA, did not improve. Many national and regional newspaper employers coupled the introduction of new process and production technology to the removal or renegotiation of collective agreements. These changes, in every case, lessened the union's influence over the labour process, and frequently bought the unions into conflict, as employers sought to recognise only one of the two print unions for their production areas. Chastened by the events at News International

---

8   These accusations were given greater substance by Andrew Neill (1997: 187) who claimed that Dean had asked News International to take legal action against the union after SOGAT's levy ballot had been lost.

the two national unions, their chapels, branches and memberships, were also far less willing to resist detrimental changes to their terms and conditions. As one senior officer observed:

> The defeats at Messenger Newspaper Group and News International destroyed the spirit and the strength of the newspaper membership.

The position in the general print was not initially as bad, owing to the different technology that was then being employed. However by the end of the 1980s there was also a growing trend towards employers seeking single union agreements, alongside considerable reductions in staffing levels as computer controlled machinery was introduced. This trend led to another ferocious battle between the NGA and SOGAT, as they sought to retain membership in the major printing companies. This conflict formed a major part of a wider struggle between the two unions for membership numbers, as they sought to retain members. As in the newspaper sector, all of the alterations in agreements and working practices introduced by the employers also saw the unions influence over the labour process weakened.

After the unions finally merged in 1991 to form the GPMU (which is discussed in detail later in this chapter), there was a concerted effort by the new General Secretary, Tony Dubbins, to stop the membership slide and to show general print employers that the new union still possessed substantial industrial strength. As a former GPMU National Officer commented:

> At the BPIF[9] there was a growing reluctance on the employers' side to negotiate with the union. They had seen us defeated in the papers and some of their members were now starting to believe that they could act in a similar fashion. We had to show them they were wrong; so when the BPIF talks broke down in 1993, Tony recommended a rolling series of strikes against individual companies with whom we would seek individual agreements. It was a highly courageous decision to take, given the numerous problems in the union and the recent record of horrendous defeats.

---

9   The British Print Industry Federation who then negotiated on behalf of numerous general print employers.

The outcome of this campaign of industrial action was something of a curate's egg. In certain areas of the country agreements were reached which granted GPMU members significant pay increases. These individual deals also led, as the GPMU leadership had hoped, to the BPIF making a revised offer that was acceptable to the GPMU members. However the industrial action campaign was not a universal success. In a number of companies there was determined employer resistance, with members being dismissed at Revell and George, Harvest Print and Arrowsmith whilst they were taking part in strike action.

Reflecting on the period after the News International dispute, many former officers from both unions agreed that the often poisonous relationship between their unions assisted employers in their efforts to reduce union influence over the labour process. Contributors also candidly conceded that the dysfunctional relationship that existed between the two General Secretaries, both before and after the merger, only added to the unions' tendency to turn on each other as opposed to working together to protect their members' influence over the labour process. Participants from SOGAT also agreed that the conflict inside their union, which had developed into genuine hatred between some individuals, led to infighting and divisions which handicapped them in defending terms and conditions and in organising non-members, post the abolition of the closed shop.

What was also universally agreed by interviewees from both unions is that the manner of the defeat in the News International and Messenger Newspaper Group disputes played a significant role in weakening the NGA and SOGAT's financial and industrial ability to combat employer attacks upon their members influence over the labour process. Equally important, as many lay and full time officers made clear, the defeats had a depressive effect on their members' willingness to combat employers who sought redundancies and attacked their influence over the labour process. These observations about a previously militant membership, gives empirical support to Kelly's assertion that during this period many unions entered a 'vicious cycle of union ineffectiveness, worker fatalism and decline' (Kelly, 1998).

The conflicts that occurred inside SOGAT and between the NGA and SOGAT over how to protect their influence over the labour process were not predominantly ideological; instead they were more often centred on micro-political, industrial, geographical, gender and craft based issues. The empirical evidence points clearly to the fact that key strategic choices made in the period from 1980–1996, and in particular during the tumultuous periods of the Messenger and News International disputes, contributed significantly to the lack of success the unions experienced in the prosecution of these disputes and in their wider efforts to influence the labour process across the printing sector. These findings are in line with the assertions of authors (Kelly, 1998; Heery and Kelly, 1994; Kelly and Heery, 1994; Heery, 2000, 2003, 2006) who believe that union policy makers' strategic choices play a key role in shaping their union's destiny. Furthermore the evidence is also persuasive that the reasons why the two unions found it so difficult to act jointly to defend their influence over the labour process was connected not just to institutional, ideological and industrial factors but also to micro-political factors, specifically the poor personal relationship between Brenda Dean and Tony Dubbins. Similarly SOGAT's inability to remain internally cohesive over labour process issues was a reflection of not only political and industrial differences, but also of craft, geographical, gender and personal loyalties and prejudices. Whilst authors (Gennard and Bain, 1995; Bain, 1998; Littleton, 1992; Richardson, 2003) have focused on the effect of geographical and occupational loyalties on the two unions' policies and Cockburn (1984, 1991) has written of the effect of gender prejudice in both print unions, these authors have not explored the impact of micro-political factors on policy formation. As has been shown, these were influences which played an important role in shaping the unions' labour process policies.

Recruitment

At the start of the 1980s both SOGAT and the NGA relied heavily on the closed shop to recruit new members. Expansion of their membership coverage depended upon their using their industrial strength in areas such as national newspapers and the general print to secure compulsory membership agreements with companies who supplied or traded with businesses that already had closed shops. The defeats at Messenger Newspaper Group and News International resulted in a rapid escalation in the number of companies who sought to terminate closed shop agreements. This strategy the print unions found much harder to resist than in the years preceding 1980, owing to their weaker industrial position and legislative prohibitions on secondary action. These factors, alongside the extensive introduction of new technology conspired to create large falls in the print union membership numbers during the 1980s.

The scale of these membership losses was dramatic. SOGAT's membership dropped from 204,865 in 1982 to 127,176 in 1990, whilst the NGA membership also fell, they claimed, from 112,122 in 1982 to 102,820 in 1990. However these figures as one former NGA officer conceded were inflated:

> We took a clear policy decision to stay above 100,000 members. This ensured we kept our automatic seat on the General Council.

Even with this 'massaging' of the NGA figures, there is no doubt that SOGAT suffered the greater proportional drop in membership. There were a number of reasons for SOGAT's more rapid decline. In the ancillary and distribution areas of the industry, which SOGAT organised, there was a wholesale outsourcing of functions to non-union distribution, cleaning, catering and logistics companies. These developments were similar to those, that other studies have shown were occurring, at the same time, in other British industries (Beynon, 1997; Crouch, 1999; Heery and Salmon, 2000).

Employers in the general print and newspapers also started to derecognise the print unions, in some instances to enter into single union agreements with other unions, in others to move towards non-unionism. These were developments which support Kelly's (1998) contention that employers were deploying a counter-mobilisation policy. Membership also fell rapidly in advertising agencies and graphic design shops, where the need to supply unionised copy to publishers no longer applied. Allied to all these factors there were job losses in heavily unionised areas as new technology was introduced that required less labour.

However it is important to note that unlike industries such as manu-facturing and coal mining, the economic recession of the 1980s did not result in a decline in employment in printing, which rose from 467,000 in 1986 to 484,000 in 1990.[10] The major problem for the printing unions was that this growth occurred in new areas of computer driven graphical and text composition where the workforce were predominantly young and female and the employers had no tradition of union recognition. In the period from 1982 to 1987, whilst both national unions passed motions stressing the need to start recruiting in these areas, the focus was upon the major industrial conflicts that were occurring, principally in the newspaper industry. As one officer commented:

> The truth is we were fire-fighting every day. Leaving aside Warrington and Wapping, employers were having a pop at us all over the place and we were run ragged negotiat-ing redundancies and trying to head off attacks on members terms and conditions. We had no time to address what we knew was a major recruitment problem.

The scale of the membership losses and the growth of the non-union sector prompted both unions to attempt to put into place policy initia-tives designed to address the problem. Branches and chapels were urged to recruit in the expanding number of non-union companies and leaflets were produced by the national unions specifically for use in these areas. National officers were also assigned the task of co-ordinating the branch and chapel efforts to recruit, and campaign strategies were drawn up for the targeting of specific companies. The materials themselves were of a very high quality, as was seen to be befitting of printing unions, which resulted in many thousands of pounds being spent on resources for the campaigns.

However, with a few notable exceptions, the efforts of both the NGA and SOGAT to recruit non-union members proved to be singularly unsuc-cessful. Reflecting on these ineffective campaigns, national and branch officers were candid in identifying the problems that beset their efforts. Nearly every interviewee focused on the lack of experience and knowledge

10   These are Department of Employment statistics for numbers employed in the paper, printing and publishing sector.

that officers and FoC's had of recruiting members, owing to the previous operation of the closed shop. As a former NGA NC member commented:

> Recruitment was just totally alien to the FoC's and the branch officials. None of them had done it before. Half of them just didn't know where to start, whilst the other half just didn't want to know.

An NGA branch secretary, who was relatively successful in recruiting new members, commented on the culture shock that his colleagues suffered when they went out recruiting for the first time:

> If it wasn't so serious it would have been hilarious. There were these, middle aged, suited and booted NGA officers, trying to persuade a bunch of young lads and girls who worked for a £100 per week to pay £4.00 per week to be a member of the union. They had no chance, and when they were ignored or told to piss off, they hated it.

These problems in persuading younger workers who no longer had to be a member of the union, to join, was the source of considerable difficulties for those running SOGAT or the NGA's recruitment campaigns. FoCs and full-time officers of both unions found the disappearance of what Hyman (1999) describes as 'mechanical solidarity' in which new employees simply accepted the need to be a union member, difficult to comprehend. They were not used to employees being resistant to joining a union and many were uncertain how to respond. As a SOGAT branch secretary recalled:

> I spoke to one FoC and encouraged him to come with me recruiting at a new site his company was opening. He looked at me like I was mad and said: Who do you think I am – a brush salesman?

Numerous contributors stated that the attitudes they faced when they did venture out recruiting in the 1980s was often hostile. This was not only because of lack of recruiting skills or high membership subscription rates; it also related to the antagonism towards the print unions that extremely hostile media coverage had generated. The difficulties both unions faced in recruiting were further compounded by the lack of expertise that the branches, chapels and national officers had of running recruitment campaigns. Whilst the senior officers charged with organising the national recruitment campaigns had a wealth of negotiatory experience they had little, if any, direct experience of successfully recruiting workers. As unions which had for decades successfully used the pre-entry and post-entry closed shop there was simply no group of full-time officers or activists inside the union with experience of how to successfully recruit in unorganised areas. This meant that when it came to recruiting techniques it was, as one former NGA national officer commented, "a case of the blind leading the blind".

The lack of success the two unions had in recruiting members in non-union areas, along with continuing falls in membership and poor inter-union relations, resulted in a series of coordinated attempts by both unions to recruit each other's members. Which union started this conflict is open to question, with officers and activists of both unions blaming the other for instigating what became tit-for-tat 'poaching'. SOGAT reached agreements at the *Liverpool Post and Echo*, which saw its members performing functions that had previously been carried out by the NGA's members. They also signed a deal at Boxfoldia in Birmingham which resulted in their members operating Lithographic presses, which had previously been the preserve of NGA members. The NGA complained to the TUC, who engaged Professor Sid Kessler to draw up a formula to avoid these types of membership disputes occurring when new technology was introduced. He provided guide-lines as to which union's members would undertake what work following the introduction of new technology in newspapers and the general print. The NGA accepted the 'Kessler formula' as it became known, but SOGAT refused to accept the recommendations, as they feared it would allow the NGA to move into their clerical and tele-sales areas.

Angered by SOGAT's rejection of the 'Kessler formula' the NGA used the introduction of new printing machinery and the subsequent blurring of demarcation lines to recruit SOGAT members in the general print. The NGA concluded a series of single union agreements with SOGAT members being told that they would only be trained for the new jobs if they joined the NGA. By the middle of 1990 the NGA had concluded these types of agreements with 23 companies, covering many hundreds of former SOGAT members. SOGAT unsurprisingly were incensed by these actions and lodged complaints to the TUC, who requested that the NGA did not sign any further single union deals in the commercial web-offset press areas without the consent of the TUC and SOGAT. As is detailed later in this chapter this NGA recruitment policy helped to hasten the merger of SOGAT and the NGA, which took place in 1991.

The amalgamation however did not reduce the dramatic falls in membership or solve the continuing difficulty in recruiting members in the ever growing non-union areas. Membership, according to the GPMU's own figures fell from 207,000 working members at its creation to 156,000 by the end of 1994 and the various internal campaigns and efforts to recruit new members were generally unsuccessful. These recruitment and retention problems led, by the end of 1996, to the GPMU considering a further merger, just five years after the tempestuous amalgamation, which had in large part been necessitated by the inability of SOGAT and the NGA to recruit members in new sectors of their rapidly changing industry.

The empirical evidence set out above clearly supports the assertion made by authors (Dunn and Gennard, 1984; Gennard and Bain, 1995; Gennard, 1990) that the demise of the closed shop had disastrous consequences for recruitment and membership levels of both print unions. The historical success of the closed shop also meant that, after its prohibition, the unions' officers and activists had no experience or skill in direct organising. As the NGA and SOGAT both also elected or appointed officers from their own ranks, this meant that there were no officials with experience of recruiting predominantly female, white collar workers, who were not compelled to join a union. These findings are broadly supportive of Heery's (2003) thesis that unions will struggle to be 'strategically innovate' if they do not have the ability to, 'renew their leaderships with those of a different gender, generation and ideology' (Heery, 2003: 297).

Amalgamation

The perilous industrial and financial position that the NGA and particularly SOGAT found themselves in at the end of the News International dispute prompted them to restart amalgamation discussions. These had been abandoned in 1985 owing to the public acrimony that occurred between the unions over the Wolverhampton Express and Star, and the Kent Messenger disputes. The negotiations, from the start, were highly fraught owing to the tensions that existed between the unions and their senior officers. As one former SOGAT officer stated:

> Look from the start of the talks the NGA officers were generally sexist and patronising towards Dean. They made little secret of the fact that they were amazed she'd been elected GS, and simply didn't believe that she was up to the job.

On the NGA side a senior official put forward a different view of the difficulties that arose in the amalgamation discussions:

> We didn't trust Dean. We knew she had been up to no good in the Wapping dispute and we were determined to ensure we protected our interests in the talks.

In this, and other contributors' assessments of the negotiations, the focus was always on the poor personal, as opposed to political or industrial, differences between the General Secretaries. This was the case even though Dean was seen as being somewhat to the right of Bill Keys and more industrially moderate, whilst Dubbins was viewed as being to the left of Joe Wade and more militant. That these issues were not cited illustrates the dominant role that their poor personal relationship played in the negotiations. However, such was the financial, industrial and membership damage sustained by both unions during the News International dispute that the two unions did agree to attempt to reach an agreement on amalgamation within one year.

This proved to be too ambitious a schedule as difficulties soon developed in the negotiations, specifically over the new union's rulebook and constitutional structure. There were familiar stumbling blocks, with SOGAT determined to ensure that their full-time branch secretaries should be allowed to sit on the new union's NEC and that the branch structure resembled their own. The NGA on the other hand wanted to ensure that only lay officers sat on the executive and that their chapel and branch structure remained in place. There were also debates over the size of the new national executive and the number of senior officers. The dominant question, though, according to interviewees from both sides, was who was

going to be General Secretary? Over this issue there were a series of informal discussions at which a wide variety of personal political and industrial
trade-offs were floated. Resolution however was not easy to find, partly
because neither General Secretary was enamoured with the idea of working
with the other, whilst there was also an absence of trust that any informal,
pre-merger, agreement would be honoured.

By 1988 these difficulties worsened after a series of inter-union disputes
in the provincial newspapers. As has been related earlier, the NGA now
went on a membership offensive against SOGAT, the intention being to
try and weaken SOGAT to such an extent that they would be forced to
reach an amalgamation agreement. A then senior National Officer of the
NGA described the philosophy behind the NGA's policy:

> By the late 1980s we were getting seriously concerned over the failure to get the merger
> of the ground. We had gone a long way to meet their concerns, agreeing to concessions
> over the CMS branch and over subscription rates. Tony had even offered to let Dean
> be GS as long as he was able to head up the industrial side of the union. Amazingly
> she turned it down. Anyway by late '88 we were all pretty pissed off and decided that
> the only way to get them to negotiate seriously was to give them a good kicking so
> that they would realise that there was no future for them as an independent union.

This unusual pre-amalgamation policy had a number of notable industrial
successes and SOGAT were left badly damaged by membership losses,
financial problems, and now 'poaching' of their members by the NGA.
At the 1990 SOGAT conference, Tony Dubbins was invited to address
the delegates. This he did, but only after the conference had passed a series
of motions that had condemned the actions of the NGA. In his speech
Dubbins was typically blunt: he would agree to the TUC's request for the
NGA not to sign any further single union agreements, where SOGAT were
currently recognised, but only if they agreed to an amalgamation with the
NGA. As a senior former SOGAT NEC member recalls, "it was typical
NGA, basically he was saying, merge or we'll give you a kicking".

However annoyed delegates were by Dubbins' speech, the NGA were
successful in persuading the SOGAT leadership that they needed to speed-
ily negotiate a merger. As a former NGA senior officer commented:

Look whatever you think about what we did – and remember it was them, not us
that ripped Kessler up – we did succeed in stopping SOGAT from negotiating until
Doomsday. Print unionism was under the cosh and we could not afford to wait for
SOGAT. We had to take action to get an amalgamation.

Reflecting on the amalgamation negotiations a former senior SOGAT
officer observed:

Crucial errors were made by Brenda and her closest advisers. They should have taken
Dubbins hand off when he offered her the General Secretaryship. They believed,
wrongly, that our larger membership meant that she'd walk it in a ballot for General
Secretary. They totally underestimated the Machiavellian ability of the NGA to
'win' elections.

In 1990 both unions' executives finally accepted the redrafted amalgamation package. The settlement did not contain agreement over the much
debated and highly contentious, new union's branch boundaries, nor did it
deal with the vexed issue of branch and chapel amalgamation. These issues,
the amalgamation document declared, would be resolved within the new
union, by 1 January 1997. The new union's title was to be the Graphical
Paper and Media Union (GPMU). There was also an agreement that the
two General Secretaries and the two General Presidents would be the only
two candidates in the elections for the GPMU's General Secretary and
General President. The proposal was put out to a ballot of both unions'
members and after pro-amalgamation campaigns by the respective leaderships, SOGAT members voted 74,883 to 13,078 in favour whilst the
NGA membership supported the amalgamation by 51,859 votes to 19,212.
The result clearly indicated that whatever the national and local hostility
between the unions a substantial majority of members could see the logic
of an amalgamation.

As researchers of union amalgamations have made clear (Undy, 2008;
Waddington et al, 2005) it is very unusual for an amalgamation to be entered
into when the unions' leaders enjoyed such a poor personal relationship and
industrially the unions were at loggerheads. Part of the reason why the two
unions were able to amalgamate was their increasingly dire membership
and financial position. However there was also, according to contributors

from both sides, a strong belief in both the Dean and Dubbins camps that the amalgamation agreement gave them the opportunity to effectively take control of the GPMU. The basis for this belief stemmed from the agreement that there would be a 'run-off' election for the GPMU's General Secretary after the unions merged. Both leaderships calculated that if they could win the General Secretaryship they could effectively take control of the new Executive.

Dean's supporters' confidence rested on the fact that SOGAT claimed to have over 50,000 more members than the NGA, whilst Dubbins supporters believed that they could secure a higher NGA turnout and attract a substantial minority of SOGAT members votes. Part of the NGA's strategy also involved delaying the GPMU General Secretary and General President elections, for a substantial period after the merger, so that they could launch a campaign amongst SOGAT members.

Neither campaign was co-ordinated by internal political factions. Instead the two campaigns were run by senior officers who were friends of the respective candidates. Both campaigns concentrated on appealing to their own members, stressing that their current General Secretary would ensure that their craft or occupational interests would be protected, if they were elected. In canvassing for support both candidates stressed these issues, although Dubbins and his supporters did attempt to make capital out of Dean's unpopularity in the London branches. The lack of political factional influence in the elections is a reflection of these groups relative weakness in SOGAT and the NGA, where craft, industrial and personal loyalties played a more dominant role than political ideology.

To engage in their desired longer election campaign the NGA needed a credible reason for postponing the election date. They were handed an excellent opportunity when a retired SOGAT member, K. Braidwood, challenged the President Danny Sergeant's, right to hold office, because he had not stood for re-election in the previous five years. Braidwood's legal challenge was upheld and the NGA were able to delay the official vesting day of the GPMU from 1 June 1991 until 30 September 1991. The legal action also delayed the elections for the posts of General Secretary and President, and over the summer months the NGA launched a concerted campaign amongst SOGAT members. The campaign was well organised, concentrating on two specific groups; SOGAT's craft membership and those disenchanted with Brenda Dean. To this end the NGA campaigned hard in Scotland, where the SGA had merged with SOGAT and in London. As one former NGA National Officer observed:

> As far as we were concerned it was all or nothing. The whole future of the union was at stake, if we had lost then Dubbins would have resigned and all the traditions of the NGA would have been swept away.

On the SOGAT side a similarly professional campaign was also put into place, although the emphasis was on turning out the SOGAT vote rather than on persuading NGA members to vote for Dean. The election campaign, thanks in large part to Dean's high media exposure during the News International dispute, received significant media coverage.

Once voting started the NGA traditions of strong chapel organisation and internal discipline came to the fore, with NGA branch officers and FoC's, encouraged by the Dubbins campaign team, ensuring that they got their members to vote. Their tactic worked admirably with a remarkable 70% of eligible members voting in the election and many branches returning an astonishing 90% of the eligible vote. These are startling figures, especially when consideration is given to the decay that occurs in membership lists as members move between branches, leave the industry, retire or die. However the NGA's remarkable electoral performance was almost matched by SOGAT who also achieved a tremendous turnout of 65%, which considering they were an industrial as opposed to a craft union and therefore did not enjoy the same degree of membership stability and discipline was an equally incredible achievement.

At the close of voting the mood in the two camps when the numbers of votes returned was known was markedly different. The Dubbins supporters believed that they had lost; reasoning that even if they had picked up as much as 15% of the SOGAT vote their candidate would still fall short. At this stage, according to those close to Tony Dubbins, he made it clear that if this was the result, he would resign, as he would not work as Deputy General Secretary to Brenda Dean. In the SOGAT camp there was considerable satisfaction at their turnout, yet they had strong doubts as to who had won, owing to the intelligence they had received concerning how London members were voting. On 29 May 1991 the result was announced. Tony Dubbins had received 78,654 votes, whilst Brenda Dean had only polled 72,657 votes. The NGA and SOGAT branch breakdowns of how their members had voted clearly showed why Dean had lost. Whilst not one NGA branch returned a majority for Dean, nor was close to doing so, a number of major SOGAT branches in London and Merseyside had voted for Dubbins, whilst large minorities had voted for the NGA General Secretary in other London and North Western branches. Here the legacy of the News International dispute had undermined Dean, with over 25% of her own members voting for Dubbins.

In the General President's election the pattern was repeated with Bryn Griffiths polling 66,588 votes against Danny Sergeant's 51,649. The disappointment the SOGAT leadership felt at these defeats was further compounded when Moss Evans,[11] who had been appointed to decide on the location of the GPMU's headquarters, selected the NGA's Bedford offices, rather than SOGAT's headquarters in Southend. Having been defeated Danny Sergeant declined to take up his position as GPMU Vice President, whilst few other SOGAT staff moved to Bedford, allowing senior staff positions to be secured by former NGA employees. By this stage a number of former SOGAT officers recalled that they felt the GPMU was rapidly turning into an 'NGA mark two'. These assessments were given more substance when Brenda Dean announced her resignation as Deputy General Secretary. As a source close to Dean commented:

> It was no surprise when Brenda left; she was shocked at the level of hostility displayed towards her at Bedford. Dubbins went out of his way to ensure that she felt totally unwelcome and she was unable to do her job properly.

The loss of their former General Secretary was a crushing blow to Dean's supporters, many of whom were angry about the way they were being treated whilst also feeling disappointed that very few officers had stayed to, as one former SOGAT activist put it, "battle it out on behalf of SOGAT

---

11   Moss Evans was the former General Secretary of the TGWU.

members." The move inside the GPMU to create a union that closely resembled the NGA gathered pace after Dean's departure. A former SOGAT
and subsequently GPMU NEC member recalled:

> The GPMU soon bore a remarkable resemblance to the NGA. All the internal sys-
> tems, the financial procedures, the education programme and the house style of the
> journal were identical to the NGA's. The whole feel of the union was very formal,
> which was just like the NGA. There were formal hierarchies everywhere, even down
> to the different crockery for different grades of officers, and the staff calling officers
> Mr instead of using their first name. Everything good about SOGAT was lost.

Unsurprisingly, former NGA officers and activists held different views,
complaining that their democratic traditions were being undermined by
former SOGAT full-time branch secretaries being allowed to remain on the
GPMU NEC. The structural, constitutional and cultural tensions between
the former activists and officers of SOGAT and the NGA were not rapidly resolved in the GPMU. From its outset the membership, recruitment
and industrial difficulties that both unions suffered prior to their merger,
continued to grow worse. Membership continued to tumble, leading to a
decline in income, which when allied to a series of costly and unsuccessful
industrial disputes during the BPIF campaign in 1993, created further financial problems. These fiscal difficulties led the GPMU by the end of 1996, in
common with many other unions experiencing sharp membership decline
(Undy, 2008), to seek another, larger, amalgamation partner. Discussions
which, post the period covered in detail by this book eventually resulted
in the GPMU's amalgamation with Amicus in 2004.

Conclusion

This chapter set out to examine the reasons why specific policy choices
were taken by the NGA and SOGAT, in relation to the labour process,
recruitment and amalgamations, in the period from 1980 to 1996. The
empirical evidence has shown that in all three areas, numerous strategic

choices were made by the two unions' policy makers, which had a profound influence on their fortunes. Although it is clearly the case that the unions faced immense challenges that were the result of profound changes to the institutional and political context, their ability to select from a series of possible policy responses, in a manner Heery and Kelly suggest, has been demonstrated (see Kelly, 1998; Kelly and Heery, 1994; Heery and Kelly, 1994; Heery, 2000, 2003, 2006). These choices, as was particularly clear in relation to the News International dispute, had a profound impact on the eventual outcome of the dispute and the future destiny of the unions. The testimony not just of trade union interviews, but also of News International managers, has established that if the unions had made a series of different policy decisions and had been able to bridge their inter and intra-union divisions, they could at least have retained collective agreements, employment (with some considerable job losses) and recognition at Wapping. These findings are contrary to the assertions of political and institutional contextualist scholars (Bain, 1970; Howell, 2005) who do not accept that unions can assert this level of control over their own futures, when facing such a hostile political, legal and institutional environment.

The evidence has also shown that Kelly and Heery's (Kelly, 1998; Heery and Kelly, 1994; Kelly and Heery, 1994; Heery, 2000, 2003, 2006) thesis that ideology, gender and generational factors are important in deciding how policy makers respond to industrial, technological and political challenges is accurate. Furthermore there is also strong evidence that those scholars (Littleton, 1992; Richardson, 2003; Gennard, 1988; Bain, 1998) who state that SOGAT's and the NGA's policy-making was significantly shaped by a combination of craft, occupational and industrial traditions, plus the effect of formal structures and internal geographical and occupational factions, are making sound assertions. Finally, in terms of testing this book's hypothesis, the empirical evidence is extremely persuasive, that micro-political factors, specifically friendships, enmities and personal loyalties, played a powerful role in influencing policymakers' decisions. Whether all these findings are replicated in relation to the Australian print unions and the two nations' telecommunications unions, will be discussed in the next three chapters.

CHAPTER 9

The Australian Printing Unions: 1980–1996

Introduction

This chapter examines the labour process, recruitment and amalgamation policies of the Australian print unions from 1980 to 1996. It uses empirical evidence to analyse the process of policy-making, whilst it also assesses the various influences which shaped the judgements of union decision makers.

In the period under review the Australian printing unions faced substantial challenges, owing to technological innovation and increased regional competition, which resulted in considerable reductions in employment levels. These technological and economic developments occasioned employer challenges to union influence over the labour process and precipitated membership decline in traditionally strongly organised areas. An analysis of the policy choices the unions made in response, and the reasons behind their selection, lies at the heart of this chapter. The similarities and differences in the policies of the British and Australian print unions, when faced with alike institutional and economic challenges, are also considered. Finally, woven throughout the chapter, there is an examination of the effect on policy of the complex and, at times, dysfunctional relationships that existed within the various layers of the PKIU's, highly federated, policy-making structures.

The labour process

Reflecting on the way the PKIU dealt with the introduction of new technology and alterations to the labour process during the early 1980s, a former PKIU full-time officer observed:

> New technology is like a bus: either you get on it and try and influence where it takes you, or you stand in its way and get run over.

This view succinctly reflects the pragmatic standpoint adopted in the early 1980s by the PKIU and the Victorian printing unions towards the introduction of new technology and associated changes to the labour process. It was a policy which, many participants stated, had been forged following the loss of the Fairfax dispute in 1976. As a former PKIU State branch secretary commented:

> Fairfax was one of the union's strongest chapels. When they lost their dispute and the Commission[1] handed down that mongrel judgement, it made a lot of newspaper chapels and the State branches wary about having blues, over the introduction of single keystroking and other forms of new technology.

This reluctance to engage in industrial resistance resulted in PKIU chapels and branches across Australia negotiating agreements that allowed not only for the introduction of new composition and production technology but also changes to working practices. This was not a formal policy of the Federal union or State branches, but rather the result of decisions taken by a host of different chapels across Australia. Reflecting on the reasons for this lack of resistance, numerous interviewees highlighted the fact that when the employers first mooted such changes many chapels had reacted angrily, with some taking unofficial action. However, this antagonism often dissipated when employers offered substantial voluntary redundancy and early retirement packages.

---

1   The NSW Industrial Relations Commission.

In analysing why these packages proved to be so popular, contributors focused on the ageing nature of the craft membership. In many newspapers the majority of the members in the 'skilled' areas were aged over fifty, with many employees close to retirement. The reason for this age profile relates to the decline in the regional newspaper industry in the early 1970s, which, as Chapter 4 described, led to the closure of many State Capital and country town newspapers (PKIU Federal and Branch Journals 1965–1980). In order to ensure the redundant employees were placed into jobs, the PKIU entered into agreements with many of the remaining newspaper and general print employers, to limit the number of apprentices entering the industry. By the 1980s this had created a craft workforce that was considerably older than was the case in the 1960s or 1970s. When these members were offered large sums of money to retire early, many were keen to accept the offer. As one NSW officer recalled:

> The older blokes, who were in line to get big bucks, weren't interested in fighting any changes; they simply wanted to take the money and go. Across the State, where we did try to stop them, we had Buckley's chance of succeeding. In fact we were trampled over in the rush for the door.

Another FoC outlined how he had failed to get the membership to resist what he felt were draconian changes to the labour process, which the employer had linked to the introduction of new presses and single keystroking:

> The officer and I called on the chapel to resist the changes, but most of the blokes just weren't interested; all they could see were the dollar signs if they signed up for retrenchment.

These types of recollections were often repeated by PKIU officers and activists across Australia, casting further doubt on the arguments of rank and filist authors (Bramble, 2008; Fairbrother, 1990, 1996, 2000) who assert that it is union bureaucrats who act as a brake on membership militancy and industrial resistance. Instead policy in these cases was clearly shaped at the local level, as Heery and Kelly suggest (Kelly, 1998; Heery and Kelly, 1994; Kelly and Heery, 1994; Heery, 2000, 2003, 2006), in order to fulfil the wishes of a majority of members who wanted to accept severance packages.

In reaching these agreements the PKIU chapels were dealing predominantly with two companies, News Limited and John Fairfax Holdings.[2]
These companies owned the vast bulk of Australia's newspaper titles and
managed to introduce direct text inputting, new presses and changes to the
labour process, resulting in the loss of thousands of jobs, without a single
major industrial dispute. Both companies, in reaching these deals, expended
hundreds of thousands of dollars and continued to recognise and negotiate with the print unions. This pragmatic approach by Rupert Murdoch's
News Limited, is in sharp contrast to the confrontational tactics he, and
other newspaper proprietors, adopted in Britain. Why News Limited and
Fairfax chose this more pragmatic approach towards the unions in Australia
is a question that provoked a wide variety of responses.

Those interviewees and authors (Dean, 2007; Shawcross, 1992) who
spoke to Murdoch at length over this matter claim that the variation in his
companies' behaviour was owing to his anger at the way in which the Fleet
Street chapels conducted negotiations and influenced the labour process.
Authors (Dean, 2007; Shawcross, 1992; Neill, 1997) agree that he became
almost fixated on the idea that it was impossible to reach any negotiated
settlements with the British print unions, hence his decision to dismiss the
production staff and hire an alternative workforce when he moved production to Wapping. In Australia, whilst News Limited had had disputes with
the PKIU, there had not been the same history of industrial conflict. As
PKIU State and Federal officers agreed, whilst many of their newspaper
branches were powerful and enjoyed considerable policy autonomy, they
never wielded the type of control over the labour process, which the Fleet
Street chapels and branches enjoyed. As a former Fleet Street compositor,
who became a PKIU officer, observed:

> The strength of the Fleet Street chapels was such that they were a law unto themselves.
> That was never the case here. Our newspaper chapels were never that strong. For
> a start all our major papers were published in the various state capitals, thousands
> of miles apart. This meant that there was no opportunity for the type of collective
> organisation that characterised Fleet Street.

2   The company is now known as Fairfax Media and is no longer owned by the Fairfax
      family.

This lack of a powerful centre of national newspaper production, alongside the aging nature of the Australian craft workforce, and the less confrontational approach of employers, were only three of the many reasons offered for the lack of conflict over the introduction of new technology and changes to the labour process. Many interviewees also supported Cryle's (2006: 6) observation that News Limited, and to a lesser extent Fairfax, were able to convince PKIU members that the changes they proposed were necessary if the newspaper they worked on was to survive. As PKIU contributors recalled, both companies stressed to chapels that if the introduction of new technology was opposed, then the newspapers would close. These arguments carried considerable weight, as many older employees had previously worked on regional newspapers which had been shut during the 1960s and 1970s.

In addition to these economic and industrial factors the other major institutional influence put forward by contributors to explain the lack of industrial resistance was the operation of the arbitration system. During the early 1980s, across all the Australian States and at the Federal level, the arbitral system and its underpinning legislation prohibited the type of action that News International took at Wapping. The legislation also allowed the various State and Federal Industrial Relations Commissions to intervene and bindingly arbitrate in any dispute that occurred over the introduction of new technology and allied changes to the labour process. This was a very different political and legal context to that found in Britain in the 1980s, where the State was actively encouraging employers to regain control of the labour process through both policy and legislation. As a senior PKIU federal officer rather ruefully reflected:

> Look, Murdoch knew that in Australia the type of tactics he used at Wapping just wouldn't have worked. So instead, he got what he wanted, by buying our members off.

Other contributors also stressed that the ALP's holding of Federal Government Office from 1983–1996, was a factor in ensuring that newspaper and general print employers charted a pragmatic, rather than overtly confrontationist, approach when introducing new technology. The employers were aware that the Federal Government were not going to replace the legislation that underpinned the arbitral system, so they sought negotiated settlements. Contributors also stated that there was a desire for all parties to avoid the scenes of violence, at Warrington and Wapping, which had been widely reported in the Australian media. As a former senior State PKIU official observed:

> The ferocity of the Warrington and Wapping disputes shocked everyone. I believe it made the employers and our members keener to reach negotiated resolutions, rather than embark upon a more confrontational path.

It should, though, be noted that in many Australian newspapers and general print shops, agreements on the introduction of single keystroking and other forms of new technology had already been reached prior to the commencement of the Messenger, let alone the News International, dispute.

The powerful role that many interviewees ascribe to various economic, industrial and political environmental factors in explaining the PKIU's failure to resist the introduction of new technology and a weakening of their influence over the labour process, seemingly supports the view of institutional contextualist authors (Flanders, 1965; Bain, 1970; Clegg, 1976; Boraston et al, 1975; Howell, 2006) who view such environmental pressures as principal factors in determining union policy. However the active opposition of significant groups of officers and activists, to the decision of many chapels and some State branches, to adopt this non-confrontational approach indicates that there was also strategic choice in the shaping of policies, which was influenced by ideological and generational factors, in a manner suggested by Kelly and Heery (Kelly, 1998; Heery and Kelly, 1994; Kelly and Heery, 1994; Heery, 2000, 2003, 2006). This view is given greater credence by the hostile reaction to the unions' conciliatory policy position, particularly in the Victorian PKIU branch, as the consequences of the union's weakened influence over the labour process became clear. In a number of States there was an electoral backlash and industrial discontent following the implementation of these agreements. This led to Right factions losing the State Secretaryships to the Left in Victoria and NSW, and then, in the early 1990s, to the more moderate Left faction losing power in Victoria to an alliance dominated by the radical 'Pledge Left' faction.[3]

---

3   These political shifts in the leadership of the Victorian PKIU branch are described and analysed in greater detail later in the chapter, as they had a profound effect

The anger and disappointment towards this conciliatory attitude was not the preserve of various Left groups. Even officers who reluctantly supported the emollient approach admitted that they were deeply uncomfortable at the way in which the craft they had practised was made redundant without a struggle. An ex-PKIU senior officer, who was formerly a newspaper compositor, captured these sentiments:

> I grew up having the importance of my craft, and the need to protect it, drilled into me by the FoC. Then, there I was in the 1980s, going into employers and negotiating away not only jobs, but the application of the trade itself. Sure it might have been better than what later happened to the Poms at Wapping, but it left me feeling pretty bloody ordinary, I can tell you.

Given the distaste many officers and activists felt for these agreements, it is perhaps unsurprising that a sizeable proportion of those who remained in the industry started to support candidates for union office who favoured more combative industrial policies. Commenting on this shift, which was focused in the two most industrialised States, NSW and Victoria, interviewees from Left groups spoke of tapping into "latent membership discontent" over concessions which had led to fundamental alterations to the labour process.

The desire to resist further employer led alterations to the labour process was championed by the NSW branch. However their more robust policy approach ran into difficulties at the PKIU Federal Executive. As a former PKIU NSW officer recalled there was frustration inside his branch at the attitudes they encountered:

> Whenever we mounted an industrial campaign, many of the smaller states tried to find reasons not to support us. With the Vics often in total internal disarray, our members would lead the fight and the other branches would stand on the side-lines whinging about being unable to get their members to support any action. The truth is they never tried. They were as weak as piss, and they held us back.

---

on amalgamation policy of the PKIU, both within Victoria and across Australia as a whole.

Unsurprisingly the smaller states held a somewhat different view. A former official from one of the smaller State branches observed:

> NSW and some of the Victorian chapels were often unrealistic in their demands. They often sought to press through polices that they were struggling to get past their own members. Look, you've got to understand our members tended to be less militant. We were dealing with different economic and industrial conditions to Melbourne or Sydney and we could not sustain the type of action being called for by NSW.

The simmering discontent inside the federal union over the refusal of the smaller branches to change their highly pragmatic approach to alterations to the labour process, led to an increasing number of activists and officers arguing that federally the PKIU was pursuing the wrong industrial policy. They argued that the union should adopt, nationally, a more militant approach, in which employers' demands for change to the labour process, linked to the introduction of new technology, were rejected and that members should be actively encouraged to engage in industrial action. If they did take action, their argument continued, they should receive the full financial and industrial support of the whole PKIU, including if necessary, national secondary strike action. This policy, officers and activists from radical Left factions asserted, would properly discharge the union's duty to protect jobs, rather than simply ensuring that individual craftsmen received generous financial exit packages when they left the industry.

These arguments, whilst chiming with many members, did not gain majority support across all the PKIU branches. As officers and activists who supported a more pragmatic approach pointed out, their less confrontational methods had secured far more influence for the PKIU in the newspaper industry, post the introduction of new technology, than the British or American unions enjoyed. Whilst this assertion is correct, it was recognised by many contributors that Australia's legal and political environment, in which the arbitral system then played a key role, was also crucial in ensuring that employers continued to recognise the PKIU.

By the early 1990s the argument that a more robust industrial approach was needed in order to protect the union's influence over the labour process continued to gain ground in the largest two branches, NSW and Victoria. Tensions between these branches and the smaller States grew, whilst within the Victorian branch the radical Pledge Left faction gained electoral ground at the expense of more moderate Left factions. These electoral trends coincided with the PKIU continuing to lose the influence they had previously retained over the labour process, in different parts of the industry, as ever more sophisticated technology was introduced into their strongly organised areas, making many trades wholly obsolescent. As with the British print unions the PKIU also experienced great difficulty in recruiting workers in new computer design, graphics and reprographics areas, as composition and production passed into the hands of journalists and other white-collar staff, who needed only the most rudimentary keyboarding and technical skills.

The union's difficulties in retaining influence over the labour process increased at the end of 1996, when the Printing Section of the AMWU (as the PKIU had become following an amalgamation, the complex prelude to which is covered later in this chapter) faced difficulties in retaining their closed shops, owing to the legislative programme of the newly elected Federal Liberal/Country National Coalition Government. The employment legislation proposed by the Federal Government sought not only to prohibit the closed shop, but also to sweep away the arbitral system and place restrictions on the union's ability to take legal industrial action. These were measures that the Australian Prime Minister, John Howard, proudly stated were inspired by the British Conservative Government of 1979–1997 (Bramble, 2008). As it transpired this process took the Howard Government nearly a decade to introduce fully, but the Liberal/Country National's presence in Federal office, and their declared industrial relations agenda, gave encouragement to employers who were determined to keep the PKIU from organising and representing their employees.

The amalgamation that took place with the AMWU in 1994 also failed significantly to increase the former PKIU's ability to protect its influence over the labour process in those workplaces in which it was recognised. In those employers, technological developments resulted in ever greater numbers of job losses and the obsolescence of many of the processes that both engineering and printing members practised. The continuing movement of parts of the print industry overseas also continued, as firstly the ALP and then the Liberal Country/National Federal Government eliminated trade barriers. There were though some areas of the industry where there was a consolidation of union organisation, principally printing on cardboard and plastics. However as contributors agreed, this expansion did not offset their continuing loss of influence in traditional areas of strength.

By the end of 1996 the Printing Division of the AMWU had retained, unlike their British counterparts, a sizeable presence and some sway over the labour process in the newspaper industry, whilst having a similar level of influence within the general print. In both these areas of the industry the empirical evidence indicates that the PKIU's ability to affect the labour process had diminished markedly. This had occurred following the agreed introduction of new technology, which had removed the demand for specific manual craft skills, the control of which had historically granted the print unions the foundation of their organisational strength (Cryle, 2006). These developments illustrate that even a different industrial approach to the British unions, the PKIU was unable to sustain high levels of influence over the labour process.

Recruitment

In recalling the PKIU's efforts to recruit new members in the rapidly changing industrial environment of the 1980s, a former senior officer observed:

> Look in the early 80's we had no experience of recruiting. We'd operated the OK card system for years. If you wanted a job you had to have a card. That's how it'd been since Noah was a boy. When you wanted to find a new job you went to the branch office and they sent you to an employer with a vacancy, who had to take you on. When that started to change in the 1980s, our response, if we're honest, was pretty ordinary.

The organisational 'response', to which this contributor was referring, lay in the hands of the State branches, owing to the decentralised nature of the PKIU. They adopted a wide variety of different polices, including as one former PKIU Federal Officer caustically observed, "doing diddly squat". One of the reasons put forward by contributors for the considerable variations in approach to organising was the vast differences in branch membership which resulted in large discrepancies in financial and physical resources. NSW and Victoria's combined membership at the beginning of the 1980s was over 25,000 members, which equated to over 60% of the total national membership. The next largest branch was Queensland, which then had a membership of over 4,000, whilst the other State branches organised between 1,000 to 3,500 members. In the smaller branches in particular, many of the officers described the problems that they faced in balancing the requests of their current membership with the need to recruit in unorganised areas. These difficulties became more acute in the 1980s, as officers dealt with increased demands for representation, as employers sought to introduce new technology which caused mass redundancies.

The problem of balancing the demands of current members with the necessity of devoting resources to recruiting non-members was, as scholars have acknowledged, an extremely difficult conundrum for unions to resolve (Heery et al, 2000a, 2003a; Heery, 2005; Heery and Alder, 2004; Heery and Simms, 2008; Cooper, 2003; Gall, 2003; Milkman, 2000; Kelly and Badigannavar, 2005). As a former PKIU officer from a small State branch explained:

> My primary job was to represent my members, many of whom were looking to me for advice and representation. If I had ignored them I'd have been failing in my job and I'd have been out on my ear at the next election.

A number of the Branch Secretaries from the smaller States were also clear as to the enormous difficulty they had in allocating any time for their officers, or themselves, to recruit. This was owing, they said, to their negotiating and travelling workloads growing ever greater, owing to increasing rounds of job losses and demands for changes to their members' terms and conditions. In many of these States the PKIU branch only employed a small number of officers, and there were not the finances available to employ dedicated recruiters. Historically, as Chapter 4 outlined, recruitment had not been undertaken by branch officers, but had instead been delivered by compulsory unionism, with the agreements being policed by the local FoC. The Federal or State arbitration system had also been used to 'rope in' any new companies, which employed PKIU members, to the various printing industry awards. Technological developments in the 1980s meant that many employer entrants to the printing industry did not employ staff who possessed traditional printing skills. These employers were also often actively hostile to the PKIU being granted 'coverage' of their staff. As one Branch Secretary recalled:

> We were caught between a rock and a hard place. Myself and the officers barely had enough hours in the day to deal with all the retrenchment negotiations, let alone trying to recruit in companies who did not want us through the door. What we needed was an officer to recruit in these areas, but as our membership fell so did our bank balance.

In addition to the problem of resourcing recruitment campaigns, some senior PKIU officers also believed that the union's system of electing its branch officers acted as a brake on effective recruitment. They argued that elections delivered some officers who were of a poor calibre and lacked the ability to become proficient at recruitment. It was alleged this was a particular problem in smaller branches, where one large chapel could dominate elections. Even some supporters of the election of officers were on occasion exasperated by the outcome of such elections. One former State Secretary commented:

> Look, in my branch, I had an officer who was only elected because his chapel wanted shot of him and they had the numbers to get him up. He was less use to me than a one legged man in an arse kicking contest. He'd do anything to avoid the hard yards – including recruiting. All he was interested in was his pay check and blowing through every day. The only time you'd see him after five in the arvo was if there was glue on the carpet.

The problems that some senior officers felt were caused by the election of branch officers went further than the quality of the candidates. As another State Secretary explained:

> Our problem was that good officers depended upon the support of the larger chapels to get elected. If you're an officer in the run up to an election, what would you do? Spend as much time as possible in the large chapels that you represent, or go recruiting

in a non-union firm where you'll get no votes whatsoever? You and I both know that unless you're a total dill, you'll spend as much time as possible in the organised chapels.

Yet these views were hotly disputed by other senior officials who believed that the union's recruitment failures were being used as a stalking horse for an attack on the PKIU's democratic structures. This argument was succinctly encapsulated by one senior PKIU officer:

> All this talk about officers not recruiting, because they were facing elections, is just bullshit. It had nothing to do with whether officers were elected, state appointed or, as Cahill[4] was always angling after, federally appointed. We failed to recruit more members because as a union, we dropped the bundle. We had the chances to move into those areas of the print where we were poorly organised, but we all failed to spend enough time and resources putting in the hard yards.

Supporting this argument other officers also pointed out that it was perfectly possible for branches to employ recruitment officers on staff contracts, which would circumvent the need for them to be elected. This was a practice which the NSW branch adopted at the end of the 1980s, allowing them to hire recruitment officials who had not been PKIU members, but who had organising experience outside of areas where compulsory unionism was the norm. Part of the reason that the NSW branch was able to adopt this policy was that they had greater resources available to tackle the problem of low recruitment levels in the expanding unorganised areas of the industry. The Victorian branch also had resources but was mired in an internal conflict which stopped any coherent recruitment strategy being implemented.

The NSW decision to introduce recruitment officers followed a steep decline in membership and a subsequent review of recruitment in the late 1980s. The review concluded that those working in the growing unorganised areas, generally had no background in the printing industry, were predominantly young, and in many instances were women. Efforts to recruit these workers by the branch's male officers had been generally unsuccessful, and it was concluded that it was necessary for the branch to change their image

---

4   The PKIU's Federal Secretary, John Cahill.

in order to appeal to this growing cohort of non-members. A major part of the proposed solution was the appointment of Recruitment Officers, who, as mentioned earlier, would not have to be PKIU members. They would though need to possess the skills needed to recruit workers in the expanding sectors of the industry.

The proposal caused a heated debate at the branch committee. A number of delegates viewed the policy as undermining the history and democratic principles of the PKIU and the branch's own constitution. Although this proved to be a minority position, the branch sought to address these concerns by ensuring that the Recruitment Officers were employed on a lower grade to elected branch officials. The difficulties that senior officers of the NSW branch encountered, not only in diverting resources away from servicing to recruitment but also in changing the internal structures of the branch, are similar to those noted by authors (Terry, 2000; Heery, 1998, 2001; Heery and Kelly, 1990 Cooper, 2005; Costa and Hearn, 1997).

The NSW Recruitment Officers were initially assigned the role of organising non-members in those parts of the industry where the NSW PKIU branch had experienced severe recruitment difficulties. This proved an extremely difficult task, as they were visiting areas where the PKIU's branch officers had already made unsuccessful attempts to organise. A former PKIU Recruitment Officer highlighted their difficulties:

> At first we were often sent into companies where officers had already been unsuccessful. This was a total nightmare. There we were at five thirty in the morning asking these blokes whether they wanted to join the union, after they been asked and refused to join a couple of weeks before. I tell you we were lucky not to get bashed. It was only when we started to follow up leads from non-members, or from members who had got work in non-union companies, that we started to make any progress.

The greater success in following 'leads' into non-union companies also generated some tension between recruiters and some of the branch officers. As one former PKIU NSW branch officer explained:

> I was in favour of the branch appointing Recruitment Officers. However it has to be said that they generated a lot of work for us, without bringing in shed loads of

members. The reason was that most nons who wanted to join in unorganised areas usually had a problem at work and wanted union representation. This meant that we then spent more of our time representing those members rather than getting on with our own work.

These were sentiments that scholars (Terry, 2000; Willman, 2001; Heery, 1998) who studied the use of recruitment officers in a number of British unions, also uncovered amongst servicing officers particularly where the use of recruitment officers was not carefully and strategically focused on specific employer targets. Although this tension did exist in the NSW branch, the vast majority of NSW officials interviewed stated that the employment of recruiters had had a positive effect on membership numbers. It must though be noted, that even their most ardent supporters, admitted that the recruitment officers did not recruit as many members as the branch had initially hoped.

In addition to NSW hiring recruitment officers, the PKIU at a Federal and State level also sought recognition in companies that had been acquired by Corporations where they already had membership and recognition. This tactic saw an expansion in coverage, particularly in the printing on cardboard and plastic sectors of the industry, where large companies such as Amcor and Visy Pulp & Paper were acquiring smaller competitors. However these efforts to boost recruitment did not offset the continuing membership decline, with the smaller branches in particular sustaining considerable membership losses.

The internal debate that occurred in the PKIU over recruitment policies, was replicated in many other British and Australian unions, as authors have observed (Kelly and Badigannavar, 2004; Gall, 2003; Heery et al, 2000a, 2003a; Heery, 2005; Heery and Alder, 2004; Heery and Simms, 2008; Cooper, 2003; Milkman, 2000). It was indicative of the considerable problems of organisational adjustment that many unions faced, in a vastly changed industrial, technological and economic environment, where they could no longer rely on compulsory unionism. In the PKIU, as in the British print unions, the evidence is persuasive that these problems were particularly acute owing to the union's historical reliance on the closed shop to recruit members.

Reflecting twenty years later on why the PKIU's recruitment strategies failed to stop the union's membership falling in the 1980s and early
1990s, officials from across Australia cited a number of different reasons.
Without exception they stressed the immense problems the union had in
recruiting sufficient numbers to counterbalance the high levels of job losses
in their areas of membership strength. There was also unanimity that the
recruitment of workers, who were employed outside of the PKIU's traditional sectors of organisational strength, was considerably more difficult
than organising workers inside established production areas. Where the
consensus fractured was over the question of whether the decline could
have been slowed or even reversed. This question was particularly relevant,
as employment in the Australian printing industry, similarly to Britain, did
not shrink to the same extent as the PKIU's membership.[5]

Those who felt that the PKIU could, with the correct recruitment
policies, have reversed the decline cited a number of internal factors that
hindered recruitment. A number of interviewees highlighted the fact that
because of the pre-entry closed shop, officers and activists lacked the necessary skills and confidence to recruit effectively. They went on to point
out, as had NGA and SOGAT officials, that the senior officers who were
directing the organising campaigns had no experience of co-ordinating
recruitment operations and were therefore unable to offer pertinent advice,
or good strategic leadership. The appointment of more officers with this
type of experience some felt would have made a substantial, positive, difference to the union's recruitment performance.

Other interviewees highlighted the mistrustful relationship that
existed between a number of the State Secretaries and the Federal Secretary,
John Cahill, for the lack of a coordinated national recruitment strategy.
Many of the branches viewed Cahill as a centraliser, and in retrospect a
number of State Secretaries admitted that they opposed suggestions that
the Federal union should organise and resource a recruitment campaign in
their State, simply because they distrusted the Federal Secretary's motives.

---

5   Australian Bureau of Statistics figures suggest that from 1980–1996 the Australian
     Printing Industry's employment figures shrank by approximately 10% whilst PKIU
     membership declined by over 30%.

Similarly the dysfunctional relationship that existed between Cahill and the NSW branch was mentioned as the primary reason why NSW refused to co-fund Federal recruitment officers, which would have assisted in recruiting in the smaller states. Poor micro-political as well as ideological relationships were put forward as reasons for these problems, as they also were for the lack of co ordinated recruitment initiatives by the Victorian branch. As representatives from all the Victorian factions admitted, officers and activists became so focused on factional and personal divisions, that it was almost impossible for whoever was holding office to institute a coherent branch recruitment strategy. In particular any efforts to divert branch officers away from servicing duties towards recruitment, or to take the equally controversial step of employing recruitment officers in an effort to halt membership decline, were viewed as being too politically hazardous. The result was that in Victoria there were relatively few positive steps taken to try and recruit new members in growing, unorganised areas of the industry during the 1980s.

The internal difficulties the PKIU experienced in coordinating a coherent national recruitment strategy during the 1980s and early 1990s, illustrates again the importance of not just environmental, structural and ideological factors in determining policy but also micro-political influences. By the early 1990s the relative failure of the PKIU's recruitment policies, plus the continuing membership decline and resultant financial problems resulted in the PKIU's leadership entering into a series of amalgamation discussions, which finally resulted in a merger in 1995 with the AMWU. It was hoped by the PKIU's leadership that being part of the larger AMWU would deliver more financial and physical resources for recruiting workers in developing areas of the industry. However the reality proved to be somewhat different as the AMWU, who were also experiencing a membership decline, did not place the additional recruitment resources into the Printing division that had been expected.

The historic dependence of the PKIU on compulsory unionism caused the union great organisational difficulties when they were unable to use this recruitment method in new areas of the industry during the period under review. As the evidence has shown they often lacked the skills and experience needed to execute successful organising campaigns. As with the

British printing unions the PKIU was highly resistant to changing its rules to allow for the employment of officers, particularly senior officials, who could provide the knowledge and ability to deliver successful recruitment strategies. Whilst a considerable part of this reticence was linked to the PKIU's pride and attachment to its democratic electoral traditions it also reflected ideological and particularly micro-political divisions between States and the national office; factors which meant that a national programme of employing recruitment officers was not adopted. These internal constitutional difficulties, alongside the long term reliance on the closed shop, arguably placed the PKIU and the British print unions at an organising disadvantage compared to other Australian and British unions when it came to adopting recruitment strategies in a radically altered institutional and political environment (see Heery et al, 2000a; Heery, 2003, 2005; Heery and Alder, 2004; Heery and Simms, 2008; Cooper, 2003; Gall, 2003; Milkman, 2000; Kelly and Badigannavar, 2004).

Amalgamations

At the start of the 1980s the PKIU was still in the process of attempting to convince the last two remaining independent printing craft unions, the Federated Photo-Engravers, Photo-Lithographers and Photogravure Employees Association of Australia (FPA) and the VPOU to enter into an amalgamation. The FPA membership was concentrated in Victoria and South Australia, whilst the VPOU organised workers in the Victorian newspaper industry. Previously both these unions had rebuffed approaches from the PKIU, but by the early 1980s the membership of the FPA, in particular, had fallen dramatically, as the crafts that their members undertook became obsolescent. The FPA Committee of Management decided, in the mid-1980s, that a merger was unavoidable as the union would soon be unable to meet its financial obligations. Prior to this point, as a former FPA member recalled, the union had done everything possible to avoid an amalgamation:

> We didn't want to merge, because we didn't want a bar of the various blues that were occurring within the PKIU Victorian branch.

Officers from the VPOU cited similar reasons for seeking to retain their independence, although as Chapter 4 has illustrated, there were also historic craft and demarcation divisions which separated the two unions. The concern that officers of the FPA and VPOU expressed over infighting within the PKIU Victorian branch, also engendered disquiet amongst senior officers of the Federal union and other State branches. They believed that the internal conflict was not only adversely affecting amalgamation negotiations, but also harming national industrial policies.

These anxieties developed further in the early 1980s as the then Branch Secretary, Frank Nelson, who was a member of the Victorian Centre Unity faction, became embroiled in a struggle for control of the branch with Victorian Left PKIU branch activists. The latter's campaign focused not only on the branch's poor performance but also on Nelson's management of the branch. In particular they concentrated on Nelson's dismissal of a staff member which had led to a strike by Victorian branch staff. The dismissal and strike had prompted the PKIU Federal Executive to order a federal investigation into the Victorian branch. The fact that the PKIU State Secretaries, who made up the majority of the Federal Executive, backed the investigation and subsequently the critical findings of the investigatory panel infuriated both Nelson and his Centre Unity supporters. Following the inquiry Nelson's health deteriorated rapidly and he went on long term sick leave. This left the branch without a State Secretary, and the factional conflict worsened as a series of allegations were made of theft and threats of violence. These resulted in an inconclusive police investigation. Eventually, in 1986, Frank Nelson retired on ill health grounds and at the subsequent election the Left's candidate, Ian Wenham, won the position of State Secretary. It was only at this stage that the now very small FPA finally agreed to amalgamate with the PKIU.

Securing the FPA merger assisted Wenham in his attempt to persuade the VPOU to amalgamate with the PKIU. He was aided in his efforts by officers of the NSW branch, who spoke to the VPOU and assured them that they now enjoyed a more harmonious industrial and political relationship with the Victorian PKIU. This was important to the VPOU, as by the mid-1980s they often negotiated alongside the NSW PKIU branch, as ownership of Victorian newspapers had passed into the hands of companies whose Australian operations were based in NSW.

The improvement in relations between the two branches had been driven by the NSW State Secretary, Gordon Cooke, who was keen to build an alliance with Ian Wenham, after relations between the branches had become very strained during Frank Nelson's tenure. Cooke wished to form an industrial and political alliance with Victoria on the Federal Executive, so as to ensure that NSW, the PKIU's largest branch, could not be outvoted by Victoria and a combination of smaller branches. In order to do so he sought a better personal relationship with the new Victorian Secretary.

This desire grew even stronger after the election of John Cahill, as Federal Secretary, in 1986. The NSW leadership had not supported Cahill, and he subsequently actively opposed a number of NSW policy proposals at the Federal Executive. As interviewees recalled, Cahill's relationship with NSW, and a number of the other States, deteriorated quickly after he took up office. A former PKIU Executive member attempted to explain the difficulties that arose:

> The problem with John was that he was an awful communicator. I don't believe that he set out to deliberately upset the State Secretaries, but by not consulting them and taking decisions behind their backs, that's what happened. NSW in particular, were always spewing over what they saw as a lack of consultation. To make matters worse he was a barrack room lawyer and set himself up as the union's legal officer, in all but name. This incensed the branches, especially when he attempted to run shonkey legal cases.

The disagreements they were having with Cahill led NSW to redouble their efforts to build an alliance with the Victorians. This they achieved and the improved relationship between the PKIU's two largest branches created a considerable alteration in the PKIU's internal dynamics, as the two branches combined together represented a majority of the union's membership, allowing them to effectively drive forward their own policy agenda. This meant that the third largest branch, Queensland and their State Secretary, Tom Burton, were not now able to wield the influence on the Federal Executive that they had previously enjoyed. As a State Secretary of one of the smaller branches recalled:

> Tom previously acted in the role of a power broker; delivering the smaller states' support to one or other of the big branches. Once Cooke and Wenham started to work closely together this strength disappeared and Tommy went back to running his branch like a separate union.

However there was to be one policy issue over which NSW and Victoria disagreed profoundly; amalgamation with the AMWU. By the late 1980s there was general consensus inside the PKIU, that membership decline, and the resultant fall in income, was so great that it was necessary to seek to an amalgamation with a union from outside of the printing industry. These problems were not dissimilar to other Australian and British unions, who also sought to merge during this period (see Chaison, 1996; Undy, 1996, 2008; Waddington, 1988, 1995; Waddington et al, 2005; Griffin, 2002). What was unusual in the PKIU, as they entered into amalgamation talks, was the lack of internal consensus over a preferred merger partner. There were a variety of different unions who were favoured by the different State branches, whilst the Victorian branch remained opposed to any merger, other than that with the VPOU. Add to this the Federal Secretary's strong support for an amalgamation with the AJA, which NSW vociferously opposed, and the reasons for the divisions within the union over this issue become clearer.

These disagreements were part of a wider conflict over the industrial, institutional and political direction of the PKIU. The NSW leadership believed, by the late 1980s, that the PKIU needed to merge with a large, financially stable union, which had more centralised financial and policy-making structures. They believed that the smaller branches had proved themselves to be wholly ineffective in recruiting new members whilst they acted as a barrier to radical policy changes and were a severe drain on PKIU finances. The answer, NSW believed, was a merger with a union whose internal structures would divest the smaller branches of control of their finances, whilst removing their ability to frustrate policy initiatives.

The AMWU's[6] structure, with its greater centralisation of finances and more unified national divisional policy-making, fulfilled this desire. Merging with the AMWU also satisfied the NSW branch's wish for a partner with whom they were industrially and politically comfortable. Industrially the NSW branch had a history of working co-operatively with the AMWU, particularly in the carton and cardboard sector, which was becoming an increasingly significant employer of PKIU members. Politically there was also compatibility, with PKIU NSW State branch senior officers, being members of the same ALP Socialist Left faction that controlled the AMWU. The senior officials had also developed strong personal alliances, whilst working together in the Socialist Left faction. All of the above factors led the NSW branch to be clear that the AMWU was the only prospective merger partner with whom they were prepared to merge. This view strengthened further, following the decision of the PKIU Federal Executive to issue emergency grants (largely funded by NSW and Victoria) to two smaller PKIU branches, in the early 1990s.

On the other side of the debate those who supported either Cahill's plan for an amalgamation with the AJA, or a merger with a more decentralised union, expressed very different opinions. As a former senior Federal Officer explained:

> An amalgamation with the AJA would have allowed the PKIU to retain its identity and its influence inside what would be a merged union of equal partners. This was very different to merging with the Metals, into which the PKIU would disappear and lose its industrial identity.

6   During the merger discussions in the early 1990s the Amalgamated Metal Workers' Union (AMWU) was officially known, following an amalgamation with the Association of Draughting Supervisory & Technical Employees (ADSTE) in 1991, as the Metals & Engineering Workers' Union (MEWU). The Union then changed its name to the Automotive Metals & Engineering Union (AMEU) following an amalgamation with the Vehicle Builders Employees Federation of Australia (VBEF) in 1993, before changing its name again to the Australian Food Manufacturing and Engineering Union (AFMEU) following a merger in 1993 with the Confectionery Workers & Food Preservers Union of Australia (CWFPU).

Other senior PKIU officers did though concede that personal motives also played a significant role. As one retired Federal officer commented.

> Look, Cahill and some of the other State Secretaries knew that if we merged with the Metals, then they were as good as finished. Cahill knew that Cooke and McCarthy were mates with the Metals leadership and that none of them had any time for him. I believe that John thought that his future was much better served by a merger with a smaller union like the Journos. He had a better relationship with them and I think he felt he could be Federal Secretary of a merged Union.

The NSW leadership, whilst cool over all the prospective amalgamation partners except the AMWU, was positively hostile to an amalgamation with the AJA. There were two major reasons for NSW opposition. First, the branch's long running antipathy towards the AJA, which had been triggered by Journalists crossing PKIU picket lines in the 1976 Fairfax dispute. Secondly, the strong conviction that amalgamating with the AJA would not solve the PKIU's long term membership decline, or address the need to reconstitute the union's policy-making and financial structures.

The plethora of different potential amalgamation partners, allied to the decentralised nature of the PKIU, led to a series of informal amalgamation talks being conducted by various State Secretaries. This created considerable confusion, which finally led the PKIU Federal Executive to decide that they needed to enter into formal negotiations with only two unions, and that all other informal merger discussions in the States should then cease. A vote was taken at the Federal Executive and the AJA and the ATEA/APTU were the chosen unions. The NSW branch were so furious at this decision that they immediately made it clear that they refused to be bound by this verdict and would continue to negotiate with the AMWU.

The NSW branch's actions were similar to those of the NGA and SOGAT's London newspaper branches and chapels, who had refused to abide by national policies over the easing of demarcation lines, in the early 1980s. NSW's actions are another example of how a very powerful constituent section of a union can, in certain circumstances, simply refuse to abide by a national policy decisions and not be subject to any sanction, owing to their importance to the organisation. This is also another example of policy not residing as Boxall and Hayes assert (Boxall and Hayes, 1997) simply in the hands of a national union's leadership.

Following this contentious Federal Executive, the NSW branch made a major effort to convince the Victorians to support an AMWU merger. They did so in the knowledge that if they could gain Victorian support then they would have a majority at the PKIU's supreme governing body the Federal Council, where delegate numbers reflected State's membership levels. However the Victorians were not enamoured of the prospect of a merger with the AMWU. Even the new spirit of cooperation with their northern neighbours could not overcome the branch leadership's desire to stay as an independent printing union. A Victorian PKIU officer of the time recalled the debate that took place inside the branch:

> Look, you have to remember that our branch was dominated by Comps. At that stage the VPOU had not joined with us and our traditions were very much of the old PIEUA. We wanted to remain an independent craft union. Merging with a union like the Metals was not something that the branch wanted to contemplate. Added to that, our members thought the Victorian Metals branch were led by a bunch of hoons.

These types of derogatory remarks about the Victorian AMWU branch leadership were repeated not only by other PKIU officers but also by a number of AMWU contributors. As a Federal AMWU officer of the time colourfully stated:

> Yeah the Vics were a bunch of galahs. You had these different factions running around in the branch, all of them bashing the shit out of each other. Mate I'll tell you, half the bastards were as mad as cut snakes, whilst the other half were a bunch of biker hoons.

The commonly held perception in the Australian labour movement that the Victorian AMWU was, at best, poorly administered and politically unstable, meant that the PKIU Victorian branch felt they had good reason not to support an AMWU merger. Instead Wenham and his senior officers played what one former PKIU Federal Officer, described as "a very dangerous game", in that they attempted to give the impression to NSW that they could be persuaded to support an AMWU merger, whilst informing those who opposed the amalgamation that they would never agree to such a proposal. Asked about this policy, a former senior Victorian officer was candid:

> At the time we didn't want an amalgamation with anyone but the VPOU. If we had to have one then we certainly didn't want to merge with those dills from the Victorian AMWU. We valued our working relationship with NSW, and therefore we didn't want to put them offside, but allowing them to bulldoze through a merger with the Metals was a step too far. We had a lot of trouble brewing in the branch, so we decided to behave tactically, supporting the AJA talks, whilst knowing that NSW would scupper any deal with the Journos.

In the short term this tactic worked. NSW did remain supportive and the joint efforts of the two branches persuaded the VPOU to finally merge in 1992. By this stage the VPOU membership had fallen dramatically and they were facing great difficulties in surviving as a viable organisation. The merger bought approximately 1,500 VPOU members into the Victorian branch which temporarily offset the branch's continuing membership losses.

At the same time as the VPOU amalgamation was finalised, the PKIU's formal national merger negotiations were running into difficulties. Neither the ATEA nor the APTU, who were engaged in complex four way merger negotiations with each other, the ETU and the PIUA, showed any enthusiasm for entering into further merger discussions with the PKIU. Negotiations with the AJA were also proving problematic, with, ironically, the AJA expressing concerns about the PKIU's federated structure, which they did not wish to see replicated in a merged organisation. These obstacles were further increased by the AJA's parallel merger negotiations with Actors Equity of Australia (AEA) the Musicians Union of Australia (MUA) and the Australian Commercial and Industrial Artists Association (ACIAA), who were all seeking to amalgamate, owing to ACTU pressure and the Federal Government's legislation. As these three unions were also federally organised, they too were worried by the size and devolved structure of the PKIU.

During 1989 the AEA, AJA, and ACIAA amalgamation talks made considerable progress and the three unions moved towards concluding an amalgamation agreement. As a former senior AJA officer admitted, the commitment of the AJA to discussions with the PKIU started to wane:

> Look, we got a bit sick of dealing with the PKIU at that time. Any agreement we
> thought we had reached with their negotiators was overturned within five minutes.
> In the end we focused on getting the MEAA[7] off the ground as the discussions with
> the PKIU became a total waste of time.

This lack of progress was largely owing to the total opposition of NSW, who continued to make it clear that they believed the only way forward, was a merger with the AMWU. Their campaign was greatly assisted by what one senior AMWU officer described as a "charm offensive" that his union embarked upon at the Federal and State level. PKIU Branch Secretaries were personally feted and reassured of their central role in any merged union's State branch structure. Nationally efforts were also made to reassure the PKIU Federal Officers that their positions were secure, and that as a centrally funded union with sound finances, that they would have an important role in overseeing the new printing division, which the AMWU would create. The promise of a new printing division, the incorporation of the PKIU's name into that of a new merged union, and the protection of the PKIU's structures and their own positions inside the AMWU, all played a part in convincing a number of branches to change their opinion and support an AMWU merger.

By 1990 the majority of PKIU branches had been persuaded to support an amalgamation with the AMWU. There was however one very notable exception; Victoria. The reason why, according to interviewees, was directly linked to the increased factional and micro-political conflict inside the branch. Although the Left had consolidated its control of the branch, after Ian Wenham won the State Secretaryship in 1986, they had failed to dislodge Ed Snell from his position of Assistant Secretary. Snell was a member of the Centre Unity faction and had been a strong supporter of Frank Nelson. After he was re-elected, thanks to strong support from his home chapel, he had been marginalised inside the branch. This position was to alter, in the early 1990s, after the election of a new Organiser, Michael Brown. Brown had been supported by the Left in his election campaign, but after his election he fell out with Wenham and aligned himself with

---

7   Media Entertainment and Arts Alliance.

the Victorian 'Pledge Left' group, who were predominantly made up of Trotskyists and Maoists. Brown also started to forge, after he left the Left faction, an unlikely personal alliance with Snell.

Even Brown's harshest critics (and there were many in the former PKIU) admit that he had great ability as a factional organiser. He and Snell's supporters started to field joint candidates in branch executive and organiser elections. Although from a craft background himself, Brown recognised that the non-craft membership in the carton and cardboard printing sector was a growing group, which received little attention from branch officers. He decided to seek candidates from this area, and to canvass extensively there for support for his and Snell's candidates. This proved to be a successful strategy and the Pledge Left/Centre Unity joint candidates started to win branch positions from the Left, whose power base was centred foursquarely in the newspaper chapels. Relations, in the early 1990s, between the two factional groupings deteriorated rapidly as smear campaigns were entered into by both groups, often involving the use of hostile anonymous leaflets, known colloquially as 'shit sheets'. The defamatory, highly personal, nature of these publications led to the dislike that existed between the leaders of the factions, turning into a strong and palpable hatred. In these circumstances Wenham and his supporters were not prepared as one officer recalled to "gamble" on persuading their supporters to back the AMWU merger.

The Left's success inside the Victorian branch, and the changes in amalgamation and industrial policy they introduced from 1986 onwards, does illustrate how the replacement of one ideological faction by another can lead to an alteration in industrial and political direction (Frenkel and Coolican, 1984; McIllroy et al, 1999, 2007; Daniels and McIllroy, 2009). However, the nature of the struggle within the Victorian branch in the early 1990s also demonstrates how ideological differences can be eclipsed by micro-political factors which in this instance resulted in improbable cross-factional electoral alliances. These developments give further credence to the hypothesis that micro-political factors, particularly personal enmities, can have a profound impact upon union policy-making.

As problems in the Victorian branch escalated, NSW officers had, by 1991, persuaded the Federal union to engage solely in amalgamation discussions with the AMWU. The one dissenting voice at both these forums was the Victorian branch, which still remained adamantly opposed. The negotiations, with the NSW senior officers very much to the fore, were successful and a draft amalgamation document was agreed in 1992. Significantly the only dissenting voice on the PKIU Federal Executive was that of Ian Wenham. The amalgamation document was approved by a specially reconvened Federal Council, in July 1992 and preparations began for a ballot of all PKIU members in early 1993.

Throughout the whole of this process the Victorian Branch was implacable in its total opposition to the merger. This included in 1991 conducting a state wide plebiscite, which produced a large majority against amalgamating with the AMWU. Wenham, according to fellow officials in the Victorian Left faction, had become even more determined to stop the amalgamation after Brown joined the Pledge Left faction, which had a strong presence in the AMWU Victorian branch. However the Victorians were constitutionally bound by the Federal Council decision not to oppose the merger. Nevertheless, as a former Victorian Branch officer admitted, they ignored this rule:

> There was no way we were going to sit idly by and allow the merger to get up. So we campaigned for a No vote.

The other PKIU branches quickly became aware that the Victorian branch was actively campaigning through a 'front' organisation named the 'Combined Chapels Committee'. Their action effectively destroyed the by now fragile alliance between the NSW and Victorian branches. As one officer close to NSW Branch Secretary, Gordon Cooke, observed:

> Gordon had put so much time and energy into improving relations with the Vics, and this is how they repaid him. He was really dirty with them, and he had every right to be.

Anger with the Victorian branch was widespread across the union and it reached boiling point when, with a day to go to the ballot, the 'Combined Chapels Committee' sent out leaflets urging a No vote to all members of the PKIU. The leaflet stated that PKIU members would be "swamped" inside the larger AMWU with which PKIU members had "nothing in common" (PKIU Combined Chapels Committee leaflet, 1993). To the dismay of the NSW branch, they received reports from other branches that the leaflet was resonating with many members. Part of the reason was that in the geographically huge, but numerically small States, only a low key Yes campaign had been waged, because no serious opposition was expected. As one senior officer from a physically vast State with a small membership recalled:

> As I travelled across the State, there was no real hostility to the Metals merger. So we never made any great effort to get a Yes vote up.

The result, when it was declared on 27 May 1993, showed the folly of this policy. Nationally PKIU members had voted by 5770 votes to 4952 to reject the merger. Across the branches there had been large disparities in the results; Queensland and South Australia returned narrow No majorities whilst Victoria returned figures of 2332 votes to 422, against the merger. Equally as important, the majorities in favour in the other branches were not as large as expected, with NSW only voting 2500 to 1600 in favour. In NSW officers and activists put this small margin down to the confusion caused amongst their members by the highly professional No propaganda. As one NSW branch officer recollected:

> After they had voted lots of my FoC's rang me up to ask why the union had changed its mind and recommended a No vote. They said they and their members had followed the leaflets advice and voted No. Quite simply they were conned.

The rejection of the merger left the PKIU Federal Executive deeply divided over how to move forward. The Western Australian branch called upon the Federal Secretary to launch an investigation into allegations that there had been balloting irregularities within the Victorian branch. Whilst the South Australians put forward the charge that the No campaign had broken the union's rules and the result should be declared null and void. Both these demands were turned down by the Federal Secretary, John Cahill, who stated that under rule he did not have the power to launch such an enquiry. His interpretation of the rulebook caused an even deeper rift between him and a number of States, particularly NSW, who had supported the Western Australian and South Australian motions.

The anger of the NSW branch officers' and activists intensified further when their Branch Secretary, Gordon Cooke, announced that he would retire at the end of 1993, partly, those close to him believed, in disappointment at the ballot result and the behaviour of Wenham and Cahill. Cooke was replaced by his Assistant Secretary, John McCarthy, who, with the full backing of his branch, decided to take an uncompromising attitude towards the Victorians and the Federal Secretary. As another State Secretary recalled:

> John MaC took no prisoners at the Federal Executive. He was determined to get the merger with the AMWU up; no matter what it took.

To attain this goal, the NSW branch privately made it clear that if the merger was not revisited, then the branch would breakaway in order to merge with the AMWU. Such an action, owing to Australia's federated industrial relations legislation and the autonomy of the PKIU's branches, was perfectly feasible.[8] As all the other branches were well aware, secession by NSW would have totally devastated the union, as it would have shorn the PKIU of their strongest industrial and financial component, making survival, or even amalgamation, extremely problematic.

As NSW applied increasing pressure, the Victorian branch's internal conflicts were worsening. By the early part of 1994 the Centre Unity/ Pledge Left factional alliance had made considerable electoral progress. Brown himself held off the challenge of the Left's Mike Duffy, for his Organiser position, whilst further gains were made by those endorsed by Brown and Snell in the branch lay and full-time officer elections. At this stage New South Wales moved to directly ensure their desire for another ballot would not be adversely affected by the power struggle in Victoria. Talks were convened by the NSW branch leadership with all the factional groups operating in the Victorian Branch. A former senior PKIU Officer recalls the meetings:

---

8   The Queensland branch of the Public Services Union (PSU) broke away from the Federal PSU and joined the Australian Liquor Hospitality and Miscellaneous Workers Union (ALHMU) in 2011.

> It was made clear to the Vics that the rest of the union would not tolerate their factional spills any longer. If they had another shit fight over the State Secretary election we would move against them federally. We told them we knew their books were so shonky we could crucify them. After a lot of persuasion we got both sides to agree that instead of retiring, Wenham would continue in office, until shortly after the merger, and that Brown's faction would not be opposed for certain officer positions.

There were similarities in this deal with that hammered out between the Left and the NSW Right, which had allowed the Right's Athol Cairn to continue unopposed as NSW State Secretary, when the Left took control of the branch during the 1970s. Although both Victorian factions had agreed to the deal, the level of distrust was such that a State Secretary nomination form was completed in favour of Brown, in case the Left put forward another candidate. To ensure the veracity of the agreement it was agreed that Brown would sign Wenham's nomination form. Shortly before the close of nominations, Brown rang the returning officer at the Victorian Electoral Commission, to check how many forms had been submitted. The Returning Officer confirmed that only one form had been submitted. Brown, believing this to be Wenham's form, did not lodge his nomination papers. However when the winner was declared, having been elected unopposed, their name was Mike Duffy. It swiftly transpired that whilst allegedly collecting signatures for his own nomination paper Ian Wenham had in fact been collecting signatures for his, younger, factional colleague, Mike Duffy.

Unsurprisingly, the Brown/Snell group were incandescent with rage. In an act of retaliation they defied Victorian branch conventions and nominated Brown, who was a full-time officer, as their candidate for the office of Branch President. Previously a lay member had always occupied the role of Branch President, although this was not stipulated by rule. Brown's election resulted in him playing a prominent part in the Victorian branch's Executive Committee, including overseeing the State Secretary's administration of the branch, whilst in his job as a Branch Organiser he was under the direction of the State Secretary. This contradictory position led, unsurprisingly, to further conflict in what had become a wholly dysfunctional branch. Outside of Victoria senior PKIU officers were also extremely angry. As a senior New South Wales's officer reflected:

> What Wenham and Duffy did was a total disaster. I don't like Brown or his mates, but to use such shonky tactics to get Duffy in, meant that everyone viewed him as being an illegitimate State Secretary. He had no authority, and all Ian achieved was the strengthening of Brown. This at a time we needed stability across the union, in order to get the Metals merger back on track.

As the Victorian branch spiralled into ever deeper internal conflict, it was significantly the NSW State Secretary, as opposed to the PKIU's Federal Secretary, who spoke to Mike Duffy and made it clear that they believed he had no right to hold office. In the words of a former PKIU Federal Executive member:

> McCarthy met Duffy and told him he was a totally illegitimate officer. He had no mandate from his members and NSW would refuse to work with unless he proved himself capable of taking the hard decision.

The "hard decision" referred to was supporting a merger with the AMWU. During the same period that NSW's John McCarthy met Duffy he also engaged in talks with Brown and Snell. At these discussions they reassured NSW that their opposition to the merger had only ever been tactical, and they were not in principle against the merger. One of the senior officials who supported the Brown/Snell group described their policy on the first merger ballot in this fashion:

> We knew that Wenham had whipped a number of key chapels into frenzy over the Metals merger, portraying it as if he was defending the existence of our union. If we had supported the Metals merger then we would have been crucified; the elections were coming up and we could not afford to let ourselves be destroyed.

At the PKIU Federal level, John Cahill, was still attempting to find an alternative amalgamation partner to the AMWU. In late 1993 he sent out a list of six unions and asked branches to rank them in order of merger preference. NSW was angry at Cahill's action but following consultation with other branches, it agreed to complete the form. The result was that the merger with the Journalists (who were now part of the MEAA) was effectively ruled out, as the MEAA came last of the six, in a majority of the branches rankings. The AMWU easily topped the poll, whilst of the other unions considered only the CFMEU, who came second, received any significant support. However the hostility of the WA and Queensland branches to the CFMEU meant that effectively only the AMWU were left as a serious amalgamation option.

Mike Duffy and what remained of the Left group in Victoria, after election defeats and the retirement of Ian Wenham were now in a weak strategic position to resist the pressure being placed upon them. After much deliberation and further persuasion Duffy decided to recommend merger with the AMWU to his branch. He did so at the April 1994 Branch Committee where, even though there was dissent, he secured a narrow majority in favour. At the subsequent Federal Executive of the PKIU there was unanimous agreement that they should hold another ballot, where they would seek endorsement of an amalgamation with the AMWU.

The 1994 campaign proved to be very different from its predecessor. There was the total absence of a No campaign, and the Yes campaign was vigorously prosecuted with the result that the amalgamation was endorsed by 9,171 votes to 1,453. Significantly none of the States voted against the merger, with Victorian members voting 2,023 to 397 in favour. The merger with the AMWU followed in February 1995, with the new union being titled the Australian Food Manufacturing, Engineering, Printing and Kindred Industries Union, although it was still referred to as the AMWU. The former PKIU membership along with AMWU members who worked in the printing and allied industries were placed into the union's newly created Printing Section.

The PKIU's eventual agreement to amalgamate with the AMWU, after the Federal Executive initially vetoed entering into merger talks, and subsequently their national membership voted to reject such an amalgamation, is supportive of the proposition that unions have the ability to make, and reverse, strategic decisions, which profoundly affect their futures (Heery and Kelly, 1988; Kelly and Heery, 1994; Heery, 2003, 2006). In the negotiations that led up to the merger the ability of key component parts of a union, in this case NSW, to reject national policy without incurring sanctions, proved to be extremely important. This provides evidence to support the hypothesis that deciding on amalgamation partners involves a more complex internal process than that outlined by some authors who place an overwhelming emphasis on a union's amalgamation strategy being driven by external environmental factors (Chaison, 1996; Undy, 1999, 2008; Waddington, 1988, 1995; Waddington et al, 2005; Griffin, 2002).

In the amalgamation of the PKIU with the AMWU the role played by micro-political factors in shaping amalgamation policy has been shown to be critical. In particular the respect that specific individuals were able to command amongst their peers played a significant role in determining who would be the PKIU's amalgamation partner. This was the case even when the officer concerned did not hold the most senior position in the union. These observations are strongly supported by the NSW State Secretary, John McCarthy's refusal to accept nomination for the post of Federal Secretary, just prior to the second AMWU amalgamation ballot. He refused, as many interviewees stated, because he believed he could be equally as effective in delivering the Yes vote as NSW State Secretary. Furthermore, as a senior officer close to McCarthy stated:

> John Mac received calls from nearly all the State Secretaries saying they wanted him to nominate against Cahill. He refused, even though he would have been a shoe in, because he viewed an election as a distraction to the main aim – the Metals merger.

As a consequence, John Cahill was re-elected unopposed as PKIU Federal Secretary and after the amalgamation became Secretary of the AMWU Printing section. However as many contributors pointed out his was very much 'office without power' as the Federal AMWU leadership continued to deal with John McCarthy, when seeking the views of the Print Section. As a former senior AMWU Officer confided:

> If it hadn't been for blokes like Gordon Cooke and John McCarthy we would have simply given up on the printers, after their first ballot. As far as we were concerned McCarthy was the real leader of the Printers and we dealt with him, before, during and after the amalgamation.

Soon after the merger took place, significant pressure was placed on Michael Duffy to step down as Victorian State Secretary, which he acceded too, whilst efforts were made to place the Divisional Secretary, John Cahill, in another post in the labour movement. This Cahill resisted, although as the above quotation illustrates, he continued to be marginalised by the AMWU leadership.[9] The PKIU branches also amalgamated at the State branch level, with the exception of the ACT branch, which was integrated into the AMWU NSW branch. Whilst the NSW PKIU branch fitted in comfortably with their long term factional allies in the AMWU NSW branch, there were problems elsewhere, most notably in Victoria. Here factional conflicts continued within the Printing Division, and they had still not been resolved by the end of 1996. There was also, as one State Secretary commented, a "considerable culture shock", for the smaller PKIU branches. They were now part of the much larger AMWU State branches, whose internal organisations were typically characterised by factional and divisional manoeuvrings. These types of machinations were unfamiliar to many PKIU officers and activists from the smaller State's, whose branches had historically seen little, if any, political factional activity.

Conclusion

This chapter set out to examine the influences which shaped the judgements of policy makers, whose collective decisions fashioned the policies of the Australian print unions on the labour process, recruitment and amalgamation. The evidence gathered has shown that the industrial, economic and political environment within which the unions operated did play a

9   Cahill, although he remained in office was to be defeated in a controversial election for the Federal Printing Divisional Secretary post, in 1998, by the Victorian branch's Michael Brown. His defeat occurred after NSW and their allies had, again, chosen not to oppose Cahill for what would have been his last term in office, before retirement. Following Brown's election, Cahill successfully took legal action over a leaflet that made libellous allegations against him, and which was received by every Printing Division member the day they took delivery of their ballot paper. Subsequently the AMWU Printing Division Executive and the union's Federal Executive both agreed to remove Brown from office, over this and other alleged election malpractices.

significant part in shaping union policy. It is also the case that unlike the British print unions, the Australians did not consciously decide, in any of the three policy areas, to defy the legislative restrictions placed upon them by the apparatus of the State. A number of reasons for this divergence in policy have been identified. These include the relatively dispersed, smaller nature of the print industry, the age profile of the workforce, and the Federal Government's support for the operation of the arbitral system which led Australian employers to seek negotiated settlements of labour process issues.

Whilst this evidence suggests that the theories of institutional contextualist authors (Flanders, 1965; Bain, 1970; Clegg, 1976; Howell, 2005) are more applicable to the Australian print unions than the British unions, there is also abundant evidence of a whole series of clear strategic choices being made, which are in line with Heery and Kelly's assertions that unions take decisions which have a profound effect on the direction and success of their organisations (Heery and Kelly, 1988; Kelly and Heery, 1994; Heery, 2003, 2006). The evidence has also shown that the creation of policy at the workplace, State and Federal level is the product of a complex series of interactions between policy makers, who are often operating at more than one level of a union's structure. Furthermore there is evidence that decisions taken at a national level can, in certain circumstances, be thwarted or even totally reversed by powerful minority sections. These findings strongly support Heery and Kelly's hypothesis that important strategic policy choices are made at a variety of different levels of a union's structure (Heery, 2003, 2006; Heery and Kelly, 1988; Kelly and Heery, 1994) and cast doubt on other scholars' suggestion that important strategic decisions are predominantly taken at the national level (Boxall and Hayes, 1997; Child, 1997).

The empirical evidence, when combined with that relating to the British print unions, also strongly suggests that the theories of rank and filist authors who contend that membership resistance to detrimental changes to the labour process, are stifled by officers seeking non-confrontational, negotiated compromises, is inaccurate (Fairbrother, 1990, 1996, 2000; Bramble, 1993, 2008). There is also a powerful corroboration in this chapter of the assertion that the policy of Australian print unions' was shaped by the craft, occupational and industrial loyalties of members, activists and officers (Fitzgerald, 1967; Hagan, 1966; Cryle, 2008). In addition to these influences the chapter has also shown that PKIU policy was altered by the election of officers from different political factions (Darlington, 1994, 2001; McIllroy and Campbell, 1999; McIllroy, 2007; Daniels and McIllroy, 2009). However, it is also abundantly clear from the evidence that whilst institutional, occupational, geographical and ideological factors all played a significant part in influencing PKIU policy-making, the hypothesis that micro-political factors also perform a highly influential role in policy formation is accurate. In particular the role of friendships, enmities and personal loyalties on policy makers' decisions, has been shown to be extremely important. Whether these, and the previous chapter's findings are replicated in relation to the British and Australian telecommunication unions' policy-making, is the subject of the next two chapters.

CHAPTER 10

The British Telecommunication Unions: 1980–1996

Introduction

The period from 1980 to 1996 proved to be one of seismic change for the British telecommunications industry and its then principal trade union the POEU.[1] In 1980 British Telecom (BT), as it had been renamed that year, was a Public Corporation and the monopoly provider of all domestic telephony services. By December 1984, BT had been stripped of its domestic telephony monopoly and had been privatised. This transformation of the British telecommunications industry heralded the introduction of competition into the domestic telephony market and presaged acceleration in the utilisation of new technologies, including digital, mobile and satellite systems. BT sought to deal with this rapidly changing industrial and technological environment by introducing significant alterations to the labour process, sizeable reductions in employment levels, and a total restructuring of the company's industrial relations system. All of these developments resulted in a series of major challenges for the POEU, 90% of whose members, in 1980, were BT employees.

The labour process, recruitment and amalgamation policies that the POEU and subsequently the NCU adopted in response to these political and industrial alterations are examined in this chapter. An analysis is also undertaken of the reasons why the union selected specific policy options. In addition, an assessment is made of the factors that influenced

1   The Post Office Engineering Union amalgamated with the Civil and Public Servants Association, Postal and Telecommunications Group in 1985, to form the National Communications Union.

the POEU and NCU decision makers in their policy choices. Time is also spent analysing the Mercury interconnection dispute and the POEU's campaign against BT's privatisation, both of whose unsuccessful outcomes profoundly influenced subsequent policies. The similarities and differences between the POEU's and NCU's policy approach and those of the Australian and British printing trade unions, is also considered. Finally, the chapter evaluates the influence on POEU and NCU policy of their powerful political factions, whose operations were often distinguished by bitter internal disputes, as well as cross factional conflicts.

The labour process

In 1981, the Conservative Government announced its plans, which had not been contained in the Party's election manifesto, to privatise BT. The POEU's NEC, which was then controlled by The Bloc faction, agreed that they would 'vigorously oppose' this policy. This decision achieved cross factional support, not only owing to an ideological consensus in favour of public ownership, but also, as interviewees recalled, because NEC members and officers were aware of the possible damage that privatisation could cause to the POEU's ability to influence the labour process. As a then senior NEC member commented.

> We had spent decades achieving a closed shop, decent terms and conditions and influence over how management managed our members. We knew that if BT were privatised, our facilities and local agreements would be attacked. We also knew that if competitors weren't charged the proper rate for using our network we would lose customers and jobs.

Whilst there was a broad agreement over opposing the Government's plans, there was no unanimity over the form this resistance should take. NEC members and branch secretaries who were part of the BL, pressed for the POEU to immediately ballot for a national strike. The Bloc, whose membership included the vast majority of National Officers, was more cautious. They preferred to launch a parliamentary attempt to derail the privatisation and deregulation programme.

These different approaches reflect the ideological divergence that had been developing inside the POEU during the 1970s. The differences had become increasingly pronounced, in respect of POEU's efforts to influence the labour process. High levels of factional influence distinguished the POEU from the British or Australian printing unions where craft, occupational, geographical and micro-political factors were all more influential. By 1980, the balance in the factional struggle had shifted further in the BL's favour. They had gained control of more POEU branches than at any time previously. These branches were predominantly large and based in Britain's major cities. Once elected, BL branch officers had been successful in gaining considerable improvements to their members' terms and conditions and greater influence over the labour process, often through the application of more militant tactics. This process had been aided by the GPO's increasing use, in the 1970s, of local productivity bargaining, which enabled branch officers to negotiate local pay deals. This decentralisation of bargaining structures, allied to a greater bargaining role for lay union activists, was a phenomenon that extended wider than the telecommunications industry (Flanders, 1965; Bain, 1970; Clegg, 1976; Boraston et al, 1975) and was associated, by some scholars, with similar increases in militancy in other sectors of the economy (Beynon, 1973, 1984; Batstone et al, 1977, 1978; Lane and Roberts, 1971; Darlington, 1994).

As interviewees from both factions agreed, the success of BL branches, in the face of Bloc opposition, in securing a reduced working week and the immensely popular nine day fortnight, had greatly increased their industrial confidence. Following this achievement, the BL firmly believed that the POEU had the industrial strength to defeat privatisation and deregulation. This conviction had grown further when, in the early 1980s, the BL won control of branches whose members maintained highly fault sensitive, commercial telephony equipment. The confidence of the BL is encapsulated in part of a speech that NEC member, Brian Macey, made to a POEU BL meeting in the early 1980s. He stated:

In the 1970s the NUM were the most powerful union in this country. When they took strike action they bought industry to a standstill. Well we now have great industrial strength; we can stop the banks, the stock exchange, the multi-national's and even the Government. We are the electronic miners of the twentieth Century. Whereas the NUM could stop industry, we can stop capitalism.

The Bloc's National Officers and activists believed that the BL's wish for immediate national industrial action was premature and that the union should instead seek the assistance of the Labour Party and their sponsored MP's in trying to defeat the Bill in Parliament. They also suggested that the union should launch a publicity campaign in rural areas, where the allegation would be made that a privatised BT would cut services and raise charges, owing to the higher costs of provision and lower levels of demand. The POEU's aim was to incite rural electors to lobby their Conservative MP to oppose the Telecommunications Bill. These two strategies were adopted by the Bloc controlled NEC, much to the anger of BL Executive members.

Intriguingly these polices were remarkably similar to the successful anti-privatisation campaigns run in outback Australia by the APTU. Whilst the POEU Bloc leadership did not accept they adopted this tactic as a consequence of speaking to the APTU's officers, interviewees did confirm that there was a meeting between the two unions (prior to a Postal, Telegraph & Telephone International (PTTI) conference) at which the APTU's policy was discussed. This is the first evidence, uncovered by this book, of a British union drawing directly upon the policies of their Australian counterparts.

The POEU's strategy to counter privatisation had some, short term, success. Their rural campaign lead to a small number of Conservative MP's moving amendments to the Telecommunications Bill, which when allied to a major filibuster by the union's sponsored MP's, resulted in the Bill running out of parliamentary time prior to the 1983 General Election. The Government, however, was not so legislatively hindered in their wish to introduce competition into the British Telecommunications industry. This they were able to do by simply issuing an operating licence to another telecommunications company. In 1982 they did so, allowing the Cable and Wireless subsidiary, Mercury, to operate in the British market. The Government also stated that BT would have to allow Mercury to use their infrastructure, without being allowed to charge for the costs of constructing and maintaining the telephone network. The order also stipulated that BT would have to connect Mercury into the telecommunications network. This in turn meant that POEU members would be expected to undertake the physical interconnection of Mercury. Following the announcement there was cross-factional unanimity that the union should actively oppose the interconnection of Mercury. Where this accord was to fracture was over the nature of this opposition.

The BL wished to see a clear instruction given to all members to refuse to undertake the interconnection work, and for the NEC to sanction a national strike ballot. Senior National Officers and Bloc NEC members agreed that members should not undertake the interconnection work, but they opposed the holding of a national strike ballot, for fear that a prolonged strike would bankrupt the union. These financial concerns derived from the POEU's rule book commitment to pay members the equivalent of their basic salary, whilst they were engaged in official strike action. The NEC had attempted on numerous occasions to amend this policy at POEU Annual Conferences, but their proposals had been defeated. That the POEU's leadership was unable to change this policy reflects both the independent mindedness of Conference delegates and the lack of any sustained period of national strike action.

The Bloc's refusal to support a national ballot resulted in the union's leadership being criticised for what many members and branches perceived was a lack of action. Importantly for The Bloc this anger was emanating not only from BL supporters, but also from non-aligned branches, whose support they relied on in elections held at Annual Conference. Given this discontent the POEU Bloc leadership was keen to explore policy alternatives to a national strike. Such an alternative was presented to them from what Bloc interviewees agreed was a very unlikely quarter: the BL led London International branch. The branch had written to the NEC proposing that their members should take selective strike action, which they asserted could win the interconnection dispute, without any other POEU members having to take action. The London International branch's confidence emanated from their members responsibility for the Bank of England, the Stock Exchange, the major clearing banks and the Houses of Parliament telephone services. Having received London International's proposal, The

Bloc dominated NEC agreed to accept their offer and sanctioned the selective strike action. This is yet another example which supports the theory that important national union policies can be, and often are, profoundly influenced by strategic choices made at the local workplace or branch level (Heery and Kelly, 1988; Kelly and Heery, 1994; Heery, 2003, 2006).

Inside the BL there was considerable anger at the behaviour of the London International branch. The branch's offer had been made without the agreement or knowledge of the BL leadership, and there was fury that London International had effectively allowed the POEU's leadership to avoid calling a national ballot. There was also, as BL interviewees recalled, an equally strong belief that London International was greatly overestimating their own industrial strength, in a dangerous act of hubris. The lack of communication by the London International branch with the rest of the BL was indicative of broader fissures that were appearing inside the faction, not only over Mercury's interconnection but also over general industrial tactics. These tensions were in part ideological, with disagreements occurring between Trotskyist and CPGB supporters (see also McIlroy and Daniels, 2009; Undy et al, 1996).

However, when interviewed, many BL and Bloc members highlighted two other key reasons for the different industrial approaches of BL branches and their officers. The first related to a branch's geographical location; the second to variations in senior branch officers' industrial judgement. It was stated by some interviewees that BL London branches tended to be more militant than their counterparts from outside the Capital. This was the case even where the provincial and the London branches had members of the same political group or Party holding senior branch officer positions. Reflecting on this anomaly a number of interviewees pointed to larger attendances at provincial branch meetings, which led to industrial strategy being moderated by memberships who were less ideologically committed. The reason for the larger turnouts at meetings was generally attributed to members living closer to their workplace and therefore finding it easier to participate in meetings.[2]

---

2   The empirical evidence gathered through attending numerous NCU (E) branch meetings substantiated this theory. However the attendance at many large London

Significantly a number of POEU activists, who had been active outside of London before moving to the Capital, rejected the causal link between lower branch attendance and greater militancy. Instead they pointed to the more adversarial attitude of BT's London managers who, they stated, wished to exclude the POEU branch officers from various aspects of the labour process, such as work rosters and the allocation of overtime. This led, these officers contended, to a more confrontational attitude being adopted by London branches, in order to gain influence over the labour process.

Another, sizeable group of interviewees disagreed totally with the contention that geography or managerial attitudes played a major part in explaining the divisions that occurred between BL branches. They pointed out that there were BL London branches which followed a similar industrial line to their provincial counterparts, whilst there were also branches based outside of London, which adopted a very militant approach to gaining influence over the labour process. In analysing this variance, these contributors acknowledged that the division was not ideological, but instead rested more on micro-political factors, in particular the respect members had for key senior activists. As a BL NEC member and branch secretary stated:

> The reasons for many disagreements inside the BL were not political. There was a group, including both Trots and CP members who came together and sensibly assessed how to move forward and then adopted a sensible, but still radical, approach. Then there was a minority who were often self-important and who could be easily flattered or bullied by Stanley and other Bloc members into adopting a weaker line. Then there was another group who seemed to think that world revolution could be instantly achieved, just by calling for a national strike.

A Bloc NEC member also made some intriguingly similar observations:

> Look there was a number of splits in the BL and these were not just between the CP and the Millies. There was one small group you could talk with and sometimes get them to agree with you. Then there were another group – who industrially were nobody's mugs – but who held the factional line. They came from well organised branches, and it was clear they knew what they were about. Then there was another group – who were just a bunch of head-bangers.

---

branches was often proportionally still relatively high, with over 50 members regularly in attendance at a number of the London branches meetings.

These observations whilst lending weight to the argument (McIlroy and Daniels, 2009) that Left factions are prone to internal splits, also provides evidence that there are other, micro-political, factors at work inside a faction which influence the attitudes of individual decision makers and the policy positions they adopt.

Following the NEC's adoption of London International's offer to stage unilateral action, the BL met and agreed that the NEC's response to Mercury's interconnection was inadequate and that they would call for a meeting of all branches with the national leadership, at which the demand for a national strike would be pursued. Under pressure from a number of Bloc and nonaligned branches, who supported this idea, the POEU leadership finally agreed to a series of meetings with the union's branches to discuss the interconnection dispute. At the meetings the national leadership remained resolute that they would not call a national strike ballot, however there was acceptance that there needed to be additional selective industrial action, in addition to that being taken by the London International branch, in order to disrupt the City of London's telecommunications. Whilst still disagreeing over the lack of a national ballot these proposals were endorsed by the BL, as well as by the branches concerned, and the action commenced in the spring of 1983.

The Mercury interconnection dispute

As soon as the dispute began, BT management deployed a series of counter measures, designed to undermine the action and place financial pressure on the union. The first of these steps involved managers, who possessed the relevant technical skills, being instructed to work on the inter-connection programme. Although their union, the Society of Telecommunications Executives (STE) issued instructions that their members should not undermine the POEU dispute, pressure from senior management was often sufficient for many STE members to decide to undertake the work (see also Gall, 2010). The Company also sought, as BT managers confirmed, to increase the cost of the dispute to the POEU by ordering engineers from outside London to undertake 'blacked' work. When these POEU members refused to do so, they were suspended. At the height of the dispute POEU members from as far away as Bristol were being suspended. This resulted in a rapid increase in the number of members receiving full strike pay from the union.

Inside the POEU there was increasing disquiet at the failure of the industrial action to significantly affect Mercury's connection into the telecommunications network and at the ever escalating costs of the dispute. The union, which did not possess the type of cash reserves and property assets the NGA held prior to the Messenger dispute, had rapidly depleted its modest funds and was now in a perilous financial position. The POEU's anxieties were compounded when Mercury commenced legal proceedings against the union, arguing that the interconnection boycott was unlawful, as it contravened the 1982 Employment Act's prohibition on politically motivated industrial action.

How the union should respond to these serious industrial and financial challenges caused disagreement and recrimination, not only between, but also within, the POEU's factions. The BL continued to call for a national strike ballot, but there was internal conflict over their support for selective strike action. As a former senior BL NEC member recalled:

> By this time we were bloody angry about what was happening. To have any chance of winning, what was clearly one of the most important disputes in our history, we had to take national strike action. As we had predicted the London action had not worked and we were all paying the price. Stanley just wanted an easy option, and those Muppets from London gave it to him on a plate. We should never have supported anything but a national strike, where we occupied the exchanges so management couldn't do our work.

Divisions were also occurring inside The Bloc where a number of officers and lay activists felt they were caught in an almost impossible bind. As one senior officer recalled:

> We were badly undermined by the STE members' undertaking the interconnection work. Some of us even agreed with the BL's call for a national strike, but the fact is if we couldn't afford to finance a national strike even for a few days. We were in a classic Catch 22.

As a result, The Bloc's officers and NEC members remained committed to only supporting selective industrial action and the 'blacking' of Mercury's interconnection. The two factions therefore went into the POEU's 1983 Annual Conference, putting forward different policy proposals as to how to proceed with the Mercury dispute. At the Conference, delegates supported BL motions calling on the POEU leadership to hold a national strike ballot; they then proceeded to elect a majority of BL candidates onto the NEC. The assumption, at the close of Conference, was that the new BL dominated NEC would immediately call a national strike ballot.

However the General Secretary engaged in a series of meetings with selected members of the BL, whom he hoped he could convince not to support a national ballot. At these meetings, according to those close to Stanley, he explained in vivid detail the financial ramifications for the POEU of running a national strike. Stanley's, arguments had been strengthened by the Conservative's winning the June 1983 General Election with an increased majority, dashing the POEU's hopes that the Labour Party would form a Government and fulfil their commitment to keep BT in public hands and rescind Mercury's operating licence. Instead the re-elected Conservative Government made it clear that they would immediately reintroduce the Bill to privatise BT and refused, in all their negotiations with the POEU, to substantially alter their telecommunications deregulation policy.

The General Secretary's effort, to convince a minority of BL NEC members that a national strike would bankrupt the union, was successful. To the fury of other BL members a small number of the faction's NEC members voted with The Bloc and stopped the national strike ballot. Unsurprisingly this led to further internal recriminations, whilst it also ensured that the POEU continued to prosecute the dispute in the same fashion as previously. By the autumn of 1983 the continuation of the Mercury boycott was being questioned, as more members were suspended for refusing to undertake the interconnection work, and the levels of strike benefits continued to grow. These pressures seemed to ease slightly, when at the High Court in

October 1983, Mercury's application for an injunction was denied, when the Court found that the POEU's industrial action constituted a legitimate trade dispute. However at the Court of Appeal, the Master of the Rolls, Sir John Donaldson reversed the decision, finding that the strike was attempting to affect the Government's decision to deregulate the industry and was therefore 'political'. As McIllroy (1988: 95) notes, Donaldson singularly failed to disclose his significant share holdings in Cable & Wireless, prior to hearing the case.

The Court of Appeal's judgement meant that the POEU was now liable for substantial damages, which the TUC General Council made clear they would not assist with, as they were withdrawing support for what had been ruled an unlawful dispute. This decision was in line with the TUC's refusal to support the NGA in the Messenger Newspaper Dispute, after similar judgements had been handed down. Although the TUC had not been granting the POEU substantial financial assistance, their distancing of themselves from the dispute, combined with the fines imposed by the Court, alarmed the POEU's bankers, who threatened to cap their overdraft limit. This danger, combined with the continuing lack of success in stopping the interconnection, led the General Secretary to recommend to his Bloc Executive colleagues that the Mercury action should cease. His recommendation was accepted and agreement was reached that a motion proposing the ending of the dispute be moved at the NEC. As a leading Bloc NEC member of the time recalled this was a traumatic decision for all those concerned:

> It was a terrible decision to have to make. We knew that our members were committed to the dispute and that the introduction of competitors to BT would lead to job losses and attacks on our conditions. However it was clear that if we carried on we would bankrupt the union. I saw Bryan [Stanley] close to tears over the issue, but we all knew that even if we stopped paying full strike pay the costs of defying the injunctions would have crippled us. In the end we had no choice.

At the subsequent emergency NEC the majority BL group, was divided over whether the union could continue with the dispute in the face of possible sequestration of the union's assets. The majority of the NEC BL delegates wished to continue and to escalate the action by calling a national strike ballot. However four of the BL NEC members agreed with the General Secretary that the union was heading for financial disaster if it continued with its action. After hours of debate the NEC finally voted, by a small majority, to call off the action.

The decision of the NEC, to end the dispute, created further deep divisions inside the union. Some branches refused to abide by the Executive's instruction, and continued with their boycott of inter connection work. Significantly this split did not simply run along factional lines. BL controlled branches and those whose officers were not aligned to either faction continued to refuse to undertake the interconnection work, whilst even branches which supported The Bloc, voiced dissent at the decision. Eventually, after further legal sanctions were threatened and BT managers continued to undertake the 'blacked' interconnection work, the areas in dispute ceased their unofficial industrial action.

In reviewing why the Mercury interconnection dispute was unsuccessful, interviewees from each faction and those who claimed to be factionally non-aligned, all focused on the failure to change the rule granting full strike pay as a significant strategic error. As one former BL NEC member and Branch Secretary stated:

> In retrospect it was wrong of us to oppose the rule change. Many of us did so because we believed National Office was always looking to find ways to stop members from taking action. At the time we didn't appreciate how The Bloc would use the cost of strike pay to stop a national ballot.

However, contributors agreed that getting such a change through POEU Annual Conference would have been extremely difficult, as delegates would have had to be persuaded to remove the guarantee that they would receive full strike pay when they were taking industrial action. Cross factional unanimity over why the dispute failed ceases at this point. Bloc officers and activists highlighted how hostile legislation, adverse Court judgements and the commitment of the Conservative Government to privatisation, conspired to fatally undermine the dispute. This analysis is similar to that put forward by institutional and political contextualist authors who view environmental factors as the primary determinant of union behaviour and the success or failure of their industrial strategies (Flanders, 1965; Bain, 1970; Clegg, 1976; Howell, 2005).

Many BL members however dispute this institutional analysis. They focus instead on what they believe were a series of incorrect strategic choices, which led to the failure of the dispute. Primary amongst these was the leadership's decision not to hold a strike ballot, which prohibited POEU members from undertaking an official national strike, which could have forced the Government to alter their deregulation proposals. In support of this argument BL members point to the success of the POEU's industrial action in the late 1970s which achieved the shorter working week. These views are given further credence by the memoirs of Conservative Cabinet Ministers (Lawson, 1992; Parkinson, 1992) who detail the Government's relief that there was no national strike, as they feared that industrial action could have led to a Conservative back bench revolt, which would have forced a withdrawal of what were then unpopular deregulation proposals.

The nature of the policy debate outlined above over the Mercury interconnection dispute provides more support for the argument that unions are constantly making a series of critical strategic choices, which are central to determining the success of their overall policy goals (Kelly, 1998; Heery and Kelly, 1994; Kelly and Heery, 1994; Heery, 2000, 2003, 2006). The nature of these debates, which often did not follow simple ideological lines, also adds further substance to the hypothesis that micro-political factors, as well as ideological affiliations, play an important part in determining policy direction.

The labour process: after the Mercury interconnection dispute

Interviewees agree that the failure to reach a negotiated settlement did severe damage to the industrial confidence of the POEU's activists and officers. This ebbing away of belief in the union's capacity to take effective industrial action is cited by The Bloc members as the primary reason why the General Secretary received NEC majority support, including crucially a minority of BL members, when he proposed that the union should not take industrial action in protest at the privatisation of BT. Instead the union simply heightened their anti-privatisation campaigns, which had been launched in 1981.

The privatisation of BT was the precursor, interviewees from both management and the POEU agreed, to a sea change in the management of industrial relations and the labour process. BT's management sought to divest themselves of all vestiges of the old Whitley bargaining structure and the consensual, pragmatic approach, with which it was associated. Senior BT management stated to their junior managers and supervisors that their business ethos had now fundamentally altered. As an STE activist recalls:

> At meetings it was made clear to us that we needed to take control of the business. In fact my boss actually said we had to ensure that we regained the right to manage the workforce from the POEU.

This change in managerial approach created conflict inside the POEU over how to respond. As with Mercury's interconnection, whilst there had been unanimity that the union needed to oppose privatisation, redundancies and efforts to lessen the POEU's influence over the labour process, there was disagreement over how they should do so. A majority of BL branches and NEC members were still adamant that the union should be resisting privatisation and seeking re-nationalisation, via a concerted campaign of industrial action, including a national anti-privatisation strike. The Bloc and senior national officers opposed this call, as did those BL NEC members, who had opposed action prior to privatisation.

Internal disagreements also occurred over how the POEU should respond to BT's, post-privatisation, voluntary redundancy and early retirement schemes. These deals offered long-serving employees extremely generous severance packages. As in the Australian newspaper industry, management interviewees confirmed that the schemes were intentionally made very attractive in order to avoid any wide scale conflict over the loss of thousands of staff. BT stated that they wished to lose staff in order to concentrate on their 'core' business. The 'peripheral' functions of which BT wished to divest itself included substantial parts of POEU members' work, including the excavation of buried faults and substantial elements of network construction. This work was to be outsourced to contractors, so that BT's remaining engineers carried out only skilled maintenance and construction tasks.

In scenes remarkably reminiscent of those in the Australian printing industry, these redundancy proposals were initially met by membership opposition. There was anger at the large scale job losses and at the replacement of BT employees by contractors. This resentment resulted, in a number of instances of local unofficial industrial action. However, as numerous contributors commented, this hostility quickly started to dissipate when members realised how much money they would be entitled to if they accepted a severance package. Here, as with the Australian printing unions, the POEU's efforts to oppose redundancies started to founder, owing to a lack of membership support. The strong similarities in the responses of the respective memberships provides yet more evidence that the rank and filist contention that officials are constantly acting as a brake on membership militancy, is unsound (Callincos, 1983; Cliff, 1970; Offe et al, 1985; Fairbrother, 2000; Bramble, 1993, 2008).

Reflecting on his efforts to fight the 'release' programme a BL branch officer highlighted the way in which he felt BT's financial inducements also started to change the collective industrial mood of the membership:

> Once a lot of our long-serving men realised they could leave with over £70 or £80K, they simply weren't interested in fighting. Whilst even amongst younger members it was hard to convince them that they'd not be better off letting a contractor dig their holes. As for opposing privatisation – well that also became harder, once their free shares started to rocket in value.

This last point was highlighted by a number of officers and NEC members, as to why they felt opposing privatisation, job losses and detrimental changes to the labour process, was futile. Free shares in BT had been issued to all employees when the Company was privatised and rose sharply in value after flotation, owing to the Government's initial share price proving to be a gross underestimate of BT's market value (Parker, 2009: 321). As POEU branch and national officials recalled, a significant number of members had also taken the opportunity to buy additional pre-privatisation shares at a discounted price, which resulted shortly after the flotation in many of them possessing shareholdings worth many thousands of pounds.

There was, though, no consensus amongst participants that the issuing of free shares and the offer of redundancy packages had a significant impact on the membership's willingness to take industrial action. Those who supported the call for national strike action point out that less than three years later, when the vast majority of members still held large shareholdings and many staff were still opting to take redundancy packages, the union's membership voted for a national strike. In explaining why, in their view, the union did not hold a ballot, BL members were quick to highlight what they viewed as a collective failure of nerve by the union's leadership and elements of their own faction. As a senior BL NEC member stated:

> The General Secretary and NEC should have been honest and told the members that the only possible way we could stop the Government's privatisation plans was with a national strike. We also should have said to the members that if they voted for action, we would not be able to afford to pay them the equivalent of their basic wages in strike pay. I am certain, from the responses I received to this proposal from members across the country, that we would have won a vote – on those terms.

Other activists supported this position, whilst also stressing that by not holding a ballot, members were effectively being denied the right to choose whether to fight privatisation. As a 'non-aligned' branch secretary commented:

> A strike might have been lost, or even the vote might have been lost, but at least with a ballot we'd have had the opportunity to decide one way or the other.

The BL Executive group's failure to deliver a strike ballot owing to their split, contributed substantially, interviewees agreed, to the faction losing control of the NEC at the following election. Owing to the provisions of the 1984 Trade Union Act, the NEC could not now be elected by Annual Conference delegates. Instead the Executive was now elected by a postal ballot of all members. This change assisted The Bloc, whose supporters were less likely to attend branch meetings where previously Conference delegates had been elected and in many cases mandated. The BL's electoral misfortunes continued when, following Bryan Stanley's retirement as General Secretary their candidate, Phil Holt, lost to Bloc member and Newcastle under Lyme MP, John Golding.

These results saw The Bloc, now renamed Members First (MF), having full control of all the key POEU national officer posts, as well as the NEC. This allowed them to adopt a pragmatic, non-confrontational approach to BT's desire to dilute the POEU's branches influence over elements of the labour process. These industrial tactics led, according to many BL supporters, to a grateful BT management allowing MF use of the Company's internal staff communication system to distribute propaganda. Whether or not it was officially sanctioned, the MF literature was unquestionably disseminated through the internal BT system, which resulted in all union members receiving leaflets which focused negatively on the Trotskyist allegiances of some BL candidates. In the subsequent 1986 NEC election the tactics proved highly effective, with the BL retaining only one seat on the NEC. As leading BL member recalled:

> We took a fearful hammering in 1986. Members First all but wiped us out. A number of us though realised that their appeasement policy towards management would end in tears and that the branches and members would soon find that their terms and conditions were being sold down the river. We were right, as the 1986 pay round demonstrated.

The cause of the problems alluded to above, was BT's wish to tie their 1986 pay offer to more flexible work rosters. These entailed compulsory earlier starts and later finishes, without any additional compensatory payments. The company also envisaged that what was by now NCU (E) branches would play a diminished role in negotiating work patterns, which were to be decided, following consultation as opposed to negotiation, by the relevant managers.

The national leadership's relatively emollient approach to these proposals incensed the BL branch activists. They organised a 'writing in' campaign in which BL branches faxed letters to the union's negotiators, detailing the alternative strategy they felt the leadership should be following. Each of these letters was then forwarded, by fax, to every branch office, thereby allowing the BL to communicate its views on the negotiations to the union's activist base. This campaign was viewed, by the BL, as a counter to MF's use of BT internal communication system, and interviewees from all sides agreed that it was an effective way for the BL to disseminate information to the whole union. Complaints about the way the national leadership was conducting the negotiations were, importantly, not confined to BL branches. Non-aligned and even MF controlled branches, all started to write in criticising the concessions the union's negotiators were making. This campaign had a detrimental effect on MF unity, with prominent members openly disagreeing with each other over how to conduct the negotiations. The dissenters, including the MF supported Deputy General Secretary, Eric George, now started to criticise John Golding's handling of the negotiations.

By the autumn of 1986 the patience of many branches with the negotiations, and those conducting them, ran out. Unofficial over-time bans were put in place by a number of prominent BL branches. As a result members in West London were suspended and the unofficial action escalated as branches reacted angrily to the suspensions. Reluctantly the General Secretary and NEC agreed to call a national ballot over BT's offer, which still contained the highly controversial changes to working practices. The membership voted in favour of strike action and with BT refusing to alter its position, on 26 January 1987 the national strike commenced. As a then MF NEC member stated:

> Golding overestimated his ability to get more out of BT – whilst he underestimated the members' anger with the strings attached to the deal. By allowing the negotiations to drag on and on, believing he could negotiate a better deal, he created a vacuum that led to frustration amongst the members and then unofficial action. This led to splits inside the MF and Golding lost control of the situation.

After less than a week of national strike action, BT made an improved offer. Controversially the NEC decided to suspend the industrial action, whilst they held a consultative ballot on the Company's proposal. This decision incensed a large number of branches, as it allowed a substantial backlog of faults to be cleared, thereby alleviating the pressure on BT. The offer was narrowly accepted, but so great was the hostility of a substantial number of branches to the agreement that they continued to take unofficial industrial action. Significantly this only ceased when BT reached local agreements with the individual branches over rosters and the continuing role of branch officers in overtime allocation and roster patterns.

The internal difficulties that the dispute's prosecution had exposed inside the MF faction increased, as a tabloid expose of John Golding's sado-masochistic liaisons with prostitutes, led the MF NEC group to agree with the BL that he had to be forced to resign. After Golding's departure a resurgent BL won back control of the NCU (E) NEC and their candidate, Tony Young, was successful in the General Secretary election. However Young's victory was not universally welcomed by members of the BL, many of whom viewed him as being too moderate. His nomination as the BL's candidate had followed a national selection meeting, where the faction's desire to be 'open' to all members had been exploited by elements of the NCU (C) Section, who affiliated dozens of new BL members at the door of the meeting. As NCU (C) officers admitted they had instructed these 'new' BL members to vote for the most moderate of the candidates: Tony Young. This they were able to do thanks to the lack of any prohibition on new affiliates participating instantaneously in BL affairs. Remarkably, given that a majority of NCU (E) BL members had not supported him, the faction accepted the legitimacy of Young's selection and the faction went on to campaign for him in the General Secretary's election.

Young's industrial approach proved to be a grave disappointment to the BL. They had hoped to build on the 1987 strike with a co-ordinated campaign to regain a greater influence over the labour process along with improvements to pay and conditions. Instead as one MF member wryly recalled they discovered that Young had swiftly become "less militant than The Bloc" over a whole series of industrial issues. The BL therefore sought, once again, to build a more militant approach from the branches upwards. Their campaign was, in part, successful with a number of branches adopting a more combative approach, as BT tried in the late 1980s and early 1990s to make changes to the labour process and to wrest influence away from the NCU branches.

The ability of branches to influence directly their members' terms and conditions and the labour process, started to grow again in the late 1980s, as BT devolved large parts of its operation down to semi-autonomous divisions and geographical regions. It was often now NCU (E) branch officers who were conducting local negotiations with various BT subsidiaries, rather than such discussions being undertaken at a national level. Whilst 'framework' agreements were reached nationally, how these often broad agreements were applied, was the subject of local discussions. The divergent results of this approach to bargaining were most evident in relation to BT's introduction of their Customer Service Improvement Programme (CSIP), which pursued even greater flexibility in Engineers working patterns.

After a National agreement had been reached over CSIP (following another split in the BL NEC group) negotiations at branch level took place over the programme's implementation. These negotiations were accompanied, in some areas, by branch led unofficial industrial action in protest at the terms of the national agreement. By the conclusion of the local 'implementation' negotiations there was a marked variation in how CSIP was applied across the country. Those branches which adopted a more militant attitude, secured more advantageous 'implementation' agreements for their members, than those who had adopted a less combative approach. By the mid 1990s, the number of local negotiations supplementing national framework agreements was increasing rapidly as BT broke into an ever growing number of trading divisions and subsidiaries. Marked variations in the nature of these local agreements were also becoming apparent, with some branches achieving considerably more favourable settlements. It was noticeable that, as with the CSIP implementation, the majority of the branches which achieved these more advantageous arrangements had either threatened, or had actively engaged in, different forms of industrial action.

In analysing the reason for why some branches displayed greater militancy than others, a number of authors make a straightforward causal link to the control of branches by the BL (Undy et al, 1996: 238; Parker, 2009). However this book has found that many of the branches who were most militant in resisting detrimental changes to working practices, and were successful in gaining advantageous local agreements, had officers who were not members of either NCU faction. Further research revealed that these 'non-aligned' branches possessed a number of similarities. All of them enjoyed high levels of membership activity, their branch meetings were well attended, and there was clear respect amongst the members for the views of senior branch officials. Although the branch leaderships were not factionally aligned they all clearly held similar convictions, including a commitment to public ownership, a desire to strongly influence the labour process locally, and a strong belief in the efficacy of industrial action. A senior NCU National Officer, in considering the behaviour of these non-aligned branches observed:

> There was a closeness and trust there, which fostered industrial strength and coherence. In each one of those branches, the officers worked hard for the members and were straight with them. In return, the members trusted them and backed them 100%. This type of relationship builds over time and results in members following the advice of the branch rather than that of the national union or BT managers.

This officer's assertions, that trusted branch officers played a central role in shaping the policy views of their members was supported by other interviewees. These arguments provide support for the assertions of authors who declare that officers and senior lay activists play a key 'interest formation' role in shaping their members views (Kelly, 1998; Heery and Kelly, 1994; Kelly and Heery, 1994; Heery, 2000, 2003, 2006; Hyman, 1997).

In seeking to explain why these non-aligned branches displayed levels of militancy equal to or greater than BL branches, a number of contributors argued that although they were ideologically radical, they declined to participate in the BL, for a variety of personal reasons. Interviews with the branch officers concerned suggest that in some instances, this was true. However in other cases officers stated that they held views that were not in keeping with what they perceived as the radical political views of BL members. These contributions give credence to Daniels and McIllroy's observation that many Left union factions have difficulty in uniting activists and members who hold a broad range of political views and are members of diverse political parties (McIllroy, 2007; Daniels and McIllroy, 2009).

The evidence outlined in this chapter has clearly shown that the POEU's and subsequently the NCU's ability to influence the labour process diminished considerably over the period from 1980 to 1996. In large part, this decline has been shown to be linked to adverse changes in the industrial and political environment, in a fashion that institutional and political contextualist scholars predict (Flanders, 1965; Bain, 1970; Clegg, 1976; Howell, 2005). However there is also overwhelming evidence that the strategic choices made by the national union and its branches, particularly surrounding their readiness and capacity to take effective industrial action, greatly affected the union's ability to retain influence over the labour process (see Kelly, 1998; Heery and Kelly, 1994; Kelly and Heery, 1994; Heery, 2000, 2003, 2006). The evidence for this assertion is clearest in relation to the increased devolvement of bargaining in BT during the late 1980s and early 1990s, when the level of union influence over the labour process became closely tied to the local branch's industrial strength and willingness to take effective industrial action.

Recruitment

At the start of 1980, the POEU was operating a long established and highly effective series of post-entry closed shops. These ensured that all those staff employed on BT's engineering grades became members of the union. Owing to the GPO's and then BT's role as the provider of all domestic telephony services this effectively meant that the POEU enjoyed 100% membership density amongst those workers it sought to organise. This in turn led to the union having to expend less time and energy on physical recruitment than even the British and Australian print unions, which efficiently operated pre-entry closed shops. The Conservative Government's abolition of BT's domestic telephony monopoly and its subsequent prohibition of the closed shop dramatically altered this benign institutional environment and forced the union to address difficult questions surrounding the recruitment of non-BT staff.

Following the announcement by the Conservative Government in 1981 that they would licence Mercury to operate in Britain, the Cable and Wireless subsidiary immediately offered the POEU recognition and check-off facilities. Whilst this statement was officially welcomed by the union, it sparked a heated internal debate over whether Mercury staff should be admitted to the POEU. Many branches and NEC members stated that they felt it was morally wrong for them to take into membership employees of a company whose entry to the industry they were actively resisting. Other

NEC members, particularly from the BL faction, held the view that the POEU should aim to be an industrial union and should therefore recruit Mercury workers.

Reflecting over a decade later on this debate those who supported refusing admittance to Mercury staff, concede that, with hindsight, it may seem a somewhat bizarre and self-defeating policy. However as a former National Officer recalled there were good reasons for this position being adopted at the time:

> It seemed illogical to recruit Mercury staff whilst opposing Mercury entering the industry. If we had been successful inevitably all their staff would have been made redundant. How, in all conscience, could you recruit workers you were aiming to make redundant?

Other activists and officers point to the ill-will that there was amongst the POEU membership towards the Mercury workforce, as one former Bloc NEC member stated:

> The membership viewed Mercury workers as the enemy. If we had recruited them, our branches would have refused to represent them or have them in meetings.

A BL NEC member of the time, who took the view that Mercury staff should be recruited, reflected on the debate from a different perspective:

> Look many members and Bloc activists had a company union mind-set. They failed to differentiate between an employer and its workers. My view was that we should aim to be an industrial union and unite all telecommunication workers. The fact that we were campaigning for the industry to be in public hands shouldn't have stopped us from organising Mercury.

Other BL interviewees developed this theme pointing out how other trade unions, who experienced privatisation and deregulation in the 1980s and 1990s, immediately sought to organise workers in the various competitors who entered their industries. They also stressed that they believed that many of the arguments made against organising Mercury workers were excuses, manufactured to mask a reluctance of officers and activists to undertake any organising. As one BL National Officer observed:

> I heard every excuse imaginable, and too be honest they were all bollocks. It wouldn't have been difficult to create separate Mercury branches whose members would have been represented by Mercury officers. The truth is lots of our officers and activists simply weren't prepared to do the hard work involved.

This caustic analysis, whilst expressed less harshly, was repeated by many BL contributors and a number of non-aligned and even MF National Officers and activists. As one Branch Secretary who was a member of MF candidly stated:

> As a Branch Sec I'd never had to recruit anyone. We all felt that if the union agreed to take Mercury workers in then Head Office would look to us to recruit them. In all honesty it wasn't something I was comfortable with doing, and yes it probably influenced my opposition to recruiting them into the union.

This type of starkly honest, self-assessment was certainly not universal amongst MF branch officers. Instead a number of them highlighted potential contractual problems if BT employees were asked to undertake non-BT recruitment, whilst others focused on the fact that recruiting Mercury staff would divert branch resources away from servicing members. All of these reasons were dismissed as excuses by those POEU activists who supported the idea of organising Mercury workers. They pointed out that there was, in reality, no micro-management of the use of facility time by BT and that many POEU branches had sufficient officers on release to cover representational duties, whilst also recruiting.

The reasons put forward by some POEU officers and activists for not undertaking Mercury recruitment were very similar to those tendered by Australian and British print union officers for not recruiting in developing, unorganised, areas of their industries. Studies undertaken by other authors of union organising campaigns also documented similar levels of reluctance by officers and activists to recruit in unfamiliar unorganised areas (Heery et al, 2000a; Heery et al, 2003a; Gall, 2007; Waddington and Kerr, 2000; Milkman, 2000). Where however the POEU differed from the printing and other TUC and ACTU unions was that, following a Bloc inspired motion at the NEC, the refusal to recruit Mercury workers became official union policy. The public justification being that the Labour

Party had committed itself to revoking Mercury's operating licence, if they won the 1983 General Election, and it would therefore be wrong to recruit staff, which you were campaigning to make redundant.

The POEU's hopes that the questions surrounding recruiting Mercury workers would disappear with the election of a Labour Government were dashed when the Conservatives were re-elected. Instead of rescinding Mercury's licence, the Conservatives permitted a whole raft of companies to provide telecommunication services in Britain. A number of these organisations grew rapidly as consumption of new electronic mail and mobile telecommunication services burgeoned. Meanwhile a privatised BT continued to rapidly shed large numbers of workers as they concentrated on 'core' services and contracted out large areas of their operations. As a result of these job losses and the refusal to recruit workers in other telecommunication companies, membership levels of the POEU and then the NCU started to fall rapidly, with the union losing over 50,000 members by 1988. This was at a time when the numbers employed in the telecommunications sector was rising.[3]

The POEU though continued to refuse to recruit in BT's competitors until 1988 when, following the re-election of the Conservative Party in 1987 and further substantial membership losses, the NCU NEC finally agreed to start to try to recruit members in BT's competitors. This decision was only arrived at after many lengthy and acrimonious debates at the NEC. Large parts of the MF faction remained adamantly opposed to Mercury recruitment, as did a number of branches, not all of whom were led by supporters of MF. Owing to the NCU's structure, which relied so heavily on lay branch officers, the national leadership initial intention was that the physical organising would be undertaken by the branches. However efforts to get the branches to recruit non-BT employees were not universally successful. Sizeable numbers of branch officials informed the national union that local BT managers would not allow them to spend their time recruiting non-BT staff. When the POEU nationally asked BT

---

3   1980–1988 British Government, Department of Trade and Industry statistics for
     telecommunications.

management to verify these claims, they, perhaps unsurprisingly, supported these assertions. However many interviewees cast doubt on this reason for not recruiting. As a BL Branch Secretary recalled:

> Look my manager had no idea what I did all day, and frankly he didn't care. So long as we were on hand for negotiations and representations, they didn't monitor us at all. I went out recruiting and organising, and no one was in the least bit bothered. No, Bloc branch officers deliberately asked the question, knowing that the official answer would be no.

As a consequence of BT's 'refusal' to allow branch officers the facility to recruit outside of the company, the NCU had to centrally resource recruitment in Mercury and the other telecommunication companies. The campaign swiftly ran into difficulties owing, as many interviewees recalled, to the hostility of Mercury and other telecommunication companies staff. As one National Officer candidly admitted:

> It was hardly surprising that after five years of treating Mercury staff like lepers that they told us to piss off when we finally decided to try and recruit them.

Mercury, having performed a total *volte face* on union recognition, as soon as they had gained an operating licence, also hampered NCU recruitment initiatives. They barred officers from their premises and made all employees aware of the NCU's historic antipathy towards Mercury.

In these unusual and extremely problematic circumstances it is unsurprising that the NCU recruitment teams made little progress. However the NCU's organising difficulties extended to the other telecommunication employers. In seeking to explain why this was the case, those involved in the recruitment campaigns point to the hostility of the employers, the difficulties in speaking directly to prospective members, and a lack of branch assistance. As a senior NEC member recalled:

> In the early 1990s it felt like we were trying to square the circle. As membership shrank we were short of resources for recruiting, so our membership continued to shrink further. We were caught in a vicious downward spiral.

These difficulties in resourcing successful recruitment programmes, in unions experiencing rapid falls in membership were shared by both countries print unions, as well as other British and Australian unions in the 1980s and 1990s (Heery et al, 2000a; Heery et al, 2003a; Gall and Mackay, 2001; Gall, 2002, 2004, 2007). The recruitment tribulations the NCU were experiencing outside of BT, also now started to affect the union's organisation inside the Company. BT's increasing use of contractors to perform work previously undertaken by their own staff, weakened the ability of the NCU, at national and branch level, to take effective industrial action. The desire of the national union to organise these contractors also proved to be problematic, as they proved to be almost as difficult to recruit as staff in BT's competitors. The NCU's efforts were not helped by the fact that those NCU (E) branches that were willing to help organise BT's contractors, often had little direct contact with the contractors' staff.

By the end of 1996 BT's employment levels had fallen from 238,000 in 1983 to just over 140,000. As interviewees candidly admitted, the NCU had sustained an almost identical percentage drop in membership, owing to the lack of success of their organising outside of BT. This rapid membership decline was not dissimilar to that suffered by the Australian and British print unions, as they too struggled to adjust to a radically altered political and institutional environment in which their sole and highly efficient recruitment tool, the closed shop, was undermined. These type of membership losses also occurred, as studies have shown, in other British and Australian unions who were heavily dependent on compulsory unionism (Zappala, 1991; Dunn and Gennard, 1984; Heery et al, 2003a; Gall and Mackay, 2001; Gall, 2004, 2005).

Added to these environmental difficulties, the NCU also found it extremely difficult to reconcile themselves to organising on an industry wide, as opposed to a company, basis. The refusal for over five years to recruit Mercury workers for ideological reasons created a lack of organising purpose, and a perception of hostility towards all non-BT telecommunication workers, which proved to be an enormous handicap, when they finally tried to recruit in these companies. These decisions by the POEU and the NCU, when coupled to a hostile political and industrial environment, resulted in the NCU being unable to stop their membership decline and led to them seeking another amalgamation. Here, as with their labour process policies, there is overwhelming evidence that the union's strategic decisions profoundly influenced their recruitment performance.

Amalgamation

At the beginning of the 1980s the POEU was engaged, once again, in preliminary discussions with the UCW over a potential merger. These negotiations broke down (as they had done at various times since the 1920s), because the two unions were unable to resolve questions concerning the new union's internal structure and rulebook. The POEU's BL faction was particularly disappointed at this failure, and persuaded the NEC to make it clear to other telecommunications unions that they were still keen to explore the possibility of forming an industrial union, through a series of mergers. As many POEU interviewees agreed, they were surprised when they received an approach, not from another union, but instead from the Civil and Public Servants Association, Postal and Telecommunications Group (CPSA P&T Group). This Group organised approximately 35,000 white collar BT and National Girobank staff, in a discrete, largely self-governing, division of the CPSA.

The CPSA P&T Group amalgamation

The P&T Group's former officers stated that their approach to the POEU was prompted by the CPSA's ever more acrimonious internal factional conflicts. By the early 1980s the P&T Group's leadership had decided that these conflicts had become so damaging that they needed to remove themselves and their members from the CPSA. A former P&T officer explained their thinking:

The CPSA weren't known as the Beirut of the union movement for nothing. By 1981 the CPSA BL and the Right had become totally obsessed with doing each other over, rather than representing the members. Things had become so bloody awful we decided that we had to get out.

In taking the decision to extricate the Group from the CPSA the P&T leadership also decided that they needed to attain protection from 'poaching', by transferring into another TUC affiliated union. Such a transfer was highly unusual within the British union movement and presented the P&T Group with some major problems. Firstly, they needed to convince their members that they not only needed to leave the CPSA, but that they should then join another union. Secondly the CPSA had to be persuaded not to block the Group leaving for another union. Finally another union had to be found who would allow the Group to affiliate on terms that the P&T leadership and membership found acceptable.

The P&T Section leadership addressed the last of these points first and made their approach to the POEU. Initially the POEU senior officers, whilst interested, were slightly sceptical about the P&T Group's approach. However after the election of a BL dominated NEC in 1983, a markedly more enthusiastic attitude was adopted, owing to the faction's ideological commitment to industrial unionism. Their enthusiasm was not shared by parts of the MF, who expressed concerns at what they viewed as the industrial weakness of the P&T membership. The BL dominated POEU NEC though ignored these apprehensions and formally opened merger discussions with the CPSA P&T Group. In the negotiations the P&T section made it clear that they wanted sufficient autonomy in order, as they described it, 'to protect their members' interests'. The POEU NEC felt able to accede to this request and an 'in principle agreement' was reached between the two parties.

The agreement granted the P&T Group its own Division, to be known as the National Communications Union (Clerical) Section (NCU (C). The NCU (C) was to have a separate Sectional Executive, which would have decision making autonomy on all sectional issues and a National Sectional Conference. Unusually the NCU (C) was also to be granted an effective policy veto at the new union's conference, with a clause in the draft rulebook which stated that if over 50% of the NCU (C) delegates opposed a motion, it would fall, no matter the overall majority in favour. This was a remarkably favourable deal for the much smaller P&T Section as studies of British amalgamation agreements make clear (see Undy et al, 1985; Undy et al, 1996; Undy, 2008).

In recalling the discussions that led up to the offer, a POEU NEC member reflected ruefully:

> Looking back the deal we offered the Clerics was ridiculously generous. We effec-
> tively gave away our members right to make policy. Yet at the time we felt that if we
> could just reassure the Clerics that they wouldn't be swamped in a merger, then they
> they'd be happy to integrate. Well we were totally wrong. The only thing the Clerics
> officers and branches were interested in was themselves.

The P&T officers and activists, who negotiated the deal, freely admit that they were surprised at the munificence of the POEU's offer, which was beyond anything they had expected to achieve. In reflecting on why such a generous offer was made to them, a number of P&T Officer's and activists focused on what they felt were paternalistic and slightly patronising attitudes amongst the POEU leadership. As a former P&T officer recalled:

> I had the feeling that they saw us as the poor country cousins, who needed to be
> reassured, that we would be treated well in our new home. The inference being that
> once we had merged together, full integration would take place. We were happy to
> allow them to think this, but privately we were determined to keep the autonomy
> we had secured.

Prior though to any merger with the POEU taking place, the CPSA had to be convinced that they should release the P&T Group. Such a voluntary separation is unusual in British trade unionism (Undy, 1996; Gennard and Bain, 1995) and it is a testimony to the negotiating skills and the cohesion of the P&T Group they were able to persuade the CPSA's leadership to allow their 35,000 members to leave for another union. How they managed this feat has not been publically commented upon, but interviewees from the P&T Group did give some insights into the discussions. As one officer recalled:

At the time the CPSA NEC elections were on a knife edge. Both sides knew that our members were loyal to us and if we asked them to leave the CPSA the majority would do so. The Right's leadership also knew that if they tried to stop us, we'd tell our members to vote for the BL, which would almost certainly lead to them losing power. So letting us go was, for them, the lesser of two evils.

Having secured the reluctant agreement of the CPSA that the P&T Group could leave, the proposal was then put to the Group's membership. They voted overwhelmingly in favour, and the amalgamation with the POEU took place in 1985.

The P&T's influence on the newly created NCU's policy-making was, thanks to powers granted to them in the amalgamation agreement, profound. The NCU (C) leadership were determined not to give up any of their autonomy and the NCU (E) hopes that greater integration would quickly follow the merger were dashed. The operation of the new sectional structures added considerably to the administrative costs of the NCU, which owing to job losses in BT's engineering and clerical areas, now had a rapidly declining membership. Although the NCU (E) and the NCU (C) Executives did finally merge in 1990, the two Sections continued to operate separate branches and Sectional Committees.

The union's financial problems continued to worsen and in the early 1990s they became so acute that the General Secretary, Tony Young, produced a plan that proposed drastic cuts in the size of the NEC and the NCU (C) officer core, plus an ending of union funding for NEC members who were on full-time paid release. These proposals were all rejected. So too were further suggestions that the number of NCU (E) and NCU (C) branches should be radically reduced. As a senior official of the time recalled:

At the time there were numerous factional and occupational interests jockeying for position inside the NCU. There was a high level of paranoia, plus a lack of clear, strong, leadership. Any proposal to save money was viewed, by one group or another, as an attack on their political powerbase, and so all the proposals were rejected.

The rejection of all his proposals for cost cutting measures, allied to the continuing decline in membership, led the General Secretary to inform the NEC that the NCU would not financially be able to continue indefinitely as an independent union. In these circumstances he and other NCU senior officers recommended that the union sought a further amalgamation. The NCU (E) and the NCU (C) Sections reluctantly accepted the logic of this argument and agreement was reached that the Union should seek a merger partner. Industrially the logical union to merge with, in the majority of activists and officers minds, was the UCW. They still organised some BT telephony staff, whilst the NCU (E) continued to organise the Post Office's postal engineers. It was also hoped that, what interviewees described, as a 'cordial' relationship between the two unions General Secretaries would assist in the negotiations. The UCW reacted positively to the suggestion of a merger, even though they had not lost members to the same extent as the NCU owing, in part, to the Government's proposals to privatise the Post Office having been rejected by Parliament.

Negotiators from the two unions worked together to draw up possible structures for a new organisation, and discussions were held on these proposals at the unions Executives and Conference's. Inside the NCU there were concerns, amongst the BL NEC members and branches, about what they viewed as the UCW's anti-activist culture and lack of branch autonomy. This was coupled to anxiety over the UCW's political position on the Right of the Labour movement, which owing to the UCW larger size, could lead to the BL being marginalised in a new union. However the BL's ideological commitment to forming an industrial union, allied to an appreciation of the UCW members' proven willingness to take industrial action, meant that they supported the merger in principle. They were though determined to negotiate a structure that would free the UCW membership from what they viewed as their current internal political and industrial straight jacket.

The NCU MF also harboured concerns about the prospect of a merger with the UCW. They were apprehensive that a merger with the UCW would leave the NCU engineering members in a minority, with policy being imposed upon them by the postal membership. Interestingly their branches, in common with those of the BL, also disliked the structure of the UCW, which they felt gave full-time officials undue influence over branch affairs and the conduct of local negotiations. The UCW record in having reduced by a quarter their number of branches, during the early 1990s, also worried the smaller MF branches.

All of these different factional anxieties, along with comparable concerns in the UCW, had to be dealt with, if an amalgamation agreement were to be reached. The negotiators answer was to put together a package that consciously left aside, until after the merger, a number of contentious issues. An official of the NCU who worked extensively on the amalgamation commented:

> We knew there were issues which could wreck the merger. So we agreed to 'park' them until after we had amalgamated. That way, it was possible to get the various factions and sections to move forward, in the knowledge that in merging they would not be losing out.

The list of items, that the negotiating teams suggested should be left until after a merger had been entered into, was extensive. It contained a series of problematic questions, including: Would the new union elect or appoint National Officers? Where would the union's headquarters be located? What levels of policy autonomy would be granted to the branches? None of these questions were addressed in the draft merger proposals, which were finally put before the respective unions NECs. Instead there was a proposal that the merger agreement would enshrine the right of both unions to unilaterally block any changes to the rulebook and structure after the merger. These guarantees were accepted by the NEC's of both unions and also by the NCU Engineering and Clerical Sections. They all endorsed the proposed merger document and agreed to recommend a Yes vote in a ballot of their members.

The lack of controversial proposals in the merger agreement was also sufficient to ensure that the NCU's political and occupational factions did not oppose the merger. In the absence of serious opposition the official pro-merger campaign was successful; the NCU membership voting 41,539 to 6,957 in favour, whilst the UCW's members supported the amalgamation by 53,800 votes to 6,539. Shortly thereafter, on 26 January 1995, the NCU and the UCW officially merged, to become the Communications Workers Union (CWU). Commenting on the merger, a number of interviewees made similar comments, which are encapsulated in the observations of a former senior NCU (E) official:

> It was a victory for the leaderships of both unions. They had succeeded in achieving
> a merger that had proved to be impossible for over a hundred years. Yet in truth it
> was a merger in name only. We were Noah's union. We had two GS's, two NEC's and
> two Head Offices. The only thing we had one of was a bus, which shuttled between
> Greystoke and Clapham[4] every day.

Achieving agreement over the difficult issues that had been left unresolved, prior to the merger, proved to be difficult. By the end of 1996, potential solution's to all of the 'parked issues' had been proposed and then rejected, by one or more of the constituent groups, who continued to jealously guard their autonomy.

In analysing the amalgamations that created the NCU and the CWU what is striking is their dissimilarity. The empirical evidence has shown that the creation of the NCU was the result of an unforced, strategic choice by the CPSA P&T Group, whilst the CWU's creation was the forced consequence of a combination of adverse industrial, political and financial factors. The impetus behind the CWU's formation was similar to that which led to the British and Australian print unions to merge, along with many other unions (Undy, 1996, 2008; Chaison, 1996; Waddington, 1988, 1995; Waddington et al, 2005). The evidence that environmental factors played a major part in the CWU's creation support the arguments of those scholars who view trade union amalgamation policy as being shaped largely by the economic and political environment (Undy, 1996, 2008; Waddington, 1988, 1995; Waddington et al, 2005; Howell, 2005; Chaison, 1996). However the reasons that lay behind the NCU's creation do not fit readily with the institutional, economic, legislative or industrial explanations of amalgamations. Instead a dominant role was played by occupational loyalties, political factionalism and personal allegiances, as the P&T Group was extricated from the CPSA and joined with the POEU. These findings not only support the theory that important policy decisions can be taken primarily for ideological reasons (see Heery and Kelly, 1988; Kelly and Heery, 1994; Heery, 2003, 2006; Kelly, 1988; Darlington, 1994, 2001; McIllroy and Campbell, 1999; McIllroy, 2007; Daniels and McIllroy, 2009)

---

4   Greystoke House was the NCU's Head Office in Ealing, whilst Clapham was the
     location of the UCW's Headquarters.

but also provides evidence of the importance of micro-political influences in amalgamation policy formation.

Conclusion

In common with the British and Australian print unions, this chapter has shown how POEU and NCU policies, in all three key areas, were principally fashioned in response to what were seismic shifts in the political, industrial and technological environment. The empirical evidence has demonstrated how these contextual forces played a significant role in constraining the POEU's and NCU's policy choices. Whilst this is supportive of the premise of institutional and political contextualist authors (Flanders, 1965; Bain, 1970; Clegg, 1976, 1979; Howell, 2005), the evidence has also established that although the POEU and NCU were in part constrained by the political and institutional environment, they were also able to make a series of strategic policy decisions, which helped to shape that environment and determined their industrial and political success. This substantiates the theory that unions have the ability to make strategic choices, at both the local and national level, which have a significant bearing on their success, as Heery and Kelly have suggested (Kelly, 1998; Heery and Kelly, 1994; Kelly and Heery, 1994; Heery, 2000, 2003, 2006).

More evidence has also been produced, particularly in relation to BT's post privatisation redundancy programme, that the rank and filist hypothesis that union members are constantly being restrained from acting in a more militant fashion, by conservative full-time officials, is seriously flawed (Bramble, 1993, 2008; Callincos, 1982, 1983; Freeman, 1985; Cliff, 1970; Beacham, 1970; Offe et al, 1985). The influence over decision makers of political factions has also been shown to be considerably greater in the POEU and the NCU, than in the Australian and British printing unions. The information gathered illustrates as well how the two dominant factions in the POEU and NCU played a leading role in shaping union policy by influencing the behaviour of policy makers.

However the evidence also indicates that the factions did not exert the totally dominant influence over policy-making that some authors have suggested (Undy et al, 1996; Parker, 2009). Instead, policy-making was the result of a more complex process in which factional loyalties were only one of many different influences, which affected decision making and policy choices. These included occupational, political and branch allegiances, along with micro-political factors, such as friendships, animosities, loyalty and trust in respected officers. All of these factors have been shown to have played a significant part in shaping POEU and NCU policy, which bears out the central hypothesis of this book.

CHAPTER II

The Australian Telecommunication Unions: 1980–1996

In this chapter the Australian telecommunication unions' labour process, recruitment and amalgamations policies are analysed. This evaluation includes an appraisal of the various influences which shaped the judgments of the unions policy makers. A comparison of how the ATEA and the APTU responded to similar institutional challenges is undertaken, whilst the reasons for similarities or differences in approaches are sought.

During the period under review the Australian telecommunications industry altered substantially, due to rapid changes in the technological, industrial and political environment. The development of digital, satellite, and microwave technology reduced employment levels in Telecom Australia (TA) and led to a decline in the union membership. Although Federal Government plans to privatise TA were repulsed by the unions until after 1996, the industry's deregulation in 1992 presented the unions with many serious industrial and recruitment difficulties. These problems were augmented by TA's desire to respond to the fast changing technological environment, by seeking higher levels of productivity and greater control over the labour process. The ability of the ATEA and the APTU to respond to these challenges, in a co-ordinated manner, was greatly inhibited by bitter occupational and factional enmities, the sources of which are also explored in this chapter.

The labour process

At the beginning of the 1980s the ATEA and the APTU had achieved a considerable level of influence over the labour process. Membership of local and national joint negotiatory committees, which were similar to the British Whitley Councils, granted the unions a formal role in the establishing of staffing levels, the instituting of new working practices and the introduction of new technology. Equally important the industrial strength of both unions in Sydney and Melbourne had accorded them even greater local influence over the labour process. The foundation of this influence was the operation of unofficial, but nevertheless highly effective, closed shops across all TA's manual grades. These informal arrangements meant that by 1980 both unions enjoyed density rates of nearly 100%. This compared favourably with the density levels achieved by the POEU's operation of official post-entry closed shops. These findings support the assertions of authors who state that it is the implementation, as opposed to the status, of a closed shop that determines its effectiveness (Dunn and Gennard, 1984; Gennard and Bain, 1995).

In addition to the unofficial closed shop, the two unions also enhanced their control over aspects of the labour process via the strong enforcement of demarcation lines. This was particularly the case, interviewees asserted, in Melbourne and Sydney, where both the ATEA and APTU policed their national demarcation lines with considerable zeal (Bamber et al, 1997). Tensions surrounding demarcations had though become considerably worse in the 1970s after (different) Left factions took control of the ATEA Victorian and NSW branches. This led to factional as well as occupational conflicts between the unions, as the APTU branches continued to be controlled by the Right. The confluence of these factional and occupational inter-union tensions, allied to an increased propensity of particularly the ATEA members to take industrial action, resulted in a series of demarcation disputes.

Outside of Sydney and Melbourne demarcation lines were not so tightly enforced by either union and there were fewer disputes. Significantly this was the case in other parts of NSW and Victoria (as well as the rest of Australia), where there was generally greater flexibility. This was partly owing to the need for greater demarcation flexibility in rural areas, if the network was to remain operational. The lack of demarcation rigidity was also part of a different approach to the management of the labour process in rural NSW and Victoria. Informal agreements were common which granted union members greater autonomy over their working patterns than their colleagues in the State Capitals. An APTU lay activist, who moved from Sydney to a small NSW country town, recollected these different approaches:

> Because the demarc lines were less rigid in the bush, we often did some of the techs work and they frequently did some of ours. This would never have happened in Sydney, but remember we didn't have managers looking over our shoulders all day, like they had. If we wanted a longer smoko we took one. All the bosses wanted us to do was to get the faults fixed – and we did that bloody well.

This flexibility in the ATEA and APTU's attitudes belies the impression given by some scholars that the NSW and Victorian branches were totally committed to rigidly enforcing nationally agreed occupational demarcation lines (see Bamber et al, 1997).

The negotiation by both unions of local arrangements, which reflected their members wish to trade demarcation adherence for an increase in self-management, is illustrative of a wider propensity of State branches to be flexible in making important strategic choices at the local workplace level. These findings are similar to those relating to the NCU, whose local branches would often also negotiate distinctive arrangements for the implementation of national agreements. The flexibility of the NSW and Victorian branches provides further empirical support for authors who argue that unions have the ability and willingness to make important strategic choices, and decide policy priorities, at the local workplace level (Hyman, 1997; Heery, 2003).

In 1982 TA's ratio of staff to customers, which was higher than in Britain or the USA, was cited by elements of the Liberal/National Coalition Federal Government as a reason to consider deregulation and privatisation. TA was charged by the Federal Government with making operational

savings. They proposed making substantial cuts in staffing, whilst introducing new technology and securing increased flexibility and productivity
from their workforce. This plan was approved by the Federal Government
in 1982, and they also stated that they would consider suggestions that
Australia should follow the British lead and deregulate the telecommunications industry, if they were re-elected.

The ATEA and the APTU vigorously opposed all of these proposals.
Keeping TA in public hands they believed to be crucial to their continuing ability to protect their influence over the labour process. To this end
they lobbied the ALP to ensure that they would oppose privatisation,
deregulation and the proposed job cuts if they were elected in 1983. The
APTU also reactivated their previously successful anti-deregulation and
privatisation campaign in the rural electorates of Country National Party
MP's. These political efforts resulted in both the Coalition and the ALP
stating they had no plans to privatise TA. However, worryingly for the
unions, the ALP refused to criticise TA's plans for making extensive staff
cuts or to rule out deregulation.

The ALP won the 1983 Federal election and to the unions' anger immediately endorsed TA's cuts to staffing, whilst also announcing they were
considering deregulating the telecommunications industry in order to
improve services and reduce costs. Worse still from the unions perspective,
they also stated they would not rule out privatising TA (Bamber et al, 1997).
As many union interviewees recalled this was viewed as a betrayal by the
ALP Federal Government and it marked the start of a thirteen year struggle over the future of TA. Throughout the period the unions' pursued two
separate, yet linked, policies in an effort to influence Federal Government
telecommunication policy.

First, the two unions launched publicity campaigns, independently of
each other, which sought to galvanise public opposition to the Government's
telecommunication plans. These campaigns focused on the unions' joint
claim that subsidised line provisions and the untimed flat rate charge for
local calls would be abolished after deregulation. The unions' efforts elicited
considerable support, with opinion polls regularly indicating, throughout
the period, that a majority of Australian voters were opposed to both the deregulation of the nation's telecommunications industry and the privatisation

of TA (Keavney, 1990: 35). Secondly, the unions' sought to apply informal pressure internally within the ALP. As one ATEA National Officer stated:

> We lobbied, cajoled and threatened ALP Ministers, Senators and MPs, in order to dissuade them from privatising TA.

These efforts were made, arguably, more potent by the existence of State labour movement factions, which covered a multiplicity of unions and the ALP. This was unlike Britain where individual unions tended to have their own discrete ideological factions, whose links with like-minded factional groups, in other unions or the Labour Party, were less formal. The cross labour movement nature of the factional organisations allowed the State leaderships of the telecommunication unions to campaign inside the faction to which they were aligned. The various State Left factional groups supported the unions' anti-privatisation and deregulation position; however in many of the Right factions there were major disagreements over the issue. This was particularly the case in the powerful NSW Right faction where, contributors recalled, there were clashes between ALP Ministers and the APTU NSW officers over the issue.

According to senior ALP figures the twin pronged strategy the unions adopted played a considerable part in getting the Federal Government to shelve its deregulation and privatisation plans. These were being spearheaded by the then Treasurer Paul Keating. In recalling the decision to withdraw privatisation and deregulation plans for TA a number of ALP and union interviewees focused specifically on the role of senior NSW Right factional figures in getting the policy dropped. As a NSW APTU officer confided:

> Look, you need to remember that the NSW Right effectively controlled the ALP parliamentary caucus. Richo[1] was the numbers man, and he was generally pretty close to us. We were able to convince him to put the hard word on Keating, that if he kept on he could lose factional support for his plans to kick Hawke out of office.

---

1   Graham Richardson, ALP Federal Minister (1983–1988) and leading member of the NSW Right faction.

The agreement by the Government to withdraw its proposals came at a price, with ALP Ministers insisting that TA now had to become more profitable and efficient. This led to TA proposing a further series of job cuts and changes to working practices. These plans, whilst they were officially opposed by both unions, exposed divisions in the ATEA and the APTU over how they should respond. There were groups in both unions, who believed that concessions were needed if TA was to remain the sole provider of domestic telecommunications. As one ATEA Federal officer stated:

> Look we knew that there had to be changes to working practices and a reduction in head count. There were demarc lines which had to go if we were to remain a viable operation.

Whilst this was the view of many parts of the ATEA and APTU there were branches and local areas that actively opposed TA's proposals. However, this resistance was often undermined by members accepting management's voluntary redundancy and early retirement packages. These findings undermine Bramble's (2008) implication that the failure of the telecommunication unions to resist job losses was simply the fault of the unions' leadership.

The Government desire for TA to be more 'cost effective' led to the commissioning of McKinsey's, to advise on how TA could operate more efficiently. Their report recommended a "more proactive managerial approach", which included new bargaining arrangements, the unilateral introduction of new technology, plus the introduction of individual contracts and performance related pay for higher graded staff. These proposals sought to overturn many of the agreements that TA had reached with the unions, including the 1983 'technological change agreement', which had been widely praised for the conflict free introduction of new technology (Davis and Lansbury, 1989; Matthews, 1987). The agreement, which encompassed joint TA and union working parties and the use of a panel of independent experts to assess the introduction of new equipment, was scrapped as part of TA's adoption of McKinsey's recommendations.

These changes in TA's attitude created difficulties inside the ATEA and APTU for those officers' who favoured a cooperative approach. As TA management actively disengaged from joint working parties and adopted a more bellicose approach towards the unions it became increasingly difficult for senior federal officials to justify the sort of moderate industrial attitude, which the ALP had stated was a prerequisite if deregulation and privatisation was to be avoided. Senior officials now came under considerable criticism, particularly within the ATEA, over their lack of a robust response to attacks on staffing levels and terms and conditions of employment. These criticisms often emanated from the NSW and Victorian branches who wished to see more robust industrial tactics, similar to those which they had adopted locally.

Whilst the condemnation of the ATEA's federal negotiators did lead to the replacement of senior officers, the call for national industrial action in response to TA management's bypassing of procedural agreements and unilaterally imposing job losses was not endorsed. Seeking to explain why this was the case, interviewees pointed out that members were all too aware, by the late 1980s, that the new telecommunications technology was robust and that any short-term industrial action would be ineffective. They also focused on the manner in which members had become disenchanted and rather than wishing to fight management plans for job losses, they now wanted to leave, what many viewed, as a failing organisation.

This view gathered strength during the early 1990s, when TA's determination to hit Federal Government targets for improvements in profitability and reductions in costs, led to continuous offers of voluntary redundancy and early retirement. The scale of the job losses was profound with TA's workforce shrinking from 94,000 in 1982, to 67,000 in 1993. As both ATEA and APTU officials explained, the situation was made worse by what they and their members viewed as wholly inept management, many of whom had been recruited from outside of the Australian telecommunications industry. An ATEA officer pithily encapsulated many officers' views of these foreign managers:

> These clowns came in from the U.S and fair dinkum they didn't have a bloody clue about running the joint. I'll tell you they let so many blokes go, they shit-canned the whole operation. By the early 1990s we couldn't cope with day-to-day faults, let alone a real bad storm.

Many contributors were similarly disparaging about the lack of operational and technical knowledge of the new managers, who often attempted to impose labour process changes without local consultation, let alone negotiation.

Although TA's new managerial approach did not spark a national dispute it did result in local industrial action, predominantly in the ATEA's most militant areas. These disputes often revolved around what State officers described as 'idiotic' or 'irrational' unilateral changes to rosters and working practices. As ATEA and APTU officers made clear, whilst industrial action was taken in some instances, on other occasions, when their members were not adversely affected, they simply decided to stand back and allow naive managers to make changes that led to serious operational failures. As local lay representatives stated, previously they would have intervened and informed inexperienced managers of the pitfalls of specific proposals, now relations had become so poor that they simply allowed mangers to impose changes that undermined the service. The subsequent spectacular rise in the number of customer complaints corroborated the unions' argument that staff cuts and unilateral changes to working practices were detrimental to providing a good service. The unions were though infuriated when TA's response to the large number of complaints was to hire significant numbers of contractors to undertake the work previously performed by ATEA and APTU members.

Aside from their anger with TA, the telecommunication unions' were also irate that the ALP Federal Government had not intervened, to force TA's management to change their provocative approach. This resentment was to turn to fury in 1991, when the new ALP Prime Minister, Paul Keating, announced that the Federal Government was granting Optus[2] limited entry to the Australian telecommunications market. Officers from both unions were adamant that the Government's announcement broke

---

2   Optus was a consortium, the overwhelming majority of which was owned by Bell
     South and Cable and Wireless. The Company was initially limited to competing
     only in the overseas and the long distance telephony markets. This restriction was
     lifted by the 1996–2007 Liberal/National Coalition Federal Government.

an informal agreement that TA would remain the sole national provider of all Australian telecommunication services, so long as the unions made concessions over working practices and job losses. Senior union officers believed they had met their side of the bargain, but that the Government had acted in bad faith.

The ATEA and APTU engaged in debates at their respective Federal Executives over how to respond to the Federal Government's announcement. There were suggestions, particularly in the ATEA, that support for the ALP should be withdrawn. This view however was rejected, as the majority of delegates felt it was crucial to support the ALP at the forthcoming Federal election, as the alternative was the return of the Liberal/National Coalition, which was wholeheartedly committed to privatisation and the total deregulation of the telecommunication industry. The unions instead decided to try and generate pressure on the Federal Government by launching a campaign against deregulation inside the parliamentary caucus and at the Federal ALP conference. Additionally the telecommunication unions threatened to withdraw their support for the latest Accord, which was already failing to attract the endorsement of a number of ACTU affiliate unions. At the State level the unions also sought to persuade the labour movement factions, to whom they were affiliated, to oppose the deregulation. This was particularly relevant in NSW where the APTU made strenuous efforts to persuade the NSW Right to press for the reversal of the deregulation proposal.

None of these different strategies resulted in the Government dropping its deregulation plans. There were however assurances that the deregulation would only be partial, and that in future TA would be prohibited from making an employee redundant and then hiring a contractor to undertake their work. The Federal Government also promised to force a transformation in TA management attitudes towards the unions, with the ATEA and the APTU being granted a more positive role. Whilst the ALP's commitment to stop TA's wide-spread use of contractors was translated into a new redundancy agreement, TA management refused to alter their approach to the unions. As TA managers admitted, part of the reason for this was senior management's belief that the ALP would lose the 1993 Federal election and that a Liberal/National Government would almost instantaneously privatise TA. This conviction, led them to continue to disregard anything, including the unions, who stood in the way of 'stripping out unprofitable elements of the business' in preparation for flotation (Bamber et al, 1997).

In 1993 the ALP defied the odds and won the Federal Election. Almost immediately senior managers of what had become Telstra (created after the Federal Government's merged TA with the Overseas Telecommunications Corporation), started to leave the organisation. A major managerial reorganisation took place, in which former Liberal Party Minister, Ian Macphee, was appointed to oversee Industrial Relations. Although he was a former Liberal Party, Minister of Employment, Macphee had a reputation of working constructively with the unions. After Macphee's appointment Telstra adopted a markedly more conciliatory attitude to the unions, which he christened the 'participative approach'. This 'approach' encompassed wide scale consultation over a host of labour process issues and was officially launched at a conference of senior Telstra managers and union leaders, at Lorne, Victoria, in March 1994. Such was the transformation in the attitudes of the managers, that the union officers in attendance christened the conference "The love-in at Lorne".

The change in TA's approach received contrasting responses from what had become, following the ATEA and APTU's merger, the two divisions of the Communication Workers Union (CWU). The CWU operated a federated structure, which allowed the Postal and Telecommunications (P&T) section, which was previously the APTU, to warmly embrace the new Telstra policy, whilst the Telecommunication and Services (T&S) section, formerly the ATEA, were free to respond more cautiously. At a national level both divisions welcomed the ability to participate more fully in negotiations and consultations with TA over any plans they had to introduce new technology and changes to the labour process.

There was though a wider dichotomy of responses to the 'participative approach' at the State level. Having spent the late 1980s and early 1990s being effectively marginalised, a number of P&T branches reacted very positively to management's, new, accommodating attitude. They were happy to accept invitations to meet formally and informally, in order that they could discuss a whole raft of different Telstra policies. The officers involved were adamant that embracing Telstra's 'participative policy' worked to the benefit of the members as it enabled them to spend time with managers, when they could explain and convince them of the union's position on a variety of issues. In support of these assertions they pointed to a number of agreements they reached over working practices and the introduction of new technology. The decision of many P&T branches to engage so totally in the 'participative approach' was controversial. A number of the T&S branches, and elements within the P&T division itself, were unhappy over the close relationships some branch officers formed with managers. An officer from the NSW T&S branch outlined the criticisms of their P&T counterparts:

> Look the Linies got so close to Telstra management you couldn't prise them apart. We had their members on the phone spewing at the way their own branch officers were siding with management against them over a whole host of issues. They were also real dirty about their officers going out on the grog with management.

The NSW and Victorian T&S branches adopted a cooler attitude to TA management, attending formal meetings and negotiations but not engaging, to the same extent, in informal events. This policy, the officers felt, kept relations on a more professional basis and helped to stop any accusations of collusion. It also, they believed, assisted the branch in gaining better agreements, as Telstra managers were aware that they could not simply reach an agreement by 'persuading' branch officers over dinner to agree to their proposals.

Across the rest of Australia, whilst there were policy differences between the two division's branches, there was not the same level of divergence, with both division's branches generally welcoming the 'participative approach'. However these branches also shared the view that the new managerial attitude did not make a significant difference to Telstra's policies and that the adoption of a less hostile attitude towards the union was somewhat contrived and would disappear with a change of Federal Government.[3]

---

3 These assumptions proved to be well founded. Telstra management adopted a highly combative approach towards the CWU in the years following the election of the Liberal/National Coalition Government in 1996.

The two CWU divisions' different approaches to Telstra's participative approach, particularly in NSW and Victoria, are indicative of a wider ideological variation in labour process policies. The APTU and subsequently the P&T division, sought to use their internal political influence in the ALP, and their powers of persuasion with TA/Telstra management, to attempt to protect and enhance their influence over the labour process. Their stated preference was to work with management in a cooperative manner and it was only if this approach failed would they call for industrial action. This reflected the ideological position of the dominant Right factions whose members made it clear that they felt that a cooperative approach, when it was possible, was the most effective way of influencing policy in the publically owned Telstra.

This view was in contrast to the T&S division, particularly in the Left controlled NSW and Victoria branches. Here there was a strong belief that only by deploying, or threatening, industrial action was it possible to enhance union influence over the labour process. There were though disagreements within the T&S division over the extent to which officers should engage in informal meetings with Telstra managers or participate in joint working parties. Those officers and activists who held more radical views were generally wary of such meetings and in participating in joint decision making forums.

These empirical findings substantiate the views of scholars who assert that the operation of strong ideological factions, in both Australian and British telecommunication unions, played an important role in determining policy direction (see Bamber et al, 1997; Undy et al, 1996; Parker, 2009; McIllroy et al, 2007; Daniels and McIllroy, 2009). Yet closer scrutiny of the evidence has also shown that there were subtle variations in labour process policy, inside State branches which were dominated by a single political faction. These disparities in labour process policy have been shown to be fashioned by the views of the local area officers and activists whose opinions were shaped not only by ideology but also by specific geographical and micro-political factors. Such findings, which are similar to those relating to variations in POEU/NCU branch policies, support the assertions of those authors who state that union policy can be extensively shaped at a local level by local activists and officers who decide in conjunction with their members their interests and priorities (Kelly and Heery, 1994; Heery, 2003; Hyman, 1997). The influence upon those policies of micro-political factors as well as well as ideological and institutional factors is supportive of the central hypothesis of this book.

Recruitment

Prior to 1992, when the Federal Government removed TA's domestic monopoly, the ownership of all of Australia's domestic and overseas telecommunications resided solely in the hands of the Federal Government. Within these Government owned institutions, most prominently TA, the unions had long established unofficial closed shops, which efficiently recruited Australia's manual telecommunication workers. Union success in persuading the ALP Federal Government to retain TA in public ownership meant that even by the late 1980s they had to dedicate relatively little time or energy to recruiting members. However the Federal Government's controversial partial deregulation of the industry in 1992 and TA's increasing use of contractors meant that both unions could no longer depend on informal closed shops to recruit all of Australia's telecommunication workers.

The union response to this altered environment was not dissimilar to the POEU reaction to comparable political and institutional changes. Both the ATEA and the APTU opposed Optus being allowed to operate in Australia and sought the prohibition by the Federal Government of TA's use of contractors. However this hostility did not manifest itself in a formal refusal to recruit Optus employees. Instead what had become, by 1992, the CWU met Optus management and discussed recruitment, representation and collective bargaining arrangements. These discussions took place in the period between the company being given leave to operate and its starting trading. Optus stated that they wished to conclude a single union Enterprise Bargaining Agreement with the CWU, which would grant the union sole recognition and recruitment rights. Assurances were also given that there would be no barriers to the union recruiting Optus staff, with pay-role deduction and officers' entry to company premises being guaranteed. In this spirit of co-operation, an agreement was entered into by the CWU and Optus, which set out the intention of the company to recognise the CWU, grant recruitment facilities and establish an Enterprise Bargaining Agreement. Significantly, in the context of Australia's legalistic industrial relations system, this agreement was not legally binding.

This 'Heads of Agreement' package, as it was known, succeeded in ensuring that CWU was granted formal membership 'coverage' of Optus, much to the disappointment of other unions who organised in TA. Believing that their provisional agreement with company and the coverage award would effectively guarantee them high membership levels, the two CWU divisions now became embroiled in a heated debate as to who was to organise the Optus membership. The argument was, according to interviewees, made considerably worse because Optus' main operations were to be in Sydney and Melbourne, which meant that the two divisions NSW and Victorian branches were involved in the discussions. Their poor relationship meant that reaching an agreement over which branch the Optus members should be placed into in the two States, proved to be problematic. After many months of debate, a federally brokered compromise was eventually reached which split the potential membership between the divisions, with the Victorian P&T branch and the New South Wales T&S branch organising Optus employees in their respective States, whatever work they undertook.

Most bizarrely there was also an agreement that neither division would have Federal coverage of Optus. This meant that the CWU Federal Officials could not negotiate with the company over their Australia wide operations and there would be no national coordination of Optus members. The deal was not universally welcomed at the time, with many interviewees believing that the arrangement was flawed. As one senior Federal official declared soon after the compromise was agreed:

> It's a really shonky compromise that won't work and makes us look like a bunch of galahs to prospective Optus members. To be honest it's a total bloody disgrace and it's typical of the pig's arse that we are making of our dealings with Optus.

This proved to be a perceptive comment, as the union encountered considerable difficulties in its dealings with Optus and in recruiting their employees. These difficulties started after Optus' had achieved the integration of their operation into the network, at which point they reneged on their promises of union recognition, check-off and unimpeded access to their workforce. The respective divisional branch officers in NSW and Victoria also found it difficult to recruit Optus workers when they were able to speak to them. As the officers concerned stated, many Optus staff that had refused to join the union referred to hostile statements the CWU had made about their employer, which Optus had reproduced and sent to every employee. A number of officers involved were also candid enough to admit that they had no previous experience of recruiting and were uncertain as to how to respond when faced with employees whose initial response was to refuse to join the union. As one Optus worker who became a CWU member commented:

> Every criticism of Optus that the CWU made was twisted by management. Management stated at staff briefings that the CWU wanted to close Optus down, and if you joined the union you were funding an organisation that wanted to retrench you, so lots of workers just refused to join.

In addition to producing negative publicity, Optus management were also accused by the union of intimidating employees who wished to join, and of actively discriminating against staff who became CWU activists. This combination of a lack of recruiting skills and a hostile employer, hindered recruitment in Optus and by the end of 1996 the CWU had made little progress in establishing a substantial membership. Reflecting on their Optus recruitment policy many interviewees, from both divisions, admit they had been foolish not to insist on an agreement which guaranteed recognition and some form of unofficial closed shop. Such naivety was ruefully reflected upon by a senior CWU T&S Federal officer:

> At the time there seemed no need to press for a tighter agreement. In all our dealings with Telstra, they had always honoured agreements. What we failed to realise was that Optus simply wanted to get their system linked into Telstra's. Once that had been done, they felt safe to give us the flick.

The trusting manner in which CWU dealt with Optus over recruitment and recognition is at least partly explained by the union's relationship with TA. Over many decades TA, even when in dispute, had generally honoured all its verbal agreements. Not to have done so, as union and management interviewees pointed out, would have been counterproductive for the company as serious industrial action would have followed. In dealing with Optus, the CWU's lack of experience in negotiating with employers other than TA contributed to their serious error in not insisting on a binding agreement. This said, it should be noted that after the election of a Liberal/ National Coalition Federal Government in 1996, the legal underpinning of such recognition and coverage agreements was removed (Cooper and Ellem, 2011).

Inside the CWU the breakdown of the collective agreements with Optus, and the severe difficulty that the union faced in recruiting their staff, was not universally viewed as a negative development. As with the POEU a decade earlier, there were officers, activists and members who felt that Optus employees did not belong in the same union as TA workers. This perception reflected in part the close identification of many members with their employer. However unlike in Britain this view did not gain majority support and the leadership of the CWU remained committed to trying to organise Optus workers. In part this policy was shaped, contributors stated, by their knowledge of how the POEU's failure to try and recruit Mercury workers had proved to be counterproductive.

In order to try and address their poor organisational progress in Optus the CWU reconsidered their strategy of splitting the membership between the two divisions. Agreement was finally reached that a separate Optus national branch should be formed, with its own dedicated officer, who reported directly to the CWU Federal Executive. Even after the CWU adopted this new structure, membership did not increase rapidly. Reflecting on this, a CWU officer involved in the Optus recruitment programme stated:

> In Optus our errors hurt us badly. The message we sent out to potential members was that we were against them having a job. Then we dropped the bundle with our failure to have a proper Optus organisation with officers who knew how to recruit. By the time we put these failures right, it was too late; many of the workers were anti-union.

This assessment was substantiated by Optus success in gaining a non-union Enterprise Flexibility Agreement (EFA), thanks to the agreement of the majority of the Optus work force, in 1996. An arrangement which was to last until after the Liberal/National Coalition was removed from Federal Office in 2007.

In analysing the CWU's and its predecessors recruitment policies, the evidence has shown that the unions made a series of strategic choices, which whilst being shaped by the need to respond to significant institutional contextual alterations, were also heavily influenced by ideology, factional strength and personal rivalries. These observations are in line with those of authors who view unions as having the ability to make important strategic decisions which are affected by policy makers' beliefs values and ideology (Kelly, 1998; Heery and Kelly, 1994; Heery, 2000, 2003; Hyman, 1997; McIllroy and Campbell, 1999; McIllroy, 2007; Daniels and McIllroy, 2009). The findings also support the central tenet of this book's hypothesis that micro-political as well as institutional, occupational, craft and ideological factors colour the policy choices of union decision makers.

This section has demonstrated that the Australian telecommunication unions, in common with the other unions featured in this book had enormous difficulty in recruiting in areas where they became unable to operate the closed shop. The evidence suggests that these problems were linked to a lack of recruitment skills amongst officers and activists, which could not be readily addressed, as both unions constitutions demanded they elected officers from amongst their own ranks. These findings bear out Heery's analysis that unions which cannot easily and effectively change the nature of their leadership and officer cadre with those of a different gender, generation and ideology, often face great difficulty in revitalisation (Heery, 2003: 297). These findings also provide further evidence that unions such as the British and Australian telecommunication and printing unions who relied so heavily on compulsory unionism, found it even more difficult to adjust their organising strategies in order to cope with the radically altered industrial environment of the 1980s and 1990s, compared to unions who had previously operated in sectors where compulsory unionism was not ubiquitous (see also Zappala, 1991; Dunn and Gennard, 1984; Heery et al, 2003a; Gall and Mackay, 2001; Gall, 2002, 2003).

Amalgamations

At the start of 1980 TA recognised fifteen trade unions, who all organised different discrete occupational or grade based groups of employees. It was not until the mid-1980s, when many of the smaller supervisory and occupational unions felt compelled to merge with either the ATEA or the APTU that this organisational pattern started to alter. Unlike many of the other union mergers featured in this book, these amalgamations were not principally a response to reductions in membership numbers, financial difficulties or the obsolescence of specific occupations. Instead the amalgamations were driven by ACTU and Federal Government policy, which sought to create large industrial unions. In order to achieve this goal the Federal Government eventually passed the 1988 Industrial Relations Act which withdrew many of the protections afforded by the Federal arbitration system (see Griffin, 2002; Davis, 1999; Bramble, 2008; Dabscheck, 1989). Prior though to the passing of this legislation the ACTU and ALP's Federal Government's desire for industrial unionism had encouraged TA to make it clear to the many small supervisory and occupational unions that their collective representational role was in question.

These dramatic changes in the political and institutional context forced the small unions in TA into a series of merger negotiations with the ATEA and the APTU. Prior to this time the smaller unions operating in TA had rebuffed amalgamation advances from the ATEA and the APTU. As interviewees from these unions stated, these rejections had in part been informed by fears that their members' interests would be ignored if they became part of a larger union. They also agreed that it was TA's operation of a Whitleyist industrial relations system that allowed them to operate effectively, even though they were numerically very small. Significantly though senior officers of a number of the smaller telecommunications unions claimed that the principal reason why they had not joined either of the larger telecommunications unions was the dysfunctional relationship that existed between the ATEA and the APTU. As a former senior officer of the ATPOA (Australian Telephone and Phonegram Officers Association) stated:

> We were wary of becoming involved in the demarcation and political brawls that the techs and the linies were constantly involved in. Our preference was to remain independent, but the ACTU and the Feds actions made that impossible.

Aware of the wariness of other unions to amalgamate with them, both the APTU and the ATEA embarked during the mid-1980s on what Undy (2008) has characterised as a 'pro-active approach' to amalgamation. Both larger unions Federal and State leaders made advances to the small occupational unions, offering them a variety of different assurances and inducements in order to achieve an amalgamation. The APTU efforts resulted in the concluding of a series of amalgamations, predominantly with small postal and telecommunication, supervisory and retail unions. However the numbers of members these unions organised were very small and the benefit to the APTU in membership terms was negligible. The ATEA in contrast had, by the mid-1980s, decided to concentrate on trying to achieve a merger with the second largest of the unions which organised solely in TA, the ATPOA.

The ATEA's amalgamation with the ATPOA

The ATPOA represented predominantly women workers who occupied telephonist and other white-collar, non-managerial roles. By the mid-1980s the union had received amalgamation approaches from a number of larger unions including the ATEA and the APTU. As former ATPOA officers recalled, from the outset they made it clear to all parties that they only wished to enter into an amalgamation if their autonomy as a section was protected. Whilst a number of unions were keen to accommodate the ATPOA, the union which was prepared to offer them the most autonomy was the ATEA. The ATEA's merger proposal included guaranteeing the ATPOA a disproportionately large number of seats on the union's Federal Executive, plus extensive policy-making autonomy for a newly created ATPOA section. As one ATEA official who opposed the amalgamation terms observed:

> We ended up making an offer that would allow the operators tail to wag the tech dog.

Reflecting on the discussions that preceded the merger, former ATPOA officers made a series of observations that were remarkably similar to those made by CPSA P&T Group officers when describing their talks with the POEU. These are encapsulated in one ATPOA senior officer's recollections:

> There's no doubt the ATEA thought of us as a pack of Sheilas who knew nothing about negotiating. They were convinced that if they could just get us to merge then we'd be happy to give away the autonomy the merger deal gave us. Well they were mistaken!

The views of the ATEA officers in describing their amalgamation negotiations with the ATPOA also bear a marked resemblance to those of their British counterparts in the POEU. As a former ATEA official recalled:

> We gave the ATPOA a whole host of concessions in order to encourage them to merge. For example, they had a disproportionately large number of seats on the Federal Executive. Then, after the merger, they went shonkey on the understanding that they would integrate more fully.

The similarities in the merger agreements of the ATEA/ATPOA and the POEU/CPSA P&T Group, are striking. In both instances the male dominated, occupational craft union offered considerable autonomy to the smaller, predominantly female, occupational union, on the assumption that, once merged, it would be straightforward to assimilate them into an integrated structure. That both the ATEA and the POEU were prepared to make such concessions, without any written agreement detailing when or how the integration would occur, is illustrative of a shared belief that their merger partner's desire for autonomy was based on a fear of being subsumed rather than a real desire for policy independence. Interviews have indicated that amongst the ATEA leadership, as with the POEU, there seems to have been an underestimation of the negotiating capabilities of the officers of the smaller merging unions, which led to an assumption that they would be prepared to concede to further structural integration after an amalgamation took place.

Whether this misapprehension by the ATEA's negotiators was caused predominantly by sexism, occupational elitism or simple micro-political artlessness is difficult to quantify. The ATPOA's negotiators believed that the ATEA underrated their capabilities because they were women, who represented a white-collar, predominantly female, trade union. Whilst this analysis is vigorously denied by ATEA officers, many of them do agree that if they had been contemplating a merger with, for instance, the APTU, they would never have offered the concessions that they did to the ATPOA.

The evidence surrounding the ATEA's amalgamation discussions with the ATPOA does suggest that there was at least a subconscious degree of sexism and associated occupational elitism in the ATEA leadership's approach. These observations substantiate the analysis of a number of feminist authors, who document how male trade unionists display both conscious and unconscious gender prejudices in their policy judgements (Dickens, 2000; Cockburn, 1983, 1991). Ironically in this instance, as with the POEU's merger negotiations with the CPSA P&T section, the under-estimation of the negotiating skills of the predominantly female led unions, led to these unions securing very favourable amalgamation agreements.

The amalgamation agreement between the ATPOA and the ATEA was overwhelmingly endorsed by the members and the two unions formally merged in 1988. This amalgamation meant that the vast majority of the smaller telecommunication unions had now amalgamated with either the ATEA or the APTU. However, both these unions remained under pressure from the Federal Government and the ACTU to merge not only with each other but also with an even larger industrial union. Although the two unions had experienced severe membership losses during the 1980s, it was apprehension at the suggestion that they could be forced into a merger with a union the ACTU selected that triggered their amalgamation discussions with one another and other unions.

The APTU's amalgamation with the ATEA

The initial amalgamation discussions between the APTU and the ATEA proved to be extremely difficult as their relationship, particularly in NSW and Victoria, had become more dysfunctional during the 1980s. In large part this was due to an increasing number of conflicts over demarcation lines which had become blurred following the introduction of new technology. As both unions campaigned to retain, or gain, coverage of new or amended tasks, inter-union resentment flourished. A flavour of this antipathy can be found in the comments of an APTU activist:

> The IT skills that I had and used went far beyond that of the average tech. Half of them bludged around all day pretending it was difficult to pull a faulty phone out of a socket and plug in a new one. A trained monkey could do a lot of the techs work. It made me spew, and Telecom hadn't the guts to put it right.

This type of complaint was oft repeated by other APTU activists and members, whilst equally strong contrary views were put forward by ATEA members and activists. This antipathy over coverage cemented, as contributors from both unions admitted, deep-seated prejudices which had been fostered in many members from the moment they entered a specific telecommunications trade. As a former senior ATEA Officer reflectively recalled:

> From when I started work at 15, we were always told that Linies were a bunch of dills. In hindsight these sorts of prejudices played a massive part in keeping our unions divided.

These tensions made the progression of any preliminary amalgamation discussions both difficult and slow. However they accelerated after the ACTU Congress passed a motion calling on all small and medium sized unions to merge, which then prompted the Federal Government to amend the 1988 Industrial Relations Act, so that federally registered unions with up to 10,000 members could potentially be deregistered by the AIRC (Davis, 1999). As a senior officer of the APTU recalls, the pressure being placed on the two telecommunications unions was now very intense:

> We were being put under the pump by Kelty[4] and the ALP. They made it clear that if we did not enter into the ACTU amalgamation programme then there would be open slather on our union. This could involve further changes in legislation, and even the possibility that our coverage at Telstra and Australia Post could be placed in jeopardy.

---

4   Bill Kelty – ACTU Secretary from 1983–2000.

The ACTU and ALP threats generated considerable anger in both tel-ecommunication unions at what they viewed as a bullying and dictatorial approach. In addition they deeply resented being told that not only should they merge, but they should then go onto become part of the AMWU or the Public Services Union (PSU). Equally as angry at what Australian scholars agree was unprecedented interference by the ACTU and the Federal Government in the internal affairs of sovereign unions were two other medium sized Federal unions, the ETU and the PTEU (D. Kelly, 1993; Griffin, 2002; Davis, 1999). These four unions now formally met and agreed to devise a merger that would protect them from the ACTU and Federal Government sanctions, but which would also enshrine their individual autonomy.

These four way negotiations proved to be extremely problematic for the ATEA and the APTU. Early in the negotiations the ETU and the PTEU both insisted that there could only be one Communications division in any new union and that the ATEA and APTU needed to merge before they would consider an amalgamation. This was an unwelcome development for both the ATEA and the APTU, which had wished to remain in sepa-rate divisions; however, they did proceed, owing to their desire to protect themselves from the Federal Government's and ACTU's plans. These formal negotiations were beset from the start by animosity between the NSW and Victorian branches. As a former ATEA NSW State officer recalled:

> Look we all know there were demarc blues with the linies and yes, there were times when we spat the dummy over the shonkey deals they did with the bosses. But you know this wasn't the real reason why we disliked the bunch of mongrel bastards so much.

The source of the animosity being referred to was the alleged interfer-ence by the respective NSW and Victorian branches in the other union's affairs. These allegations, which centred upon the provision of financial and material support to candidates who stood against the respective State leaderships in branch elections, were admitted to by various officers from all four branches. However, none of these officers confessed to assisting in the production of the highly scurrilous leaflets, known as 'shit sheets', or to engaging in vote collecting or ballot-rigging in the other union's

State elections. After a number of interviews with many of the key participants, it did though emerge that those who had engaged in such behaviour were often were funded by the other State branch. Unsurprisingly
knowledge of these actions created a dysfunctional relationship between
the branches senior officers, which is encapsulated in a NSW APTU's
officer's comments:

> Yes we supported candidates who ran against the no-good mongrels who ran the
> techs. They were always interfering in our elections, so when the opportunity pre-
> sented itself we had no compunction in giving them a bloody good serve.

What also emerged was the personal, rather than the political, nature of
the antagonism that existed between the officers. Although the NSW and
Victorian branches respective leaderships were all factionally aligned, issues
relating to ideology were rarely cited by officers and activists in explaining why they so deeply disliked the leaders of the other union's/section's
branch. Instead they focused on the personalities and a perceived lack of
trustworthiness of the individuals concerned. The words of one senior
ATEA officer encapsulate these sentiments:

> Look it was never really about factions or politics. I didn't trust the linies, because
> they were led by no good, deceitful bastards.

These personal, and often very powerful, divisions played a major part in
ensuring that the NSW and Victorian branches remained at loggerheads
throughout the amalgamation discussions. Interviewees from both unions
agreed that this position would have scuppered the amalgamation process
had it not been for the intense external pressure the two unions were under.

In analysing these schisms what is striking is the manner in which
factional divisions, which were often cited by contributors from outside
NSW and Victoria to explain the respective branches rivalries, were often
a mask for more complex, micro-political, divisions. These observations
are further strengthened by the fact that in other States where ATEA and
APTU branches were controlled by different factions, there was not the
same rancour that so characterised relations between the Victorian and
NSW branches. This nuance in inter-union relations is ignored by those

authors who ascribe variations in policy, and animosity between unions and their branches, simply to ideological differences (Bramble, 2008; Frenkel and Coolican, 1984; Bamber et al, 1997).

By 1991, even though their NSW and Victorian branches were still at loggerheads, the ATEA and the APTU finally agreed an amalgamation package. This was only achieved after many hours of meetings, which were described by one former senior APTU Federal official "as absolutely bloody awful". At the meetings, some contributors claim, the NSW and Victorian branches had to be actively persuaded that they must accept an amalgamation. This characterisation of the discussions is hotly disputed by both unions NSW and Victorian branches, whose officials were adamant that they were not forced into accepting a merger. As one senior official of the NSW APTU stated:

> We didn't need anyone to tell us that we had to merge with the techs in order to avoid those bastards from the ACTU stitching us up. Don't listen to any bullshit that the Feds forced us to merge. We agreed, when we had ensured that our branch was protected. There would have been no merger if we had had to merge with Cooper's[5] branch.

These comments reveal tensions, once again, between the two Federal unions and their two most powerful branches over where the locus of policy-making power resided. Detailed research and interviews with all those concerned suggests that owing to their size and financial strength, the respective Eastern States branches decision to support merger was not forced upon them, instead it only took place when they were satisfied that the final agreement protected their branch autonomy. This evidence gives further support to the assertion that national union policy is often significantly shaped by decisions of local and regional policy makers as well as those who hold national office (see Kelly, 1998; Heery and Kelly, 1994; Kelly and Heery, 1994; Heery, 2000, 2003, 2006).

---

5   Col' Cooper the State Secretary of the NSW ATEA branch in the early 1990s and later the Federal Secretary of the CEPU Communications Division.

The provisional amalgamation agreement included a guarantee that there would be two separate autonomous divisions within the new union; the Telecommunications and Services section (T&S) for all the former ATEA and ATPOA members, and the Postal and Telecommunications (P&T) section, which would accommodate all the former APTU members. Both sections would have full policy-making autonomy, with separate sectional State branches. The new union was to be named the Communication Workers Union (CWU), and upon its creation it was agreed that it would immediately seek to finalise a further merger with the ETU and the PTEU. The amalgamation agreement was put to the respective memberships, and in the absence of any serious No campaign the merger was overwhelmingly endorsed by both unions' members. Commenting on this success, one ATEA officer dryly observed:

> It's hardly surprising the merger got up. There wasn't a No campaign because in reality there was nothing to oppose. We kept totally separate sections, and branches. In truth we were largely still two unions.

The formation of the CWU in 1993 did not herald a cessation in hostility between what was now the T&S and P&T branches in NSW and Victoria. Accusations in 1994 of widespread ballot rigging and the unconstitutional collecting of uncompleted ballot papers by NSW P&T branch officers, led senior P&T officials to accuse the NSW T&S branch of secretly supporting those making the allegations. The controversy that surrounded the NSW P&T branch then grew more serious when their Branch Secretary, Alan Jarman, unexpectedly left his post at very short notice. All of these events threatened to disrupt national merger discussions with the ETU and the PTEU, owing to the acrimony they had generated between the respective CWU divisions NSW branches. However at the CWU Joint Divisional Executive, there was unanimity that it was imperative to try and finalise an amalgamation agreement with the ETU and PTEU, in an effort to protect themselves from any ACTU or Federal Government sanctions.

The decision to firstly form the CWU and then to continue to seek an amalgamation with the ETU and the PTEU, even when relations between the two most powerful branches of the ATEA and APTU were so poor, is illustrative of the powerful environmental and political pressures the unions were under. Whilst the merger to form the CWU does therefore support the contention of institutional contextualist authors (Chaison, 1996; Bain, 1970) that the environment is the key force in shaping union behaviour, including mergers, the ability of the ATEA and the APTU to enter into what was an amalgamation in name only also demonstrates the ability of unions to make important strategic choices, even when faced with powerful institutional pressures (see Heery and Kelly, 1988; Kelly and Heery, 1994; Heery, 2003, 2006).

The CWU amalgamation with the ETU and the PTEU

The amalgamation discussions between the CWU, the ETU and the PTEU proceeded far more smoothly than those which preceded the formation of the CWU. As a result there was remarkably swift progress between discussions formally opening and an amalgamation agreement being put before each union's members. Reflecting on the reasons for this brisk progress, a former official of the CWU P&T Division commented:

> It's hard to stuff up a merger, when there isn't any merger occurring. We were all looking for a port in a storm and that's what forming the CEPU provided.

The highly federated nature of the new organisation, which was to be known as the Communications, Electrical and Plumbing Union[6] (CEPU), was evident in the amalgamation agreement. The deal ensured that all three unions were granted their own sections, which had total policy and financial autonomy. The three sections also retained their own separate state branches, national headquarters and independent representation at

---

6   The full title of the union was the Communications, Electrical, Electronic, Energy, Information, Postal, Plumbing and Allied Services Union of Australia. Many Australian unions adopted such lengthy official titles as they believed it would be useful in any disputed membership coverage claims, before the Federal and State Industrial Relations Commissions.

all bodies to which they affiliated, most notably the ACTU and the ALP. Recruitment and representation of members would also be undertaken separately and companies, where more than one CEPU sections had coverage, would continue to be represented by officers of the separate sections.

Such an extreme level of sectional autonomy was unusual, even in Australia, where a substantial level of autonomy for State branches was common. The draft constitution of the CEPU also guaranteed that there would be no alteration to the CWU's sectional structure, with the T&S and the P&T sections continuing to be allowed to operate autonomously of each other. Representation of the CWU was also to be split, with T&S and P&T State Secretaries having guaranteed seats on various CEPU as well as CWU Federal bodies.

Having agreed amalgamation terms in early 1994 the Federal Executives of the three unions recommended the merger to their respective members. There was concern amongst both P&T and T&S officers that CWU members would fail to see the merits of a merger. A campaign was therefore launched which stressed that the amalgamation was a pragmatic way to defend their union's against hostile Federal Government and ACTU policies. Contributors stated that this policy was highly effective in dispelling members concerns and the amalgamation was agreed, by overwhelming majorities, in all three unions. The amalgamation followed in 1994 and it achieved its principal purpose of creating a union large enough to comply with the Federal Government's and ACTU's amalgamation policies (Griffin, 2002).

However, the merger bought few, if any, other benefits. The management and policy-making autonomy of the three divisions meant there was no sharing of any resources. All three divisions remained in separate headquarters, with discrete divisional branches occupying separate offices. They also operated under their divisional titles and had their own membership services and officer corps. Such was the autonomy of the divisions that, as interviewees stated, the respective senior Federal officers rarely spoke to their opposite numbers, let alone discussed joint policy initiatives. As one CEPU T&S State Secretary wryly observed in 2008:

> We merged with the Plumbers and Electrician's did we? Can't say I ever noticed.

The mergers to form firstly the CWU and then the CEPU were very clearly entered into as direct responses to powerful external political and institutional pressures. They were designed to protect the unions from efforts by the Federal Government and the ACTU to force them into a particular form of industrial unionism. As such the amalgamations were clear attempts to subvert the efforts of the Federal Government and the ALP to strategically alter the organisational shape of Australian trade unionism (Davis, 1990; Griffin, 2002). Their success in remaining, in all but name, as four separate unions is testimony not only to the ability of unions to make independent strategic choices (see Heery and Kelly, 1988; Kelly and Heery, 1994; Heery, 2003, 2006), but also to defy the policies of the State, in a fashion not countenanced by the political contextualist authors such as Howell (2006). Whether these amalgamation choices also brought the telecommunication unions and their members' real industrial benefits is a more debatable question.

Conclusion

As with all the other unions featured in this book, the Australian telecommunication unions' policies, in all three areas, have been shown to have been profoundly shaped by their institutional and political environment. Specifically, because TA remained in public hands throughout the period under consideration, the political context has been shown to be central in determining union policies. Whilst these observations are seemingly supportive of institutional and State contextualist authors (Howell, 2005; Flanders, 1965; Bain, 1970; Clegg, 1976) who stress the role of the State and employers in establishing the parameters for union policy-making, the evidence has shown that the telecommunication unions were far from passive recipients of Federal Government policy decisions. Instead, what has been demonstrated is that the unions made a series of strategic political and industrial choices, which were successful in ensuring that the Federal

Government did not privatise TA, and delayed the introduction of competition into the industry until 1992. These findings support the theories of those authors who attest that unions' policy choices can play a central part in influencing their political and industrial environment and in determining their own futures (Kelly, 1998; Heery and Kelly, 1994; Kelly and Heery, 1994; Heery, 2000, 2003, 2006).

The policy choices of the telecommunication unions have also been shown to be profoundly shaped, across all three areas, by occupational rivalries and political factional divisions, which manifested themselves most strongly at the State as opposed to the national level. This supports the assertions of those authors who state that ideology plays a central role in determining union policy (Kelly, 1988; Darlington, 1994, 2001; McIllroy and Campbell, 1999; McIllroy, 2007; Daniels and McIllroy, 2009), and that decisions at the local as well as the national level profoundly affect union policy direction (Hyman, 1997; Heery, 2003, 2006; Heery and Kelly, 1988; Kelly and Heery, 1994).

There is also convincing evidence that Bramble's (2008) rank and filist assertion that the Australian telecommunications unions' failure to resist mass redundancies in TA was owing to the inherent conservatism and aversion to industrial action of union officers is both simplistic and fundamentally flawed. Finally this chapter has provided further evidence that micro-political factors, in particular personal animosities, have profoundly influenced Australian telecommunication unions' policies, in a manner suggested by this book's central hypothesis.

Summary and Findings

This chapter summarises the findings of this book and juxtaposes the empirical data against the theories of union policy-making set out in the literature review. In doing so it outlines the similarities and differences in the labour process, recruitment and amalgamation policies adopted by the featured Australian and British unions, whilst exploring the reasons behind their responses to the serious challenges they faced from 1980 to 1996.

The chapter goes on to highlight the significant answers the research has uncovered to the two central questions which were posed at the outset of this book: How, and why, do unions adopt specific policies? What factors explain the different behaviour of similar unions when faced with comparable policy choices? Time is also spent in considering whether the hypothesis put forward at the start of this book, that union policy-making was significantly affected by micro-political factors, such as personal friendships, loyalties and enmities, has any validity.

Structurally the chapter is similar to the literature review. Initially it juxtaposes the various general theoretical explanations of union policy-making against the empirical evidence. Then it contrasts the various hypotheses put forward in the literature, concerning the labour process, recruitment and amalgamations, with the reality of policy-making in all the featured unions.

Classical theorists

The assertion of classical theorists (Webbs, 1897, 1920; Michels, 1913) that union policy is controlled by a small coterie of union officials, who operate in an oligarchic fashion, is not supported by the findings of this book. The evidence shows that in all the British and Australian unions featured there was extensive devolvement of decision making authority to the branch and chapel lay officers, who in many instances enjoyed considerable policy autonomy. This devolution of powers occurred in both craft and occupational unions and, contrary to Turner's (1962) hypothesis that a functioning democratic process was only possible in craft unions, all the occupational unions featured also had fully operative democratic structures. The empirical evidence has also illustrated that, thanks in large part to the powers of political, occupational and geographical factions, incumbent lay and full-time officers were also regularly removed from office. This fact is at odds with the belief that an overwhelming electoral advantage is enjoyed by incumbent office holders (Webbs, 1897, 1920; Michels, 1913; Turner, 1962).

There were also examples, from all of the unions, of national policy makers engaging in negotiations and accommodations with lay officers from the local representational layers of the union, in order to ensure that any national policy was acceptable and would be implemented. These were actions which also contradict the belief that a union's senior officers are subject to some form of 'veneration' and can therefore easily disseminate policy downwards (Michels, 1913; Webbs, 1897, 1920).

Rank and filism

Authors who adopt a rank and filist view of union policy-making assert that gaining effective control of union policy-making is dependent on the successful mobilisation of shop stewards and members in order to challenge 'unrepresentative union officialdom' (Fairbrother, 2000). This belief in the need for a 'challenge from below' is part of a wider, dichotomous view of the roles of full-time officers and lay officials (Fairbrother, 2000).

This book's findings supports the assertion that the development and politicisation of lay activists is important if unions are to effectively build and sustain influence over the labour process. However the evidence clearly indicates that a far more complex and interdependent relationship exists between full-time officers and lay activists. In all of the unions studied there was a high degree of cooperation and mutual reliance between lay officials and the full-time officer core. This applies to efforts to gain, or protect, influence over the labour process and to recruit new members, particularly since the demise of the closed shop.

There was no evidence, even in relation to amalgamation policy, that there existed a simple dichotomy between full-time officers and the lay activists. Instead, support for, or hostility towards, a specific policy was often found to equally divide officers and lay activists, with their views often corresponding to their occupational backgrounds or political beliefs. There have though been times when a concerted politically motivated 'challenge from below' has wrought a radical change in policy. The rise of the POEU BL in the 1970s resulted in an increase in local, member-led, industrial militancy, which in turn secured a greater control over the labour process. But the research has also revealed other instances where the full-time officer cadre was more proactive than lay activists in attempting to secure, or protect, influence over the labour process.

The findings of the book therefore indicate that, contrary to the assertions of rank and filist scholars (Callincos, 1982; Cliff, 1970; Fairbrother, 2000; Bramble, 2008), policy formulation was not profoundly influenced by a simple struggle for control between full-time officers and lay activists. Instead, policy in all three areas has been shown to be more heavily influenced by the often abstruse and multifaceted relationship which exists between officers and lay members. Their relationships have been revealed to be shaped by occupational, craft, geographical, political and micro-political factors, which cut across and outweigh any supposed dichotomy of interests between lay and full-time officials.

Political factionalism

The earliest proponents of the political factionalist argument (Lipset et al, 1956; Edelstein and Warner, 1975) asserted that for there to be any form of democratic policy-making in trade unions there needed to be an effective political opposition to the incumbent leadership. Without such an opposition these authors held that oligarchical powers would be enjoyed by the national leadership (Edelstein and Warner, 1975).

The research has shown that political factions do play an important role in ensuring that union memberships are provided with a choice, at national and local elections, between candidates who are proposing different ideological policy approaches. However the evidence has also revealed how other internal groups, whose uniting element was an occupational, geographical, or individual allegiance, also collectively influenced policy and stood 'slates' of candidates in elections. The extent of policy influence these organisations exerted inside a union varied considerably, with those unions in which political factions were weak, seeing occupational and geographical groups exerting considerable control. Importantly these groups ensured that in every one of the featured unions, where political factions were not capable of fielding candidates for senior lay and full-time officer positions, elections were contested and alternative policies were put forward. The operation and influence of these often powerful and well organised groups also helps to explain why, in answer to the question posed by Daniels and McIlroy (2009), political factions of the Left or Right struggle to gain and retain control over policy-making in some British and Australian unions.

Institutional contextualism

Those authors who adopt an institutional contextualist viewpoint stress how collective bargaining structures and the policies of the State and employers largely determine the nature of union organisation and policy formation

(Bain, 1970; Clegg, 1976). This work also emphasises the secondary nature of union organisation, with authors asserting that it is only with the active acquiescence of the State and employers that unions are able to function effectively on behalf of their members (Bain, 1970). These arguments have been developed by other scholars who argue that only when employers are persuaded of the economic benefit to themselves of, for example, adopting equal opportunities in the workplace, will they start to engage with unions over issues such as equal pay and improved conditions for part-time workers (Dickens, 1999).

This book's findings have shown that whilst collective bargaining structures, employer policies and Government programmes all play a substantial role in shaping the context in which unions take policy decisions, they are not always the primary causal factor in determining union behaviour. Examples have been outlined, from all the featured unions, of the adoption of industrial policies which have forced employers to involuntarily make concessions over the control of the labour process. Similarly instances have been documented where the unions have defeated or subverted employer and State efforts to fundamentally alter the industrial or political environment. A clear example of this phenomenon is the successful campaign by the Australian telecommunications unions to derail the Federal Government's plans to deregulate and privatise TA during the 1980s.

The research undertaken for this book has also shown that similar unions, when faced with comparable challenges, do not always behave in a homogenous manner, but instead are able to adopt dissimilar policy responses, which affect their fortunes as organisations. The decision of the PKIU's newspaper chapels to reach negotiated agreements over direct text inputting by journalists, as opposed to their NGA's counterparts total refusal to countenance such a change in the early 1980s, is a significant example of such divergent policy responses. This evidence suggests that institutional contextualist authors underestimate the ability of unions to exercise autonomy in their policy-making.

State contextualism

In common with institutional contextualist authors those scholars who favour a State contextualist explanation for union behaviour also believe in a form of external determinism (Howell, 1999, 2005; Dickens and Hall, 2003). They stress the pre-eminence of the State in regulating the national industrial relations framework and the inability of unions to make autonomous policy choices. This control is provided by the State's legislative, judicial and policing powers, which can limit the ability of unions to engage in industrial militancy and resist alterations to the labour process. State contextualist authors consequently argue that unions are dependent upon the Government adopting a benign attitude towards their activity, if they are to operate successfully (Howell, 2005).

The evidence outlined in the empirical chapters suggests that the State often plays a crucial role in shaping the environment in which unions operate, primarily through the deployment of its legislative powers. This is particularly the case in terms of union recruitment and labour process policies, where hostile legislation prohibiting compulsory trade unionism, necessitated radical changes to union policy. Where central Government occupies the role of the employer this influence, State contextualists scholars argue, increases even further (Howell, 1999, 2005).

This book has however shown that all the unions featured have, at different times, actively resisted State policies. The level of union success in opposing State policies has varied considerably, with the relative unity, industrial strength and political resolution of the union and the Government involved, determining the outcome of such struggles. This ability of unions to actively resist the will of the State and, on occasion, to be successful in altering Government policy, calls into question the State contextualist view that 'trade unions have little ability to act autonomously of the State' (Howell, 2005: 79).

Strategic choice

The claim that unions are able to make independent 'strategic choices' between policy options, which profoundly affect their overall performance, is asserted by a number of authors (Boxall and Hayes, 1997; Boxall, 2008; Child, 1997; Heery and Kelly, 1988; Kelly and Heery, 1994; Heery, 2003, 2006; Hyman, 1997). These scholars however are divided over the level at which strategic policy decisions are made, and whether there is one, logical set of choices a union needs to make to ensure its future success. Some authors (Boxall and Hayes, 1997; Boxall, 2008; Child, 1997) assert that it is at a national level that unions invariably make key strategic decisions and that whilst they are able to choose between a series of policy approaches, the only sensible set of policy choices is to embrace 'partnership unionism' in the context of neo-liberalism (Boxall and Hayes, 1997: 587).

Other strategic choice authors (Heery and Kelly, 1988; Kelly and Heery, 1994; Heery, 2003, 2006; Hyman, 1997) adopt a different approach, arguing that strategic policy choices can be made at the local as well as the national level. They also assert that policy makers' decisions are affected by their values, gender, generation and ideological views, whilst being shaped by the political factions and complex social interactions with other activists and members. Some of these strategic choice authors (McIllroy and Campbell, 1999; McIllroy, 2007; Daniels and McIllroy, 2009; Kelly, 1988) go on to stress the key role of ideology and political factions as the primary source of variation in the policy choices of union activists and officers.

The evidence gathered for this book strongly supports the central assertion of both strands of 'strategic choice' scholarship, that unions are capable of making policy choices which manifestly influence their fortunes as organisations, and the ability effectively to represent their members. In each of the unions studied, evidence has been produced of clear choices being made between different policy options. The selection of specific policies has also been shown to have had a profound effect on the fortunes of the unions, in all three key areas.

Turning to the question of where policy authority resides within unions, the evidence unequivocally supports those authors who assert that important policy choices take place at the local as well as the national level (Heery and Kelly, 1988; Kelly and Heery, 1994; Heery, 2003, 2006). In every union featured there was a considerable level of local policy-making autonomy at either the branch or chapel level. This autonomy was particularly ubiquitous in relation to the labour process, but it was also present, on occasion, in relation to recruitment and amalgamation. There were also numerous examples of national decision making being the result of complex interactions between national officers, regional officials and lay activists, rather than simply reflecting the unitary decisions of a union's national leadership.

The evidence also powerfully supports the contention that strong political factions and the ideological views of policy makers have had a profound effect on decision making in the majority of the featured unions. This is in line with the assertion of a number of scholars (Kelly, 1988; Heery and Kelly, 1988; Kelly and Heery, 1994; Heery, 2003, 2006) that the values, gender, generation and ideological views of policy makers play a significant part in colouring their policy choices. Where this book diverges from and adds to this strand of strategic choice scholarship is in its assessment that there is a greater breadth and richness of influences on policy choices, than is overtly acknowledged in this literature. These influences encompass the workings of internal factional groups, whose basis was geographical, occupational, or personal loyalty, rather than explicit ideological principles. In all the featured unions, to a greater or lesser degree, such groups have influenced policy makers and successfully organised 'slates' of candidates in lay and full-time officer elections.

The research for this book has also revealed how individual policy makers' decisions have been shaped by micro-political factors, particularly loyalties, friendships, and enmities. Owing to a historical reluctance of union officers and activists to admit to third parties that such emotions coloured their judgements, the important role of these micro-political factors has previously gone unrecorded in the work of strategic choice authors.

The labour process

The definition of the labour process that has been used throughout this book involves the control of the recruitment and regulation of labour, the operation of the production process (including the introduction of new technology), and the ability of employers to deskill and fragment their employees' work (Braverman, 1974; Burawoy, 1979). In all of the empirical chapters the focus has been on the ability of different unions to influence these various elements of the labour process.

The substantive findings have revealed how all the Australian and British telecommunication and printing unions developed their influence over all aspects of the labour process in the period up until 1980. In doing so all of the unions were successful in increasing their control over the recruitment and the regulation of labour, by using their industrial strength to attain compulsory union agreements across large parts of their respective industries. Whilst the nature of these agreements differed, with the two nations' print unions operating pre-entry closed shops and the telecommunication unions organising post-entry closed shops, the outcome – high union density levels – was identical.

One of the principal debates in the labour process literature relates to whether the increasing application of the closed shop was important in allowing unions to exert greater control over the wider labour process. One group of authors (McCarthy, 1964; Dunn and Gennard, 1983, 1984; Gennard et al, 1979; Gennard, 1990; Gennard and Bain, 1995) assert that the development of the closed shop represented a conscious strategic choice by unions to strengthen their influence over the labour process. Compulsory unionism, these authors state, was achieved in the face of employer resistance or reluctant acquiescence. They conclude that the closed shop, and in particular the pre-entry closed shop, was effective in delivering increased influence over the labour process by overcoming employer resistance to union organisation. Other scholars (Weeks, 1990; Hart, 1979) argued that, on the contrary, the growth in closed shops merely reflected the desire by employers and the State, during the 1960s and 1970s to avoid multi-unionism, which led to inter-union disputes and 'leapfrog' bargaining. The closed shop, Hart (1979) argued, was widely welcomed by employers as it allowed senior union officers to reach 'necessary', but unpopular, collective agreements with companies, without the fear members would leave for a rival union. The evidence, set out in this book, of the alacrity with which employers across all the featured industries sought to rid themselves of the closed shop, when they were able to do so, undermines these arguments.

Alongside the increasing application of the closed shop during the 1960s and 1970s, this book has also illustrated how increased levels of political and industrial radicalism in the featured unions resulted in a greater willingness of activists and members to engage in industrial action. Crucially this action, across both nations' telecommunication and printing sectors, was highly effective as it caused substantial levels of disruption. This combination of factors radicalised union policy-making and allowed all the unions to gain greater levels of influence over all elements of the labour process. In addition, the unions were also successful in achieving considerable increases in wages and improvements to terms and conditions of employment, often in the face of uncoordinated and maladroit employer and State resistance.

The difficulties all of the unions had in retaining this level of labour process influence when the economic, political, industrial and technological climate changed, are outlined in detail in the empirical chapters. Significantly, this trend started first in the Australian printing industry in the late 1970s, where the PKIU lost a dispute at the *Sydney Morning Herald* over the unilateral introduction of direct text inputting by journalists. This defeat owed much to the lack of support the PKIU chapel received from the AJA, and the unsupportive intervention of the NSW Industrial Relations Commission, who found in favour of the employer. Unlike the other featured unions, the PKIU by the mid-1970s was already facing a significant contraction of Australia's relatively small, regionally centred printing industry. These factors, when added to the alacrity with which many of their older members accepted employer offers of generous severance packages, led the PKIU at Federal, State and chapel level, to seek negotiated accommodations over the introduction of new technology. In return, the union was successful in retaining their representational role and the avoidance of compulsory redundancies in companies in which they were organised. They did however find it difficult to extend the pre-entry closed shop into new areas of the industry where new employers no longer had any requirement for the skills their members possessed and refused to hire union labour.

Rank and filist authors such as Bramble (2008) have argued that the PKIU's leadership approach, at this time, represented a betrayal of the interests and the wishes of their members. The research undertaken for this book finds this to be a wholly unfounded assertion. Across Australia the evidence is overwhelming that at the local chapel level, State officers and FoCs urged their members not to accept agreements which coupled enhanced severance packages with detrimental changes to conditions and a diminished role for the PKIU chapel in the labour process. The packages were though accepted, because a majority of members ignored their officers' objections and endorsed the agreements.

In Britain the election of a Conservative Government in 1979, which was ideologically committed to curbing union influence and abolishing compulsory unionism, led to both the printing and telecommunications unions facing efforts by both the State and employers to curb their influence over the labour process. Specifically in terms of the printing industry, evidence has been presented which demonstrates that British newspaper employers and the Government actively co-ordinated industrial and legislative policy in order to limit the ability of the printing unions to use secondary action and secondary picketing. This collusion was also to eventually result in the Police being instructed to assist both Messenger Group Newspapers and News International in their industrial disputes, in a manner which substantiates Kelly's (1990) assertion that there was a counter offensive by employers and the State, against trade union influence over the labour process (Kelly, 1990).

The British print unions sought to deal with these co-ordinated attacks upon their influence over the labour process in a fashion dissimilar to the PKIU. They chose to resist efforts to undermine their control of the labour process through the deployment of industrial action. A large part of the reason for this variation in policy was that the larger, geographically less dispersed, and industrially more powerful British printing unions had been successful throughout the 1970s and early 1980s in defending their influence over the labour process. This gave them the confidence to engage in a series of disputes, most famously at Messenger Group Newspapers and News International. A significant element of the conflicts involved official secondary action and secondary picketing, the newly introduced legislative restrictions on which the judiciary and the Police applied with zeal. These constraints, when added to the employers' ability to use pre-press and production facilities that no longer required craft skills, have been shown to have played a large part in undermining the policies adopted by the print unions to retain influence over the labour process.

It is though a key finding of this book that these factors did not inevitably lead to the print unions' defeats in the Messenger and News International disputes, nor that they were destined to lose, to the degree that they did, their influence over the labour process. Whilst the empirical evidence has shown how prosecuting successful industrial disputes was extremely difficult in the 1980s, it has also revealed how a series of policy misjudgements, alongside deep-seated internal and inter-union divisions, denied the unions more favourable outcomes. The evidence has also exposed how the schisms within and between the unions, which contributed to their comprehensive Messenger Group and News International defeats, then encouraged other employers to attack the print unions ability to retain influence over the labour process (Gennard, 1990; Gennard and Bain, 1995).

There are authors (Cockburn, 1983, 1991; Wajcman, 2000) who argue that this loss of influence over the labour process was the result of craft unions historically behaving in a fashion that created a gender segregated industry, which created widespread resentment and disunity. These discriminatory practices, they assert, contributed to the divisions between craft and non-craft unions which eventually led to their loss of influence over the labour process (Cockburn, 1991). This view is robustly rebutted by other scholars, most notably Gennard (Gennard et al, 1979; Dunn and Gennard, 1983, 1984; Gennard, 1990), who ascribes the underrepresentation of women in skilled printing trades to historical societal norms, and dismisses the notion that the pre-entry closed shop was anything other than a powerful, positive tool for recruitment and influencing the labour process. The findings of this book have demonstrated that whilst sexism existed within the printing unions, the basis for the profound internal and inter union divisions, which so undermined unity within and between the printing unions, had their foundations instead in deep seated craft and occupational prejudices, which along with political and personal enmities, were more powerful than divisions based primarily on gender.

The British telecommunication unions also suffered from the 'counter offensive' against their influence over the labour process in the early 1980s. This attack was incorporated in the British Government's larger commitment to deregulate the telecommunication industry and privatise BT (Bamber et al, 1997; Parker, 2009; Undy et al, 1996). These were policies which the POEU strongly opposed, but over which, as this book has shown, they had great difficulty in agreeing a coherent and effective response. This problem has been attributed by many authors (Parker, 2009; Undy et al, 1996; McIlroy, 1988) to the union being deeply divided along ideological lines. The cause of the heightened division being the growing strength of the POEU BL, who were challenging the long term national policy-making control of The Bloc. This schism led, it is asserted, to the POEU adopting what proved to be a series of ineffective policies in response to deregulation, privatisation and management efforts to reduce the union's influence over the labour process (Undy et al, 1996; Parker, 2009, McIlroy, 1988). This book has shown that this is too simplistic an explanation. Whilst POEU policy was profoundly affected by the factional struggle taking place inside the POEU during the early 1980s, the empirical evidence has revealed that policy conflicts often took place within the two factions and were caused by geographical, industrial and micro-political disagreements.

In the 1980s the Australian telecommunication unions also had to deal with a Federal Government who wished to deregulate the industry, privatise the national carrier and make significant changes to the labour process. However, unlike Britain, Australia had a Labor Federal Government. In common with the POEU the two largest unions in TA, the ATEA and the APTU, vigorously opposed the Federal Government's plans, as they shared the POEU's belief that such policies were not only economically and ideologically misguided but were also potentially very damaging to their influence over the labour process. In order to counter the Federal

Government's deregulation policy the unions were able, thanks to their ALP affiliations, to influence the policy not only through formal meetings with Ministers but also, more importantly, through the informal channels of the ALP's powerful internal political factions. This policy approach, unlike the POEU's, was successful in delaying deregulation until 1992 and in blocking privatisation altogether until after the ALP lost office in 1996. The success of the Australian unions anti-privatisation and deregulation policies has been shown to be directly linked to the far greater political influence they were able to exert compared to the POEU, owing to the ALP holding Federal Government office.

This success came though at a considerable price. National agreements were entered into by the Australian telecommunication unions which allowed increased demarcation flexibility and job losses. These were changes which, much to the anger of the unions, were followed in the late 1980s and early 1990s by further detrimental alterations to working practices and reductions in staffing, which were arguably proportionately more draconian than in the privatised BT. It is a central finding of this book that, in common with all the other featured unions, the telecommunication unions' efforts to resist these detrimental changes were hampered by members accepting generous voluntary severance packages, which were tied to collective agreements that diminished union influence over the labour process.

As this section has shown all the featured unions, in both nations, had great difficulty during the 1980s and 1990s in defending the influence they had gained over the labour process during the 1960s and 1970s. In both countries the unions found it difficult to resist employers' efforts to regain influence over the labour process. However in the Australian telecommunication industry a clear example was revealed of unions successfully altering the intended policy of the Federal Government in a manner which contradicts the assertion of State and institutional contextualist authors (Bain, 1970; Howell, 2005).

A further key finding of this book is that all the unions had difficulty in adopting coherent, timely and effective policy responses to the considerable labour process challenges they faced. In part this was owing to the complex, multi layered, nature of labour process policy-making, which frequently involved negotiation and accommodation between the different tiers of the respective union's structure. It also reflected the way in which labour process policies were shaped by a rich and diverse set of ideological, occupational, geographical and micro-political factors, whose fluctuating strengths, and often contradictory perspectives, resulted in policy makers often failing to implement clear and effective strategies.

Amalgamations

Many authors who have reviewed British and Australian union amalgamations concur that the vast majority of union mergers are entered into owing to adverse external factors which create financial and membership decline (Undy, 1996, 2008; Waddington, 1988, 1995; Visser and Waddington, 1996; Waddington et al, 2005; Chaison, 1996; Davis, 1990, 1999; Griffin, 1994, 2002). The empirical findings of this book partially support these assertions. Many of the mergers featured were prompted by falling membership and resultant financial difficulties, with smaller craft or occupational unions, whose strong preference had been to remain independent, being forced into amalgamations with larger unions.

It has also been shown that larger unions who for decades had spoken in broad terms about the benefits of merging together to form an industrial union, but whose dysfunctional industrial and micro-political relationships had kept them apart, were also finally propelled together by extreme financial and membership crises. SOGAT's merger with the NGA is a prime example of this trend. This book has also uncovered convincing evidence to support Undy's (1996, 2008) assertion that there are reasons other than financial deficits and membership declines for unions amalgamating. In a number of mergers political considerations were the primary cause. The CPSA P&T Group's decision to leave the CPSA and join the POEU, in order to extricate themselves from what they viewed as destructive factional environment inside the CPSA, being a good example.

The approaches a number of the featured unions made to smaller organisations also supports another of Undy's (2008) claims that, since the 1960s, larger unions have adopted a more pro-active approach to seeking amalgamation. SOGAT's approach to the smaller craft union, the SGA, is an example of this tactic. It is a finding of this book that this was a policy which could often cause problems for the larger unions, with their own members and activists. This was owing to resentment that could be generated when activists became aware of the often remarkably generous levels of autonomy that was being offered to the smaller union in order to secure an amalgamation. Antipathy often grew after the amalgamation, when merging unions proved themselves unwilling to voluntarily relinquish the policy autonomy they had been granted.

In Australia amalgamations were driven not only by membership and financial problems but also by political considerations and the pro-active efforts of larger unions to encourage smaller unions to amalgamate. The major difference in Australia was the far greater role played by the State in encouraging amalgamations during the 1980s and 1990s. Prior to this point, as Griffin (2002) notes, merger activity had been relatively limited. This was largely due to the membership protections offered to small unions by the Federal and State Industrial Relations Commissions and Courts. When the ALP Federal Government radically altered this policy and initially encouraged and then compelled small unions to amalgamate, there was a considerable increase in merger activity. This book has shown how this change in Federal Government policy resulted in many of the telecommunication unions amalgamating with either the ATEA or the APTU, often on very generous terms, owing to the inter-union rivalry between the ATEA and the APTU. It is another important finding of this book that smaller unions often benefit from such rivalries in securing amalgamation agreements in a fashion that the literature does not fully address (Undy, 1996, 2008; Waddington, 1988, 1995; Waddington et al, 2005; 1999; Griffin, 1994, 2002).

The Federal Government's desire to create industrial unions, also led to a form of amalgamation which had seldom been seen before in either Australia or Britain. This type of merger involved unions forming only the loosest of federations to avoid the strictures of legislation. The ATEA and

APTU entered into this sort of merger, initially with each other, and then with the ETU and PTEU: the purpose being, as interviewees confirmed, to ensure that they were not forced into a 'full' merger with another partner of the ACTU's choice. That an amalgamation can occur where there is no merger of any functions or roles is an important aspect of Australian union amalgamation policy, detailed by this book, which many scholars have failed to address (Bramble, 2008; Davis, 1999; Griffin, 2002). This type of merger also represents another example of unions actively subverting the industrial relations wishes of the State, in a manner which challenges Howell's (2005) Statist analysis of union behaviour.

Another area of union amalgamation policy which is not extensively focused upon in the literature, but has been shown to be of considerable importance in shaping amalgamation policies, has been the role of micro-political factors. Whilst a number of authors (Hagan, 1966; Waters, 1978; Undy, 2008) do note that personal relationships play a part in determining amalgamation policy, they do not credit micro-political factors with the important role they have exercised in the featured unions. In each of the unions, the relationship between senior officers of prospective merger partners has been shown to be critical, not only in deciding whether an amalgamation takes place, but also in shaping the structure of a new union. The fact that amalgamation negotiations are typically conducted by a small number of senior national officers, with other decision-making tiers of the union having a lesser role than in labour process and recruitment policy formulation, is a significant reason why micro-political factors play such a prominent part in shaping amalgamation policies.

Recruitment

The empirical chapters have shown how, by the late 1970s, the enforcement of compulsory unionism across their industries allowed all the featured unions to enjoy very high membership density levels. By the mid-1980s the recruitment challenges all the unions faced had altered significantly. There had been dramatic industrial and technological alterations, resulting in large scale redundancies in well organised areas, and a development of new areas of the industry where the unions had no organisational base. These factors, combined with legislative restrictions on the closed shop, led to debates inside all the unions over recruitment strategies.

These organisational difficulties and debates were repeated in other Australian and British unions and became the focus of much scholarly attention (Heery, 1998, 2001, 2003; Heery and Kelly, 1990; Heery and Alder, 2004; Heery and Simms, 2008; Cooper, 2005; Gall, 2003; Terry, 2000; Willman, 2001; Kelly and Badigannavar, 2004). In all the featured unions, settling on a coherent and effective recruitment strategy for the poorly organised, yet rapidly expanding, areas of their industry proved to be problematic. Few of the featured unions' officers and activists had experience of organising without the assistance of compulsory unionism, and there was a very limited pool of practical knowledge and experience of direct physical recruitment for them to draw upon. These were problems that affected many Australian and British unions during the 1980s and 1990s (see Gall, 2003; Heery, 1998, 2001, 2003; Cooper, 2005; Cooper, 2003, 2005; Heery and Kelly, 1990), but they were exacerbated in the unions featured in this book by the hostility that many members, activists and officers felt towards recruiting employees in the new areas of their industries.

This antagonism was particularly strong in the telecommunications unions, where hostility towards companies entering the deregulated industry manifested itself as antipathy towards their employees. In Britain this led to a period of five years when the union officially refused to recruit Mercury staff. This ultimately self-defeating policy gained majority NEC support because the POEU leadership believed it would be morally wrong to recruit members in an employer they wished to see closed. However it is a key finding of the book that many activists and officers supported the refusal to recruit Mercury staff, because they were apprehensive and uncomfortable with the idea of physical recruiting. The Australian telecommunications unions, whilst they did not formally refuse to recruit outside of TA, also suffered from activists and officers resisting recruiting Optus employees. This antagonism was coupled to lengthy internal wrangling over which section Optus members should be placed into, which tended to overshadow the actual recruitment of members. As with the POEU, the Australian union officers and activists also admitted that when they did try and recruit outside of TA, they found the process difficult and avoided undertaking such recruitment whenever possible.

In Britain and Australia the initial company entrants to the deregulated telecommunications markets had originally indicated to the unions that they wished to enter into co-operative 'partnership' agreements. The Australian unions agreed to this type of arrangement with Optus, in a manner advocated by those authors who assert that a 'partnership' with employers is the most effective way for unions to build their membership (Ackers and Payne, 1998; Basset, 1986; Bassett and Cave, 1993; Bacon and Storey, 1993; Osterman, 1999). The evidence has shown how Optus, along with other similar companies in Britain and Australia, quickly divested themselves of their 'partnership' agreements once they had achieved entrance into the market, actions which illustrate a key weakness of the partnership approach to union organising.

After Optus and other British and Australian new entrant companies opted out of their union 'partnership' agreements, they all adopted an aggressively anti-union attitude. In doing so they exploited the unions' campaign for the Government to re-regulate the sector, by informing their staff that the unions wanted them to lose their jobs. These tactics, along with a lack of recruitment knowledge and enthusiasm amongst union activists and officers, led to a poor organising performance by the unions in these companies. These types of problems were not dissimilar to those in other British and Australian unions where specialist recruitment officers were deployed (Heery, 1998, 2001, 2003; Cooper, 2005; Cooper and Carter, 2002; Heery and Alder, 2004; Heery and Simms, 2008; Gall, 2003). However, as has been revealed in earlier chapters, the close affinity the majority of officers and activists had for their national carrier and the hostility they had for their competitors, made recruitment outside of BT or TA exceptionally difficult for the telecommunication unions.

The print unions in Britain and Australia also struggled to adapt their recruitment strategies to the rapidly changing industrial landscape of the

1980s and 1990s. The decline in the levels of employment in the traditionally well organised manual pre-press and production areas, and the expansion in employment in the predominantly unorganised, computer aided design and production sector, created a major membership crisis and a substantial recruitment challenge. Allied to these problems the British unions were no longer able to enforce their highly effective recruitment tool, the pre-entry closed shop. Whilst the same prohibitions on compulsory unionism did not exist in Australia, the PKIU also had to cope with a significant rise in the number of employers who refused to operate the closed shop, because they no longer required the craft skills which members possessed.

Membership decline in both countries caused the unions to rethink their organising strategies in order to recruit workers in the unorganised areas of their industries. These attempts proved to be less than successful, as full-time and lay officers who had always depended on the pre-entry closed shop had little knowledge of the tactics and techniques that were needed if non-union employees were to be persuaded, rather than compelled, to join a union. This lack of recruitment skill and experience, as with the telecommunication unions, often led to poor organisational outcomes which left many officers and activists, who had participated, viewing recruiting as an unpleasant and highly unwelcome 'new' activity that they wished to avoid.

In all the featured telecommunication and printing unions low levels of recruitment in the 1980s prompted a reassessment of their recruitment strategies. This led, in a tentative and halting manner, to the featured unions all starting to explore the use of recruitment officers. However there was significant resistance in many of the unions, as officers and activists objected to recruitment officials not having to be elected, or to have previously been a member of the union. These difficulties were added to by the even greater problem the unions encountered with the planning and logistical delivery of recruitment projects, where all the unions displayed a lack of expertise in running efficient organising campaigns. This resulted in largely unfocused, scattergun, recruitment strategies which were singularly unsuccessful.

It is a central finding of this book that this lack of a cohesive and effective national recruitment strategy and the unwillingness of the unions to appoint, from outside their own ranks, senior officers with a proven track record of leading successful recruitment campaigns, was a serious strategic error. This, when added to the failure to adequately train and then motivate activists and officers to undertake recruitment, explains the telecommunication and printing unions' poor organising performance in what were growing industries.

Conclusion

As the empirical chapters have shown, all the featured unions faced a historically turbulent period from 1980 to 1996, during which they made a series of dramatic alterations to their labour process, amalgamation and recruitment policies. The substantive findings have corroborated Kelly's (1990) assertion that union policy makers had to deal with a counter-offensive by the State and employers, designed to regain control over the labour process. The evidence has also revealed that the unions adopted a series of policies which were not fully successful in resisting this counter-offensive, owing not only to the adverse institutional, political and technological environment, but also to their own internal divisions, which affected their ability to apply their policies in a coherent and unified fashion. These divisions, as the empirical evidence has shown, related to the rich, multi-layered and complex nature of union policy-making, and the host of ideological, occupational and micro-political conflicts, which existed within every union.

The substantive research has also shown that whilst the labour process decisions the unions made were framed by the political and institutional context in which they operated (Clegg, 1976; Bain, 1970; Howell, 2005), they also made a series of important strategic choices, at both the national and local level, which affected their success as organisations, in a manner that supports the assertions of Heery and Kelly (Heery and Kelly, 1988; Kelly and Heery, 1994; Heery, 2003, 2006). The success of the Australian telecommunications unions in opposing the Federal Government's plans to privatise TA has also revealed flaws in the argument that unions do not have the capacity to alter the policies of the State (Howell, 2005).

This book has also documented the enormous difficulties that the featured unions had in adapting their recruitment policies to deal with the loss of the closed shop and the expansion of new areas of their industries. The unions' lack of officers and activists with recruitment skills, and their internal difficulties in making constitutional adjustments to allow for the employment of those who could help renew their organisations, were major reasons for their poor recruitment performances. As unions with such a heavy historic reliance on the closed shop the evidence has also shown that the featured unions were at a disadvantage compared to unions who were more familiar with organising without the benefit of compulsory unionism (see Heery et al, 2003; Gall, 2003).

The evidence gathered in relation to amalgamation policies suggests that the unions, whilst often motivated to amalgamate owing to dwindling membership and financial difficulties, in a manner that a number of scholars have suggested (Undy, 1996, 2008; Waddington, 1988, 1995; Waddington et al, 2005), also merged for political and micro-political reasons. Additionally, a substantive finding of the book is that some amalgamations were not 'true' mergers; with the Australian telecommunications unions successfully engaging in an amalgamation with two other unions, where no organisational unification took place. This accommodation between the four unions was entered into, so that they all could avoid being forced into amalgamations with other unions by the ACTU and the Federal Government. In making choices over amalgamation partners, the book's research has also illustrated how unions' amalgamation policies are influenced by a more complex mix of ideological, industrial and particularly micro-political considerations than the literature has previously acknowledged (Undy, 1996, 2008; Waddington, 1988, 1995; Waddington et al, 2005).

Union policy-making has been revealed by this book to be the result of a rich and varied process, involving negotiation and accommodation between different tiers of decision makers who are all influenced by a wide variety of ideological, occupational, geographical and micro-political factors. The levels of complexity surrounding the creation and application of policy have also been shown to be considerably greater than is credited in much of the literature (Bain, 1970; Howell, 2005; Boxall and Hayes, 1997; Willman, 2001). Evidence has also been provided which substantiates the assertions of scholars that union policy is affected by the beliefs, values and ideology of individual officers and activists (Hyman, 1997; Kelly, 1998; Heery and Kelly, 1994; Kelly and Heery, 1994; Heery, 2000, 2003, 2006). Finally this book has provided strong empirical evidence to support the hypothesis that micro-political factors, particularly friendships, personal loyalties and enmities, profoundly affect the policy choices of individual decision makers.

CHAPTER 13

Conclusion

At the outset this book sought to answer two central questions: How, and why, do unions adopt specific policies? What factors explain the different behaviour of similar unions, when faced with comparable policy choices? In order to assist in gaining answers to these questions, the following subsidiary questions were posed: Who makes policy? How is policy formed? How is policy implemented? What are the internal and external influences on policy makers? How successful were the policies the unions adopted? In attempting to answer these questions this book also sought to test the hypothesis, which had been developed whilst I was working as a BIFU National Officer, that micro-political factors, such as personal friendships, loyalties and enmities, affect policy-making to a far greater extent than has been acknowledged in the literature.

In order to address these questions and assess the validity of the hypothesis, a detailed study of policy-making in the Australian and British telecommunications and printing unions was undertaken. This research, which is set out in chapters 4–11, provides a rich source of evidence, from which it has been possible to answer the research questions, test the validity of the hypothesis, and to juxtapose the research findings against existing theories of policy-making. In this concluding chapter the key findings of the research are highlighted, whilst the wider implications for the union movement are contemplated, and the implications for the policy-making literature are considered.

The first significant finding of this book relates to how policy is created. Across all the featured unions' policy formulation was the product of a complex and multifaceted process, which involved negotiation over the locus of policy authority between officers and activists who occupied different representational roles in the various tiers of union structures.

Authority did not, as the classical theorists (Webbs, 1897, 1920; Michels, 1915) suggest, simply reside at the national level with a small coterie of senior officers. Instead, in each of the unions, national policy makers were engaged in a constant process of formal and informal negotiation with officers and activists from other layers of their union in order to reach accommodations that would allow policy to be applied.

This book also uncovered numerous examples of policy formulation being wholly or partly devolved to the unions' branches or chapels. This devolution occurred on some occasions because of pure logistical necessity, but in other instances it was owing to a conscious ideological commitment to decentralise the locus of policy-making. Yet there were also countervailing examples, where national lay and full-time officers sought to centralise rather than devolve parts of the policy-making process, often owing to their perception that local lay officers were failing to adequately address a major industrial challenge. These contradictory trends reflect the manner in which the locus of policy control shifts between various tiers of a union's decision making structure for a variety of internal and external ideological, logistical, institutional and legal reasons. This ebb and flow in the location of policy authority has been shown to be highly dynamic, with different layers of a union's structure seeking to attain, retain, or hand over control of specific policies at different times. That there was such a rich complexity to this process, in all the featured unions, undermines the arguments of rank and filist authors who posit that there is a straightforward struggle for policy authority between full-time officers and lay activists. (Bramble, 2008; Fairbrother, 2000)

A further important finding relates to the ability of local union organisations and lay officers to subjectively interpret, subvert, or simply ignore, national policies. Across all the unions featured there are examples of powerful branches and chapels behaving in this manner. The most common of these forms of resistance was the subjective interpretation of national policies at the local level. In these instances local representatives interpreted the wording of a policy to suit the beliefs and aspirations of themselves and their members, whilst still averring that they were following national policy. In other instances there was a more flagrant flouting of union policy with powerful branches or chapels unashamedly altering national policy to match their own ideological or industrial purposes. Whilst the national union and the employer were frequently aware of these subversions of policy, they would often choose to ignore this behaviour, owing to the organisational and industrial strength of the branch or chapel concerned. Finally, there were occasions when branches or chapels explicitly stated that they would refuse to implement national policy. These instances always involved powerful local organisations, such as the Fleet Street chapels or a major Australian State branch, whose size and industrial strength was such that the national union was unable to either impose policy or discipline those involved. These complexities in the process of policy implementation often led to major inconsistencies in policy, which handicapped the efforts of national unions to make radical changes in direction.

This book has also revealed a number of reasons why unions make specific policy decisions. The first relates to the impact of external influences on union policy and the ability of unions to make independent strategic choices. It has been shown that all of the unions featured were clearly and powerfully influenced in their selection of policies by external environmental factors, such as institutional, political and technological forces. Whilst this evidence is supportive of the assertions of authors (see Bain, 1970; Clegg, 1976; Howell, 2005) that the environmental context shapes union policy, the empirical evidence has also shown, very clearly, that unions are able to make key strategic policy choices which not only affect their own destinies, but can also alter the political and institutional environments. These findings strongly corroborate the arguments of Heery and Kelly that unions have the ability to make a series of policy choices, at both a local and national level, which profoundly affect their success as organisations (Heery and Kelly, 1988; Kelly and Heery, 1994; Heery, 2003, 2006).

The second concerns internal influences on policy direction; here the evidence has revealed that across all of the unions featured, informal factional groups have played a key part in determining policy. These informal organisations took a number of different forms, with ideological, occupational and geographical factions often operating alongside groups whose basis was allegiance to a specific individual. A number of the organisations, particularly the Left political factions, operated openly, whilst others were more shadowy, often going to considerable lengths to keep their membership and their operating processes secret. This book has established that the effect that these various informal groups had on policy was often profound. In many of the unions it was impossible to win an internal union election without the support of one or other of these bodies, whilst they were often able to exert considerable influence over individual decision makers' policy choices. Whilst this role has previously been charted in relation to political factions (Undy et al, 1981; Parker, 2009; McIllroy, 2007; Daniels and McIllroy, 2009) the impact of non-ideological factional groups has gone largely unreported in the literature, and is a key finding of this book.

The third and final significant finding as to why unions select specific policy options relates to the influence that micro-political factors have in shaping policy makers' decisions. This book has shown that across labour process, recruitment and, most prominently, amalgamation policy, micro-political factors, specifically friendships, loyalties and enmities have had a considerable impact. These factors have previously not received significant coverage in the literature, owing in large measure to the understandable reticence of policy makers to admit that their decisions were driven by friendships or enmities, rather than industrial logic or ideological beliefs. The documenting of the role of these micro political factors is one of the original contributions of this book to the study of union policy-making.

There are some wider implications for the Australian and British union movement, which can be derived from the substantive findings of this book. It is clear that from 1980–1996 that the less overtly hostile attitude of the ALP Federal Government towards the labour movement provided the Australian unions with a more favourable legislative and institutional environment in which to operate than that found in Britain. This clearly assisted the Australian telecommunication unions in their campaign to keep TA in the public sector, whilst helping the print unions to retain bargaining rights with companies such as News Limited, who became aggressively anti-union in the USA and Britain. The benefits to the unions of operating under a Social Democratic as opposed to Conservative administration have therefore been illustrated.

However, it should be noted that the shared neo-liberal economic policies of the ALP and the British Conservative Governments created similar challenges for the telecommunication unions in particular, as both Governments sought to privatise and deregulate their industries. The ability of the Australian unions to effectively combat these plans, by use of their informal micro-political influence on key ALP Federal Ministers, as well as through their formal role as Labour Party affiliates has been shown to be highly significant.

The difficulties all of the unions encountered in successfully repulsing the efforts of employers to undermine their influence over the labour process, illustrates very clearly how universally problematic it is for unions to effectively tackle hostile employers, when technological advancements have undermined the industrial strength that their members possess. These difficulties have been revealed to be greatly exacerbated if the unions involved are unable to respond in a united and coherent fashion, owing to ideological, occupational, or micro-political divisions. This book has revealed how unions, which have highly complex, multi layered, democratic structures, have great difficulty in changing policy direction when their industrial or organisational circumstances radically alter. These characteristics are shared by the overwhelming majority of British and Australian unions, which explains why it often takes a perilously long period for unions to adapt their labour process or recruitment policies to radically altered environments (see also Heery et al, 2003a, 2003b; Gall, 2003).

In assessing the contribution of this book to wider debate over union policy-making it is clear that the evidence produced has been supportive of Heery and Kelly's assertion that trade unions are able to make a series of important strategic choices at the local as well as the national level. Their allied assertions that the policy stances of officers and activists are greatly influenced by their personal beliefs, values and ideology, have also been reinforced by the findings of this book (Heery and Kelly, 1988; Kelly and Heery, 1994; Heery, 2003, 2006). The book's research also bears out the claims that the workings of political factions have a profound effect on union policy direction (Undy et al, 1981, McIllroy et al, 1999, 2007; Daniels and McIllroy, 2009; Parker, 2009). Additionally, one of the original contributions of this book is the documenting of the role played by the less visible, but often as powerful, geographical, occupational, or personality centred factions.

The evidence gathered has also illustrated how the rank and filist assertion (Fairbrother, 2000; Bramble, 1993, 2008) that there is a perpetual and uncomplicated struggle between senior full-time officers and lay activists, for control of union policy-making, is erroneous. Similarly declarations by some institutional contextualist authors (Bain, 1970; Howell, 2005), that a union's destiny is essentially determined by their political and institutional environments, have been shown to be flawed.

The final and most important contribution of this book, to the policy-making debate, has been the demonstration that there is major gap in the literature concerning the significant role played in trade union policy-making by micro-political factors, in particular friendships, loyalties and enmities. This is a serious omission which this book has successfully addressed.

List of Participants

In order to protect the identities of participants, which was guaranteed prior to interview, the following list does not identify contributors by name or union. It does however indicate the post the interviewee held and whether they were from a British or Australian union.

British Unions

Position in union	Number of interviewees
General Secretaries	5
National Presidents	4
National Officers	33
National Executive/Council Members	26
Regional Officers	9
Branch Secretaries	23
FoCs/MoCs	15
Other branch and chapel officers	9
Lay members	4

Australian Unions

Federal Secretaries	7
Federal Presidents	5

Federal Officers	14
State Secretaries	26
Federal Executive Members[1]	7
State Branch Officers	37
FoCs/MoCs and State Delegates	13
Lay members	5

Miscellaneous interviewees

Managers	9
Academics	5

46 contributors were interviewed twice, whilst 27 participants were interviewed three times or more.

---

1   In all the featured Australian unions the State Secretaries sat on the Federal Executive Committee.

List of Original Sources

Trade Union Journals

Australian Telecommunication Unions

CEPU Journals	1994–2012
CWU Journals	1993–1994
ATEA Journals	1976–1993
APTU Journals	1981–1993
PTTA Journals	1953–1976
NSW CEPU T&S Branch Journal	1993–1996
NSW ATEA Branch Journal	1979–1993
Victoria ATEA Branch Journal	1982–1993
NSW APTU Branch Journal	1983–1993
NSW CEPU P&T Branch Journal	1993–1996

British Telecommunication Unions

CWU Journal	1995–2012
NCU Journal	1985–1995
POEU Journal	1973–1985

Australian Printing Unions

AMWU Journal	1995–1997
PKIU Journal	1974–1995
NSW PKIU Branch Journal	1967–1995

British Printing Unions

Unite Journal	2008–2012
Amicus Journal	2005–2008
GPMU Journal	1992–2005
SOGAT Journals	1967–1992
NGA Journal	1973–1992

National/Federal Conference Reports and Papers

Australian Telecommunication Unions

CEPU, CWU Division Federal Conference Reports	1994–1996
CWU Federal Conference Reports	1993–1994
ATEA Federal Conference Reports	1975–1993
APTU Federal Conference Reports	1980–1993

British Telecommunication Unions

CWU National Conference Reports	1995–1997
CWU Telecommunications Section Conference Reports	1995–1997
NCU Annual Conference Reports	1985–1994
NCU (E) Annual Conference Reports	1985–1994
NCU (C) Annual Conference Reports	1985–1994
POEU Annual Conference Reports	1972–1984

Australian Printing Unions

AMWU Biennial National Conference Report	1996
PKIU Federal Conference Reports	1971–1995

British Printing Unions

GPMU Biennial Conference Reports	1992–2005
NGA Biennial Conference Reports	1976–1991
SOGAT Biennial Conference Reports	1978–1991

In addition to these official union publications, I was also granted access to the minutes, circulars and briefing papers of some of the featured unions National/Federal, State and Branch Executives/Committees. These documents, along with the private papers of a number of officers and activists, were shown to me on the basis that they would not be directly quoted from, and the sources of the information would not be divulged. Supplementing all of these documents I was also permitted to attend the National/Federal Executive of four of the unions, numerous State and branch meetings and the meetings of some political factions.

Glossary

Arvo	afternoon
Bashed	assaulted
Black/Blacking	refuse to handle, boycott
Blow through	leave rapidly
Blue	argument, fight or strike action
Chance, Buckley's	no chance
Cut snake, mad as a	very angry
Diddly squat	nothing, zero
Dill	idiot or fool
Dirty	angry
Dropped the bundle	failed to grasp an opportunity
Fair dinkum	true, genuine
Fair go	a fair chance
Flick, give the	get rid of something
Galah	fool, silly person. This derogatory term refers to the Galah bird whose antics and squawking is commonly perceived as foolish
Hard yards	hard or difficult work
Hoon	derogatory term used to describe someone engaged in loutish behaviour
Mongrel	a despicable person
Ordinary	very poor
Retrenchment	redundancy
Serve	verbal attack
Shit canned	destroyed or dismissed
Shonkey	dubious or underhand
Smoko	originally a smoking break, now often used to refer to any short break from work

Spat the dummy   Lost their temper

Spew/Spewing   vomit, or intense anger

Stone   Originally a table with a smooth surface on which page forms were composed. It also came to refer more generally to areas of a print shop where compositors worked

Bibliography

Ackers, P. and Payne, J. (1998). 'British Trade Unions and Social Partnership: Rhetoric, Reality and Strategy', *International Journal of Human Resource Management*, 9: 529–50.

Bacon, N. and Storey, J. (1993). Individualization of the Employment Relationship and the Implications for Trade Unions, *Employee Relations*, 15 (1): 5–17.

Bain, G. (1970). *The Growth of White Collar Unionism*. Oxford: Oxford University Press.

Bain, P. (1998). 'The 1986–7 News International Dispute: Was the Workers' Defeat Inevitable?' *Historical Studies in Industrial Relations*. Spring 1998: 73–105.

Bamber, G., Shadur, M. and Simmons, D. (1997). 'Australia'. In H. Katz (eds) *Telecommunications: Restructuring Work and Employment Relations Worldwide*. Ithaca and London: ILR Press.

Bassett, P. (1986). *Strike Free*. London: Macmillan.

Bassett, P. and Cave, A. (1993). *All for One: The future of the unions*. Fabian pamphlet No 559, London Fabian Society.

Batstone, E. (1988). *The reform of Workplace Industrial Relations – Theory, Myth and Evidence*. Oxford: Clarendon Press.

Batstone, E., Boraston, I. and Frenkel, S. (1977). *Shop Stewards in Action*. Oxford: Blackwell.

Batstone, E., Boraston, I. and Frenkel, S. (1978). *The Social Organisation of Strikes*. Oxford: Blackwell.

Batstone, E., Ferner, A. and Terry, M. (1984). *Consent and Efficiency; Labour Relations and Strategy in the State Enterprise*. Oxford: Blackwell.

Beacham, A. (1970). *Economics of Industrial Organization*. London: Pitman.

Bealey, F. (1976). *The Post Office Engineering Union – The history of the Post Office Engineers 1870–1970*. London: Bachman and Turner.

Bealey, F. (1977). 'The Political system of the Post Office Engineering Union', *British Journal of Industrial Relations*, XV No 3: 78–91.

Beynon, H. (1973). *Working for Ford*. Wakefield: EP Publishing Ltd.

Beynon, H. (1984). *Working for Ford, second edition*. Harmondworth: Penguin.

Beynon, H. (1997). 'The changing practices of work'. In R.K. Brown (ed.) *The Changing Shape of Work*. Basingstoke and London: Macmillan.

Blissett, E. (1989). *Industrial Relations in Coventry*. Coventry: Coventry City Council.

Boraston, I., Clegg, H. and Rimmer, M. (1975). *Workplace and Union*. London: Heinemann.

Boxall, P. and Haynes, P. (1997). 'Strategy and Trade Union Effectiveness in a Neo-liberal Environment', *British Journal of Industrial Relations*, 35 (4): 567–91.

Bramble, T. (1995). 'Deterring Democracy? Australia's New Generation of Trade Union Officials', *Journal of Industrial Relations*, 37 (3): 401–26.

Bramble, T. (2008). *Trade Unionism in Australia: A history from flood to ebb tide*. Melbourne: Cambridge University Press.

Braverman, H. (1974). *Labor and Monopoly Capital: The Degradation of Work in the Twentieth Century*. New York and London: Monthly Review Press.

Brown, W. (ed.) (1981). *The Changing Contours of Industrial Relations*. Oxford: Blackwell.

Bryman, A. (2004). *Social Research Methods*. New York: Oxford University Press.

Bryman, A. and Bell, E. (2007). *Business Research Methods*. New York: Oxford University Press.

Bundock, C.J. (1959). *The story of the National Union of Printing Bookbinding and Paper Workers*. Oxford: Oxford University Press.

Burawoy, M. (1979). *Manufacturing Consent: Changes in the Labor Process under Monopoly Capitalism*. Chicago: University of Chicago Press.

Cahill, Justice. (1977). *John Fairfax and Son Limited v PKIU*, Demarcation Awards, Industrial Case of New South Wales 5th October.

Callincos, A. (1982). *Is there a future for Marxism?* London: Macmillan.

Callincos, A. (1983). *Marxism and Philosophy*. Oxford: Clarendon Press.

Callow, J. (2012). *GMB @ Work – The Story behind the Union*. London: Evans Mitchell Books.

Callus, R., Moorhead, A., Cully, M. and Buchanan, J. (1991). *Industrial Relations at Work: The Australian Workplace Industrial Relations Survey*. Canberra: AGPS.

Carter, B. and Cooper, R. (2002). 'The Organising Model and the Management of Change: A Comparative Study of Unions in Australia and Britain', *Relations Industrielles/Industrial Relations*, 57 (4): 712–42.

Carter, B. and Poynter, G. (1999). 'Unions in a Changing Climate: MSF and Unison Experiences in the New Public Sector', *Industrial Relations Journal* 30 (5): 499–513.

Chaison, G. (1996). *Union mergers in Hard Times – The View from Five Countries*. New York: Cornell University Press.

Child, J. (1997.) Strategic Choice in the Analysis of Action, Structure, Organisations and Environment: Retrospect and Prospect, *Organisation Studies* 18 (1): 43–76.

Clegg, H.A. (1970). *The System of Industrial Relations in Britain*. Oxford: Basil Blackwell.

Clegg, H.A. (1976). *Trade Unionism under Collective Bargaining: A theory based on a comparison of six countries*. Oxford: Basil Blackwell.

Clegg, H.A. (1979). *The Changing System of Industrial Relations in Britain*. Oxford: Basil Blackwell.

Cliff, T. (1970). *The Employers' Offensive: Productivity deals and how to fight them*. London: International Socialist Group.

Cockburn, C. (1983). *Brothers – Male Dominance and Technological Change*. London: Pluto Press.

Cockburn, C. (1991). *Brothers – Male Dominance and Technological Change 2nd edition*. London: Pluto Press.

Coglan, F. and Ledwith, F. (1996). 'Sisters Organising – Women and their Trade Unions'. In F. Coglan and F. Ledwith (eds) *Women in Organisations: Challenging Gender Politics*. Basingstoke and London: Macmillan.

Cohen, S. (2006). *Ramparts of Resistance: Why Workers Lost Their Power And How To Get It Back*. London: Pluto Press.

Colling, T. and Dickens, L. (1998) 'Selling the case for gender equality: deregulation and equality bargaining', *British Journal of Industrial Relations* 13, (3): 309–16.

Colling, T., and Dickens, L. (2001). 'Gender Equality and Trade Unions: A new basis for mobilisation?'. In M. Noon and E. Ogbandona (eds), *Equality, diversity and disadvantages in employment*. London, Palgrave.

Cooper, R. (2001). '"Getting Organised?" A white-collar union responds to membership decline', *Journal of Industrial Relations*, 43 (4): 422–37.

Cooper, R. (2003). 'Trade Unionism in 2002'. *Journal of Industrial Relations*, 45 (2): 205–23.

Cooper, R. and Ellem, B. (2009). 'Fair Work and the Re-regulation of Collective Bargaining' *Australian Journal of Labour Law*, 22 (3) 284–99.

Cooper, R. and Ellem, B. (2011). *Trade Unions and Collective Bargaining in an Era of Change*. Sydney: The Federation Press.

Costa, M. and Hearn, M. (1997). *Reforming Australia's Unions*. Sydney: The Federation Press.

Crouch, C. (1999). *Social Change in Western Europe*. Oxford: Oxford University Press.

Cryle, D. (2006). *Murdoch's Flagship: 25 years of The Australian Newspaper*. Melbourne: Melbourne University Press.

Dabscheck, B. (1989). *Australian Industrial Relations in the 1980s*. Melbourne: Oxford University Press.

Dabscheck, B. (1995). *The Struggle for Australian Industrial Relations*. Melbourne: Oxford University Press.

Daniels, G. and McIlroy, J. (2009). *Trade Unions in a Neoliberal World: British Trade Unions under New Labour*. London: Routledge.

Darlington, R. (1994). *The dynamics of workplace unionism – Shop Stewards organisation in three Merseyside plants.* London: Mansell Publishing Ltd.

Davis, E. (1990). 'The 1989 ACTU Congress: Seeking Change Within'. *Journal of Industrial Relations*, 32 (1): 100–10.

Davis, M. (1999). 'Is bigger better? Union size and expenditure on members', *Journal of Industrial Relations*, 41 (1): 3–34.

Dean, B. (2007). *Hot Mettle – SOGAT, Murdoch and Me.* London: Methuen Publishing Limited.

Dickens, L. (1998). *Equal Opportunities and collective bargaining in Europe: illuminating the process.* Dublin: European foundation for the improvement of living and working conditions.

Dickens, L. (2000). 'Still Wasting Resources? Equality in Employment'. In S. Bach and K. Sisson (eds) *Personnel Management: A Comprehensive Guide to Theory and Practice.* Oxford: Blackwell.

Dickenson, M. (1982). *Democracy in the trade unions: Studies in membership participation and control.* St Lucia, QLD: Queensland University Press.

Dickenson, M. (1984). *To Break a Union – The Messenger, The State and the NGA.* Manchester: Booklist limited.

Dunn, S. and Gennard J. (1984). *The Closed Shop in British Industry.* Basingstoke and London: Macmillan.

Edelstein, J. and Warner, M. (1979). *Comparative Union Democracy: Organisation and Opposition in British and American Unions.* NJ: Transaction Books.

Edwards, P. (1983). *Control, Compliance and Conflict: Analysing Variations in the Capitalist Labour Process.* Coventry: Industrial Relations Research Unit, University of Warwick.

England, J. (1979). 'How UCATT Revised its Rules: An Anatomy of Organisational Change'. *British Journal of Industrial Relations*, 17 (1): 1–18.

England, J. (1981). 'Shop Stewards in Transport House: A comment on the incorporation of the rank and file'. *Industrial Relations Journal*, 12 (5): 16–29.

England, J. (2008). 'The General Executive Council of the Transport and General Workers Union: A profile of members'. *Historical Studies in Industrial Relations.* Spring/Autumn 2008: 239–69.

Ewing, K.D. (2006) (ed.). *The Right to Strike: From the Trades Disputes Act 1906 to a Trade Union Freedom Bill 2006.* Liverpool: Institute for Employment Rights.

Fairbrother, P. (1990). 'The Contours of Local Trade Unionism in a Period of Restructuring' in P. Fosh and E. Heery (eds), *Trade Unions and their Members: Studies in Union Democracy and Organisation.* Basingstoke and London: Macmillan.

Fairbrother, P. (1996). 'Workplace Trade Unionism in the State Sector'. In P. Ackers, C. Smith, and P. Smith (eds) *The New Workplace and Trade Unionism.* London: Routledge.

Fairbrother, P. (2000). *Trade Unions at the Crossroads.* London: Mansell.

Fairbrother, P. (2002). 'Unions in Britain: Towards a New Unionism?' in P. Fairbrother and G. Griffin. *Changing prospects of trade unionism: Comparisons between six countries,* London: Continuum.

Fairbrother, P. and Stewart, P. (2003). 'The Dilemmas of Social Partnership and Union Organisation: Questions for British Trade Unions', in P. Fairbrother and C. Yates, *Trade unions in renewal.* London: Routledge.

Fairbrother, P. and Yates, C. (2003) 'Unions in crisis, unions in renewal?' In P. Fairbrother and C. Yates. *Trade Unions in Renewal.* London: Routledge.

Fitzgerald, R.T. (1967). *The Printers of Melbourne – The History of a Union.* Melbourne: Sir Issac Pitman and Son.

Flanders, A. (1965). *Industrial Relations: What is wrong with the system?* London: Faber.

Fosh, P. and Heery E. (1990). *Trade Unions and their Members.* Basingstoke and London: Macmillan.

Frege, C. and Kelly, J. (2004). 'Union Strategies in a Comparative Context', in C. Frege and J. Kelly (eds) *Varieties of Unionism: Strategies for Revitalisation in a Globalising Economy.* Oxford: Oxford University Press.

Frenkel, S. and Coolican, A. (1984). *Unions against Capitalism? A Sociological Comparison of the Australian Building and Metal Workers Unions.* Sydney: George Allen & Unwin.

Gall, G. (2004). *Union Organizing: Campaigning for trade union recognition.* London: Routledge.

Gall, G. (2005). 'Union Organising in the "New Economy" in Britain' *Employee Relations,* 27 (2): 35–73.

Gall, G. (2007). 'Trade Union Recognition in Britain: An Emerging Crisis for Trade Unions?' *Economic and Industrial Democracy,* 28 (1): 27–43.

Gall, G. (2010). *Making and Keeping the Connection – A History of Connect and its Principal Predecessors.* London: Connect.

Gall, G. and Mackay, S. (2001). Facing "Fairness at Work": Union Perception of Employer Opposition and Response to Union Recognition' *Industrial Relations Journal,* 32 (2): 94–113.

Gardner, M. (1989). 'Union Strategy: A gap in union theory'. In B. Ford and D. Plowman, *Australian Unions: An Industrial Relations perspective.* Melbourne: Macmillan.

Geary, R. (1985). *Policing Industrial Disputes: 1893 to 1985.* Cambridge: Cambridge University Press.

Gennard, J. (1990). *A History of the National Graphical Association.* London: Unwin Hyman Limited.

Gennard, J. and Bain, P. (1995). *A History of the Society of Graphical and Allied Trades.* London: Routledge.

Gennard, J. and Haywood, G. (2008) *A History of the Graphical, Paper and Media Union.* London: Unite the Union.

Griffin, G. (2002). 'Union mergers in Australia: Top down Restructuring', *Working paper No 80, National Key Centre in Industrial Relations.* Melbourne: Monash University.

Griffin, G. and Scarcebrook, V. (1989). 'Trends in Mergers of Federally Registered Unions, 1904–1986'. *Journal of Industrial Relations,* 31 (2): 257–62.

Hagan, J. (1966). *Printers and Politics – A History of the Australian Printing Unions 1850–1950.* Canberra: Australian National University Press.

Hart, M. (1979). *Union recognition in America – the legislative snare.* Coventry: University of Warwick.

Healy, G. and Kirton, G. (2000). 'Women, Power and Trade Union Government in the UK'. *British Journal of Industrial Relations,* 38(3): 343–60.

Heery, E. (1996). 'The New Unionism'. In I. Beardwell (ed.) *Contemporary British Industrial Relations.* Oxford: Oxford University Press.

Heery, E. (1998). 'The Relaunch of the Trade Union Congress', *British Journal of Industrial Relations,* 36 (3): 339–60.

Heery, E. (2002). Partnership versus Organising: Alternative Futures for British Trade Unionism. *Industrial Relations Journal,* 33 (1): 20–35.

Heery, E. (2003). 'Trade Unions and Industrial Relations' in P. Ackers and A. Wilkinson, *Understanding Work and Employment.* Oxford: Oxford University Press.

Heery, E. (2005). 'Sources of Change in Trade Unions'. *Work, Employment and Society.* 19 (1): 91–106.

Heery, E. (2006). 'Union Workers, Union Work: A Profile of Trade Union Officers in the UK'. *British Journal of Industrial Relations,* 44 (3): 445–72.

Heery, E. and Adler, L. (2004). 'Organising the Unorganised', in C. Frege and J. Kelly (eds) *Varieties of Unionism: Strategies for Revitalisation in a Globalising Economy.* Oxford: Oxford University Press.

Heery, E. and Kelly, J. (1990). 'Full Time Officers and the Shop Steward Network: Patterns of Cooperation and Interdependence', in P. Fosh and E. Heery (eds) *Trade Unions and their Members: Studies in Union Democracy and Organisation,* Basingstoke and London: Macmillan.

Heery, E. and Kelly, J. (1994). 'Professional, Participative and Managerial Unionism: An Interpretation of Change In Trade Unions', *Work, Employment and Society,* 8 (1): 1–22.

Heery, E., Kelly, J. and Waddington, J. (2003) 'Union revitalisation in Britain'. *European Journal of Industrial Relations,* 9 (1) 79–99.

Heery, E. and Simms, M. (2008). 'Constraints on Trade Union Organising in the United Kingdom'. *Industrial Relations Journal,* 39 (1): 24–42.

Heery, E. Simms, M., Delbridge, R., Salmon, J. and Simpson, D. (2003a). 'Trade Union Recruitment Policy in Britain'. In G, Gall (ed.) *Union Organising*, London: Routledge.

Heery, E. Simms, M. and Delbridge. R. (2003b). *The Organising Academy five years on*. London: TUC.

Heery, E. Simms, M., Delbridge. R., Salmon, J. and Simpson, D. (2000a). 'The TUC's Organising Academy: An Assessment' *Industrial Relations Journal*, 31 (5): 400–15.

Heery, E. Simms, M., Delbridge. R., Salmon, J. and Simpson, D. (2000b). 'Union Organising in Britain: A Survey of Policy and Practice'. *International Journal of Human Resource Management*, 11(5): 986–1007.

Hinton, J. (1973). *The First Shop Stewards' Movement*. London: Allen & Unwin.

Howe, E. and Child, J. (1952). *The Society of London Bookbinders, 1780–1951*. London: Sylvan Press.

Howell, C. (1999). 'Unforgiven: British Trade Unions in Crisis'. In A.Martin and G. Ross (eds) *The Brave New World of European Labor*. New York: Berghan Books.

Howell, C. (2005). *Trade Unions and the State – The construction of Industrial Relations in Britain, 1890–2000*. Princeton and Oxford: Princeton University Press.

Hyman, R. (1971). *Marxism and the Sociology of Trade Unionism*. London: Pluto.

Hyman, R. (1972). *Strikes*. London: Fontana Collins.

Hyman, R. (1975). *Industrial Relations – A Marxist Introduction*. London: Macmillan.

Hyman, R. (1979). 'The Politics of Workplace Trade Unionism'. *Capital and Class*, 8: 54–67.

Hyman, R. (1984). *Strikes – 3rd edition*, London: Fontana.

Hyman, R. (1997). 'The Future of Employee Representation'. *British Journal of Industrial Relations*. 35 (3): 309–36.

Hyman, R. (1999). 'Imagined Solidarities: Can Trade Unions Resist Globalisation?' In P. Linisk (ed.) *Globalisation and Labour relations*. Cheltenham: Edward Elgar.

Hyman, R. (2001). *Understanding European Trade Unionism: Between Market, Class and Society*. London: Sage.

Katz, H. (1997). 'Introduction and Comparative Overview'. In H. Katz (ed.), *Telecommunications: Restructuring Work and Employment Relations Worldwide*. Ithaca and London: ILR Press.

Keavney, J. (1990) *Telecommunications: The time for truth – the myth of deregulation*. Sydney: Booth Printing.

Kelly, D. (1994). 'Trade Unionism in 1993'. *Journal of Industrial Relations*, 36: 135–46.

Kelly, J. (1998). *Rethinking Industrial Relations: Mobilisation, Collectivism and Long Waves*. London: Routledge Paul.

Kelly, J. (2003). 'Union Revitalisation in Britain', *European Journal of Industrial Relations*, 9 (1): 79–97.

Kelly, J. (2004). 'Social Partnership Agreements in Britain: Labour Co-Operation and Compliance'. *Industrial Relations Journal*, 43 (1) 257–92.

Kelly, J. and Badigannavar, V. (2004). 'Union organising campaigns'. In J.Kelly and P. Willman (eds), *Union Organisation and Activity*. London: Routledge.

Kelly, J. and Badigannavar, V. (2005). 'Why Are Some Union Organizing Campaigns More Successful Than Others?' *British Journal of Industrial Relations*, 43 (3): 515–35.

Kelly, J. and Heery, E. (1989). 'Full-Time Officers and Trade Union Recruitment', *British Journal of Industrial Relations*, 27 (2): 196–213.

Kelly, J. and Heery, E. (1994). *Working for the Union*. Cambridge: Cambridge University Press.

Lane, T. and Roberts, K. (1971). *Strike at Pilkingtons*. London: Fontana.

Lansbury, R. and Spillane, R. (1983). *Organisational Behaviour: The Australian Context*. Sydney, Longman, Cheshire.

Lawson, N. (1992). *The View from No 11: Memoirs of a Tory Radical*. London: Bantam.

Lewis, S. (1986). 'Picketing' in S. Lewis (ed.), *Labour Law in Britain*. Oxford: Blackwell.

Lipset, S., Trow, M. and Coleman, J. (1956). *Union Democracy: The Internal Politics of the International Typographical Union*. New York: Doubleday.

Littleton, S. (1992). *The Wapping Dispute*. Avebury: Aldershot.

McCarthy, W.E.J. (1964). *The Closed Shop in Britain*. Berkeley, CA: University of California Press.

McIlroy, J. (1988). *Trade Unions in Britain Today*. Manchester: Manchester University Press.

McIlroy, J. (2007). 'Always Outnumbered, Always Outgunned: the Trotskyists and the Trade Unions', in J. McIlroy, N. Fishman and A. Campbell (eds) *The High Tide of British Trade Unionism*. London: Merlin Press.

Martin, R. (1968). 'Union democracy: An Explanatory Framework'. *Sociology*, 2 (2): 82–124.

Martin, R. (1975). *Trade Unions in Australia: Who Runs Them, Who Belongs, Their Politics, Their Power*. Ringwood, VIC: Penguin.

Martin, R. (1980). *Trade Unions in Australia: Who Runs Them, Who Belongs, Their Politics, Their Power. 2nd edition*. Ringwood, VIC: Penguin.

Melvern, L. (1986). *The End of the Street*. London: Methuen.

Michels, R. (1915). *Political Parties: A sociological study of the oligarchical tendencies of modern democracy*. Reprinted (1959) New York: Dover.

Milkman, R. (2000). *Organising Immigrants: The Challenge for Unions in Contemporary California*. Cornell: Cornell University Press.

Murray, G. (1994). 'Structure and Identity: the Impact of Union Structure in Comparative Perspective' *Employee Relations*, 16 (2): 24–40.

Neill, A. (1996). *Full Disclosure*. London: Macmillan.

Offe, C. (1985). *Disorganized Capitalism: Contemporary Transformations of Work and Politics.* Cambridge: Polity Press.

Osterman, P. (1999). *Securing Prosperity.* Princeton, NJ: Princeton University Press.

Parker, D. (2009). *The Official History of Privatisation, Volume 1: The formative years 1970–1987.* London: Routledge.

Parkinson, C. (1992). *Right at the Centre: An Autobiography.* London: Weidenfeld and Nicolson.

Richardson, M. (2003). Leadership and Mobilisation: 'SOGAT in the 1986–87 News International Dispute' *Historical Studies in Industrial Relations,* Spring 2003: 73–93.

Shawcross, W. (1992). *Rupert Murdoch – Ringmaster of the Information Circus.* Basingstoke and Oxford: Pan Books.

Silverman, D. (1984). *Interpreting Qualitative Data: Methods for Analysing Qualitative Research.* London: Sage.

Silverman, D. (2000). *Doing Qualitative Research: A Practical Handbook.* London, Sage.

Terry, M. (1995). 'Trade Unions: Shop Stewards and the Workplace', in P. Edwards (ed.) *Industrial Relations: Theory and Practice in Britain.* Oxford: Blackwell.

Terry, M. (2000). 'Unison and the quality of public service provision: any lessons from the rest of Europe?'. In M.Terry (ed.) *Redefining Public Sector Trade Unionism: Unison and the Future of Trade Unions.* London: Routledge.

Terry, M. (2003). 'Employee Representation: Shop Stewards and the New Legal Framework', in P. Edwards, *Industrial Relations: Theory and Practice in Britain. 2nd edition.* Oxford: Blackwell.

Thomas, C. and Wallis, B. (1998). 'Dwr Cymru/Welsh Water: a Case Study in Partnership', in P. Sparrow and M. Marchington (eds) *Human Resource Management: The New Agenda.* London: Financial Times Management.

Tomkins, M. (1999). Trade Union Amalgamations: Explaining the recent spate of mergers in Australia. *Labour & Industry,* 9 (3): 61–77.

Turner, H.A. (1962). *Trade Union Goals, Structure and Policy.* London: Allen & Unwin.

Undy, R. (1996). 'Review Essay: Mergers and Union Restructuring: Externally Determined Waves or internally Generated Reforms?' In *Historical Studies in Industrial Relations.* September 1996: 125–37.

Undy, R. (2008). *Trade Union Merger Strategies: Purpose, Process and Performance.* Oxford: Oxford University Press.

Undy, R., Ellis, V., McCarthy, W.E.J. and Halmos, A.M. (1981). *Change in Trade Unions.* London: Hutchinson.

Undy, R., Ellis, V., McCarthy, W.E.J. and Holmes, A. (1985). Recent merger movements and future union structure. In W.E.J. McCarthy (ed.) *Trade Unions.* Harmondsworth: Penguin.

Undy, R., Fosh, P., Morris, H., Smith, P. and Martin, R. (1996). *Managing the Unions.* Oxford: Clarendon Press.

Waddington, J. (1988). 'Trade Union Mergers: A Study of Trade Union Structural Dynamics', *British Journal of Industrial Relations*, 26 (2): 409–30.

Waddington, J. (1995). *The politics of bargaining: the merger process and British trade union structural developments 1892–1987.* London: Mansell.

Waddington, J. (2003). 'Trade union Organisation', in P. Edwards (ed.) *Industrial Relations: theory and practice in Britain. 2nd edition.* Oxford: Blackwell.

Waddington, J. and Kerr, A. (2000). 'Towards an Organising Model in Unison? A Trade Union Membership Strategy in Transition'. In M. Terry (ed.) *Redefining Public Sector Trade Unionism: Unison and the Future of Trade Unions.* London: Routledge.

Waddington, J. and Whitson, C. (1997). 'Why Do People Join Unions in a Period of Membership Decline?' *British Journal of Industrial Relations*, 35 (4): 515–46.

Waddington, J., Kahmann, M. and Hoffmann, J. (2005). *A Comparison of Trade Union Merger Processes in Britain and Germany: Joining Forces.* London: Routledge.

Wajcman, J. (2000). 'Feminism Facing Industrial Relations'. *British Journal of Industrial Relations*, 38 (2): 183–201.

Waters, F. (1978). *Postal Unions & Politics – a history of the amalgamated postal workers' union of Australia.* St Lucia, QLD: University of Queensland Press.

Watson, D. (1988). *Mangers Of Discontent – Trade Union Officers and Industrial Relations Managers.* London: Routledge.

Webb, S. and Webb, B. (1920). *The History of Trade Unionism 1666–1920.* London: Longmans, Green and Co.

Webb, S. and Webb, B. (1897). *Industrial Democracy.* London: Longmans, Green and Co.

Wedderburn, K.W. (1986). *The Worker and the Law, 3rd Edition.* Harmondsworth: Penguin.

Willman, P. (2001). 'The Viability of Trade Unionism: A Bargaining Unit Analysis', *British Journal of Industrial Relations*, 39 (1): 97–117.

Zappala, G. (1991). *The Closed Shop in Australia: Concepts and Coverage.* Sydney: University of Sydney.

Zeitlin, J. (1979). 'Craft Control and the Division of Labour: Engineers and Compositors in Britain, 1890–1930', *Cambridge Journal of Economics*, 3 (3): 263–74.

Zeitlin, J. (1983). 'Trade Unions and Job Control: A Critique of "Rank-and-Filism"', (abstract of conference paper), *Bulletin of the Society for the Study of Labour History*, 46, 1983: 6–7.

Zeitlin, J. (1989). '"Rank and Filism" and Labour History: A Rejoinder to Price and Cronin', *International Review of Social History*, 1989: 37–53.

Index

Trade Unions Past, Present and Future

EDITED BY CRAIG PHELAN

This series publishes monographs and edited collections on the history, present condition and possible future role of organised labour around the world. Multidisciplinary in approach, geographically and chronologically diverse, this series is dedicated to the study of trade unionism and the undeniably significant role it has played in modern society. Topics include the historical development of organised labour in a variety of national and regional settings; the political, economic and legal contexts in which trade unionism functions; trade union internationalism past and present; comparative and cross-border studies; trade unions' role in promoting economic equality and social justice; and trade union revitalisation and future prospects. The aims of the series are to promote an appreciation of the diversity of trade union experience worldwide and to provide an international forum for lively debate on all aspects of the subject.

Volume 1   Craig Phelan (ed.): Trade Unionism since 1945: Towards a Global History. Volume 1: Western Europe, Eastern Europe, Africa and the Middle East.
467 pages. 2009. ISBN 978-3-03911-410-8

Volume 2   Craig Phelan (ed.): Trade Unionism since 1945: Towards a Global History. Volume 2: The Americas, Asia and Australia.
364 pages. 2009. ISBN 978-3-03911-950-9

Volume 3   Pablo Ghigliani: The Politics of Privatisation and Trade Union Mobilisation: The Electricity Industry in the UK and Argentina.
293 pages. 2010. ISBN 978-3-03911-961-5

Volume 4   Heather Connolly: Renewal in the French Trade Union Movement: A Grassroots Perspective.
260 pages. 2010. ISBN 978-3-0343-0101-5